MADISON'S MILITIA

MADISON'S MILITIA

THE HIDDEN HISTORY OF THE SECOND AMENDMENT

CARL T. BOGUS

OXFORD
UNIVERSITY PRESS

OXFORD
UNIVERSITY PRESS

Oxford University Press is a department of the University of Oxford. It furthers
the University's objective of excellence in research, scholarship, and education
by publishing worldwide. Oxford is a registered trade mark of Oxford University
Press in the UK and certain other countries.

Published in the United States of America by Oxford University Press
198 Madison Avenue, New York, NY 10016, United States of America.

CIP data is on file at the Library of Congress

ISBN 978–0–19–763222–2

DOI: 10.1093/oso/9780197632222.001.0001

1 3 5 7 9 8 6 4 2

Printed by Sheridan Books, Inc., United States of America

For William and Dov

CONTENTS

Introduction

A NIGHTMARE HAD been haunting Carolinians. In the fall of 1734, readers of the *South Carolina Gazette* learned of three separate revolts on sailing ships transporting Africans to bondage in the New World. In all three incidents, the Africans killed the ship's captain, and in two of the incidents the Africans took full control of the ship and its cargo. A few months later, the paper reported that Black slaves had revolted on St. John in the Virgin Islands and "entirely massacred all of the white people on that island, consisting of about two hundred families, and were very inhuman in the executions and murders."[1] These incidents were more than concerning—they were downright frightening—in a colony (or province as South Carolina was then formally known) in which nearly two-thirds of the residents were enslaved Blacks.[2]

The nightmare turned real in the still-dark, early morning of Sunday, September 9, 1739, on the banks of the Stono River, about fifteen miles due west of Charleston (or as it was then called, Charles Town).[3] About twenty slaves broke into Hutchenson's Store, which was probably a barn-like building serving as both a general store selling foodstuffs, clothing and shoes, tools, and other goods, and a warehouse for rice bound for export from the docks in Charleston.[4] The slaves' leaders were named Jemmy and Cato. No one today knows much about them, but, according to his descendants, Cato's masters had taught him to read. That was not commonplace; Whites were afraid that reading could give slaves ideas. These slaves had not come to steal food, drink, or clothes. They had come for guns and ammunition. They decapitated two White men who were, for reasons unknown, in the closed store, and put their severed heads on the front steps, publicly announcing for all to see that they were in open rebellion.[5]

The armed band of slaves marched west on Pons Road. Some speculate they were heading for Spanish Florida. During the preceding year, Spain issued a royal edict promising freedom to escaped slaves who made their way to Florida. But Gracia Real de Santa Teresa de Mose, the northern outpost where Spain established a community of free Blacks, was about 275 miles away. If the slaves' primary goal was to get there, one assumes they would have moved as quickly and surreptitiously as possible. That was not what they did. On eight occasions, they left Pons Road to invade the homes of plantation owners and other colonists.[6] Once they were driven off; and once, a slave hid his master and told the rebels he was not at home. The rebels pillaged the other six houses, set them ablaze, and killed everyone inside—a body count totaling forty slave owners and family members before the day was through.

The targets were not indiscriminate. The rebels attacked the home of the largest plantation owner in the area, and those of two other major plantation owners, too; but they passed by the home of at least one other very large plantation owner. They attacked the homes of two justices of the peace; but when they passed Wallace's Tavern, they left the proprietor alone because, they said, "he was a good man and kind to his slaves."[7]

We can confidently conclude the rebels were not trying to reach freedom in Spanish Florida because they did not try to conceal their whereabouts. Just the opposite: They beat drums, flew banners, and called out "Liberty!" to other slaves, exhorting them to join the insurrection. Their ranks swelled to somewhere between sixty and one hundred. They had come from eight different plantations.[8]

No one knows how large the rebellion would have grown if not for a bizarre coincidence. A group of five White men, on their way to Charleston for the South Carolina Assembly's new legislative session, happened to ride within eyesight of the rebels. One member of the group was Dr. William Bull II, the lieutenant governor of South Carolina and one of the province's officials most concerned about the potential for slave insurrections. In a letter just four months earlier, Bull had warned that the colony's "Negroes, which were their chief support, may in little time become their enemies, if not their masters, and that this government is unable to withstand or prevent it."[9] One can only imagine Bull's horror as he saw a sizable group of armed slaves in open rebellion.

Bull spurred his horse on to the Presbyterian Church at Wiltown Bluff, a couple of miles south, where Sunday services were in progress.[10] A few weeks earlier, the Assembly had passed the Security Act, which required all White males who were responsible for bearing arms in the militia—that meant all able-bodied White men between the ages of sixteen and sixty—to take guns and ammunition with them to church on Sundays and on Christmas. While the Security Act would not formally take effect for three more weeks, planters hardly needed the penalty of a fine to stimulate compliance. This was, after all, exactly the eventuality they long feared. When Bull arrived at the church, therefore, an armed contingent of militia was already there.

Leaving frightened women and children at the church, the men rode off in pursuit of the rebels. By four o'clock in the afternoon, perhaps as many as one hundred armed and mounted militiamen, led by Captain John Bee, found the slaves in an open field about ten miles southwest of where the lieutenant governor had spotted them earlier. They dismounted and attacked the rebels on foot.[11] Some slaves fled in the face of the advancing militia; more than forty stood their ground and fought. Witnesses say that the battle was intense and that the slaves appeared skilled in the use of arms and fought in military formation, but the militia—better armed, better trained, and outnumbering the slaves who fought—prevailed. Twenty-one Whites died in the battle. Forty-four slaves died in the battle or were captured, questioned, and executed on the spot. The planters took pride in not torturing the slaves and instead giving them an "easy death," but they, too, decapitated those they killed and placed their heads on pikes along Pons Road. Forty-four heads, spaced some distance apart, provided a chilling display. Slaves who returned to their plantations were, if identified, also immediately shot or hanged. There was a second, smaller battle six days later when militia found a group of slaves who had escaped the initial engagement. A few slaves continued to evade capture, including one who was caught and hanged three years later.[12]

Had the Stono rebels harbored some hope—even just a glimmer—that the rebellion would be large enough to repel the inevitable counterattack by the militia and somehow survive? Maybe; desperate people will believe what they must. But in their hearts, they must have known that was unrealistic. Even if the rebellion had become large enough, and well-armed enough, to repel the first assaults, militia would come from further and further away—from all of the South Carolina Low Country, from farther-flung areas in western South Carolina, from Georgia and from North Carolina, too, until the rebellion was destroyed. The word of the rebellion would spread among Whites faster than among enslaved Blacks because Whites had horses. And the Whites would show no mercy. All the rebels could reasonably hope for was to kill as many Whites as possible before they themselves died free. The Stono Rebellion was, in short, a suicide mission.

None of this was lost on the White population. As historian Peter Charles Hoffer observed, after the Stono Rebellion no White "could ever fool himself or herself again that slaves were content in their chains."[13]

There had, however, been fears of slave uprisings in South Carolina long before the Stono Rebellion. In 1734, a visitor to the colony recorded in his diary that slaves "are generally thought to watch [for] an opportunity of revolting against their masters, as they have lately done in the islands of St. John and St. Thomas."[14] Prior to Stono, South Carolina had an extensive slave patrol system. Groups of five men, led by Captains of Patrol, made regular rounds, usually on horseback, to stop and question slaves who were not where they should be, ensure that groups of slaves were not meeting or assembling, search slave quarters for weapons and other contraband, and administer punishments—from whippings to hangings—to slaves violating the rules.

Slave patrols were considered so essential to the security of the colony that patrollers were authorized to enter plantations, conduct inspections, and mete out punishments without the consent of plantation and slave owners. Men who volunteered for patrol duty were excused from militia drills. But Stono—then the largest slave rebellion on the American mainland—caused South Carolina and the South as a whole to heighten slave control measures. The South Carolina legislature directed that for at least three months, or until all of the Stono rebels were captured, "completely armed" militia patrol both banks of the Stono River every night.[15] And henceforth, patrols became the direct

responsibility of the militia, with every militiaman required to participate.[16] Several militia garrisons were also established. The garrisons
were not located at points that were important strategically to defend
the colony from invasion; they were placed in the interior at points
useful for slave control.[17] According to one student of South Carolina
military history, the Stono reforms completed a transformation of the
militia "from a vital defensive agency to one whose principal duty was
the supervision of slaves."[18]

For a while, Georgia took a different approach. Within a year of the
Stono Rebellion, it banned slavery within its colony.[19] A South Carolina
merchant, asked for his opinion, said Georgia was foolish. Whites could
never work as well as Blacks in the rice fields because the work was too
laborious and the heat too intense, and, therefore, "without Negroes,
Georgia can never be a colony of any great consequence."[20] For two
decades, Georgia's farmers watched their counterparts amass great
fortunes on the rice plantations of South Carolina and the tobacco
plantations of Virginia. The risks were undeniable; but the enticement
became irresistible. In 1755, Georgia was ready to make its pact with the
Devil: it repealed its prohibition on the use of slave labor and adopted
South Carolina's slave control system, lock, stock, and barrel.[21]

What has any of this got to with the origins of the Second
Amendment? We're coming to that.

* * *

Here is what the Second Amendment says:

> A well regulated Militia, being necessary to the security of a free
> State, the right of the people to keep and bear Arms shall not be
> infringed.

This book deals with these questions, and these questions only: Why, in
1789, did James Madison write what became the Second Amendment
to the United States Constitution? What did he want to accomplish?
Why, after making a few changes to his initial draft, did Madison's
colleagues in the First Congress adopt the Second Amendment and
propose it to the states?

Although I am a lawyer, this book is about history, not law. In the main, I shall avoid legal issues and arguments. For example, lawyers debate whether, in interpreting either the main body of the Constitution or its Amendments, courts ought to take into consideration what the men who wrote the provisions intended. Some argue that courts should focus on the text of the provisions and ignore "original intent." Others argue that courts ought to give great weight to the intentions of the framers—in this case, Madison and his colleagues in the First Congress. Still others believe that courts should ignore the intentions of the framers and focus instead on how those who ratified the provision— in this case, state legislatures—understood the provision. And some maintain that what matters more than any of that is how the people at large understood the provision. These arguments can resemble debates about how many angels can dance on the head of a pin. For example, those who want to place the greatest weight on the intentions of the ratifiers, or the understanding of the people, can wind up arguing whether that should include legislators or people in the states of Massachusetts, Connecticut, and Georgia—three states that were part of the Union when Congress proposed the Bill of Rights but did not ratify the amendments (including the Second Amendment) until 1939. This book will not deal with such questions. If you are reading this book, I assume that you care why James Madison and his colleagues in the First Congress wrote the Second Amendment without arguing why you should care.

Nor am I going to analyze or debate how courts or other legal scholars have interpreted the Second Amendment. Suffice it to say that historians often criticize judges, lawyers, and legal scholars for doing "law office history," which means picking and choosing particular quotations and facts, and ripping them out of context to reach a desired conclusion.[22] I am proud that, years ago, when I presented my thesis about the Second Amendment in a law review article, Professor Don Higginbotham, then the leading historian on military affairs in eighteenth-century America, held it up as an exception to the rule; that is, it was a historically contextualized argument by a lawyer.[23] He also said my thesis was worthy of additional research. This book is the product of many years of additional thought and research, and I am committed to keeping faith with the principles expressed by the late

Professor Higginbotham. I shall try to present history as it should be presented: focusing on people and the circumstances that caused them to think and act as they did. Happily, history is colorful, and putting facts and statements in context means placing them in the larger narrative in which they occurred—that is, to tell stories.

James Madison never explained why he wrote the Second Amendment or what it meant. Nor did his colleagues in the First Congress. That does not mean that we have embarked on a futile quest. Nor does it mean that the Amendment is doomed to be a Rorschach test on which everyone projects their own thoughts. The most reliable method of deducing why people acted as they did is to understand the imperatives that confronted them at the time. We do this all the time, especially when listening to politicians. We don't have to be psychoanalysts or professional historians to do this successfully. We are, after all, human beings, and by putting ourselves in the shoes of other human beings, we can often understand what motivated them to do what they did. This can often lead us to a more reliable conclusion than simply accepting what someone claims their motives were. But we have to understand—truly understand—the times, circumstances, and imperatives of James Madison and other key players. Moreover, Madison and his contemporaries lived in a different time than do we. Their world—eighteenth-century America—was not our world. So stepping into their shoes will take time and care. We need to bear in mind that, as one historian ably put it, "The Founders wrote the Second Amendment to solve their own problems, not ours."[24]

There is nothing special about the method we shall follow. Historians agree that interpreting a text, statement, or idea—in this case, the Second Amendment—requires understanding the context in which it was made, who made it, and why. According to the famous historian Quentin Skinner, it is not sufficient "to concentrate simply on a given idea or a given text in itself."[25] Skinner stressed that we must recognize that ideas and statements constitute a response to immediate circumstances, and it is therefore essential to study "the context of other happenings which explains them."[26]

The absence of explanations from James Madison and his colleagues means that there is no direct evidence about what the Founders intended. There is, however, considerable circumstantial evidence that bears upon the question. As someone who taught Evidence for decades in law school, I know that there is a common misperception about the relative strengths of direct and circumstantial evidence. Many people assume circumstantial evidence is weaker than direct evidence. Not so. One type of evidence is not inherently stronger or weaker than the other. The difference between the two is that direct evidence does not require making an inference from the evidence itself to a conclusion drawn from the evidence, whereas circumstantial evidence does require an inference. Here is the classic law school example. Suppose the question is whether it snowed last night. If Joe testifies that he went outside at midnight to walk his dog, and during that walk he saw it snowing, that is direct evidence. However, if Joe testifies that when he walked his dog after supper there was no snow on the ground, but that when he walked his dog again just before breakfast this morning there was a foot of snow as far as the eye could see, an inference must be made from the evidence—no snow last night, a lot of snow this morning—to reach the conclusion that it snowed during the night. That is circumstantial evidence.

In that example, the direct and circumstantial evidence are of equal strength. (As sensible people, we can disregard outlandish possibilities such as someone had thousands of truckloads of snow delivered to play a practical joke on Joe.) In many instances, circumstantial evidence is stronger than direct evidence. We used to assume, for example, that eyewitness testimony was the gold standard in evidence, but we have learned from painful experience and rigorous studies that eyewitness testimony is often unreliable. People are often mistaken about what they believe they saw, not to mention that some people lie. So do not be put off by my telling you that we will be relying on circumstantial evidence. In fact, having to rely on circumstantial evidence is going to make our exploration more interesting.

Historian David Hackett Fisher has some useful observations about attempts to discern motives. He says that motives "are usually pluralistic, in both their number and their nature."[27] By that he means that people usually have a number of reasons for doing a particular thing. "[A] man who does something does it for every reason he can think of, and a few unthinkable reasons as well," Fisher writes. By this he means, people have conscious and unconscious motivations, "which tend to coexist and interact." I do not take Fisher to mean that we cannot try to discern those motivations and how much weight each had. A man asked a woman to marry him. Was he motivated because he loved her, because she was wealthy, because he was on the rebound from being jilted by a previous lover, or because of a combination of factors? In trying to sort that out, we would consider circumstances such as whether he treated the woman the way people treat those whom they love, how materialistic he was, how long ago his former lover broke up with him, and so on. We may have more faith in the inferences we draw from circumstantial evidence of this kind than from what the man himself claims was his reason for proposing marriage. Fisher puts this even more starkly. He writes: "There can be no primary, direct evidence of any past motive. But there is a tacit logic of inference which can attain a high degree of probable accuracy."[28] We will not, therefore, be doing anything unusual in deducing James Madison's motivations through circumstantial evidence.

In a sense, this is a mystery book. The mystery is why James Madison decided to write the Second Amendment. In a classic mystery, the author does not tell you who did it, and why they did it, at the beginning of the tale. But while we will be engaged in an exploration to solve a kind of mystery, it is not practical in this case to save the solution to end. So let me describe my thesis.

On Monday afternoon on September 7, 1787, the delegates who were still in attendance at the Constitutional Convention in Philadelphia after four grueling months of difficult and sometimes contentious debate, formed a line in accordance with the geographies of their states—North to South, with the two New Hampshire delegates going first, and the two Georgia delegates last—to sign the product of their work: the proposed Constitution of the United States. Of the fifty-five delegates who had attended some portion of the Convention, forty-one remained. Of those, thirty-eight signed. Three refused. It was three o'clock when they finished. Some made their way from the building we today call Independence Hall to City Tavern for a celebratory drink and to share a meal together.[29] It is said a woman in the street called out to Benjamin Franklin to ask, "Doctor, what have we got? A republic or a monarchy?" and Franklin replied, "A republic, if you can keep it."[30]

But, by its own terms, the Constitution would not be adopted until at least nine states ratified it. The Constitution required that each state elect delegates for a convention to make that state's decision. Two of the three men who had refused to sign—Elbridge Gerry of Massachusetts and George Mason of Virginia—vowed to do everything in their power to prevent ratification.[31] Over the next year, a battle ensued between federalists, who favored ratification, and antifederalists, who opposed it. As we know, three federalists—Alexander Hamilton, James Madison, and John Jay—wrote a series of newspaper articles supporting ratification, which were later collected and published as *The Federalist*. Meanwhile, antifederalists were writing their own newspaper articles denouncing the Constitution and urging that it be rejected.[32]

When Virginia convened its Ratifying Convention in Richmond on Monday, June 2, 1788, ratification was in doubt. Eight states had ratified, but it looked as though if Virginia failed to ratify, there might not be a ninth. Besides, without Virginia, could the Union even be feasible? It was the largest state, the wealthiest state, and home to George Washington, Thomas Jefferson, James Madison, and other nationally prominent figures. With everything on the line, the Richmond Convention was an event of the highest drama. Moreover, among the many prominent delegates were federalists James Madison, John Marshall, and Henry "Light Horse Harry" Lee, and antifederalists Patrick Henry, George Mason, and James Monroe. So many spectators showed up that the proceedings were moved to a larger building. There is something else unusual about the Richmond Convention for its time: We have a reasonably good transcript—totaling nearly five-hundred pages—of the debates.

Patrick Henry, George Mason, and the other antifederalists raised many arguments against ratification. One of the accusations they flung at Madison was that he and his fellow delegates at the Constitutional Convention had handed Congress a terrible weapon: the ability to subvert the slave system by "disarming" the militia. It is impossible to state how terrifying for Virginia, or for other states with large slave populations, any prospect of rendering the militia weaponless could be. The South was petrified about potential slave insurrections. The militia was both a deterrent against rebellions, and its defense should rebellions occur. Madison thought this was an unreasonable fear. If Congress failed to arm the militia, the states or the people themselves could arm the militia, he argued. But Henry implied that Congress might not merely neglect to arm the militia; it might deliberately disarm the militia. Why would it do this? Because, Henry suggested, the North hated slavery, and the Constitution had deprived Congress of the authority to abolish it directly. This may have been a wild theory; but as we know too well, people can be susceptible to such theories, especially if they are fearful. Patrick Henry, moreover, was a powerful persuader. He was, in fact, widely considered the greatest orator then living in America, and when Madison suggested the states could also arm the militia, Henry unmercifully, and effectively, ridiculed him.

Meanwhile, one of the antifederalists' other objections to the Constitution—and probably the objection with the widest appeal—was that it did not contain a bill of rights. And Madison was then opposed to a bill of rights.

By a thin margin, the federalists ultimately prevailed in the Richmond Convention. Madison, however, had been bloodied by the antifederalists. Seizing the opportunity to finish off an opponent while he was weak, Patrick Henry devised a Machiavellian scheme to end Madison's political career. To save himself, Madison reversed his previous position and promised Virginia voters that, if they sent him to Congress, he would write a bill of rights. He followed through on that promise; and when Madison wrote what became the Second Amendment, he did so to solve the problem that Henry raised. That is, Madison wrote the Amendment to assure his constituents in Virginia, and the South generally, that Congress could not deprive states of armed militia. Madison could not give states the authority to arm the militia without contradicting the main body of the Constitution, so, in effect, he provided that if Congress did not arm the militia, the people could do so themselves. And, in fact, this is how militias were generally armed. States simply decreed that militiamen would furnish their own arms.

An interesting thesis, you might say, but where is your evidence? That is what this book is: a presentation of evidence supporting that thesis. I hope you will find the various pieces of evidence intrinsically interesting in their own right and the entirety of the evidence powerfully persuasive.

My thesis is, of course, controversial. If I asked you what image you most associate with the Second Amendment, you might think of the

Minuteman at Lexington, with a musket in his hands. I am arguing that the more accurate image is that of the musket in the hands of the militiaman on slave patrol in the South.

Most professional historians will, at the outset, find my thesis jarring. They agree that Madison wrote the Second Amendment to guarantee an armed militia. That is undeniable from its text. But, by and large, historians believe Madison wanted to protect an armed militia to reduce the need for a standing army. They believe that the Founders considered standing armies a potential tool of tyrants, and therefore dangerous. I do not argue that view is flatly wrong. As David Hackett Fisher said, people often act for a multiplicity of motives. Nevertheless, I shall argue that the "No Standing Army!" motive is exaggerated. The Revolutionary War destroyed faith in the militia as a military force and an instrument of national defense. Lexington and Concord were, in fact, the last clear militia victories of the war. The militia repeatedly proved incapable of standing their ground in battle. As we will see, the militia was so consistently terrible that, in considering how to array their forces for battle, Continental Army generals talked about surrounding militia with Continental soldiers and ordering the Continentals to shoot the first militiamen to bolt. And it was not just Continental Army officers who considered the militia unsuitable for combat; the highest ranking militia officers thought so, too. While some politicians continued to make Fourth of July speeches glorifying the militia after the war, I believe the evidence will persuade you that it is a mistake to take those speeches at face value. Knowledgeable people knew this rhetoric was nothing more than political cotton candy.

At the same time, everyone understood that the militias were effective and essential for slave control. If we had to assign relative values to these two motives for protecting an armed militia, the slave-control motive would outweigh the "No Standing Army!" motive by a factor of at least ten to one.

Here is how we will proceed. The first three chapters of this book will take us to June 1789, and the Ratifying Convention in Richmond, Virginia. We will not only examine the most relevant arguments, but learn something about the backgrounds, personalities, and agenda of the participants. As already mentioned, the Richmond Convention had an unusually skilled and diligent person transcribing the proceedings, so you will be able to hear much of what James Madison, Patrick

Henry, and other delegates said in their own words. This chapter will also examine the Declaration of Rights adopted at the very end of the Richmond Convention, which included a right to bear arms provision and other closely related provisions. I believe you will discover that these provisions have very different connotations when you read them after listening to the debates that immediately preceded them.

The next three chapters will step back in time to provide background and insight about what was in the minds the delegates at the Richmond Convention and the Founders as a whole. These chapters provide a great deal of the context that is necessary to understand their thinking, their statements, and their motives. Chapter 4 will examine just how afraid people in the slaveholding states were of insurrections. It will explore the reasons and parameters of their fears, and the role the militia played in both deterring insurrections and suppressing them, if and when they did occur. Chapters 5 and 6 will describe some of the main battles of the Revolutionary War. These chapters will demonstrate that when Madison wrote the Second Amendment, he and his colleagues in the First Congress believed that militias were worthless for national defense and absolutely essential for slave control.

Chapter 7 will pick up the story after the Richmond Convention. This part of the story deals with Patrick Henry's scheme to extinguish Madison's political career, Madison's contest against James Monroe to win election to Congress, and the promise Madison made to voters to write a bill of rights, should they choose him as their representative. This chapter will also examine the right-to-bear-arms provisions that then existed in four state constitutions. This, together with the Virginia Declaration of Rights discussed at the end of Chapter 3, will familiarize us with the most prominent right-to-bear-arms provisions that Madison had in front of him when he sat down to draft his own provision for the Bill of Rights.

Chapter 8 will recount what happened during the First Congress. It will follow Madison's original draft of what became the Second Amendment through the process in both the House and the Senate, to its ultimate adoption. The House then kept a record of debates, so that we will be able to read what members said about the right-to-bear-arms provisions they were considering. We will also be able to gain additional insight from comments participants in these events made in letters to friends and others at the time, including their own thoughts about Madison's motives.

Chapter 9 will take another and even longer step back in time. We shall travel back almost exactly another one hundred years to the Glorious Revolution of 1688, and the English Declaration of Rights which grew out of that revolution. Although this may seem like a long way to travel, in time and in distance, from the Richmond Convention of 1788 or the First Congress in 1789, I think you will find this last trip to be both intriguing and essential. The American Founders were all born, raised, and educated as members of the British Empire. The Glorious Revolution was as familiar to them as the American Revolution is to us, and they understood and revered the English Declaration of Rights as much as we revere our Bill of Rights. Many of the Founders, in fact, thought of the American Revolution as "a sequel to" the Glorious Revolution.[33] The English Declaration of Rights contains the original right-to-own-arms provision—the provision that inspired American analogs, including the Second Amendment. It is impossible to understand what James Madison or the other American Founders thought about a right to bear arms without taking this final trip.

Until this point, we shall have examined only events that occurred before Madison and the First Congress wrote the Second Amendment. After all, no one knows the future, and Madison's thinking in 1789 could not have been influenced by later events. Chapter 10, however, will peer at bit into the future, that is, into events that occurred after Madison wrote the Second Amendment. There are two reasons to do this. First, sometimes what people do later can throw additional light on their previous actions and motives. Suppose we wish to know why Alice accepted Bruce's proposal of marriage. Was it for love? We can make a better guess about Alice's motives if we learn that she broke off the engagement after learning that Bruce had given away most of his wealth to charity. The second reason for peering a bit into the future is to satisfy some natural curiosity. Our final chapter, therefore, will focus on what the American Founders did—and did not do—with the militia after adopting the Second Amendment. We will, fittingly, end with James Madison in the White House. A short Conclusion will offer final thoughts.

I

Showdown in Richmond

MONDAY, JUNE 2, 1788, was a bright, sunny day in Richmond, Virginia.[1] So many people flocked to the State House to watch the convention that would decide whether the Commonwealth of Virginia would ratify the Constitution that officials delayed proceedings for a day to move to the largest building in the city, a two-year old structure popularly known as the New Academy on Shockoe Hill. The overwhelming interest should not have been a surprise. People then watched debates for entertainment, and this debate was going to be a battle of titans.

In one corner were the federalists, who wanted Virginia to ratify the Constitution and join the Union. In the other were the antifederalists, who wanted Virginia to decline to ratify and remain an independent state or, perhaps, join a separate union of southern states. Everything was on the line. If Virginia ratified, there would be a new Constitution, a new nation, and a new government. If Virginia decided not to ratify, probably none of those things would come into being. The Constitution had to be ratified by nine states. Although eight states had already ratified, it appeared that without Virginia there would not be a ninth.

Rhode Island ratifying was out of the question.[2] The smallest state was so opposed to a new Union that it had not even sent delegates to the Constitutional Convention in Philadelphia. It feared that the large states would politically dominate a new national government. Influential Rhode Island Quakers were repulsed by the slavery compact in the Constitution. Even more importantly, the Constitution would make it impossible for Rhode Island to continue its pro-debtor fiscal policy. Many Rhode Islanders went into debt during the Revolutionary War. Now, after the war, deflation was effectively increasing the size of their debts. Adding insult to injury, speculators had purchased many of the debts. Similar issues led to Shays' Rebellion in Massachusetts (which we will discuss in just a moment); but while Massachusetts protected creditors, Rhode Island took the opposite approach. The state reversed deflation by issuing more paper money, and it allowed debts to out-of-state creditors—but not to Rhode Islanders—to be paid with this depreciating currency. That so outraged a Boston newspaper that it proposed that "Rogue Island," as it chose to refer to its neighbor, "be dropped out of the Union or apportioned to the different States that surround her."

More to the point, Rhode Island's policies would violate the new Constitution in at least two ways. First, the Constitution forbade states from henceforth issuing their own currency or requiring that anything other than gold or silver be accepted as legal tender. Second, the Constitution did not allow states to discriminate against citizens of other states. Rhode Island expressed its contempt for the new document by ignoring the Constitution's requirement that ratification be decided by a state convention and instead put the question up for a public referendum. Among those who bothered to go to the polls, the result was 237 for and 2,708 against ratification. The federalists, therefore, wrote off Rhode Island as a lost cause. The smallest state would, in fact, not join the Union for nearly two more years—after President Washington refused to visit during his tour of New England states, after the U.S. Senate passed a bill banning all trade with the renegade state, and after Providence and Newport threatened to secede from Rhode Island and join the Union by themselves.

Prospects for ratification by North Carolina also seemed bleak. Back in January, while he was busy writing sections of *The Federalist*, James Madison had heard "that North Carolina had postponed its convention until July so it could see what Virginia did." That turned out to be correct. North Carolina scheduled its convention to begin on July 21, well after the start of Virginia's convention on June 2. As time progressed, federalists became increasingly worried that North Carolina might not ratify regardless of Virginia's decision. The strongest objection, by far, was to Congress's taxing power. Under the Articles of Confederation,

Congress had no power to levy direct taxes. It could only request monies from the states, and states often spurned those requests. Antifederalists worried that if Congress could levy taxes payable only by hard money—that is, currency backed by gold or silver, which did not exist in North Carolina, or by those metals themselves—people would be unable to pay and would have their lands and slaves seized and auctioned off to pay the federal taxes.

Even if Congress were empowered to assess appropriations from the states, antifederalists wanted the states to retain the exclusive taxing power to tax their own residents so that, for example, the North Carolina legislature could accept farm produce in payment of taxes. Antifederalists also raised a smattering of other objections to the Constitution, including the absence of a declaration of rights and the prohibition of religious tests as qualification for holding public office, which they warned might lead to "pagans, deists, and Mahometans" holding public office. And typical of hypocrisy that was widespread in the South, some North Carolinians decried the Constitution prohibiting Congress from ending the "abominable" slave trade until 1808, even as they simultaneously argued that abolishing slavery itself was unthinkable. Predictions that North Carolina would not ratify proved correct. When its ratifying convention finally met and voted—five months after Virginia—ratification was defeated on a vote of 184 to 83. And it would take nearly another year and a half after that for North Carolina to finally ratify and join the Union.

New Hampshire had originally convened a ratifying convention on February 13, 1788.[3] The federalists originally had been optimistic and spread the word that the Constitution would experience smooth sailing, but they misread sentiment beyond Portsmouth and other towns along the state's short Atlantic coastline where merchants hoped that a strong national government would be a boon to commerce. About a quarter of towns sending delegates to the convention instructed them to vote against ratification. As was the case in other states, there was particular concern about giving the national government broad taxing power. During debates at the convention in Exeter, federalists thought they had persuaded some of those delegates about the merit of ratification; nevertheless, previously instructed delegates insisted they could not vote to ratify without returning home for new instructions. Realizing they then lacked the votes to prevail, the federalists moved to adjourn the convention to a later date, which they barely won by a vote of 56 to 51. Federalists portrayed this as a temporary setback, but they now lacked credibility. "In truth, the outcome in New Hampshire was anything but certain," writes historian Pauline Maier.[4] The ratifying convention would not reconvene until mid-June so that, George Washington believed, it could see what Virginia would do. Meanwhile, federalists lobbied hard for towns to release their delegates from their instructions to vote against ratification, but they succeeded in only one of twenty-six towns.[5]

Prospects for ratification were even worse in New York State. The state's governor, George Clinton, was both opposed to ratification and extremely powerful. Historians describe him as the "number-one enemy of those who fought for the Constitution,[6] and more powerful "in his state than any other governor in America."[7] Clinton was New York's first governor, and he took full advantage of a new state constitution that, especially for the time, gave the governor special prerogatives. Clinton, for example, only had to stand for election every three years while governors in some states, including Virginia, were elected for only one-year terms. Even more importantly, the new state constitution gave New York's governor broad patronage power. Not only could Clinton appoint judges, sheriffs, militia officers, and many other county officials, he could also appoint the mayors of New York City and Albany. All of these people were, of course, loyal to the man who appointed them. Clinton became so formidable that he ran unopposed for governor in 1780, 1783, and 1786. Clinton would ultimately be elected governor seven times and Vice President of the United States twice.

Well before the Constitutional Convention, Clinton—an original model of a political boss who jealously guarded his power—opposed strengthening the central government. Under the Articles of Confederation, Congress had no taxing power, and thus no way to fund operations of the central government beyond requesting money from the states—requests that states generally ignored. To create a funding stream of some sort, Congress proposed amending the Articles to empower it to impose duties on imports. The Articles, however, could only be amended by unanimous consent of the states, and with some political subterfuge Clinton repeatedly sank the congressional proposal. Rather than Clinton leading the fight, two surrogates in the General Assembly (one of whom was the mayor of Albany) were the front men. And rather than opposing the proposal per se, they insisted on conditions that Congress could not accept. Meanwhile, soon after Congress made its proposal, New York started levying its own duties on imports arriving in the Port of New York. Since many of those imports were shipped to other states, consumers in other states wound up providing New York with a significant share of its revenue. This enhanced Clinton's in-state popularity. So did his policy of seizing lands from families that had supported the British during the war and selling them off at low prices to small farmers.

Clinton literally grew fat and rich on graft—rich enough to own, among other things, eight slaves. Clinton was also a lawyer, but you would not know by how he dressed. He presented himself as a man of the people and dressed more like "a fishmonger or stevedore."[8] For two reasons, Clinton and Alexander Hamilton became archenemies. One reason was personal. Hamilton married a daughter of one the New York State's wealthiest patricians, Philip Schuyler, and Clinton constantly made political hay by railing at the state's aristocratic families, including the Schuylers. The other reason was ideological. Hamilton wanted a strong national government; Clinton did not.

Clinton came out against the Constitution almost immediately after the Philadelphia Convention adjourned, claiming that it would throw the country "into confusion."[9] This infuriated Hamilton, who believed the governor did not even give the Constitution a fair hearing. He responded by attacking Clinton in a New York newspaper. "[S]uch conduct in a man high in office argues greater attachment to his *own power* than to the *public good*," Hamilton wrote.[10] A Clinton surrogate immediately responded by calling Hamilton "a superficial, self-conceited coxcomb" in another New York paper.[11] Realizing the importance of the ratifying battle in New York, Hamilton then recruited James Madison and John Jay to join him in writing a series of essays defending the Constitution, to be published in New York newspapers. These eighty-five essays were later published in book form under the title *The Federalist*, but their original purpose was to persuade the people of New York, and the delegates representing them, to support the Constitution at the state's ratifying convention. Their efforts appeared to have failed however. When Alexander Hamilton saw the results of the special election of delegates to the New York Ratifying Convention—nineteen delegates were federalists, and forty-six, including George Clinton, were antifederalists—he immediately wrote Madison as follows: "As Clinton is truly the leader of his party and inflexibly obstinate, I count little on overcoming by reason. Our only chances will be the previous ratification by nine states, which may shake the firmness of his followers."[12]

If Virginia failed to ratify, where would the ninth state be found? If another ninth state were found, could the new nation successfully exist without Virginia—the most populous and affluent state? And could the United States cohere if Virginia remained outside the Union, thus geographically separating states to the north and the south?

The issue to be decided by Virginia's Ratifying Convention could, therefore, not have been more consequential. And the cast of characters who would debate the issue could not have been more colorful. Not only did they loom large at the time, many of them remain famous today. They included two future presidents—James Madison and James Monroe, and even three future presidents if we include George Washington, who although not a delegate to the convention helped influence its proceedings from backstage. The cast of characters also included John Marshall, who was fated to become the fourth chief justice of the United States Supreme Court and is regarded today as the most influential justice in the long history of the Court. It included Patrick Henry, who was regarded as the best orator of his time and had famously helped rouse a nation to revolution by crying, "Give me liberty or give me death!" The 170 delegates to the Ratifying Convention also included individuals who were then famous but are unknown to most Americans today. Two of them who will become particularly important for our purposes were Edmund Randolph, who was then governor of Virginia, and George Mason, the author of the Virginia Declaration of Rights of 1776, who is still well known in Virginia and is the namesake of one the Virginia's major public universities.

It is worth spending a little time getting to know a bit about these men.

While it is their differences that will become especially important, let us quickly note what they had in common. They were, of course, all

Virginians. They had all come from venerable families or married into venerable families and were part of the state's aristocracy. They were, with the possible exception of Patrick Henry, well-educated. A number of them had gone to college—James Madison to Princeton, and John Marshall, Edmund Randolph, and James Monroe to William and Mary—but going to college was not then de rigueur and the others had benefitted from rigorous study under private tutors and were well read. All of these men knew each other. James Madison and Patrick Henry were distantly related through marriage. James Madison and James Monroe were close friends, and would remain close friends throughout their lives, even when they ran against each other for a seat in Congress. George Washington and George Mason were neighbors—Washington's home at Mount Vernon was about twelve miles on horseback from Mason's home at Gunston Hall, and even closer by boat—and they sometimes visited one another. All of these men were wealthy, and in large measure their wealth depended on slaves. While we don't know precisely how many slaves they each owned at the time of the Ratifying Convention in 1788, we can make rough estimates based on what we know about how many slaves they owned at other times. In all likelihood, George Mason,[13] James Madison,[14] James Monroe,[15] John Marshall,[16] George Washington,[17] and Patrick Henry[18] all owned at least one hundred slaves at the time of the Ratifying Convention.

James Madison would lead the federalists. Everyone knew that Madison had been a principal architect—perhaps *the* principal architect—of the Constitution. There was nothing imposing about his stature. Madison stood five feet and six inches, had a small frame, a pale complexion, and dressed simply and always in black. He was naturally shy, and sometimes his voice quavered when he began speaking; sometimes he spoke so softly his audience leaned forward to hear him.[19] Yet his brilliance shone bright. "[F]ew men possessed so rich a flow of language," said Edward Coles, who while a young man served as Madison's secretary and later became governor of Illinois.[20] Madison was not merely skilled at expression, both written and oral; his powers of reasoning and analysis—especially when it came to matters of political science—may have been unmatched, even among the other most supremely gifted Founders such as Benjamin Franklin and Alexander Hamilton.

John Marshall, a lawyer and member of the Virginia House of Delegates who had already earned a reputation as a fine debater, had also been elected as a delegate to the convention and was known to be a federalist. Marshall would, of course, go on to become Chief Justice of the United States Supreme Court. More than two centuries later, Marshall is still considered the most influential chief justice in American history.

Assisting from backstage was George Washington. No one was more of a federalist than Washington, who from his wartime experience well understood the need for a strong national government. While Washington himself declined to serve as a delegate to the Virginia Ratifying Convention in order to preserve his carefully curated persona of a statesman who transcended debates, his behind-the-curtain influence on the proceedings was palpable.[21] One historian writes that even though he "never set foot in the convention hall," Washington "dominated the exhausting drama" nonetheless, and at times the antifederalist responses seemed to be attempts to reply as much to Washington as to Madison and other federalists in their presence. Washington persuaded Madison to stand for election as a delegate to the convention so that Madison could lead the federalist effort, was in close communication with Madison throughout the convention, and hosted Madison at Mount Vernon for four days immediately after the convention so that Madison could recover from exhaustion.[22] As we will see much later, however, this alliance between Washington and Madison—so consequential at this stage—would not survive Washington's transition from federalist to Federalist and Madison's transition from federalist to Republican. That, however, is years in the future.

Two other notable Virginians were not in attendance. One was Richard Henry Lee, who on June 7, 1776, had famously offered a resolution before the Second Continental Congress declaring: "That these United Colonies are, and of right ought to be, free and independent States, that they are absolved from all allegiance to the British Crown, and that all political connection between them and the State of Great Britain is, and ought to be, totally dissolved." He had also served as president of the Second Continental Congress. Lee was a skilled orator and opposed to ratification. He did not attend the Virginia Ratifying

Convention for health reasons.[23] Thomas Jefferson, author of the Declaration of Independence, was then minister to France and also absent. During debate, both sides would try to claim Jefferson supported their position. Patrick Henry would claim that Jefferson wrote a letter urging four states to decline to ratify until a bill of rights was added to the Constitution. James Madison would object to Henry using any outside authority in debate, but would then himself say that he was acquainted with Jefferson's sentiments and knew that, if Jefferson were present, he would vote for ratification.[24] Edmund Pendleton, the president of the Virginia Ratifying Convention, would even more effectively rebut Henry. Pendleton produced a copy of the letter to which Henry had referred and read passages from it in which Jefferson said that failing to ratify the Constitution would be "an incurable evil."[25] The federalists were fortunate Lee was absent, and the antifederalists were fortunate Jefferson was absent.

Antifederalists at the Convention would be led by Patrick Henry and George Mason. Among those supporting them would be thirty-year-old James Monroe.

The antifederalists expected their ranks to include the state's popular, thirty-four-year-old governor, Edmund Randolph. After all, Randolph was one of only three delegates to the Federal Convention in Philadelphia who refused to sign the Constitution. What the antifederalists did not know, however, was that James Madison had been quietly but assiduously working for months to bring Randolph into the federalist camp.[26] Madison warned Randolph that while Patrick Henry was making a lot of noise about the absence of a bill of rights and the need to protect liberty, all of that was pretext and Henry's real objective was to create a Southern confederacy.[27] Madison also asked Randolph to reflect on the company he would keep in antifederalist ranks. Those opposing ratification either had dark ulterior motives, such as Patrick Henry, or wanted to protect their parochial interests. Do not allow these people to carry "on their opposition under the respectability of your name," Madison pleaded.[28] By contrast, Madison argued, the federalists were enlightened, cosmopolitan men who understood that a strong national government was essential for many purposes, including commerce. Nearly all "men of intelligence, patriotism, property, and independent circumstances" supported ratification, argued Madison.[29] How Randolph stood would carry considerable weight with many of the 170 delegates. He had given up much for the revolution. Randolph's father had been a Loyalist who sailed to England with his wife and daughters when the revolution succeeded.[30] As events got underway in Richmond, Madison secretly hoped that Randolph might surprise the antifederalists.

Any attempt to win over George Mason, who had also refused to sign the Constitution in Philadelphia, would have been a fool's errand. Mason was one of the other two men who refused to sign the Constitution in Philadelphia, but the sixty-two-year-old George Mason was nothing like Randolph. Edmund Randolph was earnest, curious, and open-minded. He sometimes wavered on important issues, but that was because he recognized the competing sides of issues and struggled to discern what was best. George Mason never wavered. Convinced of his own brilliance and rectitude, he was a man who always had to have his way. He was not a man to reconsider his views, and he was temperamentally incapable of compromising. George Washington described his bullheaded neighbor this way: "Pride on the one hand and want of manly candor on the other will not, I am certain, let him acknowledge an error in his opinions."[31]

As Washington's remark suggests, these two neighbors were not fast friends, especially not from Washington's point of view. In fact, over the course of the years Washington had twice accused Mason of engaging in underhanded dealings in transactions they had with each other.[32] (Washington was not the only person who questioned Mason's ethics over the years.[33]) Nevertheless, Mason tried to preserve a relationship with his illustrious neighbor, and the ever-polite Washington maintained a cool, civil relationship with his neighbor. But Washington was very much put off by Mason's conduct during the Constitutional Convention. He thought that Mason "rendered himself obnoxious in Philadelphia by the pains he took to disseminate his objections."[34] If Mason in Philadelphia was bad enough, for Washington, the Virginia Ratifying Convention, at which Mason would be even more vehement, would wind up being the last straw.[35] Washington tolerated one more visit by his neighbor to Mount Vernon after that, but Mason finally got the message. Mason told his son that while he still regarded George Washington with great esteem, he believed that his opposition to the

Constitution in Philadelphia and Richmond had extinguished his relationship with his neighbor.[36]

Mason may have been egocentric, quarrelsome, and even litigious, but there was no denying he was a man of high intelligence and well read about matters of political philosophy.[37] He was something of an intellectual. Mason's biographer described him as "[i]rritable and acerbic," but also "independent and incorruptible," and someone who "always inspired more respect than affection."[38] In one way, his cantankerousness helped him. Because Mason did not have a personality suitable for a political career—and knew it—he had no ambitions for political office, and what he said about issues was unencumbered by political calculations. This combination of traits allowed Mason to be an acceptable but never widely popular member of legislative bodies and conventions. He was elected to such bodies a number of times, but it was often "with great difficulty" or because he was essentially drafted after other potential candidates declined to stand for election.[39] But once included, Mason's service could be consequential. In the Fifth Virginia Convention, which assembled in Williamsburg in May 1776, Mason was appointed to a committee with more than thirty members, including James Madison and Edmund Randolph, tasked with writing a plan of government and bill of rights. True to form, Mason did not like working with his fellow committee members, whom he considered "useless" people who would "in all probability have a thousand ridiculous and impractical proposals."[40] So Mason retired to his room at the Raleigh Tavern to write the documents himself.

For a declaration of rights, Mason produced a draft of thirteen provisions, which the committee expanded to eighteen provisions and then contracted to sixteen before settling on a final draft. When it was time to introduce the declaration on the floor of the convention, Mason, who was then himself little known and not self-confident about his speaking skills, asked Patrick Henry to do that.[41] There is no doubt that Mason's first draft was highly influential in the final result, and it is not unfair to say that George Mason was the principal author of the Virginia Declaration of Rights. It is a bit much, however, to call him *the* author of the document. Yet that is how he is often identified. Mason, himself, is responsible for the frequent misconception; he exaggerated his own role in a letter two years later.[42] Such was the nature of George Mason.

It is worth pausing for just a moment to observe that one section of the Virginia Declaration of Rights of 1776 is one of many puzzle pieces that are relevant to solving our mystery about why James Madison wrote the Second Amendment twelve years later and what he wanted to achieve. Later we will compare this provision with a comparable one in a list of proposed amendments to the United States Constitution promulgated by the Virginia Ratifying Convention. The comparison will be particularly interesting because, as we will see, George Mason will also be the principal author of that document. For right now, I am just going to set forth that section and make two brief observations. Here it is, labeled number thirteen of sixteen rights:

> That a well-regulated militia, composed of the body of the people, trained to arms, is the proper, natural, and safe defense of a free state; that standing armies, in time of peace, should be avoided as dangerous to liberty; and that in all cases the military should be under strict subordination to, and governed by, the civil power.[43]

The two brief observations are these. First, the section is about the militia and a fear of standing armies, but it is not a right to bear arms of any kind. Second, the section was promulgated on June 12, 1776, after the Battles of Lexington and Concord and Bunker Hill but only about one year into the seven-year Revolutionary War.

Mason's role as the principal author—or, as many came to believe, *the* author—of the Virginia Declaration of Rights greatly enhanced his stature. Mason's work on government structure also very much influenced the convention's final product, but many considered that product seriously flawed. By contrast, the Declaration of Rights was widely circulated and hailed as an important revolutionary document, and it is his association with that document that established Mason as a prominent Virginian.[44] Thereafter, Mason was elected to the Virginia House of Delegates, during which time he nominated Patrick Henry to be the state's first governor.[45] After the war, the Virginia legislature appointed Mason to a special committee to negotiate with Maryland jurisdictional and navigation issues involving the Potomac River.[46]

Then, in December 1786, Virginia sent Mason—along with George Washington, James Madison, Edmund Randolph, and three others— to represent it at the Federal Convention to be held in Philadelphia.[47]

Why did Mason refuse to sign the Constitution? He had a hodge- podge of reasons.[48] He objected to Congress having the authority to enact laws regarding commerce and navigation by majority vote; he wanted a supermajority of two-thirds to be required for such laws. He thought the president was too powerful. He had originally proposed that executive authority be divided among three presidents. When that went nowhere, he argued that the president should be required to seek approval for executive decisions from a council of states of some kind. He also wanted a privy council—comprised of two members from the North, two from the middle states, and two from the South—to ap- prove presidential appointments rather than giving that authority to the Senate. He thought the office of vice president both unnecessary and a dangerous blend of the executive and legislative branches as the vice president would preside over the Senate. He thought the House was too small. He wanted Congress to have the authority to enact *expo facto* laws, but he did not want Congress to have the authority to grant monopolies. He predicted that the under the Constitution the govern- ment would start out as a "moderate aristocracy," which would evolve into either "a monarchy, or a corrupt, tyrannical aristocracy."[49]

Two of Mason's objections are, for our purposes, worthy of special mention. Mason wanted the Constitution to include a declaration of rights. He specifically wanted guarantees of liberty for the press and jury trials in civil cases, and a prohibition against standing armies in time of peace. Mason did not mention any concern about a right to bear arms.

Mason also objected to the provision prohibiting Congress from abolishing the slave trade until 1808. "I hold it essential in every point of view that the general government should have the power to prevent the increase of slavery," Mason told the Convention.[50] Why? Mason decried the evils of slavery, but his concern always seemed more fo- cused on the slaveholders than the slaves. "Every master of slaves is born a petty tyrant," he lamented. Slavery, he proclaimed, eroded "all the finer feelings of the Soul" and would ultimately "bring the judg- ment of heaven on a country." Even on this, how sincere was Mason—a man who owned three hundred slaves and never freed any of them, even in his will?[51] Mason's concern with ending the slave trade probably had more to do with Virginia's economic self-interest. Virginia had a slave surplus, and its slaveholders could profit by exporting slaves to other states. Meanwhile South Carolina and Georgia were aggressively importing more slaves from Africa, and Virginia wanted to eliminate the competition. The provision allowing Congress to end the slave trade (but, of course, not slavery itself) after twenty years was a compromise between the slave-exporting states of Virginia and Maryland and the slave-importing states of South Carolina and Georgia.[52] Mason, of course, was allergic to compromises. There is, however, another reason Mason gave for his displeasure for protecting the slave trade for another twenty years, one he was surely sincere about. Mason feared that increasing the number of slaves in the South increased the risk of slave insurrections. As he put it, importing more slaves from Africa would "render the United States weaker, more vulnerable, and less capable of defense."[53]

In many ways, Mason's lack of affinity for everything in the final document was typical. The Constitution was a complex instrument and the product of numerous compromises. Every delegate could point to things he disliked. James Madison, for example, believed the Grand Compromise between the large and small states—in which only one congressional chamber allocated seats in proportion to population while the other would give tiny states such as Delaware and Rhode Island equal representation with the large states—violated republican principles and created a permanent "rotten borough" system of the kind that plagued the British Parliament.[54] He thought this so important an issue that at one point during the convention he urged large states to refuse to capitulate. Madison wanted the president elected by the people, not by state legislature. He believed in a strong executive and wanted supermajorities of three-quarters to be required to overrule presidential vetoes, instead of the two-thirds majorities required by the final document.[55] Perhaps most important of all, Madison wanted Congress to have the power to "negative"—that is, veto—any state laws "in all cases, whatsoever."[56] Richard Beeman writes that "Madison fervently believed that this constituted the heart and soul of his plan for a new government."[57] Not getting it was a bitter pill to swallow. Yet

Madison swallowed it. He realized that creating a charter for a new government required political compromises, and making compromises between large and small states, and slave and free states, was enormously difficult. Madison said he thought it "impossible to consider the degree of concord which ultimately prevailed as less than a miracle."[58] That, however, was not George Mason's disposition. In one of his last speeches to the Convention, he declared that he would "sooner chop off his right hand than put it to the Constitution as it now stands."[59]

Following the Philadelphia Convention, Mason privately circulated to friends a pamphlet titled *Objections to this Constitution of Government*.[60] It was soon widely circulated; in October 1787, a Philadelphia printer published it, and newspapers also reprinted it. At about the same time, Alexander Hamilton recruited James Madison and John Jay to collaborate in writing *The Federalist*. Meanwhile, George Washington sat down to write a letter to someone who, Washington feared, would be critical in the coming fight over ratification. A master of diplomacy and suasion, Washington decided to begin with a short letter with a soft sell approach. Washington wrote:

Dear Sir:
In the first moment after my return I take the liberty of sending you a copy of the Constitution which the Federal Convention has submitted to the People of these States. I accompany it with no observations; your own Judgment will at once discover the good, and the exceptionable parts of it. . . . I wish the constitution which is offered had been made more perfect, but I sincerely believe it is the best that could be obtained at this time; and, as a Constitutional door is opened for amendment hereafter, the adoption of it under the present circumstances of the Union, is in my opinion desirable.

From a variety of concurring accounts it appears to me that the political concerns of this Country are, in a manner, suspended by a thread. [Because the community looked up to the Convention] if nothing had been agreed on by that body, anarchy would soon have ensued, the seeds being richly sown in every soil. I am &c.[61]

Washington sent that letter to the man he knew to be the most powerful politician in Virginia: Patrick Henry.

Patrick Henry "has only to say, let this be law—and it is law," Washington told James Madison as they were strategizing about how to get the Constitution ratified.[62] It was not a compliment. Washington was commenting on Henry's ability to get whatever he wanted through the Virginia Assembly, and Washington did not believe that what Henry wanted was in the best interests of America.[63] But Washington's assessment of Henry's power was accurate. Virginia had elected Henry its first governor in 1776, and although Henry was generally regarded as an ineffective wartime governor—both by many Virginians at the time and by historians today—the state reelected Henry governor a total of four additional times, during two different periods (1776–79 and 1784–86), often by acclamation.[64] Henry, therefore, was not powerful because he was governor; he was periodically governor because he was powerful.

But it was not his political power that made Patrick Henry so formidable in this time. He might be able to call the shots in the Virginia Assembly, but the ratifying convention was not the Assembly. That was, in fact, why the Framers did not want state legislatures to decide whether to ratify the Constitution. State politicians would want to preserve their power, not yield so much of it to the national government. And political bosses often wielded enormous control over state legislatures. So the Framers bypassed this as much as possible by requiring ratification by special conventions. Voters would elect delegates to their conventions for this one purpose. In this particular setting, therefore, Henry's political power was at least somewhat diminished. What made Patrick Henry so formidable nonetheless were his rhetorical gifts. Henry was widely considered America's greatest orator.

It had been in his very first trial, as a green twenty-seven-year-old lawyer, that Henry had begun to earn that reputation. The case involved a dispute between Virginia parishes and their ministers. Traditionally, parishes had paid their ministers in pounds of tobacco. In 1758, the Virginia legislature passed a law, called the Twopenny Act, to permit parishes to pay their ministers in Virginia currency instead. The amount of their salary was to be the cash equivalent of what, on average, they had been paid in tobacco over the past six years, during which time tobacco had averaged two pennies per pound. There had, however, been a drought. Much less tobacco had been harvested, tobacco prices soared, and the ministers were getting paid far less in cash than what they would have received in tobacco under normal market prices. Ministers all over Virginia sued their parishes. One of the most prominent of these plaintiffs was Reverend James Maury. In addition to being a minister, Maury was also a distinguished scholar who privately tutored the sons of some of Virginia's most prominent families to prepare them for college. One of his students had been Thomas Jefferson. Considering how highly regarded and well-connected Reverend Maury was, it was no surprise he won his case.

The court scheduled a second trial to determine the amount of damages. The vestrymen's attorney told them there was nothing to be done. The market price of tobacco was well known and indisputable, the jury would calculate damages, and that was that. It was not even worth his time to try the case. The farmers in the parish were going to have to pay Reverend Maury so much more that they might be forced into bankruptcy, however, and they desperately looked around to find some way to reduce damages. Someone came up with the idea of hiring Patrick Henry, then twenty-seven years of age. Almost surely the farmers did not decide to retain Henry for his legal ability. Henry had been at the bar for three years, and he spent most of that time at his desk writing deeds and wills. He had never tried a major case in court.[65] They picked Henry for his family connections: his uncle and namesake, Reverend Patrick Henry Sr., officiated at The Fork Church in St. Martin's Parish, where he drew large audiences who wanted to hear his galvanizing sermons; and young Patrick's father, John, was a magistrate in the very court the case was going to be tried. Maybe none of this would affect the jury, but perhaps Patrick might catch some kind of procedural break from the court. As noted, the farmers were more or less desperate.

Patrick Henry Sr. traveled to the courthouse, eager to see his nephew's first significant court appearance, but no sooner had he stepped from his carriage than young Patrick asked him to leave. Whatever for? asked the puzzled uncle. "Because I am engaged in opposition to clergy, and your appearance there might strike me with such awe as to prevent me from doing justice to my clients," young Patrick replied. The parson stepped back into his carriage and returned home. Not only was he disappointed; he was also worried that his nephew might be too nervous for his first major trial.

By all accounts, Patrick Henry looked reasonably able during most of the trial. He made appropriate objections during jury selection and the examination of witnesses. But when he was called on to deliver his closing argument to the jury, Patrick Henry rose to his feet—and then nothing. He stood there, silent. Everyone waited politely at first. Then there were nervous fidgeting and furtive glances. Many were embarrassed for the frozen young man, though perhaps the plaintiff and opposing counsel may have been secretly delighted at the young man's plight. After a long time, Patrick Henry tilted his head back, as if gazing to heaven, pursed his lips and—still no words emerged.

Maybe it should be no surprise, some must have thought, that young Patrick Henry was in over his head. He had attended school only until age ten, after which he was homeschooled, part time, by relatives. Although he been taught to read Latin, Greek, and French and studied mathematics as well as Roman, English, and American history, homeschooling apparently ended by age fifteen.[66] At the age of twenty-four, he spent six weeks studying law on this own to prepare for the bar exam, which was then orally administered by a panel of lawyers. According to Thomas Jefferson, the lawyers who examined Henry only signed his license with great reluctance and one member of the panel, George Wythe, who was later Jefferson's law teacher and perhaps the original source of this story, refused to sign.[67] It is said that while Patrick Henry stood mute, his father, who was the presiding magistrate among the six justices who sat together at a long table (all of whom were related to the Henry family in one way or another) sunk lower and lower in his chair in humiliation. Finally he could wait no longer. Judge John Henry had to do what he had to do, so he reached for gavel to declare summary judgment for Reverend Maury. And at that moment his son began to speak.

Everyone was transfixed. The young attorney was rhetorically brilliant. At times he shouted in indignation; at other times his voice fell to a whisper. He startled everyone with his bravery. He accused Reverend Maury and clergy of the established Anglican Church with un-Christian greed. "Do they manifest their zeal in the cause of the religion and humanity by practicing the mild and benevolent precepts of the Gospel of Jesus?" the young Henry demanded. "Do they feed the hungry and clothe the naked? Oh, no gentlemen!" Instead, these "rapacious" men of God were ready to snatch the last cornbread "from the hearth of their honest parishioner."[68]

Patrick Henry spoke about natural rights and the compact between a monarch and the people. He argued that the Twopenny Act had been necessary for the economic survival of the community. When he declared that the King of England had broken faith with his people by annulling the Act, opposing counsel cried "Treason!" and demanded the court take action. But it was too late; Patrick Henry had success-fully stoked the emotions of nearly everyone in the courtroom, in-cluding even judges who are normally impervious to emotional appeals. When the young defense counsel sat down, Judge John Henry quietly instructed the jury that as Reverend Maury's right to compensation had already been decided in a previous trial, it was their duty, and their only duty, to determine the amount of compensation. But his son had already addressed that point. He had told the jury that while they were required to award the plaintiff damages, and the amount of damages would be entirely up to them, they should not award Reverend Maury more than a single penny. After only five minutes of deliberation, that is exactly what the jury did.

It is said that Henry had been so effective at rousing passions against the ministers that, as soon as the court adjourned, all clergy in attend-ance "fled from the house in precipitation and terror."[69] Meanwhile, farmers hoisted Patrick Henry on their shoulders and carried him from the building as a conquering hero.

The Parson's Cause, as the case is known, was instantly famous. Everyone in a legal scrape now wanted to retain this young lawyer, and he continued to hone his skills through courtroom experience. When word got out that Patrick Henry was trying a case, people flocked to see him. Two years after the Parson's Cause, Henry was elected as dele-gate to the Virginia House of Burgesses. Almost immediately after his arrival, and in disregard of House custom that new members should allow some time to pass before they began making speeches, Henry rose and delivered a speech denouncing the Stamp Act and proposing five then highly radical resolutions. Henry argued that only the colony's own legislature could tax its inhabitants and England's attempts to im-pose direct taxes were destroying "British and American freedom."[70] When Henry said King George the Third had broken the sacred covenant between a monarch and his people, he once again drew cries of "Treason!" This only provided Henry with additional rhetorical fuel. "If this be treason, make the most of it," Henry declared. Some members cheered; others were aghast. Following a frenzied debate, Henry's resolutions passed. That surprised most members, even though the margin was only one or two votes. Perhaps even more of a surprise was that two of the colony's largest planters—Richard Henry Lee and George Washington, both pillars of Virginian aristocracy—voted with the majority. This event was an early and significant milepost on the American road to revolution.

Observing Henry's Stamp Act speech from just outside the door of the House of Burgesses was a twenty-two-year-old law student, Thomas Jefferson, who later recalled hearing "the splendid display of Mr. Henry's talents as a popular orator. They were great indeed; such that I have never heard from any other man."[71] We will return in just a moment to an important refinement of Jefferson's assessment of Henry's rhetorical skills, but first let us leap briefly ahead ten years to Patrick Henry's most famous and consequential speech—the one he delivered on March 23, 1775, to the Second Virginia Convention.

In the ten years since Henry's Five Resolutions Speech, there had been the Boston Massacre; Rhode Islanders had burned the British revenue schooner HMS Gaspee, and the British search for the perpetrators gave rise to the Committees of Correspondence among the colonies; the Boston Tea Party had taken place; and the First Continental Congress had convened. Paul Revere's ride and the Battles of Lexington and Concord were about one month in the future. It was therefore a very different time than Henry's Stamp Act speech. Colonies were preparing for war. The royal governor had dissolved Virginia's House of Burgesses, and the First and Second Virginia Conventions were, in essence, a convening of the Burgesses in defiance of that edit.[72] Nevertheless, many delegates still hoped to avoid war with the mother country when they met at St. John's Church in Richmond. When Henry introduced resolutions that Virginia "be put in a posture of defense" and its militia be armed and disciplined—that is, trained—he was accused of imprudently inviting armed conflict. In response, Henry rose and, "with an unearthly fire burning in his eye," made a speech that, together with Thomas Paine's *Common Sense*, ranks as one of the two most ringing call to arms propelling America to open revolution.[73] "The war has actually begun," Henry declared, and then concluded with what became some of the most famous words of the American Revolution:

> Our brethren are already in the field. Why stand here idle? What is the gentlemen wish? What would they have? Is life so dear or peace so sweet as to be purchased at the price of chains and slavery? Forbid it, Almighty God! I know not what course others may take, but as for me, give me liberty or give me death![74]

When Henry sat down, the delegates responded in the most profound way possible: it was silent. This was not a moment for cheering. It was a moment for grave commitment. Henry's resolutions passed.[75]

This was the man James Madison had to debate successfully at the Virginia Ratifying Convention to prevail. That would be a herculean task, but not an impossible one. For as powerful as Henry's oratorical gifts were—and there is no denying they were formidable—Henry was master of a particular kind of oratory. Patrick Henry had perfected his skills making arguments to juries. That requires a particular approach. A jury consists of a dozen individuals who may see things quite differently. Good trial lawyers therefore often address the same point from a variety of angles, and an argument from one vantage point can often be inconsistent with an argument from a different vantage point. Lawyers "argue in the alternative" to judges, too, but they are then careful to point that out. But unlike judges or philosophers, jurors are seldom linear thinkers, and trial lawyers seldom flag for juries when they are arguing in the alternative. Trial lawyers also learn from experience that appeals to emotion are often more potent than appeals to logic. Good trial lawyers are psychologists more than logicians, and creating emotional appeals was Patrick Henry's special gift. Sometimes those who listened to Henry's speeches found themselves powerfully moved but later wondered why. Thomas Jefferson was one of those people. After listening to several of Henry's speeches, Jefferson questioned whether he would even classify Henry's oratory as eloquence. While he was listening to him, Jefferson found Henry's remarks "impressive and sublime" and "directly to the point" and was personally "delighted and moved, but I have asked myself when he ceased, what the devil has he said?"[76]

Patrick Henry's oratory, therefore, often lacked sticking power with critical listeners. It would be a mistake, however, to think of him as just a blowhard. Although he had been largely homeschooled, Henry had a rigorous, classical education, and he was capable of crafting legal arguments for judges based on a careful study of legal doctrine and precedents.[77] A judge before whom Patrick Henry appeared in a highly complicated case reported that he was "astonished how Mr. Henry should have acquired such a knowledge of maritime law, to which he had never before turned his attention," and said he had never heard a lawyer make "a more eloquent or argumentative speech."[78] That capacity often surprised opponents who were unfamiliar with him. In fact, Henry often deliberately acted the part of a country bumpkin before taking an overconfident opponent apart.[79]

Nevertheless, it was on substance that James Madison would have the advantage. Few people could construct as well-thought-through an argument as he. And no one—absolutely no one—knew the Constitution as well as Madison. Madison was proud that during the more than four months that the Constitutional Convention had been in session in Philadelphia, he had not been "absent a single day, nor more than a casual fraction of an hour in any day."[80] Not only did Madison listen carefully to all of the debates, he took detailed notes of them and spent long evenings at his desk using those notes to write out in full each speaker's remarks. Madison, himself, gave some of the most influential speeches during the convention and was the architect of the Virginia Plan, which became the fundamental framework of the document. Madison also wrote twenty-six of the essays in *The Federalist* (which today is often referred to as *The Federalist Papers* and considered "the most important work in political science that has ever been written, or is likely ever to be written, in the United States").[81] By contrast, Patrick Henry had not attended the Constitutional Convention. Indeed, he had refused to do so. So Madison could be confident that Henry could not hold a candle to him when it came to knowledge and understanding of the document.[82]

Yet it was always a mistake to underrate Patrick Henry. And as it would turn out, Henry would inflict a severe political wound to

Madison during the debates at the Ratifying Convention—a wound that Madison would attempt to salve by writing the Second Amendment.

* * *

When on September 5, 1774, Patrick Henry had stood before the Continental Congress in Philadelphia, he proclaimed, "I am not a Virginian, I am an American." It is a fascinating remark to recall because everything Henry stood for at the Virginia Ratifying Convention in Richmond four years later was precisely the opposite.

In Philadelphia, Henry had argued: "Government is dissolved. Where are your landmarks, your boundaries of colonies? We are in a state of nature, sir. . . . The distinctions between Virginians, Pennsylvanians, New Yorkers, and New Englanders are no more." It was classic Henry because it was an argument fashioned for a particular purpose. The question then on the floor in Carpenter's Hall in Philadelphia was whether each state was going to have an equal vote in the newly constituted body or whether each state would be given votes in proportion to their population of their total wealth. Virginia was the most populous and most wealthy state, and if votes were allocated proportionately, Virginia would have the most votes. That is what Henry wanted. Ironically, Henry had declared "I am not a Virginian" in service of promoting the interests of Virginia.

Now eighteen years later, when after procedural issues were out of the way and substantive debates began on the third day of the Virginia Ratifying Convention in Richmond, Henry wasted no time announcing his central thesis: that Virginia was more important than a new national republic, and a national government was a danger to Virginia. This was to be Henry's overarching theme throughout the Convention; the Constitution was fatally flawed because it created a Union—a real nation—rather than continuing a confederation among thirteen sovereign states. The state legislatures did not give their delegates that authority when they sent them to Philadelphia; they only sent their representatives to consider revisions to the Articles of Confederation. But the delegates had betrayed that charge. "What right," Henry asked, "had they to say, *We, the people?* . . . Who authorized them to speak the language of, *We the people*, instead of, *We, the states*?"[83] How bad— indeed, how malicious—was the proposed Constitution? Later during the Convention, Henry would call the Constitution "the most fatal plan that could possibly be conceived to enslave a free people."[84] Thus, while some antifederalists were open to ratifying the Constitution if only particular defects could be corrected, Henry was clearly opposed to a Union under any circumstances. He would spend many hours attacking particular aspects of the Constitution—empowering the national government to directly levy taxes, omitting a bill of rights, establishing a seat of the national government "ten miles square" under the exclusive jurisdiction of Congress, creating too powerful a president who would surely devolve into a despot, creating a federal judiciary that would diminish and displace state courts—and he hoped to persuade delegates who did not like particular aspects to vote against ratification now in the hope of getting modifications. But to Henry himself particular objections were not the point; they were merely one example after another of a model of government that should be rejected root and branch. The core problem was that the new constitutional design would destroy liberty.

Did Henry wish for Virginia to remain sovereign and independent on its own, or did he wish to make it the linchpin in a Southern confederacy, as Madison suspected? Rumors flew "out of doors"—that is, outside the Convention—and were sometimes obliquely alluded to in debates, but Henry never answered that question on the floor of the Convention, or, as far as can be determined, anywhere else. One thing is certain: Henry was unalterably opposed to creating a Union.

"I wish to hear the real, actual, existing danger, which should lead us to take those steps, so dangerous in my conception," Henry remarked. "Disorders have arisen in other parts of America; but here, sir, no dangers, no insurrection or tumult have happened; everything has been calm and tranquil." Ironically, later in the Convention, Henry will seek to play upon fears of insurrections in Virginia. At this juncture, however, he is suggesting a national government will make Virginia less safe.

Henry's reference to disorders alludes to Shays' Rebellion in Massachusetts, an armed uprising by former Continental Army soldiers and militiamen who had fought in the Revolutionary War and could not repay debts they incurred while fighting for America. As previously mentioned, Rhode Island faced similar issues but adopted pro-debtor policies. Not Massachusetts. With the assistance of the Massachusetts judicial system, creditors were executing on those loans, foreclosing on homes and small farms and threatening those who could not repay loans with debtors' prison. After the state legislature rejected their many entreaties, veterans in western Massachusetts began to obstruct debt collectors and close courthouses by force of arms. Led by Daniel Shays, this body of armed dissidents, who called themselves Regulators, grew large enough to present a threat to the state government. Massachusetts raised an army to confront the Regulators. Things reached a climax in January 1787, when Shays led 1,500 armed men to the Springfield Armory to seize the weapons stored within. General Benjamin Lincoln, who led the Massachusetts army, anticipated Shays' move. The Armory was well defended, and the Regulators were repelled by warning shots and then artillery fire. Four died and twenty were wounded.

Although the state government ultimately prevailed, the episode illustrated the potential vulnerability of states facing peril. Under the Articles of Confederation, there was no national government or national force to come to their rescue. Many American statesmen saw Shays' Rebellion as a wake-up call, and it helped provide impetus for scrapping the Articles of Confederation and writing a new Constitution. George Washington, for example, remarked that he was "hoping that good may result from the cloud of evils which threatened, not only the hemisphere of Massachusetts but by spreading its baneful influence, the tranquility of the Union."[85] James Madison felt the same.[86] Patrick Henry was essentially saying we, Virginia, do not have such problems, so let's not become part of a Union that requires us to pull another state's fat out of the fire.

Henry mentioned "insurrections," too. He was alluding to the threat of slave insurrections. While on the surface Henry was suggesting Virginia need have no fear of insurrections, his remarks later in the Convention will show that Henry did not really believe that. What he believed was that a national government might constrain Virginia's ability to deal with insurrections on its own.

George Mason quickly followed up on the overarching theme of Virginia First. Mason argued that only one government—state or national—could effectively have taxing authority because the people would not permit themselves to be "doubly harassed." (History, of course, would prove Mason wrong about this. Americans today are taxed by federal, state, and local governments.) The Constitution gave Congress the power to levy direct taxes. "This power," Mason darkly warned, "is calculated to annihilate the state governments."[87] Modern conspiracy theorists have nothing over George Mason, who was suggesting that the Founders' secret objective was to destroy state governments altogether. The federal judiciary, too, would lead to "the annihilation of state governments," though how it would do that was left unsaid.

Mason also argued that "popular governments can only exist in small territories." Only monarchies and despotic governments can govern countries of extensive size, and any government that attempted to do so would inevitably wind up "destroying the liberties of the people." So far anyway, history has proved Mason wrong on this point as well. Mason made one seemingly critical admission—"I candidly acknowledge the inefficacy of the Confederation"—that should have logically caused him to compare the relative strengths and weaknesses of the Articles of Confederation with those of the proposed Constitution, but he did not go there. Instead, as he had in Philadelphia, he went on to complain about one thing after another that he did not like about the Constitution, including especially on this day that the House of Representatives was too small. Mason never grappled with the alternatives, namely, either continuing under the ineffectual Articles of Confederation (which could not be amended without unanimous consent of thirteen states, including obstreperous Rhode Island), or, should at least nine states ratify, being left out of the new United States.

* * *

The surprise on the third day was that Governor Randolph declared himself in favor of ratification. Politicians are forever loath to say they changed their minds. That is true today; and it was true then. Randolph, therefore, offered a not entirely coherent explanation about why, a little more than nine months earlier at Independence Hall in Philadelphia, he had refused to sign the Constitution but was now in favor of ratifying it. He had not signed in Philadelphia because he wanted amendments, Randolph explained. He would make the same choice again. Yet "the spirit of America depends upon a combination of circumstances which no individual can control." He still wanted improvements, explained the governor, "but I never will assent to any scheme that will operate a dissolution of the Union, or any measure which may lead to it." It may not have been a clear explanation about why he had changed his position without changing his mind, but one thing was clear: Randolph was unequivocally in favor of ratification. Madison was surely pleased.

But the convention had just begun. There was a long way to go.

2

Debate in Richmond

IN THE MIDDLE of the fourth day, Patrick Henry took the floor, and he held it so long that the other delegates might have wondered if he would ever again yield it. This was not to be Henry's longest speech at the Virginia Ratifying Convention—later he would stay on his feet continuously for a full seven hours[1]—but it was something of a prelude of what was to come. And over the course of the Convention, Henry, although only one of 168 delegates, would take up 20 percent of the total time.[2] As was characteristic of him, on this occasion he moved from topic to topic, sometimes devoting only a few sentences to one subject before turning to another. He could not have been working from any organized system of notes; his speech resembles a free flow of consciousness. He began with rights not protected by the Constitution—rights of conscience, trial by jury, freedom of the press—and then uttered what has become one of this most famous pronouncements: "Liberty, the greatest of all earthly blessings—give us that precious jewel, and you may take everything else!"[3] He was willing to assume that the leaders of the new United States would be intent on depriving the people of liberty at every turn. Some of his examples involve topics that are important for our purposes.

"Have we the means of resisting disciplined armies, when our only defense, the militia, is put into the hands of Congress?" Henry asked. It is a curious question for two reasons. First, it assumes that the militia, if controlled by Virginia, would be able to resist disciplined armies. As we will see, the potency of the militia had been an article of faith before the

Revolutionary War, but that faith was utterly demolished during the war. In fact, when in May 1781 a British army commanded by General Charles Cornwallis was invading Virginia from the south, leading citizens, apoplectic at the prospect of relying on the state militia for defense, sent an urgent petition to the state Assembly noting that while the militia had previously "been considered as the natural strength of a nation," experience had shown otherwise and other measures were necessary to defend the state. "[I]t is impossible that an army, chiefly composed of troops without experience, should meet an army of veterans upon equal terms," they observed.[4] The second reason Henry's question was curious is because it assumed that if Congress were to control the militia, it would somehow be destroyed. Henry, in fact, had a particular reason why he feared that might occur, but he did not reveal that quite yet. Instead, he moved quickly on to other topics.

One of Henry's remarks is worthy of mention, not because it is directly relevant to our inquiry about the origins of the Second Amendment but because it reveals a weakness of Henry's freewheeling, ad lib approach. Henry complained that the Constitution was too difficult to amend. It would take legislatures in two-thirds of the states to even propose amendments, Henry noted. That meant that "a bare majority in [just] four small states may hinder the adoption of amendments."[5] True enough. But all of the delegates understood quite well that one reason the Philadelphia Convention decided to scrap the Articles of Confederation entirely was that the Articles could only be amended by consent of all of the states. Just one small state could block vitally important amendments. Indeed, just one small state—petty Rhode Island—had been doing so with regularity. These kinds of sloppy arguments might work with some jurors, but they were unlikely to work with delegates who had been elected to the Virginia Ratifying Convention. Quite the contrary, most delegates were surely thinking, "But that's a good reason to prefer the Constitution over the Articles of Confederation! Getting nine of thirteen states to agree may not be easy, but it is much easier than getting all thirteen to states to agree." This was not Henry at his best. He was only weakening his credibility for when he would turn to issues that would truly concern his audience.

Henry also brought up the question of a standing army in this speech, which is something directly related to our inquiry. "A standing army we shall have, also to execute the execrable commands of tyranny," Henry declared. As previously mentioned, professional historians believe that the Second Amendment was all about protecting armed militia in order to avoid the necessity of having a standing army. Let's take up the issue of standing armies now as some background is necessary to explain what Patrick Henry meant by his remark.

In eighteenth-century England, Whig ideology held that standing armies were dangerous to liberty. The Whigs were more of a political faction than a political party. In fact, they were really a collection of factions following different leaders with slightly different ideas. Edmund Burke, for example, was considered a Rockingham Whig because he belonged to the faction led by the Marquis of Rockingham.[6] As a general matter, however, Whigs believed in a constitutional monarchy, personal freedom and private rights, religious toleration, and a balance of power between the Crown and Parliament but with parliamentary supremacy. They were liberals of the day. They traced their philosophy back to John Locke and the English Bill of Rights of 1688, in which Parliament set forth rights that the king had to accept. (The English Bill of Rights itself will become important to our inquiry because it contained a right to possess arms, with which the American Founders were well familiar. We will deal with that important document, and the Glorious Revolution which produced it, in Chapter 9.) Whig ideology held that standing armies were a threat to liberty. That was largely because the king controlled standing armies and often used them to intimidate Parliament. Standing armies—that is, armies maintained in peacetime—therefore upset the balance of power between the Crown and Parliament. Because Parliament represented the people and protected their freedoms, the Whigs believed that standing armies were a threat to liberty.

Whig dislike for standing armies was further exacerbated by English kings employing foreign mercenaries in their armies. These mercenaries had no relationships with or affinities to the British people and thus did not have the same qualms about mistreating the people as English troops had.

American revolutionaries were generally devotees of Whig ideology. "No taxation without representation" was a Whig principle. American mistrust of standing armies, rooted in Whig ideology, became even more intense as British forces became increasingly perceived in America as a hostile occupying force. Moreover, as American revolutionaries were trying to coax the colonies to take up arms against Britain, which had one of the most powerful armies and navy in the world, it became useful to promote—and believe in—the idea that citizen militia could defeat a professional army. The argument was that citizen militiamen would be superior soldiers because they were more virtuous than professional soldiers. We can add to the mix that England did, in fact, engage Hessian mercenaries in the Revolutionary War, and thus other of the dreaded evils of standing armies became realized in America.

Hence, before the war—and during the earliest days of the war, when the militia won victories at Lexington and Concord—American antipathy for standing armies was strong. But that did not last. Faith in the citizen militia did not stand up to reality. By the end of the war, there were not many knowledgeable Americans who still believed that a citizen militia could effectively fight against a professional army. There was still plenty of soapbox rhetoric praising the militia and wailing about the evils of standing armies—particularly by politicians in Fourth of July–type speeches—but most knowledgeable Americans no longer took it seriously. Especially when it counted.

One time it counted a great deal was at the Constitutional Convention in Philadelphia. The Constitution gave Congress the power to raise armies and a navy, and it also gave Congress the lion's share of power over the militia. To be specific, here are the provisions set forth in Article I, Section 8 of the Constitution:

The Congress shall have the Power . . .

To raise and support Armies, but no Appropriation of Money to that Use shall be for a longer Term than two Years;

To provide and maintain a Navy;

To make Rules for the Government and Regulation of the land and naval Forces;

To provide for calling forth the Militia to execute the Laws of the Union, suppress Insurrections and repel Invasions;

To provide for organizing, arming, and disciplining, the Militia, and for governing such Part of them as may be employed in the service of the United States, reserving to the States respectively, the

Appointment of the Officers, and the Authority of training the Militia according to the discipline prescribed by Congress.

Thus, the Convention decided to leave it up to Congress, as a matter of policy, how much to rely on standing armies and a navy and how much to rely on the militia. The only restriction is that Congress cannot fund armies for more than two years at a time.

George Mason and Elbridge Gerry of Massachusetts, who would be the third delegate to refuse to sign the Constitution, wanted further restrictions. Mason said he hoped that there would not be standing armies in times of peace except perhaps for a few garrisons.[7] Elbridge Gerry said he wanted to limit the army in times of peace to three thousand men.[8] When Gerry made that statement, George Washington supposedly demolished it with a stage whisper suggesting that the Constitution also limit foreign invading armies to three thousand men.[9] Jonathan Dayton of New Jersey remarked that "preparations for war are generally made in peace; and a standing force of some sort, for ought we know, [might] become unavoidable."[10] Charles Pinckney of South Carolina said he had "but a scanty faith in militia" and that "[t]here must be also a real military force."[11] These delegates knew something of which they spoke. Dayton had served in the Continental Army during the war and saw action in the Battle of Yorktown. Pinckney had served in the militia and fought in the Battles of Savannah and Charleston. Following these remarks—and whatever snickering ensued from Washington's side remark—neither Gerry nor anyone else had the temerity to make a motion restricting the size of peacetime armies.

Later during the Philadelphia Convention, James Madison offered a motion proposing to add the following to the Constitution: "As the greatest danger is that of disunion of the states, it is necessary to guard against it by sufficient powers to the common government, and as the greatest danger to liberty is from large standing armies, it is best to prevent them, by effectual provision for a good militia."[12] Madison was suggesting—somewhat between the lines in this language, but quite expressly in debate on the Convention floor—that federal control was the best hope for an effective militia. "The states neglect their militia now," he told the Convention.[13] Edmund Randolph agreed, noting that members of the state legislatures were too interested in courting popularity "to enforce proper discipline" over the militia.[14] Even this modest attempt to include in the Constitution a nonbinding expression of sentiment disfavoring standing armies was overwhelmingly rejected. Only three states supported it; nine were opposed.

Still later in Philadelphia, George Mason tried yet again. Following the language in the Constitution giving Congress the power to organize, arm, and discipline the militia, Mason proposed adding: "And that the liberties of the people may be better secured against the danger of standing armies in time of peace."[15] This was defeated by a vote of 9 to 2.[16]

So this principle of Whig ideology no longer had much support in America as a whole after the Revolutionary War. Perhaps Patrick Henry thought it had more support within Virginia. After all, in Philadelphia three Virginians—Madison, Mason, and Randolph—voiced concerns about peacetime armies. But while Henry and other antifederalists often mentioned the bugaboo of standing armies, they seldom dilated on the evils of standing armies per se. Rather, they made standing armies and militia two sides of the same coin. While they repeatedly associated standing armies with tyranny, their real emphasis was on the militia side of the coin. Their theme, often more darkly suggested than explicitly set forth, was that Congress would rely on standing armies rather than militia for national defense, with the consequence that Virginia would lose control of an effective militia. The militia might decay through neglect—or something far more nefarious may happen. They hoped this theme would resonate because everyone in Virginia understood that, regardless of how ineffective they might be against an invading army, the militia was absolutely critical to the Commonwealth of Virginia.

Patrick Henry wasted little time deploying this line of attack. When he rose on Thursday, June 5, the second day of substantive debates at the Convention, he rattled off many objections to the Constitution— its failure to protect rights of conscience, jury trials, and freedom of the press, among them—and then turned to the double-sided coin. We are going to lose control of our militia, he warned, though his first, brief suggestion was that this would leave Virginia vulnerable to foreign attack. "Have we the means of resisting disciplined armies, when our only defense, the militia, is put in the hands of Congress?" he asked.[17]

He then immediately veered off onto other topics for quite a while before returning again to the double-sided coin, first rather obliquely. "Your arms, wherewith you could defend yourselves are gone," Henry declared, followed shortly by, "[a] standing army we shall have, also, to execute the execrable commands of tyranny," followed in turn shortly by "you will not have a single musket in the state for, as arms are to be provided by Congress, they may not furnish them."[18] If these comments, interspersed with unrelated remarks, seemed too disjointed to be entirely clear, Henry soon put things in context:

> Let me here call your attention to that part which gives the Congress power "to provide for organizing, arming, and disciplining the militia, and for governing such part of them as may be employed in the service of the United States—reserving to the states, respectively, the appointment of the officers, and the authority of training the militia according to the discipline prescribed by Congress." By this, sir, you see that their control over our last and best defence is unlimited. If they neglect or refuse to discipline or arm our militia, they will be useless: the states can do neither—this power being exclusively given to Congress. The power of appointing officers over men not disciplined or armed is ridiculous; so that this pretended little remains of power left to the states may, at the pleasure of Congress, be rendered nugatory. Our situation will be deplorable indeed.[19]

What was Henry driving at? Without spelling it out in so many words, he was raising the specter of the federal government using its newly acquired powers over the militia to subvert the slave system indirectly. He was suggesting that Congress, controlled in the future by an abolitionist North, might use its constitutional authority to arm the militia to, in effect, disarm them. He did not need to explain further why that would render Virginia's situation "deplorable." Everyone in Richmond would have understood this to be the import of his remarks.

When proceedings resumed on the next morning, Friday, June 6, Edmund Randolph attempted to turn Henry's argument on its head. Virginia was indeed vulnerable, he suggested, but this meant it needed to be part of a strong Union that could come to its aid. Virginia could easily be invaded by sea, and it was menaced by "cruel savages" to the west who might be induced by foreign enemies to attack Virginians, noted the governor.[20] Then he dealt in greater length with the more pressing concern:

> There is another circumstance that renders us more vulnerable. Are we not weakened by the population of those we hold in slavery? The day may come when they may make impression upon us. Gentlemen, who have been long accustomed to the contemplation of the subject, think there is a cause of alarm in this case: the number of people, compared to that of whites, is an immense proportion: their number amounts to 236,000—that of whites only to 352,000.[21]

In due course, Randolph turned to the capability of the militia to protect Virginia from these threats. First, he noted that Virginia itself did not have enough militiamen to defend against a foreign invasion but that the other states, collectively, had enough. His phraseology was suggestive. Randolph first said that the total militia could "be a good army," but he then immediately corrected himself by saying "or they can very easily raise a good army out of so great a number," thereby suggesting that merely summoning militia might not produce a good army but that militiamen could be fashioned, with training and discipline, into good soldiers.[22] That, of course, is the key distinction between militia and professional soldiers. Both before and after the Revolutionary War, militiamen were required to show up for periodic drills. However, militia drills were notorious for often not taking place or being lackadaisical when they were held. In many places, militia drills were largely excuses for drinking and companionship. And even at their best, militia drills consisted of amateurs training amateurs. By contrast, professional soldiers underwent sustained, rigorous training that taught military skills and inculcated a discipline that impelled men to follow orders, even when those orders placed them in harm's way.[23] Randolph gingerly expanded on the capability of the militia as a fighting force. "Who are the militia?" he asked.[24] "Can we depend solely upon these?" The governor began with obligatory praise of the valor of the state's militia. "I will pay the last tribute of gratitude to the militia of my country: they performed some of the most gallant feats during the last war," Randolph said. He then damned the militia with faint praise by saying—not that they acted nobly during the war—but that they "acted as nobly as men inured to other avocations could be expected to do."[25] "[B]ut, sir," he concluded, "it is dangerous to look to them as our sole protectors."

Later in his speech, Randolph argued that if Virginia failed to ratify and stayed out of the Union, it would be able to confederate with only North Carolina. Both states, he said, were weak, "oppressed with debts and slaves," and unable to "defend themselves externally, or make their people happy internally."[26] Congress, he argued, needed the authority to both repel invasions and quell internal insurrections. While Randolph reminded the delegates that under the Articles of Confederation, Congress was unable to respond to Shays' Rebellion in Massachusetts, they well understood that in Virginia the gravest danger of insurrection was from its large number of slaves.

The next morning Francis Corbin took the floor. Corbin, then only about twenty-nine, was a federalist who hailed from Middlesex County, an area east of Richmond along the Chesapeake Bay. He was not a veteran of the war—in fact, his bona fides as a revolutionary were not rock solid—but he hailed from a wealthy family and was extremely well educated. His father, a Loyalist, had taken the family to England at the start of the Revolutionary War and enrolled Francis in the best schools in the land. Francis studied at Canterbury, an elite prep school believed to be the oldest in England, and then at Cambridge University. He was admitted to the study of law at Inner Temple.[27] While in England, Francis Corbin petitioned the king for financial assistance because his father could no longer furnish it. Corbin returned home in 1783, the year England and America formally ended the Revolutionary War by signing the Treaty of Paris, to reclaim his family's extensive estates.

Corbin claimed to be an American patriot who had been too young to remain behind when his family fled to England, but his situation was further complicated by other family relationships. Corbin's sister Elizabeth married Carter Braxton, a man from another wealthy and prominent Virginia family.[28] Braxton had signed the Declaration of Independence. That would normally have been pretty good revolutionary credentials, but Braxton had been a moderate when it came to going to war with Britain. He had tussled with Patrick Henry in 1775 when Henry demanded the king reimburse the colony for gunpowder seized by British troops. Braxton was so offended by Henry's demand that he arranged for his family to reimburse the colony for the gunpowder. That was not the half of it: Braxton wrote a pamphlet opposing democratic ideas proposed by John Adams and other American revolutionaries, and there were rumors that Elizabeth—Braxton's wife and Francis Corbin's sister—was a Loyalist. So not everyone accepted Corbin's claim to be a true-blue American. In light of all of this baggage, it is no surprise that both Francis Corbin and Carter Braxton would go on to have largely unsuccessful political careers. Nevertheless, Corbin had succeeded at winning election to the House of Delegates the year after his return to Virginia. It had, in fact, been on Corbin's motion that the House of Delegates voted to hold the Virginia Ratifying Convention, to which Corbin was also later elected.

Corbin carried the professional versus amateur thesis a bit further. For Virginia to have good soldiers and good farmers, Corbin said, some members of the community would have to be "exclusively inured to its defense" while other members devoted themselves to "cultivating the soil."[29] In other words, Virginia needed professional soldiers just as much as it needed professional farmers. Corbin argued that if Virginia's "defense be solely entrusted to militia, ignorance of arms and negligence in farming will ensue," and the state would have neither competent soldiers nor competent farmers. Corbin also went after Patrick Henry's great strength directly, namely, his oratorical gifts, and called attention to Henry's dramatic delivery not always being accompanied by sound reasoning. "No man admires more than I do his declamatory talents," Corbin declared, "but I trust that neither declamation nor elegance of periods will mislead the judgment of any member here, and that nothing but the force of reasoning will operate conviction."[30] Corbin's speech was well reasoned, but just how persuasive he was is another matter. Historian Harlow Giles Unger writes that Corbin's "distinct English accent, regal dress, and aristocratic airs—and his failure to fight in the war—clearly annoyed backcountry delegates."[31]

When Corbin sat down, Patrick Henry rose and invited Edmund Randolph to continue remarks Randolph began the day before. Henry said he would listen patiently to Randolph and wanted to know everything he could urge in defense of the new system of government proposed by the Constitution. It is a strange request from a man who had no intention of listening with an open mind to anything Randolph had to say. But Patrick Henry had something else in mind. He was an experienced and wily enough advocate to recognize that sound arguments were only going to go so far. Human beings are moved by a host of factors besides rational analysis. Other federalists had already accused Henry of fear mongering, and they had even uncharitably suggested that Henry's rhetorical gifts were deserting him.[32]

But Henry was not to be deterred. He recognized that one obstacle to victory was the personal appeal of the popular governor. Henry fancied himself an effective counterpuncher so he undoubtedly expected to be able to jab at whatever arguments Randolph raised. But Henry's target was not so much Randolph's arguments as the man himself. Could Henry discredit Randolph's support for the Constitution? If so, that would go a long way. And Henry had something to work with—something that surely rankled him and his fellow antifederalists: Randolph's flip. As we already know, Randolph refused to sign the Constitution in Philadelphia, but he advocated for its ratification in Richmond and had failed to offer a truly plausible explanation for his conversion. Henry and the antifederalists suspected that something had happened to cause Randolph to flip—something that Randolph did not want to admit, something concealed, something untoward. Just a smidgeon of innuendo might set delegates' minds racing. And innuendo was one of Henry's specialties. It is reasonable to suspect, therefore, that Henry's strategy here was to invite Randolph to become even more prominently associated with the federalist cause, and then to use the flip to call into question both Randolph and ratification.

If this were a trap, Randolph—himself supremely confident—had no intention of avoiding it. He took the floor and spoke for quite a long time. He particularly honed on the antifederalist argument that giving Congress the power to levy direct taxes would unduly enhance national power and diminish state power. The Articles of Confederation had denied Congress the power to tax, thereby forcing the national government into the role of beggar. When Congress decided what requisitions were needed from the states to fund national operations, it could only request that states tax their own citizens to raise the state's contribution. Henry and Mason repeatedly argued that this was preferable because the states knew best how to tax their own citizens. They further argued that Congress should only be permitted to levy taxes if and when states failed to pay requisitions voluntarily.[33] Randolph asked the delegates to consider how, even just within a state, such a system would work:

> Suppose, for a moment, the only existing mode of raising revenue in Virginia to be that of requisitions; suppose your requisitions sent on to every county; say that money is wanted; assume the most pressing language—"We earnestly entreat you; we humbly supplicate and solicit you would furnish us with one thousand or one hundred pounds, to defray the necessary charges of our government!" What would be the result of such applications for voluntary contributions? You would be laughed at for your folly, for thinking human nature could be thus operated upon. From my knowledge of human nature, and of my countrymen, I am perfectly certain this would be the case.[34]

Pressing the point perhaps more than necessary, Randolph used it to comment again on the superiority of regular troops over militia. What would be the result of a state's refusal to pay requisitions deemed essential by the national government? Civil war, Randolph answered. The national government would use the army to compel compliance, and Virginia would find itself in dire straits. "Have we any troops but militia to confront those disciplined bands that would be sent to force our compliance with requisitions?" he asked.[35]

Madison followed Randolph with a long and reasoned speech, but Madison was feeling ill.[36] Although he persevered, he was not at his most effective. According to his own description, Madison was "extremely feeble" at this point in the Convention, and federalists were worried about him and their cause. When Patrick Henry took the floor again, he ignored Madison's remarks. Henry was ready to execute his strategy against Randolph. It was a marathon speech and dealt with a multitude of issues. At one point, Henry turned to Edmund Randolph, referred to him by name, and said: "That system which was once execrated by the honorable member must now be adopted, let its defects be ever so glaring. That honorable member will not accuse me of want of candor, when I cast in my mind what he has given the public, and compare it to what has happened since. It seems to be very strange and unaccountable that that which was the object of his execration should now review his encomiums."[37] One wonders whether, when he uttered the lines that Randolph "will not accuse me of a want of candor" whether Henry put particular emphasis on the word *me*, thereby subtly emphasizing his implied accusation that Randolph lacked candor in explaining his flip of position. "Something extraordinary must have operated so great a change in his opinion," Henry declared.

This, it turned out, was a mistake. Indeed, it was nearly, quite literally, a fatal mistake. But first we must turn to a portion of Henry's long speech that deals directly with a subject that concerns us, namely, arms and the militia. Henry began by arguing that the federal government would take control of military garrisons, including magazines, which traditionally were under state control. "Are we at last brought to such a humiliating and debasing degradation, that we cannot be trusted with arms for our defense?" he asked.[38] "If our defense be the real object of having those arms, in whose hands can they be trusted with more propriety, or equal safety to us, as in our own hands." Notice the droplet of innuendo in the phrase *[i]f our defense be the real object of having those arms.* Henry, quickly and subtly, suggested that the authors of the Constitution might have something else in mind in giving the national government control of the military. Henry did not say what that true objective might be. Instead, he cunningly makes a quick and almost imperceptible suggestion, just enough to imbed a question in his listeners' minds. Then, reading from Article I, Section 8, of the Constitution, Henry said:

> The clause which says Congress shall "provide for arming, organizing, and disciplining the militia, and for governing such part of them as may be employed in the service of the United States, reserving to the states respectively the appointment of the officers," seemed to put the states in the power of Congress. I wish to be informed, if Congress neglected to discipline them, whether the states were not precluded from doing it. Not being favored with a particular answer, I am confirmed in my opinion, that the states have not the power of disciplining them, without recurring to the doctrine of constructive implied powers. If, by implication, the states may discipline them, by implication, also, Congress may officer them; because in a partition

of power, each has a right to come in for part. . . . We have not one fourth of the arms that would be sufficient to defend ourselves. The power of arming the militia, and the means of purchasing arms, are taken from the states by the paramount powers of Congress. If Congress will not arm them, they will not be armed at all.[39]

Henry quickly tied this to the antifederalist objection to giving the federal government taxing power. Henry said, "Congress, by the power of taxation, by that of raising an army, and by their control over the militia, have the sword in one hand, and the purse in the other." He pretty quickly followed this with: "Give us at least a plausible apology why Congress should keep their proceedings in secret."[40] Henry proceeded to hold forth for a while about the evils of Congress deliberating and legislating in secret. To modern ears, the concern about congressional secrecy may seem strange. In the more than two hundred years of its history, Congress has conducted nearly all of its business—and all acts of legislating—in public. In the modern age, proceedings on the floor of both chambers and many committee hearings are televised, and before that citizens had quick access to transcripts of proceedings through the Congressional Record. Members of Congress do not shun limelight; they bathe in it. However, Henry and other antifederalists in Richmond had been making hay out of the clause in the Constitution that requires each house of Congress to "keep a Journal of Proceedings, and from time to time publish the same, excepting such Parts as may in their Judgment require secrecy."[41] Among other things, they had been arguing that since Congress was only required to publish its proceedings "from time to time" Congress would keep its proceedings secret for very long stretches of time.

This portion of Henry's remarks, therefore, had an artful symmetry. He began with a subtle suggestion about dark motives of the authors of the Constitution, and he closed with another subtle suggestion that these authors had shrewdly inserted a mechanism to keep Congress's conduct secret. At this juncture, Henry did not say what these nefarious motives might be. He merely planted seeds.

Patrick Henry was followed by Henry Lee Jr., who was best known by his nickname "Light Horse Harry."[42] Although Lee was only thirty-two years of age, there was no one at the Richmond Convention whose voice was more respected on military affairs. During the war, Lee had commanded an elite corps of light cavalry and infantry known as Lee's Legion. It was a light corps because it traveled light, without tents, wagons, or baggage carried by other units, giving it speed and mobility. Its specialties included surveillance and raiding the enemy, often to disrupt chains of supply and communications. Lee's Legion was also exceedingly proficient in combat—a sort of eighteenth-century equivalent of the Green Berets. And, in fact, its troops wore distinctive green jackets. Light Horse Harry was a scion of one of Virginia's most distinguished families. He graduated from what is today Princeton University at seventeen. Under different circumstances, he would have been sent to London to study law, but America was going to war and Lee was instead commissioned as a captain in the Virginia cavalry. Within the year, that unit was absorbed into the Continental Army.

Lee's special gifts became immediately apparent. He was tough and extremely smart. He was a natural-born leader. He was both aggressive and a meticulous planner, ever eager for battle but never rushing into it without reconnoitering the enemy and the terrain. By November 1780, George Washington had promoted Lee to lieutenant colonel and placed him in command of the Legion. It was there—partly for Lee's horsemanship, partly for the Legion's characteristics—that he earned the sobriquet Light Horse Harry. Lee became instrumental in some of the war's most important battles. Congress awarded him a gold medal for his service, an honor it bestowed on only eight individuals and on none, except Lee, below the rank of general. An aptitude for the military arts must have run in Lee's blood because one of his sons, Robert E., would gain fame for commanding the Confederate Army. Also in the future, Virginia would, by turns, send Light Horse Harry to the United States House of Representatives and elect him governor. Because of his oratorical skill, Lee later would also be selected to deliver the eulogy of the first president of the United States, whom he would describe as "first in war, first in peace, and first in the hearts of his countrymen." We can be sure that delegates at the Richmond Convention listed attentively when Light Horse Harry told them the following:

> It was my fortune to be a soldier of my country. In the discharge of
> my duty, I knew the worth of the militia. I have seen them perform

feats that would do honor to the first veterans, and submitting to what would daunt German soldiers. I saw what the honorable gentleman did not see—our men fighting with the troops of that king whom he so admires. [Lee was sarcastically referring to a suggestion by Patrick Henry that equated George Washington with a king.] I have seen proofs of the wisdom of that paper on your table. I have seen incontrovertible evidence that militia cannot always be relied upon. I could enumerate many instances, but one will suffice. Let the gentlemen recollect the action at Guildford. [Lee was referring to the Battle of Guilford Courthouse, which will be described in Chapter 6.] The American troops behaved there with the most gallant intrepidity. What did the militia do? The greatest number of them fled. Their abandonment of the regulars occasioned the loss of the field. Had the line been supported that day, Cornwallis, instead of surrendering at Yorktown, would have laid down his arms at Guildford.[43]

As Lee's remarks illustrate, it was de rigueur for politicians to pay homage to the militia, even while recognizing their inadequacy as a fighting force. In Fourth of July–type speeches, politicians would, of course, praise the militia and leave it at that. After all, some militia had fought bravely and some militia had died in service of their country—not to mention that members of the militia were voters. We see here why it is a mistake to attach too much weight to speeches glorifying the militia. Lee, however, was not making a Fourth of July–type speech. His remarks had an important purpose: to remind the delegates that the militia had been tested in war and found wanting, and the Constitution had therefore wisely avoided expressing a preference for citizen militia over a standing army. Lee's evaluation of the militia as a fighting force was unmistakable; nevertheless, he carefully prefaced that evaluation with some praise.

Lee went on to challenge Henry's assertion that because the Constitution invested Congress with the power to arm the militia, only Congress could do so. "I cannot understand the implication of the honorable gentleman, that, because Congress may arm the militia, the states cannot do it: nor do I understand the reverse proposition."[44] That was simply wrong. "The states are, by no part of the plan before you, precluded arming and disciplining the militia, should Congress neglect it," Lee said. This seemed sensible, but was it really correct? Henry had a strong point when he said that when the Constitution parceled out some authority over the militia to Congress and other authority to the states, it could not really mean that they both could do the same things. If so, why the careful division of powers? This is not the last time the issue would come up.

When Lee sat down, Edmund Randolph took the floor. Almost immediately, Patrick Henry learned the rooster had come home to roost, and not how he had expected. With his voice rising to a near shout, Randolph declared:

> I find myself attacked in the most illiberal manner by the honorable gentlemen (Mr. Henry). I disdain his aspersions and insinuations. His asperity is warranted by no principle of parliamentary decency, nor compatible with the least shadow of friendship; and if our friendship must fall, *let it fall, like Lucifer, never to rise again!*[45]

To our ears today, that last phrase is cryptic, but the delegates understood it and gasped. By invoking the name of Lucifer in this fashion, the sitting governor had just challenged the first governor of the Commonwealth of Virginia to a duel.[46] Henry looked visibly shaken. Randolph then read a letter he had written to a constituent in which he said that although he had objections to the Constitution, he would vote to ratify it.[47] The apparent object of reading this letter was to show that Randolph had been consistent in this view for some time and therefore had not recently succumbed to bribery. This gave Henry a moment to reflect. Henry was then forty-eight years old but looked and acted much older. Randolph was a vigorous thirty-five. There was little doubt who had better odds in a duel.

Henry rose. Randolph, who still held the floor, allowed him to speak. The transcript of the Convention reads as follows: "[Henry] declared that he had no personal intention of offending any one; that he did his duty, but that he did not mean to wound the feelings of any gentleman; that he was sorry if he offended the honorable gentleman without intending it; and that every gentleman had a right to maintain his opinion."[48] All eyes turned back to Randolph. Would he accept this apology?

Randolph did accept it. He added, however, that if Henry had not made this concession that he, Randolph, had been prepared to "make some men's hair stand on end, by the disclosure of certain facts."[49] Now it was Henry's turn to be indignant—but not too indignant; he did not want to risk a renewed challenge to a duel. The transcript reads: "Mr. Henry then requested that, if [Randolph] had anything to say against him, he would disclose it."[50] If Randolph was going to disclose some shameful fact regarding Henry, he changed his mind. Instead, Randolph read at some length portions of two public letters he had written to constituents stating that he supported the Union, at least one of which he publicly made available to constituents before his election as a delegate to the Richmond Convention. None of this was likely to make "men's hair stand on end." Nevertheless, Randolph flung one of the letters on the clerk's table "and declared that it might lie there for the *inspection of the curious and the malicious*."[51] With that final flourish, bloodshed was averted. And the effort to discredit Randolph based on his flip of position came to an unsuccessful end.

* * *

Although a duel had been averted, tensions remained sky-high. With Randolph staunchly on their side, the federalists may have been feeling a bit better. If so, the feeling was premature. Antifederalists were preparing to launch one of their most potentially potent arguments—a nightmare scenario about slave insurrections and a "disarmed" militia. Something quite rare would come with this: James Madison would stumble in debate. America's greatest living orator would seize the opportunity to ridicule Madison, inflicting a political wound that would trouble Madison greatly.

3

Decision in Richmond

ON FRIDAY, JUNE 13, James Madison sat down to write George Washington a brief letter.[1] The good news was that Madison was feeling better physically. The bad news was that Madison was not feeling confident about how things would turn out. He reported that prospects for success appeared "less favorable" than before. Madison had last reported just after Randolph had declared himself in favor of ratification. Federalist spirits were then running strong, and Madison had described Henry and Mason as appearing to make "lame" and "awkward" arguments.[2] Madison was not so cheery now. He feared that delegates from Kentucky, then the western part of Virginia, might make the difference. In fact, the antifederalists had been hammering away on an issue important to those delegates—navigation rights to the Mississippi River—and suggesting that the Northern states would be all too willing to give those away to Spain in return for some trading advantage. Much time had been spent debating that issue. The ultimate outcome of the Virginia Ratifying Convention was going to be close one way or the other, Madison told Washington, adding gloomily, "I dare not encourage much expectation that it will be on the favorable side." Madison closed with another item of unhappy news: he heard that the delegate election in New York had favored the antifederalists.

The antifederalists were not feeling especially confident either. They also knew that, unless something changed dramatically, the Convention was likely to remain a nail-biter till the end.

Much maneuvering was also taking place "out of doors," that is, in private conservations outside the halls of the Convention. The publisher of an antifederalist Philadelphia newspaper had traveled to Richmond and was meeting privately with delegates. The word was that he was seeking to coordinate strategy among antifederalists in Virginia and New York, particularly with respect to demanding certain constitutional amendments as a prerequisite to considering ratification.[3] The Virginia legislature was also scheduled to convene on June 23. Many Convention delegates were also legislators; they couldn't be at two places at one time, and federalists feared that the Convention would disintegrate if it had not concluded its business by then. Federalists, therefore, became more insistent that the Convention proceed through the Constitution article by article, section by section, and that the chair not permit speakers to wander into areas not then under discussion. Probably to their surprise, the antifederalists agreed to this, and speeches became generally shorter and more focused.

There seemed to be an emerging clarity on the strongest themes for each side. The strongest line of argument for the federalists was that the Articles of Confederation were fatally flawed, and because they could only be amended by unanimous vote of all the states, including recalcitrant Rhode Island, the Articles could not be reformed. (Both sides competed on which had greater disdain for petty Rhode Island. Benjamin Harrison may have won this trophy for the antifederalists by declaring: "Rhode Island is not worthy of the attention of this house. She is of no weight or importance to influence any general subject of consequence."[4]) Thus, argued the federalists, the question was not whether the Constitution was perfect. Nothing is perfect. The first question was whether the Constitution is preferable to the Articles of Confederation. It was undeniably better, federalists argued, because the Articles were a disaster. The second question was whether imperfections were easier to correct in the Constitution. They were, federalists argued, because it only took nine states to agree to amendments, rather than thirteen. Moreover, other states would be just as eager to correct imperfections as would Virginia.

The antifederalists continued a scattershot approach. The Constitution was filled with perils, they argued. They characterized every objection in apoplectic terms. George Mason, for example, called the provision giving the federal government exclusive authority to impose customs and duties "one of the most wanton powers of the general government";[5] predicted with assurance that the president would "be continued in office for life";[6] said "the Vice President appears to me to be not only an unnecessary but a dangerous officer";[7] declared the provision giving the president the power to make treaties with the consent of two-thirds of the Senate "a most dangerous clause";[8] and called federal courts "disgraceful and dangerous" and said they would "utterly . . . destroy the state governments."[9] And those remarks were all on just one single and typical day.[10] Meanwhile, the antifederalists put increasing emphasis on the absence of a bill of rights. Originally, the federalists, and especially Madison, argued that a bill of rights was either unnecessary or even unwise because it could never be complete, which would open a door for arguments that rights that were not listed had been deliberately omitted and therefore did not exist. But now federalists were increasingly arguing that a bill of rights could easily be added through the constitutional amendment process.

In a long speech two days earlier, Madison had touched on many themes, including why a strong federal government was essential to both national and state safety and security. If the federal government could not derive revenue from taxes, it would not be financially able to afford an army. "The inability of the government to raise and support regular troops would compel us to depend on militia," Madison observed.[11] That would risk "national annihilation."[12] Moreover, in such a crisis the Southern states would be the "most defenseless and exposed" on account of "circumstances which render them still more vulnerable, which do not apply to Northern states."[13] Madison, of course, was alluding to the vast numbers of slaves, whom the South would be obliged to control and whom an invader might try to encourage to revolt.

During the same speech, Madison made an observation that was not only prescient but is, in hindsight, also ironic and sad. If America were weak, financially and militarily, it would be unable to stay out of European wars notwithstanding its best efforts, including a policy of remaining determinately neutral. That was because, Madison explained, as long as they could do so with impunity, combatants would seize American ships carrying property belonging to (or presumably also en route to) their enemies. The United States had to be sufficiently strong so that neither Britain nor any other power "would be willing to add us to the number of their enemies."[14] "I am no friend to naval or land armaments in time of peace," Madison added a bit later, "but if they be necessary, the calamity must be submitted to. Weakness will invite insults."[15] Madison would be proved right. In 1812, the nation would be drawn into war precisely this way. However, it would in significant part be the policies of James Madison and his Republican Party that caused America to be both financially and militarily weak.[16]

On Saturday, June 14, George Mason took up the same theme. He began by adding a new wrinkle:

> Mr. Chairman, unless there be some restrictions on the power of calling forth the militia . . . we may very easily see that it will produce dreadful oppressions. It is extremely unsafe, without some alterations. It would be to use the militia to a very bad purpose, if any disturbance happened in New Hampshire, to call them from Georgia. This would harass the people so much they would agree to abolish the militia, and establish a standing army. I conceive the general government ought to have power over the militia, but it ought to have some bounds. If gentlemen say that the militia of a neighboring state is not sufficient, the government ought to have the power to call forth those of other states, the most convenient and contiguous. But in this case, the consent of state legislatures ought to be had. On real emergencies, this consent will never be denied, each state being concerned in the safety of the rest. This power may be restricted without any danger. I wish such an amendment as this—that the militia of any state should not be marched beyond the limits of the adjoining state; and if it be necessary to draw them from one end of the continent to the other, I wish such a check, as the consent of the state legislature, to be provided.[17]

Mason's remarks gave Henry's earlier supposition a different twist. Instead of Congress leaving the state vulnerable by disarming its militia, George Mason was raising the possibility of Congress simply removing the militia from Virginia. What, he asked, if a Southern state's militia were marched to New Hampshire? The consequence of such an act was obvious to everyone in the audience: the state would be unprotected against its slaves. The idea of an insurrection in New Hampshire was not necessarily farfetched; two years earlier the governor of New Hampshire summoned two thousand militiamen to suppress disturbances in the state.[18] New Hampshire had restored order, however, without assistance from sister states. The prospect of Congress ordering militia from the Southern states to deal with disturbances in New England was implausible except, perhaps, to those profoundly mistrustful of Congress's motives. Henry and Mason were not above stoking the coals of Virginia's paranoia. "Virginia and North Carolina are despised," Henry told the Richmond Convention at one point.

In addition to adding this new possibility, Mason reiterated Henry's supposition of Congress disarming the militia. He told the Convention:

> The militia may be here destroyed by that method which has been practiced in other parts of the world before; that is, by rendering them useless—by disarming them. Under various pretenses, Congress may neglect to provide for arming and disciplining the militia; and the state governments cannot do it, for Congress has an exclusive right to arm them, etcetera. . . . Should the national government wish to render the militia useless, they may neglect them, and let them perish, in order to have a pretense of establishing a standing army.[19]

Mason went on for some time, suggesting that disarming the militia would be part and parcel of a congressional scheme to create a standing army, which was something of a non sequitur since the Constitution expressly granted Congress the power to raise an army and navy and it did not need to disarm the militia to decide to raise an army or navy. Then he continued:

> Why should we not provide against the danger of having our militia, our real and natural strength, destroyed? The general government ought, at the same time, to have some such power. But we need not give them power to abolish our militia. If they neglect to arm them, and prescribe proper discipline, they will be of no use. I am not acquainted with the military profession. I beg to be excused for any errors I may commit with respect to it. But I stand on the

general principles of freedom, whereon I dare to meet any one. I wish that, in case the general government should neglect to arm and discipline the militia, there should be an express declaration that the state governments might arm and discipline them. With this single exception, I would agree to this part, as I am conscious the government ought to have the power.[20]

Mason's stories were contradictory. On the one hand, Mason suggested that the Southern militia would be sufficiently sharp instruments that Congress might employ them to quell insurrections as far away as New England. On the other hand, he suggested that Congress would cause the militia to atrophy in order to develop political support to raise a standing army. These were inconsistent visions. Moreover, there was a fundamental flaw in Mason's theory that Congress might deliberately allow the militia to atrophy in order to use their very frailty to develop political support for a standing army. Rather than creating support for a standing army, would not weakened militia stimulate demands for reinvigorating the militia themselves?

At this point, Madison rose and offered a brief comment. "If insurrections should arise, or invasions take place, the people ought unquestionably to be employed, to suppress or repel them, rather than a standing army," he said. "The best way to do these things was to put the militia on a good and sure footing, and enable the government to make use of their services when necessary."[21] While Madison was agreeing with Mason about the undesirability of a standing army, he was saying something quite different about the militia. Mason was warning that Congress would affirmatively do something to interfere with the militia while Madison was suggesting the federal government was needed "to put the militia on a good and sure footing."

Madison's interjection was very brief, no more than a minute, and it did nothing to deflect the trajectory of Mason's argument. Mason continued with this fever dream of Congress—one house of which was to be chosen by the state legislatures, and the other house directly elected by the people—so bent upon designs of tyranny that it would do bizarre things to the militia in order to build political support for raising a standing army. Mason had still another idea for how Congress might pursue this goal. "[T]he first attempt," Mason predicted, "would be to render the service of the militia odious to the people themselves—subjecting them to unnecessary severity of discipline in time of peace, confining them under martial law, and disgusting them so much as to make them cry out, 'Give us a standing army!' "[22]

These are curiously roundabout ways of arguing that a standing army must be prevented at all costs. It would be far more straightforward to argue that the Constitution was defective because it gave Congress carte blanche to raise a standing army, and leave the militia out of this argument entirely. Madison would have replied that in Philadelphia they—Mason and Madison—proposed including admonishments against standing armies in the Constitution, but their efforts failed. To which Mason could have replied, yes, we tried, but giving Congress unbridled power to raise armies is unacceptable and delegates should vote against ratification on that basis. Instead, Mason created a tortured argument that Congress might do any number of things to the militia—some of them downright weird—as an indirect means of building political support for a standing army, and that in turn would lead to its raising a standing army. This does not make the antifederalist argument that the Constitution is defective because it empowers Congress to raise a standing army more plausible. Just the reverse. If the genuine concern was about standing armies, just stick to standing armies. Why muddle the point by arguing that degrading the militia would be a prelude to standing armies? Moreover, with all Mason's handwringing that Congress might neglect, disarm, remove, or abuse the militia, one might have thought that the militia were strong and well supported by the states. They were not. Far from it. It was universally agreed that states were not making efforts to arm or train their militia for combat. As Madison himself had observed at the Constitutional Convention, "The states neglect their militia now."[23]

This makes sense only when one realizes that all of this talk about degrading the militia is not, at least primarily, about a standing army at all. It is about the militia. As I shall establish in Chapters 4, 5, and 6, and only ask you to accept provisionally until then, Mason's audience knew that the militia were ineffective as a fighting force but indispensable for slave control. The militia did not need to be trained by the federal government for that purpose. Nor did militia have to be armed by government, state or federal. In the main, they weren't armed by government then;

they were simply required to supply their own arms. For slave control purposes, it did not matter that their arms might not be uniform or state of the art. But if the militia were somehow disarmed, that would be another matter. In eastern Virginia, where the delegates were meeting and many of them lived, the White population was the minority. Enslaved Blacks were the majority. Many of the men in the room were themselves large slaveholders; Mason himself owned more than three hundred slaves. Nothing was more important to them than slave control. That was why Virginians would fear something affirmatively being done to interfere with its militia. This is what Mason's gallery of horrors about the militia being removed, destroyed, or disarmed was really all about.

Why, then, did he not make the argument directly? Why not tell the delegates that the Constitution would enable Congress to interfere with the militia and thus with slave control in the South? Instead of weaving farfetched stories of Congress degrading the militia in order to build political support for a standing army, which Congress secretly wanted for a reign of tyranny, why not tell the delegates that Congress might degrade the militia to subvert the slave system, which many Northerners (and some Southerners) found morally abhorrent and wanted to extinguish? The answer is that slavery was considered such "a delicate subject" that public discussion of it was often frowned upon.[24] This reluctance was even greater when the subject was slave control. While these topics were not absolute unmentionables, there was a real reluctance to discuss them openly. This led to oblique, circuitous, or even somewhat encoded discussions, exactly of the kind that occurred here.

In answering Mason, Madison called the idea of a Congress bent on "mischief," dragging the militia from one end of the nation to another, "preposterous."[25] "I think there can be no ground of apprehension," he said. One imagines thin-skinned George Mason boiling at having Madison label his suggestion "preposterous." But if Mason desired vengeance, he would not need to seek it on his own. Patrick Henry would do that for him. What made Madison vulnerable were remarks that on their face did not seem particularly provocative. Madison said:

> I cannot conceive that this Constitution, by giving the general government the power of arming the militia, takes it away from the state governments. The power is concurrent, and not exclusive. Have we

not found, from experience, that, while the power of arming and governing the militia has been solely vested in the state legislatures, they were neglected and rendered unfit for immediate service? Every state neglected too much this most essential object. But the general government can do it more effectually.[26]

This was a blunder. This argument had come up before, but this time Patrick Henry was ready to seize the opportunity. He was soon on his feet, and proceeded to ridicule Madison, as follows:

As my worthy friend said, there is a positive partition of power between the two governments. To Congress is given the power of "arming, organizing, and disciplining the militia, and governing such part of them as may be employed in the service of the United States." To the state legislatures is given the power of "appointing the officers, and training the militia according to the discipline prescribed by Congress." I observed before, that, if the power be concurrent as to arming them, it is concurrent in other respects. If the states have the right of arming them, &c., concurrently, Congress has a concurrent power of appointing the officers, and training the militia. If Congress have that power, it is absurd. To admit this mutual concurrence of powers will carry you into endless absurdity—that Congress has nothing exclusive on the one hand, nor the states on the other.[27]

Henry proceeded to hold forth on the absurdity of implied concurrent powers. And indeed it was, as a constitutional matter, absurd. When the Constitution explicitly divided powers between the federal and state governments, doling out some powers to the federal government and other powers to the states, it could not possibly mean that both governments shared those powers. Surely, the printed transcript does not do this renowned orator justice. We can only imagine the timber of his voice rising and falling, the cadence and pauses that gave Henry's speeches dramatic power. Throughout much of the Convention, Henry had not been at his best. Now he was effective, and using his talents. He was a lawyer making an indisputably correct legal argument, and using his principal, and formidable, opponent as a piñata. He took his time, drew the argument out, and repeated his key point over and over again in slightly different ways. He repeatedly stressed how critical the militia was. "The militia, sir, is our ultimate safety," he said at one point.[28] "If you have given up your militia, and Congress shall refuse to arm them, you have lost everything," he said at another.[29]

Then Henry made the following, seemingly reasonable, point:

> When this power is given up to Congress without limitation or bounds, how will your militia be armed? You trust to chance . . . . If gentlemen are serious when they suppose a concurrent power, where can be the impolicy to amend it? Or, in other words, to say that Congress shall not arm or discipline them, till the states shall have refused or neglected to do it? This is my object. I only wish to bring it to what they themselves say is implied.[30]

What was Madison thinking at this juncture? Henry had suggested that all he wanted was this one modest and reasonable change in the Constitution, to allow the states to arm the militia if the federal government failed to do so. Henry's real objective, of course, was to destroy rather than reform the Constitution. Besides kicking himself for handing Henry an oratorical weapon, Madison may well have been thinking that Henry's point had merit—states ought to have a concurrent authority to arm their militia. What harm would there be in it, especially if it would relieve some of the antifederalist paranoia about Congress emasculating the militia?

A little later in the Convention, John Marshall would shrewdly attempt to repair the damage by putting the argument in practical terms. "If Congress neglect our militia we can arm ourselves, he declared."[31] "Cannot Virginia import arms? Cannot she put them into the hands of her militia-men?" Marshall was simply saying that if Congress did not give the militia arms, what would stop Virginia from doing that? Madison, however, had put the matter in legal terms. He suggested that even though the Constitution expressly gave Congress the authority to arm the militia, the states also possessed a concurrent constitutional power to arm the militia. Madison must have realized that as he had framed it, his argument was simply wrong. He would eventually try to fix this problem by writing the Second Amendment.

* * *

As the Convention began to draw to a close, the antifederalists began to sense they were in trouble. Things were still uncertain, but it felt as if things were drifting in the federalist direction. Notwithstanding the taboo about talking openly about slavery, slave control, and abolition, Henry called the Convention's attention to grim realities. "In this state there are two hundred and thirty-six thousand Blacks, and there are many in several other states," he began.[32] "But there are few or none in the Northern states; and yet, if the Northern states shall be of opinion that our slaves are numberless, they may call forth every national resource." Henry suggested that Congress might draft Blacks and provide that every Black who served in the army would be free. "May Congress not say, *that every Black man must fight?* Did we not see a little of this in the last war?" he asked.[33]

Indeed, they had seen a little of it. During the war, Rhode Island persuaded General George Washington to allow it to raise a segregated regiment consisting mostly of African Americans but also including Narragansett Indians and men of mixed race. Rhode Island promised freedom to any slaves who joined.[34] Washington had agreed because he was desperate for soldiers. Massachusetts followed suit. In August 1778, the Continental Army included 755 Black soldiers, who comprised about 5 percent of the Army's total manpower. There were precious few slaves in either Rhode Island or Massachusetts, and probably most of the Black soldiers were freemen at the time they enlisted. Later in the war, General Nathanael Greene asked permission of the South Carolina and Georgia legislatures to offer slaves freedom in exchange for joining the Continental Army. Greene could personally vouch for the performance of Black soldiers; he had seen them fight the Hessians near Newport, and he had commanded the Rhode Island's Black regiment during the Battle of Monmouth Courthouse. The Georgia legislature dispensed with the proposal without deigning to vote on it. South Carolina, however, took up the proposal as a political courtesy. General John Laurens was advocating for the proposal. Laurens hailed from a prominent South Carolina family. His father, who had recently served as president of the Continental Congress, was a planter and one of the state's largest slaveholders. John had become an ardent abolitionist, and the Continental Congress had granted him permission to recruit three thousand Black soldiers from the South, in exchange for their freedom, provided state legislatures agreed. So in deference to the Laurens family, South Carolina took a vote—rejecting the proposal, with fifteen in favor and one hundred opposed.[35] Instead, South Carolina offered to send Black slaves to serve as servants for the Continental Army, provided they were not armed, permanently retained their slave status, and counted toward the state's quota of soldiers. General Greene considered the counterproposal outrageous and rejected it. Meanwhile, the British army offered freedom to slaves who fought on their side, and about seven hundred accepted their offer (including, quite embarrassingly for America, fourteen of George Washington's slaves).[36] After the war, Britain refused American demands that former slaves be returned, even though American claimed the peace treaty required it.[37]

That is how far things had progressed along these lines during the Revolutionary War. It was, as Henry said, relatively just "a little," but it was more than enough to make the South both fearful and furious. Henry offered this history as evidence that the North would be quick to claim the authority to abolish slavery, notwithstanding assurances from Madison and other Virginians who had been delegates to the Constitutional Convention that there had been a bargain denying the federal government that authority. "[T]hey will search that paper, and see if they have power of manumission," Henry warned. He continued:

And have they not, sir? Have they not power to provide for the general defense and welfare? May they not think that these call for the abolition of slavery? May they not pronounce all slaves free, and will they not be warranted by that power? This is no ambiguous implication or logical deduction. The paper speaks to the point: they have the power in clear, unequivocal terms, and will clearly and certainly exercise it.[38]

Henry's claim that the Constitution provided clearly and unambiguously that Congress could abolish slavery was over-the-top, not to mention just plain wrong. But an argument that Congress's responsibility to provide for the national defense might be interpreted to allow Congress to enlist Blacks and grant them freedom in return for fighting for their county was not entirely implausible. His main point was not the means, however, but the end desired. "Slavery is detested," he declared.[39] "The majority of Congress is to the north, and the slaves are to the south."[40]

He and Mason had suggested many ways that Congress might employ to destroy the slave system. There was, Henry was saying, much to fear.

One scholar suggests that Henry's speech may have been a mark of desperation.[41] The tide was apparently running in the Federalists' direction. Madison was now privately calculating that the federalists had a small majority of between three and four delegates. And Henry's speech may actually have done the antifederalist cause more harm than good. He weakened his argument by overstating it; whatever implied powers one might claim to find, the Constitution did not in "clear, unequivocal terms" grant Congress the power of emancipation. "I was struck with surprise when I heard him express himself alarmed with respect to the emancipation of slaves," Madison told the delegates shortly thereafter.[42] "There is no power to warrant it, in that paper. If there be, I know it not."[43] Although Madison's argument may have been persuasive and, on the whole, reassuring, it may also have heightened Southern anxiety. If the federal government found the slave system so obnoxious but lacked the constitutional authority to attack it directly, perhaps Congress would look for ways to undermine the system indirectly.

* * *

As the Convention reached its final days, the antifederalists increasingly focused on the absence of a bill of rights. This was probably their most persuasive argument. Their strategy was to ask the Convention to declare that the Constitution should be ratified, but only after a bill of rights had been included. Madison and the federalists were deploying the counterstrategy of not opposing a bill of rights in principle but arguing failing to ratify the Constitution until the states had all agreed on a bill of rights would lead to chaos. Madison argued that if the antifederalists were right when they asserted that the desire for a bill of rights was strong everywhere, there will be little difficulty adding it through the constitutionally mandated amendment process.[44]

Although the Convention continued past the time when the House of Delegates was also in session, antifederalists did not use that as an excuse to suspend the Convention. Instead, the House of Delegates accommodated the sixty-two men who were members of both bodies by only holding brief sessions in the early morning so that the

Convention could begin in late morning, after the House of Delegates had adjourned.[45]

On Wednesday, June 25, 1788, the final day of debate, a number of delegates who had remained silent over the course of the preceding weeks rose to declare themselves. Those who declared themselves to be in favor of ratification urged their fellow delegates not to succumb to antifederalist fearmongering. Instead of antifederalists offering dispassionate reasoning and lessons from history, said James Innes, Virginia's attorney general, "horrors have been called up, chimeras suggested."[46] "When gentlemen of high abilities in this house, and whom I respect, tell us the militia may be subjected to martial law in time of peace, and whensoever Congress may please, I am much astonished," remarked Zachariah Johnson, a planter from Virginia's backcountry who had served for many years in the House of Delegates.[47] "The people are not to be disarmed of their weapons," he said.[48]

The penultimate speech—an uncharacteristically short, calm, and conciliatory one—was given by Patrick Henry. He reminded delegates of antifederalist arguments concerning taxes, treaties, and the absence of a bill of rights. The promise "of subsequent amendments is only to lull our apprehensions," he argued.[49] "With respect to your militia," Henry said, "we only request that, if Congress should refuse to find arms for them, this country may lay out their own money to purchase them."[50] "I beg pardon of this house for having taken up more time than came my share," said Henry.[51] On this, Henry was not exaggerating. The Convention had lasted twenty-two days; Henry had spoken on seventeen of those days. He had, moreover, often spoken three times a day. On one day Henry spoke five times; on another day he spoke only once but had been the only speaker because his speech lasted seven hours.[52] There had been much concern that if the Convention ratified, Henry would carry on a campaign against the Union and might go so far as to urge supporters to obstruct the new government through violence. Henry had done nothing to discourage this speculation. His biographer writes that many expected Henry to make a call to arms, and "[s]ome buckskins in the gallery were ready to cock their rifles."[53] There was great relief, therefore, when Henry concluded by stating that if he should lose, "I will be a peaceable citizen. My head, my hand, and my heart, shall be at liberty to retrieve the loss of liberty, and remove the defects of that system in a peaceable way. I wish not to go to violence."[54]

Governor Randolph had the very last word. He used it to reiterate that his refusing to sign to the Constitution in Philadelphia was not inconsistent with his voting to ratify it now. "I refused to subscribe [in Philadelphia], because I had, as I still have, objections to the Constitution, and wished a free inquiry into its merits" but now that eight states have ratified "the single question [is] Union or no Union."[55]

The delegates then voted on two resolutions. They voted first on a resolution submitted by Patrick Henry that before the Constitution were ratified the states should first consider a declaration of rights to be proposed by the Virginia Convention. This was the key vote. Everyone held their breath while the roll was called. The motion lost on a vote of 80 to 88. The second vote, taken immediately after the first, on a motion to ratify the Constitution passed 89 to 79.

The Richmond Convention was not quite done. It appointed two committees. The first was to prepare a formal declaration that Virginia had ratified. The federalists, who comprised the majority and were in control, selected only members who supported ratification for that committee.[56] They would not allow mischief with this all-important formal statement. The second committee was charged with drafting a recommended bill of rights to send along to Congress with the formal statement of ratification. The federalists, of course, could have decided not to appoint the second committee at all. Madison, however, urged his fellow federalists to look at this as a political opportunity to mollify the antifederalists.[57] Let them draft a recommended bill of rights. It meant nothing. Since Virginia was ratifying the Constitution unconditionally, a recommended bill of rights was a document without legal effect. This committee would be chaired by the esteemed law professor George Wythe, a federalist. The rest of the committee was composed of ten federalists and nine antifederalists. It included key players on both sides. Madison, Randolph, and Marshall were on the committee; so were George Mason, Patrick Henry, and James Monroe.[58]

The Convention had spent twenty-two days debating ratification. The committee writing a proposed bill of rights completed its work in two days. Truth be told, it did not have much work to do. An antifederalist caucus had been busy throughout the Convention drafting proposed amendments to the Constitution.[59] George Mason, the principal author of the Virginia Declaration of Rights of 1776, was put in charge of this effort. For five consecutive days during the Convention, Mason was absent from the hall. It is believed he was then hard at work on that effort. Eleazer Oswald, the publisher of the antifederalist *Independent Gazetteer* newspaper in Philadelphia, was in town during that time and probably included in those discussions. Oswald took a copy of Mason's draft with him when he returned to Philadelphia on June 11. Patrick Henry introduced the proposed declaration of rights during one of his last speeches to the Convention, on June 24.[60] The bill of rights or declaration of rights (the document used both terms) recommended by Wythe's committee was almost identical to the previously drafted antifederalist proposal.

The only notable change was that Mason's original proposal stated "that no particular religious sect or society of Christians ought to be favored or established" and Wythe's committee deleted the phrase *of Christians*. The Convention approved the proposed bill of rights without debate or a recorded vote.

Francis Corbin characterized the "whole business" of the recommended bill of rights as "ludicrous" and "absurd."[61] James Madison told Alexander Hamilton that many of the provisions in the proposed declaration of rights were "highly objectionable" but "could not be parried."[62] The federalists had decided to give the antifederalists what they wanted because it simply did not matter.

The Constitution had been ratified! The Union was born. Federalist delegates did not publicly celebrate in Richmond that evening however. They did not want to rub salt in antifederalist wounds. However, news that Virginia had ratified spread quickly, and that night guns on shore and ship in Norfolk harbor fired in celebration and many homes put candles in their windows.[63] Early the next morning on Saturday, June 28—two hours before dawn, in fact—a rider galloped into Richmond with startling news: New Hampshire had voted to ratify on June 21. Virginia was not, therefore, the critical ninth state to ratify and create the Union. It was the tenth.

* * *

Although delegates gave the declaration of rights short shrift and may have considered it next to meaningless, there is something worth noting for our purposes. Both the Virginia Declaration of Rights of 1776 and the Virginia's proposed declaration of rights of 1788 had the same principal author, namely, George Mason, and the second document drew heavily from the first. Section 13 of the Virginia Declaration of Rights of 1776 stated:

> That a well-regulated militia, composed of the body of the people, trained to arms, is the proper, natural, and safe defense of a free state; that standing armies, in time of peace, should be avoided as dangerous to liberty; and that in all cases the military should be under strict subordination to, and governed by, the civil power.[64]

Neither this provision, nor any other in that document, provides for a right to bear arms of any kind.

The comparable provision in Virginia's proposed declaration of rights of 1788 is almost identical—except for a new clause added at the very beginning. That provision, section 17 of the declaration, reads as follows:

> That the people have a right to keep and bear arms; that a well-regulated militia, composed of the body of the people trained to arms, is the proper, natural, and safe defence of a free state; that standing armies, in time of peace, are dangerous to liberty, and therefore ought to be avoided, as far as the circumstances and protection of the community will admit; and that, in all cases, the military should be under strict subordination to, and governed by, the civil power.[65]

What explains the addition? What changed? For the past twenty-two days, antifederalists had been arguing that Congress might disarm the militia to subvert the slave system. Whether or not they persuaded the federalists, they may have persuaded themselves. It is also important to note that the right to keep and bear arms was clearly conceived as being connected to the militia. If Mason, the antifederalists, or George Wythe's committee thought of it as something unrelated to the militia, they likely would have put it in a separate provision. They were not re-luctant to add new sections; the Declaration of Rights of 1776 had only sixteen sections and the 1788 proposals had forty, twenty characterized as a declaration of rights and twenty as constitutional amendments.

This is not to say that the idea of right to bear arms originated at the Richmond Convention. It did not. As we shall see, it can be traced back to the English Declaration of Rights of 1688. But this was the genesis and motivation of a right to bear arms in Virginia.

James Madison left Richmond both exhausted and pleased that the Constitution would be ratified. Yet Madison was worried. He may not yet have known it, but he would not have to again worry about George Mason. Mason had done grave harm to his reputation with his remarks to his fellow antifederalists in the Senate chamber.[66] His time of prom-inence was over.[67] But it was Patrick Henry who worried Madison. He told Washington that he expected Henry would work to elect a Congress "that will commit suicide on their own authority."[68] Henry's plans, in fact, were already in progress.[69] And those plans included snuffing out James Madison's political career.

4

Southern Terror

THE SURPRISE ATTACK on Fort Haldane began just after midnight on April 8, 1760.[1] The fort guarded the entrance to Port Maria Harbor on the northeast corner of Jamaica. But the attack did not come from the sea. It came by stealth out of the forest. Approximately one hundred Black slaves who worked on sugar plantations on the island, led by a slave called Tacky, sneaked up on the single British sentinel standing watch at that hour, killed him, and swept into the fort, which was largely unguarded that night. The prize was about forty muskets and pistols, four barrels of gunpowder, and a keg of musket balls. The rebels needed these munitions to succeed in their goal: a full-scale insurrection that would seize the entire island.

We do not know a great deal about Tacky himself.[2] It is believed he had been relatively recently imported from Africa, though we don't know how recently. In Ga, his name means someone from a royal family, and some believed he had been a chief in Guinea. In Jamaica, he had been a slave on the Frontier plantation not far from Fort Haldane, but most of the slaves accompanying him on the attack had come from another plantation, the Trinity estate, about a mile away.

A second and even larger attack was supposed to occur at the same time on the western side of Jamaica, but Tacky appears to have gotten the date wrong for the uprising. The most plausible theory is that the twin attacks were to take place on Whitsun Holidays, which included Pentecost, but Tacky confused Easter Sunday for Whitsunday. Some planters preferred to speculate that Tacky got drunk and began the

79

attack early on an intoxicated impulse.[3] Both attacks did occur, but they wound up not being coordinated.

Jamaica was the most lucrative colony in the British Empire.[4] It produced sugar—a great deal of sugar. England and her trading partners could not get enough of the sweetener. While sugar production doubled over the last thirty years to about six and half billion pounds per year, and also increased from sugar plantations elsewhere in the West Indies, sugar prices in London increased by about 84 percent over the same period.[5] Sugar was so immensely profitable, therefore, that supply and prices both soared. At the time of Tacky's Rebellion, there were nearly 150,000 slaves working on nearly one hundred sugar plantations on Jamaica.[6] Most plantations had at least fifty slaves, and some had considerably more than that. More than 2,000 slaves worked on one plantation, about 1,300 worked on another, and there were other plantations with hundreds of slaves.[7] The owners of the largest plantations generally lived in England and only visited their Jamaica plantations occasionally. The plantations were run by "overseers," and under them managers, who were formally called "bookkeepers."[8] Some Black slaves, called "drivers," were given special privileges in return for collaborating with the slaveholders and running work gangs on the plantations.

There were a few towns on the island, most notably Kingston and its associated port, Port Royal, which was one of the busiest ports in the New World. Between 1744 and 1746, an average of 342 ships arrived at Port Royal every year.[9] Many ships came for sugar. Many ships brought slaves from Africa. In fact, in the sixty years preceding Tacky's Rebellion, 400,000 Africans had been imported to Jamaica. Jamaica itself constantly needed more slaves because its brutal plantation conditions resulted in high slave mortality. Slaves were overworked, underfed, and severely whipped—or even dismembered—for disobedience.[10] In a typical year, two slaves died for every slave birth on Jamaica. And it was not elderly slaves who were dying; the fatalities were disproportionately high among children and teenagers.[11] Jamaica was also a major slave supplier to the rest of the New World. About one-third of all Africans imported to Jamaica were exported to Spanish provinces in South America or the West Indies, a trade that apparently continued even during periods when Britain and Spain were at war. Many slaves were also exported from Jamaica to the American colonies. In fact, the American colonies preferred slaves who were "seasoned"—that is, made more compliant and accustomed to slavery—on Jamaica and other British colonies in the West Indies to those exported straight from Africa.[12]

As was the case in the American colonies, the militia in Jamaica was ostensibly both a military force to protect the British colony against invasion from a foreign power (Spain or France) and an instrument for slave control. But in reality, it was only effective for slave control. The Jamaica militia did not have the training or the discipline of British soldiers.[13] In 1730, the royal governor of Jamaica described the militia as "indifferent" and said most militiamen were "not to be trusted with arms.[14] All able-bodied White males were enrolled in the militia, and because there were so few Whites the Jamaican militia also informally included some trusted Black and Brown men, too.[15] In addition, two British regiments were stationed on the island—the 49th Regiment was at Port Royal, and the 74th Regiment was at Spanish Town, which was more centrally located about ten miles inland to the northwest. These two regiments probably together consisted of about 1,600 British soldiers. The most powerful branch of the British forces, the Royal Navy, was principally charged with defending Jamaica from attack by other nations or pirates, but it was also available to help put down slave revolts. Jamaica occupied a strategic position in the Caribbean, and British navy vessels were constantly visiting the island. Some navy ships had contingents of marines, who were ready for deployment on land. So a slave insurrection would encounter stiff resistance.

Nevertheless, taking the island was not a pipedream. There were only about 15,000 Whites on the island, and if they could persuade other slaves to join them, they could enjoy up to a ten-to-one numerical advantage. The Whites were, of course, heavily armed, but Tacky and the rebels hoped to acquire arms themselves, as they did on their surprise attack on Fort Haldane.[16] There was, moreover, considerable precedent for successful slave revolts on Jamaica—and therein was a wild card that might well make the difference between success and failure.

There had been many slave revolts on Jamaica over the years, including a revolt by two hundred slaves in 1673 and a revolt by five hundred slaves in 1690.[17] Those revolts had been partially successful. While the slaves had not succeeded in taking the island, the British had not succeeded in extinguishing the insurrections either. Significant numbers

of former slaves—Maroons, they were called—established nearly impregnable bases high in the mountains covered with thick forests. They
acquired arms from raids on plantations, as well as through trade. At
first, the Maroons were little more than scattered gangs that often
battled each other. But in 1720 a leader known as Captain Kojo brought
together previously separate Maroon groups on the western side of the
island. Following their example, Maroon groups also coalesced on the
eastern side of the island. According to one contemporary observer, the
Maroons "began to grow Formidible by continual desertions [of slaves
from plantations] and many hundred stout able Negroes being born in
the Woods who were trained in Arms."[18] The planters worked diligently
to find and destroy the rebel bases. In 1732, they captured Nanny Town,
a settlement high in the Blue Mountains on the eastern end of the island, no more than ten miles from Kingston as the crow flies, named
after a Maroon priestess. There, planters discovered that the Maroons
had become quite established. They were, for example, growing corn,
yams, and other crops.

But by taking Nanny Town, the British won a battle, not a war.[19]
The Maroons had prepared in advance for such an eventuality; most of
them escaped—women and children going first—to other concealed
bases. Robert Hunter, the British governor of the island, who had
been governor of New York during the 1712 slave uprising there, was
alarmed. (More about slave uprisings in New York later.) At Hunter's
request, Britain transferred eight hundred soldiers from Gibraltar to
Jamaica. But the Maroons were more skilled at guerrilla warfare than
either planter militias or regular British troops. They recaptured Nanny
Town the following year, and then for good measure defeated a so-called
Grand Party of 150 British soldiers and sailors who had embarked on a
search-and-destroy mission. In April 1734, planters and British soldiers
succeeded in recapturing Nanny Town again, but only after a battle that
lasted five full days. Nanny led followers to other Maroon settlements
in the east. Meanwhile, Maroons led by Kojo on the western side of the
island were communicating with the Spanish in Cuba, who promised
them military support. The planters were now spending so much time
on militia drills that sugar production was suffering.

And so—here comes the wild card—the British negotiated a peace
treaty with Kojo and the Maroons on the western side of the island in

March 1739, and four months later negotiated a separate treaty with the Maroons and their leader Quao on the eastern end of the island.[20] The treaties granted the Maroons "a perfect state of freedom and liberty" and autonomy over 1,500 acres on the western side of the island and over similar territory on the eastern side of Jamaica. They would be allowed to hunt, grow crops, raise livestock, and even bring their products to market in British towns. But in return, the Maroons had to agree to return to the plantations any runaway slaves who reached them in the future and to "use their best endeavors to take, kill, suppress, or destroy" any future rebel forces. Thus, the Maroons had agreed to take the side of the planters in any slave uprisings. Now, more than twenty years later, would they abide by that bargain? Or would they join the insurrection and end White rule on the island?

After seizing the munitions at Fort Haldane, Tacky led the insurgents to Trinity plantation, where most of them had been enslaved.[21] There they seized more arms and sent word to slaves on nearby plantations to join the rebellion. They allowed the Trinity overseer, Abraham Fletcher, to escape unharmed because he had a reputation for treating slaves fairly. From there they marched, with growing numbers, to the Valley plantation. On the way, they were approached on horseback by Zachary Bayly, the owner of the Trinity, who gamely—or foolishly—attempted to reason with them. "Boys, don't you know me?" he called out to them, waving his hat. They did, and fired at him. Bayly turned and galloped off to spread the alarm.

At the Valley estate, the insurgents killed at least ten Whites and thirty Blacks who opposed them.[22] They then marched to the Esher plantation, several miles to the southeast. More than a dozen slaves from Esher joined the rebellion. The five Whites on the estate barricaded themselves in the main house, and a gun battle ensued. According to the one White survivor, the slaves promised not to harm the White men if they surrendered, and then broke their word and killed them all, except the survivor who only appeared to be dead. From there, they reversed course and proceeded back to the northwest to two other estates, killing another White man and setting fire to a windmill and a cane field as a signal to draw additional recruits. It was now midday, and the rebels now included about four hundred men, women, and children. According to historian Vincent Brown, the "pattern of warfare [adopted by Tacky and his followers] indicates an attempt at territorial and political control, a strategy of maneuver rather than of retreat, evasion, or escape."[23] Moreover, Tacky and other leaders probably believed a parallel insurrection was occurring simultaneously on the western side of the island.

Meanwhile, Zachary Bayly rode from plantation to plantation spreading the alarm.[24] He succeeded in gathering a militia force of about 130 men. All were armed and more than seventy were mounted on horseback. They came upon the rebels near Haywood Hall, not far from the Valley plantation. Seeing militia advancing toward them, the rebels took up positions in the woods. The rebels fired on the militia from the woods but were ineffective because they had been forced to use fishing weights as ammunition. Militia officers ordered their men forward into the woods. But here one of the glaring weaknesses of the militia became evident. As a Swiss visitor had observed a few years earlier, "the militia was littered with colonels."[25] That is, estate owners and other men of high status and wealth had purchased militia commissions. They luxuriated in the pomp, status, and title that went with high military rank but lacked military training, experience, or skill. The militia was disproportionately composed of these faux warriors. Now all of the captains, majors, and colonels on the scene decided that they should remain behind while the men of lesser rank pursued the rebels in the woods.[26] The militia only managed to kill eight and capture four rebels.

At about the time the militia had begun to engage the rebels at the border of the woods, a courier reached the seat of colonial government, Spanish Town, with news of the slave uprising. Lieutenant Governor Henry Moore, who was also acting governor at the time, promptly sent a contingent of three officers and sixty soldiers (representing a more traditional officer-to-soldier ratio) from the 74th Regiment to march by road northward toward the insurrection.[27] He also sent word to Port Royal to dispatch a detachment of the 49th Regiment to march northward by a separate road further to the east. He declared martial law—which effectively put the entire island on a military footing—and ordered the militia to be prepared to defend the towns and plantations. He declared an embargo, cutting off all shipping to the island to prevent the insurgents from receiving outside aid.

And he played the wild card.[28] Moore sent word to British officers stationed near the main Maroon villages to invoke the treaties and demand that the Maroons take up arms against the rebel slaves. And they did. Immediately. Contingents from two Maroon villages pursued the insurgents into the woods, and a combined force of the British 74th Regiment and Maroons assaulted rebels who had retreated to a cave. Tacky boldly led a counterattack but was wounded during the engagement. Further British enforcements arrived from Spanish Town, and Maroons pursued rebels into the woods and brought back severed pairs of ears as proof of kills to the British. Some rebels surrendered, and some committed suicide rather than facing punishment or re-enslavement. Tacky was killed by rebels after he refused to continue leading them. About sixteen British soldiers and four Maroons had been killed in the fighting.

The colonists, however, remained on edge. Something told them this was not the extent of things. Word of the uprising spread throughout the island both in newspapers and by word of mouth.[29] They worried this might inspire other slaves to revolt. As a warning, officials tried twenty-five rebel prisoners—40 percent of them women—and over a period of weeks hanged or burned each of them to death. Those who were hanged were decapitated and their heads placed on poles for everyone, especially slaves, to see.[30]

In late May, just around the time of Whitsun Holidays, couriers arrived in Spanish Town and Kingston with news that a revolt involving at least six hundred slaves was underway on the western side of the island.[31] The rebel leader was Apongo. The best information suggests that Apongo had been imported from the Gold Coast of Africa, where he had probably been a soldier.[32] In 1745, he became the personal slave of Captain Arthur Forrest of the Royal Navy, who was then the commander of the *HMS Wager*. Apongo was one of three Black men on the vessel, and Forrest renamed him Wager. Shortly before, *Wager* had been in Boston, where Forrest had pressed men into service with the Royal Navy against their will, resulting in a skirmish in which two men died and the ship's boatswain had been arrested and charged with murder. When the slave Wager came aboard, Forrest's vessel was assigned to patrol Jamaican waters. Six days after Wager boarded, the British warship chased a French privateer. After a battle in which two warships exchanged cannon fire, Forrest's ship captured the French vessel, took seventy-five prisoners, and offloaded them at Port Royal. Several months later, Wager saw more action when Forrest's ship, together with two British sloops, engaged in a major naval battle with two larger French warships near Hispaniola.

On July 3, 1747, the Royal Navy classified Wager as "unserviceable" and discharged him. The reason for the classification and discharge is unknown. Wager may have been ill or Forrest may not have wanted to return to England with a Black slave. The Admiralty frowned on English officers having Black slaves, and *Wager* was about to sail home. But his discharge did not make Wager a free man. Arthur Forrest was not only an officer in the British Navy; he was also the owner or co-owner of three thousand acres of Jamaica sugar plantations. Forrest's father and father-in-law had both owned plantations on the island. We can assume that when Wager stepped off the ship, he became a slave on one of Forrest's plantations because thirteen years later, at the time of the uprising, Wager was a driver on Forrest's estate, Masemure, in Westmoreland Parish, on the western end of the island.[33] Westmoreland was thick with large sugar plantations, and the overseers there were notorious for being especially brutal.[34]

It's ironic that the Jamaican slave insurrections of 1760 are generally referred to as Tacky's Rebellion as those led by Wager on the western end of the island were larger and more deadly. This branch of the uprisings began at the Masemure estate on March 25, where a dinner party was in progress celebrating Whitsun Holiday. The guests were just remarking how quiet it was when a shot rang out, shattered a window, and struck one of the men dead. Then, slaves wielding cane knives rushed the house. A few of the guests managed to escape. Later in the evening, an overseer at the Egypt plantation, about three miles to the southeast, heard a horn sounding from slave quarters. He did not then know it, but in response to the signal three to four hundred slaves from plantations in the region set out for Masemure.[35]

This branch of the rebellion followed the same strategy as did the one led by Tacky in the east—or the slave revolt in Stono, South Carolina, in 1739 for that matter—namely, move quickly, kill Whites, seize weapons, and recruit more slaves to the rebellion.[36] Encountering some resistance from other slaves at Masemure, Wager's force marched west and crossed the New Savanna River to the Delve plantation, where about two hundred more slaves joined them. From there they marched further west to the Moreland plantation, where several hundred more slaves joined the insurrection. The rebels were now approaching one thousand strong and had collected about one hundred guns. Moreland was a large plantation consisting of several estates and occupied high ground near the Hanover Mountains. The rebels took control of Moreland and made it a base.

Meanwhile, slave insurrections were breaking out on the other side of the mountains further north in Hanover Parish. There could be no doubt that the uprisings were planned and coordinated. The main group of rebels then moved further north from Moreland into the Hanover Mountains, where they established a fortified position high on a precipice.[37] The planters called this Rebel's Barricade, and the insurgents—emulating the Maroons—began turning it into a full-scale village. Women and children, especially, flocked to the Rebel's Barricade from many directions.

Terrified planters armed everyone they trusted, White or Black, and organized into militia groups. Colin Campbell at the New Hope plantation armed twelve slaves he trusted, only to see them join the rebellion.[38] Slaves at some other plantations remained loyal to their masters, however. Sporadic battles between rebels and militia erupted everywhere. Results were mixed, but according to Vincent Brown, these "early battles again showed the mediocrity of the militia."[39] Four days after the rebellion began militia assaulted the Rebel's Barricade. According to the historian Edward Long, the militia was "badly disciplined" and "struck with terror" by rebel yells.[40] They fled pell-mell in all directions, some even breaking bones by jumping down precipices in frantic efforts to escape the battle. Some abandoned their weapons in their haste, and the rebels acquired about fifty more rifles. This increased the confidence of the insurgents, and additional slaves joined the rebellion. Conversely, militiamen were deserting in droves.[41]

The British Army and Navy sprang to action. The Army marched three companies from the 74th and 49th Regiments to the combat area. The Navy sailed two sloops loaded with soldiers, munitions, and other supplies from Port Royal to the western end of the island, including fifty-eight battle-hardened marines and sixty soldiers drawn from the

49th Regiment. Together with sailors from the ships themselves, the Navy hoped to put ashore a fighting force of about four hundred. Later, a third sloop brought eighty more soldiers. The lieutenant governor again invoked the treaty with the Maroons, and once again they joined the fight on the side of the colonial forces, and perhaps once again made the decisive difference.

On June 2, the combined colonial forces—with British professional forces in the lead, militia in the rear, and Maroons protecting the flanks—again assaulted the Rebel's Barricade.[42] While the defenders fired steadily on the oncoming force, British regulars waited until they had reached the outer perimeter of the rebel's redoubt before unleashing a withering volley on the defenders, and then overran the settlement. Hundreds of rebels were either shot to death, driven off steep precipices to their death (women and children included), or taken prisoner. The British believed, however, that about four hundred rebels had escaped.

The war then entered a guerilla phase.[43] British forces, militia, and Maroons searched for rebels in the mountains and forests. Meanwhile, rebel forces struck at targets of opportunity, raiding smaller estates and still attempting to recruit more slaves to the ongoing rebellion. On June 7, rebels successfully ambushed militia in Hanover Parish on the north-west end of the island, and on the next day they successfully attacked the Jerusalem plantation in a small valley in northern Westmoreland Parish. Realizing that the militia were not up the task of either defeating or protecting them from the still ongoing insurrection, planters begged Brigadier General Norwood Witter, who was then in charge of regular British ground forces, to take command of all forces, including the hapless militia. After consulting with one of his lieutenant colonels who was also a large plantation owner in western Jamaica, Witter agreed, and he organized search-and-destroy missions combined with a pro-gram of destroying food crops to starve the rebels.

Witter's strategy was successful.[44] Rather than surrender or starve to death, many rebels chose mass suicide, including killing their chil-dren. Witter responded by promising rebels who surrendered that they would be permitted to return to servitude in their plantations. Many planters objected to this policy, however, and Witter was forced to agree that any rebel convicted of killing a White man would be put to death unless he had been promised a reprieve for taking up arms against the rebels and had then killed or forced home rebels based on that promise. Planters, ever mindful of the financial cost of losing valuable property, also extracted a promise from the colonial government to reimburse them in the sum of forty pounds for every one of their slaves whom the government executed.

Some rebels, including Wager, remained at large and still conducted raids. Meanwhile, the colony sought to reestablish rigorous control over slaves on the plantations through a robust and highly visible program of slave patrols, with militiamen riding in force from plantation to plantation to inspect slave quarters and discover whether any slaves were out of place. At the same time, the colonial government conducted grisly, public executions of rebel prisoners.[45] As Professor Vincent Brown put it, "terror was the sharpest weapon in the British armory."[46]

Colonists were still not sleeping soundly at night, however. In late June, colonists claimed to foil a planned uprising involving at least sixty slaves in Saint James Parish, on Jamaica's northern coast.[47] Most of the alleged conspirators were promptly executed. In the town of Savanna la Mar in Westmoreland Parish, colonials discovered that three coffins supposedly destined for slave burials contained not corpses but guns and swords. In early July, Wager was captured. According to one report, eighty rebels surrendered Wager in order to receive pardons for themselves. The colonial government sentenced Wager to publicly hang in chains for three days and then to be brought down and burned alive. Still, bands of rebels continued to harass colonials. A slave named Simon led an estimated fifty rebels, men and women, armed with about a dozen rifles, on a long trek out of Westmoreland Parish, across St. Elizabeth Parish, and into Clarendon Parish, during which they successfully evaded Maroons hunting them in the mountains and colonial forces looking for them in the plains and valleys, and periodically emerged to raid plantations along the way.

In June 1761, fourteen months after Tacky attacked Fort Haldane, Simon was killed or captured.[48] Some bands of rebels remained hidden in the woods, emerging intermittently to attack Whites. No event marks a definitive end of Tacky's Rebellion. There were slave uprisings on Jamaica in 1763, 1765, and one in 1766 in which twenty colonists were killed, and these may have been inspired or instigated by slaves who participated in Tacky's Revolt.[49] Nevertheless, an attack that killed a White colonist in Westmoreland Parish in October 1761 is as good a marker as any of the end of Tacky's Rebellion.

Here, then, is the bottom line. More than a thousand slaves had actively joined an insurrection.[50] The insurrection had lasted eighteen months. The rebels had destroyed an incalculable amount of property and killed sixty Whites. The entire White population of Jamaica lived in cold terror throughout the insurrection—and, one can be sure, for a very long time afterward. More than five hundred Black men and women had lost their lives, and another five hundred were transported off the island for security reasons.

* * *

The story of Tacky's Rebellion may be interesting, but is it germane to our inquiry about the origins of the Second Amendment? I believe it is.

My argument is that Southerners, including Madison's constituents in Virginia, were terrified of slave revolts and considered an armed militia essential for slave control. The key question is not how likely slave revolts were in eighteenth-century America but just how afraid Americans, and Southerners especially, were of slave revolts. Those two things are, of course, related. The more likely slave revolts actually were, the more likely Southerners were to fear them. Still, risk perception is not the same thing as actual risk. An entire cottage industry of behavioral economics is devoted to examining why human beings overestimate or understate particular risks. So did Tacky's Rebellion play into fears of insurrection in the United States?

The first thing to note is that Madison and the Founders were acutely aware of Tacky's Rebellion. The revolt was widely reported throughout the British Empire, including in the British colonies in America.[51] News of the revolt made such an impression that—a full century later—American slaveholders were still referring to potential slave organizers as "the Tackys among us."[52] If Americans were using this term a hundred years later, then Tacky's Rebellion was haunting their nightmares at the time the Second Amendment was written, twenty-eight years after the revolt.

For Southerners, Tacky's Rebellion had not happened in some far-away and exotic place, irrelevant to their own lives. Slavery in the West Indies and slavery on the American mainland were not then two, entirely separate systems. Some people operated in both theaters. Robert Hunter, for example, who was royal governor of Jamaica at the time of Tacky's Rebellion, had previously been royal governor of Massachusetts; Arthur Forrest commanded the *HMS Wager* in both New England and Jamaican waters; and slave traders sold their human wares in both places. Islands in West Indies and the American colonies were both part of the British Empire, and British subjects freely made their way from one place to the other. Alexander Hamilton, who was born and raised in the British West Indies, is one example, and some Americans had family there.[53] And as we shall discuss in more detail shortly, many slaves on the American mainland had previously been slaves in the British West Indies.[54]

American colonists first learned about Tacky's Rebellion not from newspapers but from firsthand accounts. In July 1761, for example, three ships arrived in Virginia with twenty-seven sailors who had themselves witnessed the bloody events in Jamaica.[55] The following month, another ship brought eight men from Jamaica with more recent reports. This, too, was part of the vivid immediacy of the events.

Americans reacted as if what happened on Jamaica had potential ramifications for them. For example, in the wake of Tacky's Rebellion, Jamaica slaveholders wanted to get rid of some of their most dangerous slaves—but do so at a profit. Anticipating that, Virginia adopted new duties designed to make it prohibitively expensive to import "seasoned" slaves into the colony. A cat-and-mouse game ensued. On October 26, ten ships arrived in Hampton, Virginia, with imports from Jamaica. When it had departed Jamaica, one of the ships, the *Norfolk*, listed only one kind of cargo: "Negroes." When it arrived in Virginia, the ship's master declared he was carrying rum, molasses, sugar, coffee, and other commodities, but he did not mention slaves. Perhaps *Norfolk* sold its human cargo in Georgia or South Carolina; perhaps it clandestinely offloaded slaves in Virginia out of sight of local officials. Either way, what happened on Jamaica had a palpable impact in the imaginations of Southern Whites.

Tacky's Rebellion was only one of four major slave uprisings that occurred in the Caribbean before Madison wrote the Second Amendment. Others occurred on Jamaica in 1718, St. John's in 1733, and Antigua in 1736.[56] We know that—notwithstanding the differences—slave revolts in the British West Indies repeatedly rattled Americans.[57] In fact, there was a direct correlation between slave revolts in the British Caribbean and the number of publications devoted to the problem of slavery on American soil.[58] If there had been any doubt about it, the Caribbean revolts showed that slaves were capable of organizing insurrections. And Americans feared the Caribbean rebellions might motivate their own slaves to revolt.[59] As Eugene D. Genovese put it, American "slaveholders knew of the formidable revolts in the Caribbean and took an international view of the matter, thereby displaying greater sophistication than most subsequent historians."[60]

In that last remark about "subsequent historians," Genovese alludes to something we need to take up. Comparing slavery in the South to slavery in the Caribbean has led to underestimating the risk of slave insurrections in the South.[61] Or, more precisely for our purposes, it has led to underestimating just how afraid Americans were of slave revolts. It is all too easy to unconsciously adopt this false syllogism: (1) No insurrection as large as Tacky's Rebellion—or the even larger, ultimately successful Haitian Revolution—ever occurred in the South. (2) Southerners knew that there marked differences between slavery in the West Indies and in the United States. (3) Therefore, Southerners believed that, unlike their counterparts in the West Indies, they need not fear slave insurrections. Conclusion 3, of course, does not necessarily follow from premises 1 and 2. Yet there seems to be confusion around this topic. For example, Eugene Genovese, who was just quoted earlier as saying that eighteenth-century slaveholders were more alarmed about events in the Caribbean than contemporary historians believe, also wrote: "The slaves of the Old South, unlike those of the Caribbean and Brazil, did not take up arms often enough or in large enough numbers to forge a revolutionary tradition."[62] Another historian wrote: "A great number of southerners at all times held the firm belief that the negro population was so docile, so little cohesive, and in the main so friendly toward the whites and so contented that a disastrous insurrection by them would be impossible."[63] Yet, in his very next sentence, this historian said: "But on the whole there was much greater anxiety abroad in the land than historians have told of."

Or consider these two statements, each by an esteemed historian: Edmund S. Morgan: "No white person was killed by a slave rebellion in colonial Virginia."[64] John Hope Franklin: "Before the end of the colonial period Virginia, like her neighbors, had become an armed camp in which masters figuratively kept their guns cocked and trained on the slaves in order to keep them docile and tractable."[65] It is impossible not to scratch one's head—especially if I tell you that both statements may be true.

Which is it? Were Southerners confident that their slaves would not revolt? Or did the prospect of revolts cause them to break out in cold sweats in the middle of the night? Confronting one of the sources of confusion directly will help clear things up. That is, by comparing slavery in West Indies and in the South—and thinking through what their similarities and differences would have really meant—will both clear up some of the apparent inconsistencies and help us understand just how confident or fearful Madison and his contemporaries in the United States were.

First, the demographics in the two systems were different. At the time of Tacky's Rebellion, slaves comprised 90 percent of the population on Jamaica—much higher than in any state in the Union.[66] Nevertheless, slaves constituted a sufficiently large share of the population in the South to present real risks of insurrection. At the time Madison wrote the Second Amendment, slaves comprised about 40 percent of the total population of Virginia, and a majority of the population in Eastern Virginia, where the Richmond Convention was held and where many of the Founders lived.[67] The situation was similar in South Carolina. Slaves constituted 43 percent of that state's population, but much higher portions in coastal regions.[68] In Charleston District—the second most populous district in the state—slaves constituted 76 percent of the population. Within rural coastal regions in South Carolina, slaves constituted 84 percent of the population.[69] Slaves also constituted about a third of the population in Maryland and Georgia and more than a quarter of North Carolina.[70] And once again, there were higher portions in certain areas.

Southern colonies were deeply worried about the number of slaves within their borders. At times, they attempted to cap the number of slaves within their territories. In 1735, for example, Georgia banned slavery entirely—not for moral reasons—but because it feared slave insurrections.[71] But the prohibition lasted only fifteen years. Economic considerations won out. Georgia planters envied the great wealth that their counterparts in South Carolina were able to amass as a result of slave labor, and successfully lobbied for a repeal of the prohibition.

Slaves in the South were less consolidated than on Jamaica. Consolidation matters because slaves living on the same plantation would have known each other well, known who was brave and trust-worthy, and been able to talk to one another far more easily. All of that would have would have made it easier to conspire in an insurrec-tion. Most slaves in Jamaica lived on plantations with more than fifty slaves, and as previously mentioned, some plantations were enormous. By contrast, three-quarters of the slaves in the Southern states lived on farms with no more than fifty slaves.[72] Still, many plantations in the South had large numbers of slaves. When he served in the First Congress, Madison's family owned more than one hundred slaves;[73] Thomas Jefferson had more than a hundred and fifty slaves on his estate at Monticello;[74] and George Washington had more than two hundred slaves at Mount Vernon.[75]

Another demographic difference involved where slaves were born. Were slaves born in Africa or in the New World? And if born in Africa, what part of Africa? Slave owners preferred purchasing slaves imported from the African Gold Coast (where Ghana is now located), whom they called "Coromantees."[76] Africans from this region were suppos-edly especially strong and smart. However, Coromantees were also proud, headstrong, came from tribes with strong military traditions, and in some cases were trained warriors.[77] They were, therefore, also considered especially rebellious and dangerous. Both Wager and Tacky were believed to have been Coromantees.[78] American colonialists preferred slaves who were first "seasoned" or "broken in," that is, acculturated into their lot as slaves through whippings, beatings, and physical mutilations until hope and rebelliousness gave way to resigna-tion and obedience.[79] Much of this occurred in the West Indies, which exported slaves to the American mainland.[80]

The safest slaves were considered "creoles"—Blacks who were born into slavery and knew no other life.[81] At the time of the American Revolution, 80 percent of slaves on the North American mainland had been born in Africa.[82] For Virginia, even that was too many, and in 1778 it enacted a statute banning any further imports of slaves into the state.[83] The West Indies did not have that luxury. Because of especially harsh conditions imposed by cultivating sugar, slave deaths exceeded slave births, and there was a constant need to replenish slaves with imports. In the West Indies, therefore, most slaves were born in Africa.[84] And on Jamaica, 19 percent of slaves who were being imported from Africa were particularly valuable—but also particularly dangerous—Coromantees.[85]

An important geographic difference, of course, is that Jamaica is an island, a bit smaller in total area than Connecticut. A large majority slave population might actually hope to seize and hold an island. (Indeed, in 1733, slaves took control of the island of St. John's, then a Dutch colony, for a period of six months. And beginning in 1791, slaves would begin a thirteen-year revolution in French St. Domingue, in which they would successfully seize the much larger island of Hispaniola and establish their own state.) If Tacky and Wager had begun their attacks at the same time, as intended, they may have had a longshot chance of seizing Jamaica and expelling the British. Failing that, they had at least a realistic prospect of emulating the Maroons and establishing impregnable bases in the mountains. But any slave insurrection in the South would have been a suicide mission.[86] Militia could come from farther and farther away, if necessary, until the insurrection was extinguished.

While some believe that the Stono rebels intended to make their way to Spanish Florida to become free, their conduct—taking time to invade plantation homes, set fire to the main houses, and kill Whites rather than moving as quickly as possible toward Florida—suggests otherwise. They must have known that successfully reaching Spanish Florida, 275 miles away, without being hunted down and destroyed by militia was unrealistic. Maybe they dreamed of recruiting enough slaves to create a large enough force to be able to repel militia attacks for that 275-mile march. Yet, deep down, they must have known their only realistic goal was to kill as many slave masters as possible and then die free. We can reasonably infer that was the real goal of the Stono rebels because that is what they did. That slaves might be willing to give their lives for such a goal was quite enough to fear.

Slaveholders in Virginia and other areas of the Upper South liked to think of themselves as kind, paternalistic masters, at least in comparison with their counterparts in the West Indies, and in the Deep South (particularly South Carolina), too, where slaves were more concentrated, their treatment more brutal, and their mortality rates higher.[87] Slaveholders in the Upper South generally fed their slaves better than did their Caribbean counterparts. And for the most part, they lived on plantations with their slaves, whom they knew personally, while the largest Jamaican slaveholders were absentee owners who lived in England and employed overseers to manage their plantations.[88] Slave owners in the South told everyone who would listen that slavery was a natural condition, and that in contrast to the West Indies, *their* slaves not only accepted but actually appreciated their condition. Their slaves were happy![89] The *Richmond Enquirer* said that compared to slaves in the West Indies, Virginia's slaves lived in "perfect freedom."[90]

Southerners described their slaves as "content and docile" so often that the phrase became cliché.[91] Even some twentieth-century historians bought that rubbish. Prominent historians Samuel E. Morrison and Henry S. Commager wrote: "The majority of slaves were adequately fed, well cared for and apparently happy."[92] But, of course, that was a myth. In their bones, slave owners themselves knew it was not true.[93] Content and docile people do not have to be frequently whipped. In fact, when Southern slaveholders tried to refrain from whippings, they failed. Many slaves just refused to be obedient. "The typical master went to the whip often—much more often than he himself would usually have preferred," writes Eugene D. Genovese.[94] "Even relatively enlightened planters resorted to harsh measures," Peter Kolchin writes, adding that whippings were routine.[95] Slaveholders blamed their slaves for having to be treated cruelly. A French visitor to Monticello was appalled to see the author of the Declaration of Independence carry a small whip with him into the fields and repeatedly threaten slaves with it. For his part, Jefferson lamented he was too lenient with his slaves. "I find I am not fit to be a farmer with the kind of labor we have," he remarked to a friend.[96] Like many large planters, Jefferson probably delegated the duty of administering actual whippings to his overseers rather than deigning to do that dirty business himself.[97] Moreover, whippings were often not sufficient. Castration was not an uncommon punishment. Slave owners also punished slaves by amputating ears, toes, and fingers, not to mention burning a slave at the stake for special in terrorem effect.[98] Happy slaves, indeed.

Americans certainly did not believe themselves immune from slave revolts. They experienced them. The largest insurrection on American soil, the Stono Rebellion, which took place in South Carolina in 1739 and involved as many as one hundred slaves, was discussed in the Introduction. Two others happened in a place we don't usually associate with slavery, namely, New York City. The first occurred on April 7, 1712.[99] At that time, about 40 percent of the city's White residents owned Black slaves, and slaves comprised 15–20 percent of the city's population.[100] Between twenty-five and fifty slaves, including both men and women, participated in the revolt. It is believed many of them were Coromantees. The rebels armed themselves with guns, swords, knives, and hatchets, and shortly after midnight set fire to a building. It was an ambush. As Whites flocked to the scene to fight the fire, the rebels attacked them—killing nine and wounding six more before fleeing into the woods. The next morning New York and Westchester militia sealed off escape routes from the Island of Manhattan and hunted down the rebels. They claim to have captured nearly all of the rebels. Twenty-one were executed; six committed suicide rather than being captured. New York promptly strengthened its slave laws and, among other things, added arson as a crime punishable by death.

A second insurrection occurred in New York City in 1741. There were then two thousand slaves in New York, comprising 20 percent of the city's population.[101] Sixty-five percent of New York's slaves had come from the British West Indies.[102] The insurrection—or, at least, what everyone came to believe was an insurrection—began on the afternoon of March 18. The mansion of Lieutenant Governor George Clark, which was located within Fort George, near the southern tip of Manhattan, caught fire. Alarm bells rang and a bucket brigade, comprised of men from both races, was formed. As the flames raged, a slave named Cuffee stopped handing buckets to the next man, stepped out of the line, and according to a shoemaker who was there, "huzzah'd, danced, whistled and sung."[103] It was windy and fire outran the bucket brigade. Flames spread to the Governor's Mansion, and from there to barracks and a chapel within the compound. Hand grenades in one of the buildings began to explode. A stampede began as people realized that a cache of gunpowder might blow up the entire fort. Then, the heavens intervened and New York was saved. Rain fell, extinguishing the fire.

So far, nothing was suspicious beyond Cuffee's wildly impolitic behavior. Fires were not uncommon in eighteenth-century cities. But over the next three weeks, there were nine more fires in New York City. Fires were not that common. On three days, there were multiple fires, and two of those days happened to be anniversaries of significant dates in the 1712 insurrection.[104] On the final day, April 6, there were four separate fires. A fireman fighting one of those fires spotted Cuffee inside a burning building. When Cuffee saw the fireman looking at him, he ran. The fireman gave chase. Others joined the pursuit. Cuffee was caught and taken to jail. Militia patrolled the city every night for the next three months.[105] Every building in the city was searched. Rewards were offered for information revealing "latent Enemies"—a White person would receive £100; a slave would receive freedom, and the slave's owner would receive £25 compensation; and any conspirator who gave information would receive a pardon.[106] An intensive investigation that included depositions, grand jury testimony, and trials extended over a year and a half. Just where reason left off and Salem witch trial frenzy took over is impossible to say. At the end of the day, 152 Blacks were arrested; 81 confessed (some, perhaps, after being tortured); some recanted their confessions; 30 were either burned at the stake or hanged at the gallows; 70 more were transported to slave markets and plantations in the British West Indies.[107] Whether there was a conspiracy at all, and if so, what its objective was is a mystery.[108] What we can say with certainty, however, is that New Yorkers were so terrified of their slaves that they reacted to suspicious fires that may, or may not, have been set by slaves by succumbing to mass hysteria.

If New Yorkers could be that afraid, what about Southerners?

* * *

Just how many slave insurrections were there in eighteenth-century America? Let's start at the beginning, that is, with the Middle Passage—Africans placed on ships bound for slave markets in the New World. Historians have identified 579 rebellions or attacks on slave ships or auxiliary boats, with almost 80 percent occurring between 1726 and 1800.[109] These revolts were getting a lot of attention during Madison's day; in fact, newspapers were frequently publishing stories about ship-board revolts during the 1760s and 1770s.[110]

The most famous attempt to catalogue slave revolts on American soil is *American Negro Slave Revolts* by Herbert Aptheker, published in 1943 by Columbia University Press. It was a paradigm-shattering work. As Eugene Genovese put it, Aptheker "demolished the legend of the contented slave."[111] *American Negro Slave Revolts* is, however, a controversial work. It is cited often by some and scrupulously avoided by others. It was apparently good enough for Columbia, which awarded Aptheker a doctorate in history based, in significant part, on its evaluation of its merit, for the backbone of the book was Aptheker's dissertation. But Aptheker's scholarly reputation was tarnished by the failure in his life-long quest to become a university professor.[112] Whether that was due to McCarthyism—Aptheker was an outspoken member of the American Communist Party—or to shortcomings in Aptheker's scholarship is a matter of dispute.[113]

One criticism is that Aptheker was prone to exaggeration.[114] And, in fact, *American Negro Slave Revolts* is vulnerable to an accusation along those lines. Aptheker claims his book identifies more than 250 slave plots or revolts that involved at least ten slaves with the apparent aim of winning their freedom.[115] Aptheker does, in fact, identify more than 250 incidents. And he backs up those identifications with contemporaneous newspaper accounts, letters, and other materials. However, many of the incidents are not insurrections or revolts—as advertised by the title—but plots and conspiracies that were foiled before ripening into an actual rebellion. Moreover, for many incidents it is impossible to know whether there was a genuine conspiracy or merely suspicion or rumors of a conspiracy. This is not to suggest that Aptheker fudges the differences. He doesn't. With respect to the New York fires, for example, Aptheker writes: "The hysteria of 1741 in the City of New York has been treated by some historians as arising from a complete hoax, or an un-accountable mob delusion, while others have dealt with it as resulting from a real and considerable slave conspiracy. It seems fairly certain that neither of these views altogether coincides with the facts."[116] That is entirely fair. But if the incident was more than a hoax but less than a conspiracy, does it meet Aptheker's own criteria for being included?

Or how about this one: According to an entry in the Council Journal of South Carolina on February 26, 1733, there had been reports of mysterious meetings of hundreds of slaves, as well as several "robberies and insolences."[117] Fearing a conspiracy, Charleston's militia was alerted and twelve slaves were arrested and questioned. There is no further information. A report of hundreds of slaves gathering together borders on the unbelievable. If such a thing happened, there would have been widespread panic. Fire bells would have sounded throughout the land, summoning militia from far and wide. What really happened? It is impossible to know.

Here's another example of lots of smoke but maybe no fire. On July 8, 1775, two North Carolina slaves told a slave owner that "an insurrection of the negroes against the whole people" would begin that night. A group of one hundred slave patrollers was assembled, spread an alarm throughout the area, "apprehended the suspected heads," and by night there were "near forty under proper guard."[118] It turned out that a White boat captain from the North and a particular slave had "propagated the contagion." Five Blacks were whipped and had both ears cut off. Meanwhile, a militia captain reported "negroes being in arms" near the county line. The response: "We posted guards upon the roads for several miles that night." All of the quotations are from a contemporaneous letter by the chairman of the Pitt County Committee of Correspondence, and it is reasonable to believe Whites believed—or at least feared—something was going on, but was it really? One nineteenth-century historian believed the reports that so alarmed Whites were "entirely unfounded."[119] But who can really say?

Here is one final incident catalogued by Herbert Aptheker: Near the end of the year in 1767, slaves poisoned several overseers on a plantation in Alexandria, Virginia. Three slaves were executed, and their heads were placed on chimneys on the county courthouse as a warning to other slaves.[120] This is interesting for two reasons. First, it seems this happened on George Mason's plantation. Second, it involves poisoning, which is important because poisoning, like arson, was a popular method of slave resistance.[121] Slaves poisoned their masters far more often than they engaged in open revolt. House servants were, if anything, more hostile to their White masters than were field hands.[122] Some slaves knew what roots and plants were poisonous; some employed arsenic and deadly substances from their masters' cupboards. Three slaves were convicted of poisoning Ambrose Madison—James Madison's grandfather—at Montpelier in 1732.[123] In just Orange County, where the Madison's lived, other slaves were convicted of poisoning their owners in 1737 and 1747. To prevent slaves from gaining knowledge about poisons, or access to them, South Carolina enacted legislation prohibiting physicians or druggists from employing slaves in any place where they kept medicines or drugs.[124] But determined slaves could be resourceful. When poisons were not available, some laced their master's food with ground glass.[125] In Virginia alone, and just between 1772 and 1810, at least twenty slaves for executed for poisonings.[126] Some slave owners so feared being poisoned that they used food tasters.[127]

Just how many slave revolts were there? And just how often did slaves strike back against their oppressors by poisoning them, slitting their throats in the night, or setting fire to their buildings? We will never know. Any attempt, like Aptheker's, to catalogue such incidents will be hopelessly plagued by problems of overinclusion and underinclusion.[128] The overinclusion problem results from our inability to separate the wheat from the chaff, that is, to determine which incidents were genuine acts of rebellion and which were imagined by nervous Whites.[129] The underinclusion problem results from the reluctance of the American slave-holding society to report incidents of rebellion.[130] Whites fretted that such reports, whether spread through newspapers or on the grapevine, would give slaves ideas. Southern Whites also believed that acts of slave rebellion reflected poorly on them and their slaveholding society. They were, after all, telling their Northern cousins that their slaves were content and happy.

Historian Alan Taylor says reporting slave revolts—even in so much as a private letter that might become public—violated a code of silence.[131] When faced with some act of rebellion, it was better to take firm action to repress further incidents—by punishing slaves who were suspected of being involved and implementing more aggressive patrols—while sweeping news of the rebellious act under the rug. As amazing as it sounds, the *South Carolina Gazette* did not report the Stono Rebellion, even though it occurred only about fifteen miles from Charleston, the paper's hometown.[132] That would be the equivalent today of a city newspaper not publishing news that a group of terrorists, numbering as many as one hundred, launched an attack that killed dozens of people, and were ultimately killed or captured in a battle with the National Guard. Meanwhile, news of the Stono Rebellion was widely reported elsewhere throughout the British Empire; stories about it appeared in the *Pennsylvania Gazette*, *Boston Evening-Post*, *London Magazine*, and *Scots Magazine* in Edinburgh, among periodicals.[133] No one in eighteenth-century America would have considered that odd. Southern newspapers were often reluctant to publish reports about slave insurrections—or about more common occurrences of slaves poisoning or slitting the throats of their masters in the night—for fear that slaves might be inspired by such stories.

Any catalogue of slave revolts will, therefore, almost certainly be underinclusive. There were probably acts of slave rebellion—perhaps even significant ones—about which we may never know. But we need not worry about the problem of overinclusion. That's because our primary interest is not how many revolts actually occurred but just how afraid Whites were of slave rebellions. Therefore, every report of a slave rebellion is evidence of White nervousness about slave rebellions, even if—and arguably especially if—it was only imagined. While we can never know how many slave revolts actually occurred, we can say three things with a reasonable degree of certainty: there were frequent small acts of slave rebellion, overt and covert; there was a constant cascade of rumors about plots and conspiracies of slave insurrections; and Whites were terrified of large-scale insurrections even if relatively few actually occurred.

The last point—that Southerners feared slave insurrections—is the most germane for our investigation because it bears upon the connection between the slave insurrections and the militia. The Southern militia's role was to suppress insurrections. That is why the South considered it essential to have an armed militia, and why Patrick Henry was able to make Southerners anxious that Congress might interfere with their militia. We can see now why there has been wide agreement among leading historians that the South was, in fact, terrified about the prospect of slave insurrections—as just a short sampling of statements shows. John Hope Franklin, for example, said: "Even rumors of insurrections struck terror in the hearts of the slaveholders and called forth the most vigorous efforts to guard against the dreaded eventuality."[134] Eugene D. Genovese wrote: "Most states smashed plots, real and imagined, and periodically quaked with fear without suffering substantial revolts."[135] Sally E. Hadden observed that "many whites lived in almost a 'crisis of fear' from one rumor of rebellion or insurrection to another."[136] Alan Taylor quoted a former slave as saying, "The slaveholder is well aware that he stands over a volcano, that may at any moment rock his foundation to the center, and with one might burst of its long suppressed fire, sweep him and his family to destruction."[137]

As a general matter, Southerners pretended to believe that their supposedly docile, content, and happy slaves would not revolt. In part, this was propaganda for Northerners. In part, it was a whistling-past-the-graveyard attempt to allay their own dread. But sometimes they admitted (although a bit obliquely) that they were terrified of slave insurrections. Thomas Jefferson, for example, once described how a political event that would have further swelled the number of slaves in Virginia had "like a fire bell in the night, awakened and filled me with terror."[138] It was a revealing confession. For Southerners, the first thought that leaped to mind when a fire bell rang at night was not fire—it was insurrection.[139]

* * *

Controlling a large slave population was no easy task. Yet, for the most part, the South did it successfully. By no means, of course, was it entirely successful. There were countless acts of rebellion, including arsons and murders of individual overseers and masters. There were slave revolts. And Southerners lived in constant terror. But prior to Madison writing the Second Amendment in 1791, there was no large-scale insurrection that threatened to wrest control from Whites, or resulted in mass carnage, or led to the creation of an impregnable bastion of former slaves. By contrast, all of those things occurred on Jamaica and other islands in the Caribbean. While we have described differences between the slave systems on the American mainland and on the islands of the West Indies that helped account for the South's success, it is time to focus on the bulwark of slave control, namely, the militia. Other aspects of the system—psychological, sociological, and legal—were also critical. Southerners, for example, considered it important to keep slaves illiterate.[140] If slaves could read and write, they could forge passes that allowed them to travel off the plantation, read abolitionist pamphlets, or learn about slave rebellions from newspapers. But if Southerners were somehow forced to give up their laws that outlawed teaching slaves to read or give up the militia, the choice would have been easy. The militia was the one truly essential instrument of slave control. It served the twin purposes of preventing slave insurrections and suppressing them when they occurred. Without the militia—flawed as they were—slave control would have failed.

Southern militia conducted slave patrols in all areas where there were large numbers of slaves.[141] Patrollers were armed with guns, whips, and ropes that could be used for binding hands, and they worked in groups of three to five, with a captain in charge of each group.[142] Each patrol was assigned a designated area or "beat." This is, in fact, where the terms *policeman's beat* and *patrolling* originated.[143]

Patrols were conducted day and night and on weekdays and weekends. In rural areas, patrollers were mounted on horseback, while in cities they were generally on foot.[144] Patrollers challenged all Blacks who were not on their home farm or plantation. Slaves were not allowed to leave their farm or plantation without a written pass or "ticket" signed by their master. General passes which stated simply that the holder was permitted to travel were either strongly discouraged or flatly invalid.[145] Patrollers wanted specific passes that included the slave's name, the date on which he or she was permitted to travel, where he was permitted to go, and for what purpose. For example, a pass might state that a slave from plantation A was permitted to travel to plantation B on a particular day to visit his wife. Or a pass might state that a slave was permitted to attend a church service or fetch something from town.

Patrols would do whatever was necessary to intercept Blacks traveling without permission. They would vary the times and days of the week of patrols to make them unpredictable; they would make rounds or hide and wait near paths they believed slaves might take.

Patrollers summarily whipped any Black who did not produce a valid pass (or, in the case of a free Black, identifying papers). At some times in some jurisdictions, patrollers would make examples of slaves they apprehended by administering their beatings at public whipping posts.[146] Some slaveholders objected to punishments meted out by slave patrollers because their whippings could be brutal and render slaves temporarily unfit to work or permanently maimed. Occasionally slaves died from the beatings.[147] There was often tension between slave patrols and slave owners. Slaves were valuable property, and owners did not want them damaged. Some slaveholders thought it was their prerogative to discipline their own slaves, and some considered their honor to be insulted if patrollers entered and searched their property.[148] But because slave patrols were designed, in part, as a check against lax slave owners, slaveholders generally did not fully prevail in this tug-of-war over authority. In Virginia, slave patrollers needed permission to whip slaves, but they obtained permission not from slave owners but from the local justice of the peace.[149] The general rule appears to be that patrollers were vested with the authority to enter and search property as they saw fit, even over the owner's objection.[150] In fact, at times when Southern fears were at the highest pitch, slave patrols even searched the homes of Whites, including the wealthy and powerful, without their permission, looking, for example, for slaves hidden in basements.[151]

Patrollers also routinely searched slave cabins, looking for contraband such as guns, knives, or other implements, such as scythes, that might be used as weapons, and for other goods they had no reason to possess, like linens, china, newspapers, books, or writing paper.[152] If a patroller found a gun, whether on a slave's person on in their dwelling, he was often legally permitted to personally keep it as partial remuneration for his work.[153] Patrollers would also check on whether any slaves[154] were absent from their cabins after nightfall, and be on the lookout for any gatherings of slaves.[155]

In the two largest slaveholding states, Virginia and South Carolina, slave patrols were the direct responsibility of the militia.[156] This was the case from 1721 onward in Virginia and from 1727 onward in South Carolina, and remained the case until the end of the Civil War.[157] North Carolina was somewhat different. Its slave patrol system did not begin until 1753, and the patrols were organized not by militia companies but by county courts.[158] No one is quite sure why. One guess is that because of the state's lower population density, militia companies did not routinely muster everywhere, while county courts did sit regularly and could better organize slave patrols.[159] That may be more of a distinction than a real difference because it was, of course, North Carolina militiamen who were serving as slave patrollers.[160] Slave patrols also initially had less authority in North Carolina than in her neighboring states; they could not, for example, stop Blacks who were traveling between plantations or search White homes. But that changed during the Revolutionary War, when Whites became more fearful about slave rebellions.[161] North Carolina slave patrols were then given more authority and more closely resembled their counterparts in other states.

The states took care to ensure capable people were serving as slave patrollers. They wanted "the choicest and best" to perform this critically important work.[162] Considering how onerous the work was, one might think that the elites would find ways to avoid it. That was not the case. Slave patrollers represented a cross-section of the entire male White population, including the wealthy.[163] If anything, patrol membership skewed toward the well-to-do. North Carolina had a property requirement, and for a while South Carolina required that all plantation owners, including both men and women, serve as slave patrollers.[164] Other measures also aimed at quality control. Because knowing the area well was critical, one had to live in the community for a prescribed number of years before becoming a slave patroller.[165] Historical records show that some individuals were reappointed to slave patrol duties again and again.[166] Clearly, having experienced patrollers was considered more important than equitably spreading the work. Those selected to serve received a special commission and took an oath to faithfully "discharge the trust reposed in me as the law directs, and to the best of my power."[167] No one was to take this work lightly.

The amount of resources invested in slave patrols was enormous. To some extent, of course, the intensity of slave patrolling ebbed and flowed over time.[168] Things were at the highest pitch after slave revolts or when insurrection rumors were circulating. There were other times when Southern communities complained that the militia was not adequately patrolling. But even when things were relatively lax, the operative word is *relatively*. Slave patrolling was serious business. No society would have invested—over more than a century and a half—the amount of time, energy, and treasure that the South invested in slave patrolling unless it believed it was worth it. And it was worth it. On the whole, the Southern militias were effective at slave control. The Caribbean slave revolts terrified the American South, but nothing on the scale of Tacky's Rebellion occurred on American soil.

* * *

But were the militia effective at anything other than slave control? Could they defend the state or nation from invasion by a professional army? As America was moving to war against Britain, patriots sang the praises of the militia. The citizen soldier, many claimed, would be more courageous, independent, self-reliant, and virtuous than the professional soldier. If America were to prevail over Great British by force of arms, that is what patriots had to believe. "We must all be soldiers," John Adams said in 1776.[169] "[A] well-regulated militia, composed of the body of the people, trained in arms, is the proper, natural and safe defense of a free state," proclaimed Virginia that same year.[170] Had Americans not believed that in 1776, they would not have launched the Revolutionary War. But what the Founders were to believe fifteen years later depended on how well the militia performed in that war. That is what we shall examine in the next two chapters.

5

The Militia—War in the North

THE BRITISH GROUND attack did not start until four in the afternoon.[1] It had taken most of the day to ferry 2,600 troops from Boston to the mile-long Charlestown peninsula and move them into positions for assault. Meanwhile, British warships had been firing cannonballs at the narrow neck that connected the peninsula to the mainland to prevent more American militia from reinforcing their brethren atop Bunker and Breed's Hills. And British artillery across the water in Boston's North End had fired incendiary shells into the Town of Charlestown, on the southwestern tip of the peninsula. A breeze fanned the flames, and as the attack began, the entire town was ablaze. Burning Charlestown served two goals. It removed American sharpshooters from rooftops, where they had been ready to fire upon British columns attacking Bunker Hill. And it sent a message: Going to war with the mother country will be costly. By the end of this day on June 17, 1775, fire would consume more than five hundred houses, barns, churches, stores, warehouses, and mills, not to mention wharves and the town hall.[2]

The British launched a two-pronged assault. Brigadier Robert Pigot commanded the western prong toward Breed's Hill while General William Howe personally led a column of redcoats on the right, along the shoreline, toward Bunker Hill. The only nuance was that Pigot's first advance would be a feint, designed to hold the Americans in place while Howe's column made its way along the longer route. Only after Howe's troops were ready to attack would Pigot truly surge forward.

The British estimated that American militia on the peninsula totaled between five and six thousand. If true, the Americans held a two-to-one advantage.[3] Moreover, the Americans were in entrenched positions on high ground. None of that worried General Thomas Gage, commander of all British forces in North America. Gage was confident that American militia would fold when confronted face to face by British regulars.[4] He was painfully aware of how the first skirmish of the war at Lexington and Concord turned out two months earlier. The British suffered 273 killed and wounded, nearly triple the 95 American casualties.[5] But in that engagement, the Americans had perpetrated "unmanly barbarity" by hiding behind stone walls and trees while shooting at redcoats marching nineteen miles along open roads.[6] If British troops pursued them, the militia ran away and reappeared later. This time things would be different. General Gage believed that despite their advantages in numbers and geography, American militia would not stand their ground.[7] A phalanx of British soldiers running toward them with glistening, eighteen-inch bayonets affixed to the end of their five-foot muskets was too terrifying for amateur soldiers.[8] The Americans would flee. In fact, Gage's strategy was to demonstrate that hard reality to the Americans, thereby dispelling their harebrained dream of waging a war against the British Empire.[9]

The British estimate of American strength was off considerably. There were only about two thousand militiamen on the peninsula.[10] So, the British, in fact, held a modest numerical advantage. Moreover, even before the battle began, the size of the American force was dwindling.

The Americans had spent the night and the day constructing a square redoubt with dirt walls 130 feet long and 6 feet high on the southwestern slope of Breed's Hill.[11] Why they placed their main fort there instead of on Bunker Hill, which was both considerably higher and closer to supply lines, is a mystery.[12] Perhaps they thought there was some advantage to being near the town. If so, the British reduced that idea to smoldering embers. The Americans had spent the preceding night and day building their fort and other breastworks with shovels, picks, and axes. They were tired and hungry. They had forgotten to bring food.

In the morning, the American commander, Colonel William Prescott of the Massachusetts militia contingent known as the Minutemen, realized that his left flank (the British right, where Howe would lead his column) was vulnerable and might be outflanked. He asked General William Putnam to fortify that position along the base of Bunker Hill. A call was made for volunteers to carry entrenching tools from Breed's Hill to Bunker Hill. Militiamen eagerly responded, grabbing shovels and axes. But many did not stop at Bunker Hill. They kept going north, getting off the peninsula before the battle began. According to one report, when the British assault began, only 170 men remained with Prescott in the redoubt on Breed's Hill. During roughly the same time period, 200 New Hampshire militiamen had arrived and reinforced the position at the base of Bunker Hill. Nevertheless, more militiamen were creeping away than arriving.[13]

According to lore, Prescott told his men, "Don't fire until you see the whites of their eyes." He may have said that; the phrase had been used by military commanders before. We do know that Prescott told his men to wait until the British were within about six rods (a hundred feet) before firing their first volley, and to aim at the enemy's hips.[14] Behind a field-stone fence below Breed's Hill, Colonel John Stark told his men to wait until they could see half-gaiters below the knees of British soldiers.[15] This was standard military doctrine. Smoothbore muskets had little accuracy at any distance and practically none beyond eighty yards.[16] Even within effective range, soldiers firing muskets could only expect to hit their targets around 10 percent of the time.[17] According to modern calculations, in fact, only one out of every three hundred shots fired by Americans during Lexington and Concord hit a British soldier.[18] Muskets, moreover, were entirely ineffectual at two hundred yards; if a ball hit you at that distance, it would do no more than sting. Military doctrine compensated for these limitations by having soldiers stand shoulder to shoulder and firing concentrated volleys at short distances. It took about half a minute to reload, so troops were generally arrayed in two or three ranks: one rank would fire and then kneel to reload while another rank fired. (Rifles—so named because they had rifled or grooved barrels—were more accurate, but they, like muskets, were muzzle-loaded, and rifles took even longer to reload.[19] They were also more difficult to manufacture and could not be fitted with bayonets. Consequently, rifles were used primarily by sharpshooters.[20] Contrary to myth, riflemen were seldom more than ancillary troops and rarely made a decisive difference by themselves. The brunt of causalities was inflicted by concentrated musket fire and bayonets.[21])

A column of three hundred redcoats, four or five abreast, moved toward Stark's position. They fired a volley or two as they came. At fifty yards, they lowered their bayonets and broke into a trot. As the attackers closed, the Americans unleashed a series of devastating volleys. Within moments, ninety-six British lay dead. Wounded men wailed in pain. American riflemen had been told to aim at officers, and a British captain later said that among the officers, "few had less than three or four wounds."[22] General Howe, who was personally leading his troops, had his men briefly regroup and then led them forward again, only to experience a similar result. Men all around Howe were cut down. "For near a minute, he was quite alone," a British officer remarked.[23]

During their initial feint on the left wing, Brigadier Pigot's men had suffered only light casualties, but with Howe fully engaged on the right, Pigot directly assaulted the redoubt on Breed's Hill, with similar results. One British soldier recalled that the fire from the American position resembled "a continual sheet of lightening and an uninterrupted peal of thunder."[24] The American fire was deadly, but they were using gunpowder and shot at a high rate. One captain reported firing all thirty-five rounds in his ammunition pouch. The ground was littered with bodies of British troops—some of which were heaped together for shelter from American fire.[25]

Despite horrific casualties, the British were not going to quit. Howe, the senior British commander on the scene, shifted around regiments, deployed five hundred fresh soldiers who had been held in reserve, and told supporting artillery to use grapeshot instead of cannonballs. Then, he ordered a bayonet-only attack.[26] British soldiers would not pause one or twice to fire and reload during the early stage of their advance. Instead, they would make a full-on bayonet charge from start to finish. The principal reason for firing against defenders in entrenched positions was psychological. Here, as always, the key was always to reach the enemy. The long bayonet, fixed at the end of the musket, was the principal instrument of death used by British soldiers. This time they would close with the Americans as quickly as possible.

Meanwhile, the American situation had steadily deteriorated. As historian Robert Leckie put it, "a steady trickle of desertions had drained [the defenders] like a leaking pipe."[27] Just as some escaped battle earlier by carrying entrenching tools to Bunker Hill, others were now stealing away by carrying wounded brothers to the rear, and then disappearing.[28] Fresh militia refused to come forward. One militia colonel said he was too "exhausted" from building fortifications to fight.[29] When the British began their third charge, only about 150 Americans remained in the redoubt on Breed's Hill.[30] And they only had ammunition for a single volley. Despite his urgent appeals to General Artemas Ward at militia headquarters in Cambridge, Prescott had not been resupplied with ammunition.

The final American volley was fired at point-blank range.[31] It inflicted more casualties but did not stop the British from overrunning the redoubt. There were a few more scattered shots from the beleaguered defenders before they wielded their muskets as clubs in the face of the British bayonets. Those who could run did so. Prescott made it back. Major John Pitcairn, who commanded the militia at Lexington, did not. In what would become a pattern, General William Howe did not pursue the retreating Americans.

The British drove the Americans from the Charlestown peninsula and reduced an American town to ashes. But who won the misnamed Battle of Bunker Hill? If the measure of victory is seizing the real estate that was fought over, the British won. If relative casualties are the measure, it is possible to reach a different conclusion. More than 1,000 British—40 percent of the attacking force—had been killed or wounded.[32] The dead included 92 British officers. American casualties totaled 440.[33] "I wish [we] could sell them another hill at the same price," said America's newest brigadier general, Nathanael Greene.

An eight-month siege ensued. About nine thousand British troops remained in Boston, surrounded by thirteen thousand American militiamen.[34] King George sacked Thomas Gage; William Howe now commanded all British troops in North America.[35] It was a standoff; neither side felt it could take decisive action. The British were confined to Boston, but American commanders did not believe their militia were up to a direct assault on British regulars.[36] That would change as Washington turned militiamen into Continental Army soldiers. It was not until March 1776 that American commanders believed they were ready to take on the British. They then prepared for an assault by building a strong fortress overnight on Dorchester Heights, and equipping it with heavy cannons and mortars captured from Fort Ticonderoga.[37] When dawn broke on March 5, Howe saw his predicament. British shore batteries and warships immediately opened fire on the Heights, but to no avail. It was too high for their artillery to reach. Meanwhile, American cannonballs plunged downward into British positions. A strong gale blew in, delaying the American ground assault. Howe knew when he was holding a losing hand. The gale gave him time to order an evacuation. The Americans would reclaim Boston without a battle.

While they had been in Boston, the British commandeered 368 private homes to quarter their troops.[38] Americans considered this an outrage. When, in 1765, Parliament had considered a legislation that would have allowed British troops to be quartered in public inns and private homes when military barracks were full, American objections led to a modification specifying that the only homes or barns in which troops could be quartered without the owner's consent were *empty* ones.[39] The colonies, however, were expected to compensate owners for any requisitioned buildings. Benjamin Franklin, who was then representing colonial interests in London, argued that as the Quartering Act was a form of taxations, colonial assemblies were free to comply, or decline to comply, with the Act in any manner they saw fit in light of their particular circumstances. In response, Parliament amended the law to allow colonial assemblies to enact quartering laws of their own choosing as long the laws adequately met the army's needs. The commandeering of private homes by British commanders would lead to "quartering large Bodies of Armed Troops among us" to be included as a grievance against the king in the Declaration of Independence, and, still later, to the Third Amendment to the United States Constitution, namely: "No Soldier shall, in time of peace be quartered in any house, without the consent of the Owner, nor in time of war, but in a manner to be prescribed by law."

* * *

We will discover that despite their mixed performance at Bunker Hill, General Gage would turn out to be largely correct: militia could not, in fact, stand up to a professional army. What differentiated militia and

Continentals? After all, some militia regiments were simply mustered into the Continental Army.[40] Notwithstanding the adage "the clothes make the man," giving militiamen new uniforms did not transform them into capable soldiers. What did? In a word: training.

A thumbnail description of the beginning of Nathanael Greene's military career will help illustrate the point. Greene is interesting in his own right because not only was he Washington's favorite general, but military historians consider Greene one of the best military commanders in the entire history of the United States military.[41] Greene may also have set the record for rising through the ranks—from private to general—more quickly than anyone else in American history: four months. Here briefly is his story.

Following the Boston Tea Party on December 16, 1773, King George III dispatched General Thomas Gage and a large contingent of troops to Boston to take things in hand. To the colonists, this looked like a military occupation. War seemed to be looming. In Rhode Island, fifty-four men agreed to form a militia company. One of them was Nathanael Greene, then thirty-one years of age.[42] Militia elected their officers. Greene ran for lieutenant but lost. It should not have been surprising; he had no military experience, even if he read military histories. Moreover, he had asthma and a limp, and he came from a Quaker family.[43] Stung, Greene quit, but then changed his mind and continued as a private. The group drilled three days a week under the tutelage of a British deserter.[44] This kind of diligent training under an experienced professional may have set the group apart. Following Lexington and Concord, the Rhode Island General Assembly enacted legislation to raise a 1,500-man professional army—and named Nathanael Greene as its commanding general. Why? No Rhode Islander needs to ask; the answer is political connections. Greene's brother was an officer of the Assembly. Perhaps more importantly, Greene himself had previously been a member of the Assembly and served on its Committee to Revise Militia Laws.[45]

When George Washington, the newly appointed general and commander of the Continental Army, arrived in Cambridge, Massachusetts, on July 2, 1775, he found numerous militia companies encamped and ready to join the cause. Most were from New England. Washington toured the camps and was appalled. Washington said he "found a numerous army of provincials under very little command, discipline, or order."[46] There were open latrines and "excrement about the fields."[47] Many soldiers were "exceedingly dirty."[48] One camp stood out: Rhode Island's. Tents were in straight rows; hygiene was good; equipment was properly cared for; and, most important, rather than lollygagging about the men spent their days drilling, firing muskets, and learning how to deploy in formation.[49] Greene, then thirty-three, had no military experience. He had even missed the Battle of Bunker Hill. But when Washington saw what he was doing with Rhode Island's troops, he made Greene the youngest brigadier general in the Continental Army.[50]

Greene, of course, had not turned the Rhode Island regiment into a professional-quality army. That would not have been possible. Much more training would be required. It is not easy—then or now—to turn civilians into soldiers. There are many skills to learn, and becoming proficient requires not only tutoring by experienced teachers but a great deal of repetition. Hard exercise is necessary to bring large numbers of civilians into physical condition. Most important are the psycho-logical components of military training. To some extent, individuality must be suppressed. To become prepared to make the ultimate sac-rifice, soldiers must become emotionally attached to their comrades and military units. They must be willing to lay down their lives, not only for their cause, but for their brethren. They become accustomed to immediately obeying superiors. They must become able to perform while being gripped by fear. Greene, himself, put it this way: "People coming from home with all the tender feelings of domestic life are not sufficiently fortified with natural courage to stand the shocking scenes of war. To march over dead men, to hear without concern the groans of the wounded, I say few men can stand such scenes unless steeled by habit and fortified by military pride."[51] Learning all of this—being inculcated with all of this—requires concentrated work and time. Yet militia often trained just four times a year. While getting ready for war, some semi-elite units, such as the Minutemen, had been training two times per week.[52] Now Washington's sergeants and junior officers were intensively training full-time soldiers.[53]

According to Ron Chernow, it was during his combat experience in the French and Indian War when "Washington came to believe in the need for rigorously trained, professional armies rather than hastily summoned, short-term militia."[54] So many aspects of the militia left him dismayed. The militia elected their officers, for example.[55] (How effective would basic training be today if drill sergeants had to stand for election by their trainees?) Moreover, democratic decision-making permeated militia tradition in other ways, too. New England militia not only elected their officers, they insisted on making combat decisions by consensus rather than having officers issue orders.[56] Joseph Reed, Washington's aide-de-camp at this time, undoubtedly reflected his boss's view when he said: "To attempt to introduce discipline and subordination into a new army must always be a work of great difficulty, but where principles of democracy so universally prevail, where so great an equality and so thorough a leveling spirit predominates, either no discipline can be established, or he who attempts it must become odious and detestable, a position which no one will choose."[57]

The most famous training of the Continental Army occurred at Valley Forge, from late February 1778, when Friedrich Wilhelm von Steuben arrived, until the Battle of Monmouth Courthouse in June of that year. Steuben was a veteran of the Prussian army whom Benjamin Franklin sent to Washington with a letter of introduction because Franklin believed he had something important to offer the Continental Army. Washington agreed and placed Steuben in charge of training. According to John Buchanan, among other things, "Von Steuben taught officers and men not only how to maneuver on a battlefield from column to line and back again with ease, but also how to march compactly and arrive on the field as a tightly knit force instead of in long, straggling lines, thus losing precious time in forming to fight."[58] Steuben drilled the troops every day, week after week, regardless of weather. Historians differ on just how much the Continental Army's combat performance improved as a direct result of Steuben's training; Buchanan credits him with having a major impact and David McCullough writes that the Continental Army "emerged from the ordeal of winter at Valley Forge a stronger, more disciplined force."[59] The point, for our purposes, is that just as practice makes all of the difference for a professional sports team, training makes all the difference for an army. Moreover, the better trained soldiers already are, the more effective additional training will be. Steuben was drilling Continental soldiers who, by 1778, already had considerable experience. Military historian Don Higginbotham wrote: "Steuben had gained results at Valley Forge partly because he had experienced human material to work with."[60] Militia training never equaled—or even approached—that of regular troops, which is why they were unable to perform as well in battle.

Congress created the Continental Army on June 14, 1775, by passing a law, but the process of converting militia into a professional army began in the camps around Boston after the Battle of Bunker Hill.[61] Washington said his job was to "disband one army and recruit another."[62] One year would pass before the next major engagement: the Battle of Long Island. By then, there were real differences between the militia and the Continental Army.

* * *

On June 29, 1776, American sentries on Staten Island sighted forty British warships to their south, off Sandy Hook, New Jersey, sailing toward New York Harbor.[63] Some of the ships sailed through the narrows between Staten Island and Brooklyn, and dropped anchor in the Upper Bay of New York Harbor; others dropped anchor just outside the Narrows, off of Gravesend, Long Island. British troops offloaded onto Staten Island, but otherwise the British did not make their intentions known. A second contingent of British ships arrived on August 12, and then a third on August 15. The consolidated fleet was comprised of 73 warships and 150 transports, containing 13,000 seamen and 32,000 British and Hessian soldiers.[64] It was the largest expeditionary force of the eighteenth century.

Exactly when, how, and where they would strike was unknown; but it was quite clear they had come to seize New York City. Both British and American leaders thought that New York City was the strategic linchpin of the war. John Adams said that New York was "a kind of key to the whole continent."[65] From New York Harbor, warships could sail north on the Hudson River 315 miles, well past Albany. The river separated New York from Connecticut and Massachusetts. The British had settled on a two-part strategy to win the war.[66] First, cut off New England—which Britain believed was the engine of revolutionary fever—from the rest of the colonies. Second, make forays into the South, where they believed loyalist sentiment ran high. The British believed that, with some encouragement, Southerners themselves would rise up against the rebels.

George Washington was in Manhattan trying to figure out how to defend New York City. It was, he feared, an impossible task. He had at his disposal only nine thousand men, and two thousand were then too ill to fight.[67] Moreover, the very features that made New York City strategically attractive also gave the British a seemingly insurmountable advantage. Manhattan, Staten Island, and Long Island are, of course, all islands. Warships could sail up the Hudson and cut off Manhattan from New Jersey, sail up the East River and cut off Manhattan from Long Island, and by using the Harlem River, which connects both rivers, entirely isolate Manhattan. Artillery from the warships could bombard the city proper and strategic positions on the shore. Troops could be ferried faster on water than marched on land. The British had every advantage: manpower, firepower, maneuverability, and speed. Perhaps their greatest advantage was that British and Hessian troops were professional soldiers, battle-hardened in European wars. The Americans were almost all military novices. In light of all of these considerations, Washington might have pondered whether New York City was defensible at all, but he believed the Continental Congress wanted him to defend it.[68] From the outset, one of Washington's great gifts to America was establishing the premise of civil supremacy over the military; therefore, he focused on how—not whether—to defend the city.

Commanding the British forces were General William Howe (King George had sacked Gage following Bunker Hill) and his brother Admiral Richard Howe. The Howe brothers were born to British nobility and educated at Eton. They were both Members of Parliament and friends of King George III.[69] Sir William was forty-six; Lord Richard was fifty. They each had thirty years of military experience, including considerable combat experience, and they each had distinguished themselves for competence and for courage under fire. As we have already seen, William Howe displayed great bravery during the Battle of Bunker Hill. He was now commander in chief of all British forces in North America.

Richard Howe was called "Black Dick" behind his back on account of his dour personality. Someone described him as being as undaunted and silent as a rock. While overseeing an amphibious operation in Brittany during the Seven Years War, a British army general peppered Richard Howe with questions and was nonplussed when Howe ignored him. "Mr. Howe, don't you hear me?" demanded the general. "I don't love questions," Howe replied.[70]

On both sides of the Atlantic, there were still hopes in some quarters of resolving the dispute between the colonies and the mother country peaceably. In addition to their military roles, therefore, the Howe brothers had also been appointed peace commissioners for America. There was, however, a political problem. Lord Richard and Sir William were Whigs and known to favor conciliation with the colonies. Tories controlled the government, and official policy—enthusiastically supported by King George—was to demand total submission from the Americans. (The king knew about the political positions of the Howe brothers, but he liked and promoted them nonetheless.[71]) But fearing the Howes were too sympathetic to the Americans, the government denied them any discretion. They were to offer only one thing: pardons for rebels who renounced the revolution and swore allegiance to the king and Parliament. Otherwise, they were to demand submission and require the rebels to dissolve all representative bodies and accept the restoration of royal government in the colonies.[72]

General Howe made his first military move during the early afternoon of July 12. He directed that a contingent of British ships sail north on the Hudson River past Manhattan to sever communications and supplies between American forces on the Manhattan Island from those in New Jersey and Albany, or at least threaten to do so.[73] Sir Richard was not yet on scene (as things turned out, he arrived from England with the second group of warships and troops about four hours later). Admiral Shuldham, who was the senior naval officer on the scene, recommended against taking this action. The shoreline bristled with American artillery. At the northern tip of Manhattan, twin forts—Fort Washington on the eastern shore and Fort Constitution (later renamed Fort Lee) in New Jersey—straddled the Hudson to prevent enemy ships passing between them. Both forts stood on high ground at the Hudson's narrowest point. Artillery was already in place in Fort Washington.

Sir William overruled Shuldham, and five British ships sailed north-ward, propelled briskly by both a favorable tide and wind. Rebel artillery opened fire. First came cannon fire from the western shore of Brooklyn and nearby Governor's Island. Then, other batteries opened up from Manhattan and from Paulus Hook, New Jersey. Americans fired nearly two hundred cannonballs at the British squadron. For nearly an hour, the ships sailed on without firing answering shots, seemingly unflus-tered by cannonballs whizzing through their rigging. Two frigates—the HMS *Phoenix* with forty-four guns and the HMS *Rose* with twenty guns—opened up, returning fire on American artillery positions on both sides of the river, and firing also into the heart of New York City. The ships sailed on for thirty miles, past Forts Washington and Constitution, past the Bronx and Yonkers, and finally dropped anchor where the river widens at Tappan Zee. Only four British sailors were injured; the ships suffered no more than minor damage. Meanwhile, shelling New York had reduced the city to bedlam.

If General Howe intended to begin the campaign by demonstrating the might of Britain's seasoned and professional military, he had succeeded.

Washington was worried the British squadron would disembark troops to cut off New York City from the north. He asked militia to re-pulse any attack. Hundreds of militiamen swarmed into the area, firing muskets at the ships—often from more than a mile away, well out of range. General George Clinton, a commander of New York county mi-litia, toured the western shore and described what he saw in a message to George Washington: "I found the shores guarded or rather lined by an undisciplined rabble under no kind of subordination," even though their own commanders "were active in doing all they could but had little in their power."[74] Eventually, enough order was established to enable militia to attack the British ships from row galleys (long rowboats) and launch fireships toward the British vessels to set fire to sails or rigging. One British tender was set afire, but despite some harrowing moments, the other ships remained unscathed. As days and weeks dragged on, militiamen drifted back to their farms to attend to harvest. In fact, no British soldiers were in the flotilla, and notwithstanding a few minor raids, a ground threat had been nothing more than an illusion. After menacing the surrounding area by their mere presence for more than a month, the British squadron retraced its route southward, exchanging cannon fire again with American artillery on both sides of the Hudson. The British considered the excursion a great success.

Meanwhile, the Howe brothers made a peace feeler. They sent an emissary, traveling by barge under a white flag, to deliver a letter from Lord Richard addressed to "George Washington, Esq., New York." When the emissary attempted to hand the letter to Colonel Joseph Reed, Washington's adjutant, Reed refused to accept it. "We have no person in our army with that address," he said.[75] A second attempt, similarly addressed, received the same response. The third try was the charm. This time the letter—addressed to "His Excellency, General George Washington"—was accepted, and shortly thereafter there was a brief, formal, but entirely polite meeting between Washington and Lieutenant Colonel James Paterson, Sir William's adjutant. Paterson said that General Howe was interested in exploring a settlement. Washington said he understood that Howe was authorized only to grant pardons, but those "who committed no fault wanted no pardons." America's leaders "were only defending what we deemed our indisputable rights," Washington added. "That would open a very wide field for argument," Paterson replied. But argument was not the purpose of the peace feeler. Washington had rejected the only thing the Howe brothers could offer; both sides knew there was nothing else to discuss. Washington served Paterson refreshments before returning him to the British fleet, and American escorts described Paterson as "sociable and chatty" during his return trip. Washington and the Americans had demanded, and ultimately received, what they considered the respect due them. But the war was on.

As Washington looked out at the formidable British fleet anchored in New York Harbor, he was puzzled as to why the British were not attacking. In fact, General Howe was waiting for all British forces to reach the scene. Then even after the final contingent arrived, Howe waited another week to give Hessian soldiers time to recuperate from their long journey across the Atlantic. On August 19, an intelligence report reached Washington suggesting that the British attack was imminent and that it would occur on Long Island.[76] Supplemental reports arrived stating that British troops who had been offloaded on Staten Island weeks earlier were returning to their ships. Three days later, seventy-five flatboats, supplemented by more than a dozen similar craft, began ferrying British and Hessian soldiers from ships to the beaches at Gravesend Bay, exactly where Nathanael Greene, who had reconnoitered the area some weeks earlier, predicted the British were likely to land. By noon on August 21, fifteen thousand British and Hessian troops were on the southwestern tip of Long Island.

A line of densely wooded hills, 100 to 150 feet in height, known as the Heights of Guan, stretched in a line southwest to northeast across western Brooklyn. To get to the shore across from Manhattan, the British would have to pass over these hills, through narrow passes between them, or around them. Thus, the Heights provided the Americans with a natural defensive barrier. This is where the Americans would make their stand. General Howe had personally led the British assault up Breed's Hill, and he knew well how much blood could be spilled in a direct infantry assault up a steep hill against entrenched defenders, even American troops, whom he disdained. To surmount this obstacle, British generals—General Henry Clinton was the principal mastermind of the plan—devised a three-prong attack. The first prong was on the far left. British General James Grant would lead 3,100 troops, including Scottish Highlanders, northward along a shore road running between the Heights and the coast. Clinton wanted the Americans to mistake this for the principal attack. British ships were to sail up the East River parallel to this advance, enhancing the image of this being the main British thrust. This prong, however, would be a diversion.

The second prong would be in the middle. General Leopold Phillip von Heister would march with 6,100 Hessians northward through a heavily wooded area and attack the Heights straight on. The third prong was the strategic key. It was to begin under the cover of darkness. Four British generals—Henry Clinton, Charles Cornwallis, Hugh Percy, and William Howe—would lead contingents totaling 10,275 of Britain's finest troops on a long looping march to the far right, taking them counterclockwise far to the east, and then back around in a northwest direction through Jamaica Pass on the eastern side of the Heights and behind the American left flank. If this worked, a potent third prong would attack the Americans from the rear while the Americans were preoccupied by General Grant's troops on the extreme other end of their position and by Hessians attacking straight on from their front. It was a brilliant plan, provided the Americans left the Jamaica Pass undefended. British scouting parties reported that, curiously, that seemed to be the case.

Nathanael Greene was out of commission during the Battle of Long Island. He went down with a high fever on August 15, and five days later his doctor diagnosed him as being dangerously ill with typhus. It was a great loss, not only because of Greene's native ability but because he had spent more than three weeks personally reconnoitering the area and knew it far better, and had given more thought about how to defend it, than other American commanders. Washington had replaced Greene with General John Sullivan of New Hampshire, but, after touring American positions with Sullivan on August 23, Washington must have been dissatisfied with Sullivan's preparations because the next morning he replaced Sullivan with General Israel Putnam, an old war horse from the French and Indian War. On the following day, Washington toured American positions again. What he found was a circus-like atmosphere with militia firing muskets in the air for pure amusement. Washington lectured Putnam on the "distinction between a well regulated army and a mob," and instructed him to have regimental commanders immediately crack down on the militia and ensure that when the enemy attacked the militia did not respond with "a scattering, unmeaning and wasteful fire." Putnam's semi-coherent verbal replies worried Washington, so he reduced his instructions to writing.[77]

Nathanael Greene had planned to have Americans defend the Heights of Guan from fortified positions on top of the Heights, but Washington instructed Putnam to send three thousand of his "best men" into the woods in front of the fortifications to try to prevent the British from reaching the hilltops, and to have "militia or most indifferent troops" man the fortifications on top of the hills.[78] There were at least two problems with this plan. First, American troops had to defend hills stretching six miles across, leaving the defense too thin. Second, the American troops sent into the woods were no match—either in numbers or in combat experience—for the professional Hessian and British soldiers they would encounter. Moreover, this was going to be close combat, at which British and Hessians soldiers excelled. They were extremely proficient with bayonets. American rifles lacked bayonets.[79]

Washington told his soldiers to show the enemy "what a few brave men, contending in their own land and in the best of causes, can do against base hirelings and mercenaries."[80] If he really believed that would be enough to make a decisive difference, this engagement would change his mind.

Aides awakened Washington during the night of August 26 to inform him that British troops were attacking along the shore road. That is exactly what Washington had expected. The shore road was the most direct path toward the British objective, and it avoided the hills. General William Alexander had been assigned to defend that route. Although he was born in New York, Alexander was better known as Lord Stirling, a Scottish title he claimed by inheritance even after the House of Lords decided that he had no right to use it. The House of Lords no longer carried much weight with the rebels, however. Convinced this was the main British advance, other American troops were rushed to the American right to support Continental Army troops from Maryland and Delaware that were being personally led by Lord Stirling. At this point, following the British plan, General Grant stopped advancing. That misled the Americans into believing that they had halted the main British attack.

Meanwhile, on the far other side of operations, General Henry Clinton sent a patrol to the Jamaica Pass to quietly reconnoiter. The British patrol captured a five-man mounted American patrol. Senior officers interrogated the captives. They learned the Pass itself and the route beyond were undefended. Sir Henry could hardly believe it. The route to the American rear was open. General Clinton later wrote: "The Commander in Chief seemed to have some suspicion the enemy would attack us on our march, but I was persuaded that, as they neglected to oppose us at the gorge, the affair was over."[81]

At 9:00 AM, British cannons fired, giving a signal for Gage to renew his attack up the shore road and for the Hessians to simultaneously attack the American front. The American front quickly became a bloodbath. American riflemen under General Sullivan in the woods below the hilltops found themselves all but defenseless against the Hessian and British bayonets. Their slow-loading rifles were useless in close-quarters combat. General Sullivan and his men tried to retreat up the hills, but many were butchered along the way. Horrified by the brutality they were witnessing, and terrified by the quickly advancing enemy, the "militia or most indifferent troops" who were selected to man the barricades—"this lot of rabble which parades under the name of riflemen," as described by the adjutant general of the Hessians—threw down their rifles and fled before engaging in the fight themselves.[82]

The one bright spot was that the best trained and most highly disciplined troops, who had been selected to meet what American commanders had originally expected to be the main British advance along the shore road, fought bravely and well until they were overwhelmed by British troops advancing not only in front of them but behind them as well. Some fled and some surrendered, but not before putting up a stiff fight.

More than three hundred Americans were killed and many more were wounded. More than a thousand others, including both General Sullivan and Lord Stirling, had been taken prisoner.[83] The retreating American troops found themselves trapped between the British and the East River. They quickly dug trenches.

A quick British advance might have destroyed the American army once and for all, but inexplicably there was no attack on the following day. Rain fell, and some American soldiers were up to their waists in water. None of the American troops in Long Island had tents. One-quarter of them were ill.[84] Fortuitously, weather and wind direction prevented English warships from sailing on the East River, bombarding the Americans from the west, and sealing them in.[85] Washington seized the moment to save his army. He ordered General Heath to do everything possible to give the impression he was sending reinforcements across the East River and instead to bring every boat of any kind to Brooklyn to evacuate American forces to Manhattan. When darkness fell on the windy and moonless night of August 29, American campfires were lit and then kept burning throughout the night. Meanwhile, American troops stealthily made their way to shore. "We were strictly enjoined not to speak, not even to cough," one American private said.[86] The armada of boats plied the waters back and forth, ferrying nine thousand troops to Manhattan. It was a difficult, massive, and tricky operation. At dawn, some American soldiers were still in Brooklyn, including George Washington, who had vowed to take the last boat. The weather continued to cooperate with the Americans; a thick fog rolled in, concealing the last of an entirely successful evacuation. As Washington boarded the very last boat, he heard British fire commence. The British were now attacking. They would find the trenches empty.

On September 2, Washington wrote to John Hancock, who was then president of the Continental Congress. "Our situation is truly distressing," Washington began. "The militia instead of calling forth their utmost efforts to a brave and manly opposition in order to repair our losses, are dismayed, intractable, and impatient to return. Great numbers of them have gone off; in some instances, almost by whole regiments."[87] Washington went on to complain that the militia's "want of discipline and refusal of almost every kind of restraint and government, have produced a like conduct" on the army as a whole—"an entire disregard of that order and subordination necessary to the well doing of army, and which had been inculcated before." Washington believed that "no dependence could be put in a militia" or on any other troops that were no enlisted for sustained periods of time. "[O]ur liberties must of necessity be greatly hazarded, if not entirely lost, if their defense is left to any but a permanent, standing army," said Washington, adding, "I mean one to exist during the war."

That was not only Washington's opinion. Nor was it exaggeration designed to prompt the Continental Congress into action. "The militia are passing home by hundreds in a drove, affrighted and scared of their wits," a colonel wrote exactly one week later.[88] In fact, the Connecticut militia, which weeks earlier had been eight-thousand strong, would soon be no more than two thousand.[89]

On September 15, the British invaded Manhattan, at Kips Bay.[90] Washington had assigned five brigades—mostly militia—to prevent a British landing in that area.[91] They had erected and were manning defensive barricades there. But when the British invaded, and once again, General Howe ordered his attacking troops to rely entirely on bayonets, the Americans bolted. In the words of a British captain, British and Hessians landed "without firing or receiving a shot."[92] Private Joseph Plumb Martin of the Connecticut militia found himself in a cornfield with fleeing Americans and a small contingent of British and Hessians in pursuit. "I believe the enemy's party was small, but our people were all militia, and the demons of fear and disorder seemed to take full possession of all and everything that day," Martin wrote.[93] "When

I came to the spot where the militia were fired upon, the ground was literally covered with arms, knapsacks, staves, coats, hats, and old oil flasks," he continued. In their flight, the militia abandoned sixty-seven canons—half of Washington's entire artillery.[94] Washington rode on his white horse toward the fleeing Americans. He tried to stop them, even striking officers running past him with the flat of his sword, but to no avail.

According to Washington himself: "As soon as I heard the firing, I rode with all possible dispatch towards the place of landing, when to my great surprise and mortification, I found the troops that had been posted in the lines retreating with the utmost precipitation . . . notwithstanding the exertions of their Generals to form them. I used every means in my power to rally and get them into some order but my attempts were fruitless and ineffectual, and on the appearance of a small party of the enemy, not more than sixty or seventy, their disorder increased and they ran away in the greatest confusion without firing a single shot."[95] This is when, according to legend, Washington threw his hat to the ground and famously exclaimed, "Are these the men with which I am to defend America?"[96]

* * *

In late November, Washington was leading what was left of the American army south through New Jersey. He had abandoned New York City and engaged the British three times—at Harlem Heights, at White Plains, and at Fort Washington. Now, things were dire.

Harlem Heights had been a draw. On September 16, employing a small volunteer force led by Greene as a decoy, Washington had successfully lured an advance British force commanded by General Howe into a trap.[97] The trap was to be sprung when an American force attacked the British from the rear. But the door was slammed too soon, and instead of attacking the British rear, the Americans wound up attacking its flank instead. This allowed the British advance force to retreat and rejoin the main force behind it. As a result, the plan was only partially successful. American casualties were about 120; British casualties were more than 170. It was enough, however, to give the Americans a temporary boost of morale. Following the engagement, Washington wrote a letter to Patrick Henry, who was then Virginia's governor, in which he blamed the failure to implement the trap effectively on "a want of confidence" by his troops.[98] In that letter, Washington strongly advised Henry not to rely on militia to defend the state. Washington pulled no punches; militia suffered from "an utter disregard of all discipline" and were "altogether unfit for service," he said. Washington did want to influence Henry regarding whether to use the militia "in the management of Indian affairs" but warned him that "it would be highly inadvisable" to rely on them if the state found itself "in danger from any detachment of the British Army or Marines."

A month later, fearing that the American army would be encircled in Manhattan—and on the advice of General Charles Lee, about whom more will be said shortly—Washington reluctantly yielded New York City to the British and marched his 14,500 troops north to White Plains, where he could take a defensive position on high ground (as American forces had at Bunker Hill and Long Island).[99] General William Howe led 19,000 British regulars and Hessians to meet the Americans in White Plains. Following preliminary skirmishes, the main battle took place on October 28. On the morning of battle, General Lee alerted Washington to a vulnerability in the American position: the right wing was comprised of 2,000 militia.[100] They were on the slopes Chatterton Hill, which rose to a height of two hundred feet, and they planned to array themselves behind stone walls, fences, and trees along the slope, but they had not created a fortified defense.[101]

If the British seized high ground on the American right flank, they would be able to rake American entrenchments in the center with enfilading fire.[102] Washington sent a Delaware regiment to reinforce the militia on Chatterton. Meanwhile, the battle commenced. Howe planned a straight-ahead main assault, but when he noticed Hessians making progress in attacking Chatterton Hill, he redirected the main British thrust toward that position.[103] The Delaware regiment was then arriving, but it was too late: militiamen were already fleeing in the face of a Hessian bayonet charge.[104] The right wing was gone. That caused the center to buckle, as Lee and Washington had feared. Continental soldiers retreated, firing intermittently as they withdrew. An unnerved Delaware regiment soon joined the rush to the rear. British casualties outnumbered American casualties 254 to 175—the Hessian attack on Chatterton Hill had been costly—but as the battle ended with Americans fleeing, everyone considered it a British victory.[105]

The only question—later asked by a parliamentary committee of inquiry—is why General Howe did not immediately pursue and destroy the American army as it fled in disarray. Howe would only say, "The committee must give me credit when I assure them, that I have political reasons, and no other, for declining to explain why that assault was not made."[106] This would, in fact, be one of several occasions when Howe deliberately chose not to pursue and destroy the fleeing American army, thereby effecting a coup de grâce on the American Revolution.[107] The scuttlebutt among their own subordinate commanders was that the Howe brothers "hoped to terminate the war amicably," and believed that would have been better accomplished by bringing Washington to the negotiating table rather than by massacring his soldiers and sending him and other American leaders to the gallows.[108]

The Battle of Fort Washington was the most ignominious of the three engagements. To prevent the British from controlling the Hudson River as part of their objective of cutting New England off from the rest of the colonies, the rebels had constructed two forts facing each other on opposite sides of the river. The redoubt on the New Jersey side of the river was named Fort Lee, in honor of General Charles Lee. The pentagon-shaped, earthen redoubt on the New York side was named Fort Washington. It was 265 feet above the Hudson River on Harlem Heights, and further defended by additional breastworks on steep slopes to both the north and south. The Hudson River was immediately to the west; the Harlem River was immediately to the east. The garrison was defended by 2,900 Continental soldiers commanded by Colonel Robert Magaw, who was confident he could hold it until the British suspended fighting and went into winter quarters. In his one major blunder of the war, Nathanael Greene told Washington that he doubted Howe could quickly take Fort Washington by direct assault.[109] Instead, Greene believed, Howe would take his army into winter quarters in New York and lay siege to the fort when combat resumed in the spring.

But Magaw, Greene, and Washington, who personally surveyed the scene and endorsed defending the garrison, were wrong. On November 16, Howe launched a coordinated assault by 13,000 British and Hessian troops. More than 4,000 British and Hessians attacked from the south; eight Hessian regiments made the main attack from the north; and thousands of British made two separate amphibious assaults across the Harlem River from the east. Lord Richard Howe personally accompanied forces coming from the south while Sir William went ashore with the British amphibious assault. Meanwhile, British artillery blasted away at the American positions. The defenders were quickly forced back into the earthen redoubt, where they found themselves too concentrated and constricted to move. Around 3:00 PM, the British gave Magaw an ultimatum: surrender or expect all defenders to be killed. This was his second ultimatum; he had summarily refused a similar one before battle in the early morning. This time he asked for time to consider it. That was refused, and Magaw surrendered. American casualties totaled 59 killed, 96 wounded, and most horrifically, 2,836 captured.[110] The British also captured another thirty-four canons and two howitzers.[111]

Not everyone favored taking prisoners under the circumstances. British casualties totaled 77 killed and 381 wounded. Some—particularly Hessians, who suffered the highest casualties—wanted the Americans put to the sword for refusing the first ultimatum. Howe would not allow it. His thinking was undoubtedly echoed by a British captain, who wrote in his diary: "I am of opinion it is right to treat our enemies as if they might one day become our friends."[112] But kindness did not extend far. The British treated their prisoners abysmally. They were often confined aboard prison ships in the filthiest of conditions, with little water and food and no medical care.[113] According to Rick Atkinson, two-thirds of the Americans captured at Fort Washington were dead in eighteen months.

With Fort Washington gone, there was no purpose—or ability—to hang onto Fort Lee on the opposite side of the Hudson River. The Americans grabbed what munitions and supplies they could from the fort, left the rest—including yet another dozen canons—and headed west, across the Hackensack River, with General Cornwallis and five thousand British troops only two miles behind them.[114] Washington did not know it, but Howe had ordered Cornwallis to follow but not attack the retreating Americans.

Washington spent a few days in Newark and then took what remained of his army southward. He now had only 5,140 men fit for duty.[115] A little over 2,000 of these would have their terms of enlist-ment expire on December 1—only days away—and nearly another thousand enlistments would expire on January 1. His force could no longer survive on its own. Cornwallis was now stalking him with a force that had grown to 10,000.[116] But Washington had left two other forces in New York. He had left General William Heath with 4,000 men at Hudson Highlands, about fifty miles north of White Plains, and General Charles Lee with 7,000 men in Westchester—or at least Lee had been in Westchester when Washington last heard from him. Washington now sent word to Lee to cross the Hudson with 5,000 men and join his force in New Jersey.[117] In the interim, these forces had also decreased. Lee now had only 3,000 men.[118] But no word came from Lee. With increasing desperation, Washington sent repeated orders to Lee to cross into New Jersey and join up with Washington, but Lee continued not to reply. What was going on? Lee was trying to persuade the Continental Congress to sack Washington and appoint himself commander of the American army. Washington figured this out on November 30, upon opening a letter from Lee to Colonel Joseph Reed, Washington's own adjutant, which began: "I re-ceived your most obliging flattering letter [and] lament with you that fatal indecision of mind which in war is a much greater disqualifica-tion than stupidity or even want of personal courage."[119] Washington realized that "fatal indecision of mind" remark referred to him and surmised the rest.

Cornwallis was now actively pursuing Washington with a British force numbering ten thousand.[120] In Brunswick, New Jersey, on November 30, Washington sent a letter to John Hancock. "[O]ur force was by no means sufficient to make a stand against the enemy," he wrote.[121] "[A]s yet no great number of the militia of this state has come in," he added. Two days later, two thousand men left because their enlistments expired.[122] Despite Washington's entreaties, they refused to stay. At 1:30 PM on that day, while still in Brunswick, Washington scribbled the following postscript on a letter to John Hancock: "The enemy are fast advancing; some of them are now in sight. All the men of the Jersey flying camp under General Herd being applied to, have refused to continue longer in service."[123] The New Jersey militia left even though Washington was in dire circumstances in their own state.[124] "The Jersey militia behaves scurvily and, I fear, are not worth the freedom we are contending for," Nathanael Greene wrote.[125] In fact, things were even worse than Washington and Greene then knew: nearly three thousand New Jersey men had started signing loyalty oaths to King George in exchange for pardons and promises of not having their homes pillaged by British forces.[126]

With what remained of his force, Washington raced southward. A rearguard tore up bridges and cut down trees to impede the enemy's path behind him.[127] On December 8, Washington and his battered troops crossed the icy Delaware River into Pennsylvania.[128] Fortunately, he was joined on the western shore by two thousand jittery Pennsylvania militiamen.

Washington got a break of a different sort at ten in the morning on Friday, December 13, when an ambitious, twenty-two-year-old junior British officer named Banastre Tarleton (who will become a prominent figure in our next chapter), accompanied by only two privates, captured General Charles Lee, who had left his force to spend the night in Mary White's tavern near Basking Ridge, New Jersey, accompanied by only fifteen bodyguards. Why was he there? Some believe it was for a romantic liaison with an unidentified woman.[129] No better explanation is apparent. What we do know, however, is that as part of his campaign to replace Washington, Lee had just finished writing a letter to General Horatio Gates, which began, "Entre nous, a certain great man is most damnably deficient," and then claimed that Washington had put him, Lee, in "a situation where I have my choice of difficulties."[130] The truth was just the reverse.

Charles Lee could not hold a candle to George Washington in military skill, leadership ability, judgment, prudence, courage, or integrity. But he had more military experience than Washington, and he was a relentless and effective self-promoter. Even Nathanael Greene then believed that this was "was a great loss to the American states, as [Lee] is a most consummate general."[131] And at this point in time, Washington's star had fallen. He had lost a series of engagements, without achieving any real win. The decision to defend Fort Washington had proved flatly wrong. Congress had instructed him to defend New York City at all costs, and he failed. Today, we properly consider George Washington to be one of the irreplaceable figures in American history. Yet, had he not been captured, Lee may well have replaced him.

Washington would soon prove his exceptional worth as a military commander with a daring Christmas Eve raid across the Delaware on a Hessian camp at Trenton, followed by successful engagements with British troops at Trenton and Princeton. At Princeton on January 7, 1777, a contingent of 1,100 Pennsylvania militia commanded by Colonel John Cadwalader bolted twice in the face of the enemy, even though Americans, including Continentals and militia, outnumbered the enemy.[132] Seeing what was occurring, Washington galloped on his white charger to the area of trouble, ordered Continental units to counterattack, and then—in the midst of enemy fire, with British troops no more than thirty yards way—exhorted the militia to fight. "Parade with us, my brave fellows. There is but a handful of enemy and we will have them directly," he cried.[133] A Pennsylvania officer later recalled: "I saw him brave all the dangers of the field, and his important life hanging as it were by a single hair with a thousand deaths flying around him."[134] The militia rallied "beyond my expectation," Cadwalader himself conceded.[135]

This was not the only time militia performed credibly. On January 7, Washington also reported to John Hancock that "There have been two or three little skirmishes between [enemy] parties and some detachments of militia, in which the latter have been successful and made a few prisoners."[136] In the largest of these, militia engaged a party of about fifty Hessians, and killed or wounded eight to ten and captured the rest. There were other militia victories, too. In the spring of 1775, Ethan Allen and the Green Mountain Boys, then a Vermont militia unit, captured Fort Ticonderoga, an event of considerable military significance because the Americans captured two hundred cannons and a great deal of munitions. But there had really been no fight; the fifty redcoats at the fort had surrendered without firing a shot.[137] In December 1775, eighty Virginia militiamen whipped a somewhat larger force of British regulars and sailors at Great Bridge, just south of Norfolk, inflicting casualties on sixty-six of the enemy.[138] A much longer list of militia successes during the eight-year war could be compiled. But what I have presented so far—and will present with even more telling examples in the next chapter—is representative. The record overwhelmingly demonstrates that, overall, militia were inadequate for fighting a professional army. Or, as George Washington put it in a letter to Major

General John Spencer on March 11, 1777, "[do] not depend on militia for anything capital."[139]

* * *

All of us learned something about the Revolutionary War in school, but for the most part what we learned focused mainly on the war in the North. Besides those we have already covered, the battles we are most likely to remember are Brandywine, Saratoga, Germantown, Monmouth, and Yorktown. The war in the South is not as well known. But for our purposes, it is critically important. Not only was a significant, and arguably decisive, portion of the war fought in the South, but Southerners—including James Madison—were especially well aware of what happened in their own territory. The next chapter about the war in the South is likely to hold some surprises.

6

The Militia—War in the South

IN NOVEMBER 1774, James Madison, then a twenty-three-year-old graduate of Princeton and the son of a wealthy planter who owned more than a hundred slaves, wrote a letter to William Bradford of Philadelphia, who had been his closest friend in college.[1] "If America and Britain should come to a hostile rupture, I am afraid an insurrection among the slaves may and will be promoted," Madison wrote.[2] There had already been one such plot, Madison thought. "Their intentions were soon discovered and proper precautions taken to prevent the infection. It is prudent such attempts should be concealed and suppressed," Madison continued. About seven months later, Madison returned to the subject in another letter to his friend. "It is imagined our [royal] governor has been tampering with the slaves, and that he has it in contemplation to make great use of them in case of a civil war in this province," Madison said, adding ominously: "[I]f we should be subdued, we shall fall like Achilles by the hand of one that knows that secret."[3]

The royal governor to whom Madison referred was John Murray, the fourth earl of Dunmore. Lord Dunmore had been the royal governor of New York before Britain shifted him to Virginia in 1771. Previously, the colonial Assembles paid the salaries of royal governors, but to ensure his complete loyalty to the Crown, Britain paid Dunmore itself.[4] Dunmore started dealing with slavery issues almost immediately. In the winter of 1772, floods destroyed hundreds of farms in Virginia. Some slaves—starving and desperate—began to organize, with the objective of killing their owners and seizing their farms and food.[5] Patrick Henry led a movement in the Virginia Assembly to petition the Crown to terminate the importation of more slaves from Africa. Southerners were not above shedding crocodile tears about slavery when it suited their propaganda interests, so Henry packaged his petition as being, in part, about the "great inhumanity" of the slave trade. But he was also straightforward about part of Virginia's concern, namely, that increasing the number of slaves also increased risks of insurrections and "will endanger the very existence of your Majesty's American dominions."[6] (For the same reason, the Continental Congress would later ban the importing of more African slaves "into any of the thirteen United Colonies" for the duration of Revolutionary War.[7]) Virginia, however, had yet another motive for the petition: It was a slave-exporting colony and wanted to eliminate competition from African-slave traders. Henry's petition presented Dunmore with a political problem, however. One of the investors in the African slave trade was the king of England, himself. Dunmore responded by promptly dismissing the assembly. Things continued downhill from there.

It is "imagined our governor has been tampering with the slaves," Madison wrote. He was referring to an incident that occurred on April 21, 1775, at a time many Virginians thought war was imminent. In fact, war had actually begun. The Battles of Lexington and Concord had been fought two days earlier, although neither Dunmore nor anyone else in Virginia knew that yet. What Dunmore did know, however, was that Patrick Henry stirred revolutionary fervor a month earlier with his rousing "Give me liberty, or give me death" speech in Richmond. Dunmore acted much as his counterpart in Massachusetts, General Thomas Gage, had acted in the face of an impending confrontation: Dunmore had British marines raid a militia arsenal in Williamsburg known as the Powder Horn and seize all of the gunpowder stored there.[8] Unlike the ill-fated British march to seize seven tons of militia gunpowder in Concord, Massachusetts, this British raid was successful: the militia's gunpowder was in British hands.[9] But Virginians were apoplectic. This left them vulnerable to slave revolts. Henry capitalized on their anxiety to drive Virginia further toward war. People were unlikely to go to war over duties on tea, Henry observed, but "tell them of the robbery of the magazine and that the next step will be to disarm them, and they will then be ready to fly to arms to defend themselves."[10]

Dunmore responded with what he may have thought was a clever kind of argumentative jujutsu. He claimed he seized the gunpowder for safekeeping because he learned slaves were plotting an insurrection, and he promised to return it if and when it was needed. Virginians did not know which was worse: Dunmore was lying and was therefore detestable; or Dunmore was telling the truth and had left them defenseless. Fear and anger skyrocketed. Patrick Henry led an angry mob to the governor's mansion. George Washington urged restraint and advised militia companies not to join Henry's march.[11] A couple of militia companies joined Henry's march, however. One of the men marching with the Orange County militia was young James Madison, who denounced Washington as a coward who was worried that his "property," by which he meant his slaves, "will be exposed in case of civil war."[12] Dunmore fled to a British warship and then sent word that unless the people behaved themselves, he would offer freedom to slaves who rebelled against their masters and organize a Black army to "lay the town in ashes."[13] On June 17, a Virginia assembly declared British rule at an end in Virginia and took control of the government.

On November 7, 1775, Dunmore issued a proclamation declaring all slaves who were "able and willing to bear arms" to be free upon "joining his Majesty's troops."[14] Within just a few months, eight hundred slaves ran away from their masters and made their way to British warships or Gwynn Island in Chesapeake Bay, where Dunmore established a base in order to join Dunmore's "Ethiopian Regiment."[15] Many slaves brought their families with them, and eight hundred Black women and children were also under British care. London, however, forbade Dunmore from openly encouraging a slave insurrection. That may have struck British policymakers as beyond the bounds of civilized warfare. On a more practical level, they believed widespread insurrections would destroy Southern economies. That would do Britain no good. It hoped to win the war, resume control of the colonies, and benefit from their production of tobacco, rice, and other products.[16] Regrettably, slaves who fled to Dunmore did not fare well. Most died from a smallpox epidemic, as did many of Dunmore's own troops. He had failed to inoculate them against the disease.

Dunmore, however, had a profound effect on the American Revolution. He may be ranked as one of the causes. Offering freedom to slaves who joined the British was, for most Whites in the South, beyond the pale—an act that was terrifying, outrageous, and unforgiveable. Not everyone in the South had been following Patrick Henry's call to arms. Many had been sitting on the fence. By inviting slaves to join the British, Dunmore pushed them off. Edward Rutledge, who then represented South Carolina in the Continental Congress, and would become the youngest signer of the Declaration of Independence, said that Dunmore's proclamation did "more effectually work an eternal separation between Great Britain and the colonies than any other expedient which could possibly have been thought of."[17] Rumors swept the South. A physician serving British forces in Charleston reported that the king's ministers in London were formulating plans to persuade "slaves to rebel against their masters and cut their throats."[18]

* * *

Four years later, things were not going well for the American Revolution in the South. The British had decided that their greatest opportunities lay in the South. They believed that pro-British sentiment was strong in the southern colonies and once British forces neutralized Continental Army forces in the region, Loyalists would rise up and extinguish the rebellion.[19] British forces had captured Savannah, and a subsequent American attempt to retake Savannah failed.[20] On May 12, 1780, following a long siege, Major General Benjamin Lincoln of the Continental Army had been forced to surrender Charleston, South Carolina, to British forces. That was a heavy loss. Charleston was both the richest city in America and the only major American seaport south of Baltimore. When Charleston fell, the British took 3,371 American soldiers prisoner, the vast majority of them Continentals.[21] And Tory militia were skirmishing with rebel militia throughout the Back Country of the Carolinas.

One might think that with an invading army menacing their home states, Southern militia would rally to defend their homeland, but Jon Meacham writes that "now, in wartime, militias were even more difficult to muster."[22] Or as Nathanael Greene put it while commanding American forces in the South, "It is next to impossible to draw the militia of the country from the different parts of the state to which they belong."[23] There were several reasons for this, but the principal reason—seldom mentioned but widely understood—was that the South was afraid to send most of its militia away because they were afraid that left them vulnerable to slave revolts. One time it was mentioned out loud was on March 29, 1779, when the Continental Congress adopted a resolution offering to pay the states of Georgia and South Carolina $1,000 for each slave they enrolled in the Continental Army. The reason for the proposal, explained Congress, was that the militia could not be relied upon in the war against the British because service with the army entailed a "remoteness from their habitations" that was not possible.[24] A representative from South Carolina had explained to Congress that the state was "unable to make any effectual efforts with militia, by reason of the great proportion of citizens necessary to remain at home to prevent insurrections among the Negroes, and to prevent the desertion of them to the enemy."

The resolution was never going to have any practical effect. No Southern state was going to allow slaves to bear arms, even for the defense of the state against the British. Even only one Northern state, Rhode Island, permitted it, although many Blacks capably served in New England regiments.[25] Congress's resolution meant nothing unless Georgia or South Carolina decided to act on it. Georgia, unsurprisingly, did not deign to consider it. As we have previously seen, the South Carolina legislature considered the resolution in deference to the Laurens family before overwhelmingly rejecting it.[26]

* * *

It was against this background that, on July 25, 1780, Major General Horatio Gates of the Continental Army arrived at Buffalo Ford, North Carolina, to take command of the Southern Department. It seemed like an auspicious appointment at a desperate time. If the British could eradicate the small American army then encamped by Deep River at Buffalo Ford, they would go a long way toward completing their plan. The two previous commanders that Congress sent to command the Southern Department had failed, but there were high hopes for Gates.

Horatio Gates was one of the few American commanders with significant military experience. Gates, now sixty-three, had been born in England. Although he came from modest circumstances, he had a powerful patron who helped him enter the officer corps of the British army.[27] For fourteen years, he served in various capacities in Germany, Nova Scotia, and America. Most of his assignments involved staff work, but (along with a young American militia officer named George Washington) he saw combat during the French and Indian War in a disastrous campaign led by Major General Edward Braddock, and was wounded in battle. Thereafter, Gates returned to work in military administration. He was promoted to major and promised a further promotion to lieutenant colonel, but the promise was broken and Gates's military career stalled. That may not have happened if he had the proper pedigree; one generally needed both noble birth and the funds necessary to purchase promotions in the eighteenth-century British military. Gates was bitter. In 1769, he resigned his commission, took his family to America, and became a plantation owner in what is now West Virginia, where he also served as a lieutenant colonel in the militia.

Following the shot heard around the world in 1775, Gates rushed to Mount Vernon and offered his services to the new general and commander in chief of the Army of the Colonies. At Washington's recommendation, Congress commissioned Gates as a brigadier general. Two years later, Congress made Gates commander of the Northern Department. In September of 1777, Gates won the Battle of Saratoga, defeating a British army marching south from Canada to Albany, New York. When British General John Burgoyne surrendered his army of 20,000, Gates won what was then the largest American victory of the war. At least three other individuals helped make Gates's victory possible: Continental Army Generals Daniel Morgan and Benedict Arnold, both of whom were highly effective battlefield commanders during the engagement, and General Burgoyne, whose performance had been woefully inept.[28] Gates truly deserved significant credit himself, however, and as the commanding officer of the victors he became a hero of the revolution. And so, Congress sent Horatio Gates to the South, where a hero was desperately needed.

The American army beside Deep River was tired and hungry. It had spent two months marching to its present location from Morristown, New Jersey.[29] The going had been rough. The soldiers carried no rations and had to forage for food along the way. But food had been scarce, and the soldiers went hungry for days at a time. Promised reinforcements from state militia never materialized. The first order of business for new commanders is generally to take stock of their command, but that is not what Horatio Gates did. Almost immediately upon his arrival, Gates "ordered the troops to hold themselves in readiness *to march at a moment's warning*."[30] When informed about the lack of food, Gates said that a plentiful supply of rations and rum was on its way and would catch up to them in a couple of days. His officers were dubious.

Two days later, Gates ordered the army to strike camp and begin marching for Camden, South Carolina, about seventy miles away. Gates believed that Camden was a target of opportunity, a British base defended by only a seven-hundred-man British force. That estimate was, however, based on out-of-date intelligence. The previous commander had mapped out a route to Camden. Since the army had to forage for food along the way, the planned route was through areas where foraging was likely to be fruitful and the population friendly, but Gates thought the route too circuitous and marched his force along a more direct path. This quicker route, however, was through pine barrens devoid of foraging opportunities. Promised supplies of provisions never arrived. The army became so hungry that it was approaching mutiny.[31] To make matters even worse, soldiers were fed a hastily prepared meal that wound up inducing widespread diarrhea. According to a sergeant, "men all the way as we went along were every moment obliged to fall out of ranks to evacuate."[32]

Historians are not quite sure what Gates's plan was because Gates did not share his objective with his officers. According to one view, Gates did not intend to attack Camden straight on; instead, he intended to take up defensive positions north of the city, and have other militia take up positions west and east of Camden, thereby cutting off British supply lines and forcing the enemy to surrender.[33] The British did not cooperate with Gates's plan, however. When word reached General Lord Charles Cornwallis in Charleston that a 5,000-man American army was marching to Camden, Cornwallis leaped onto a horse and rode hard, day and night, for Camden, arriving there four days later. The British force at Camden numbered not 700 but 2,239.[34] Cornwallis, therefore, believed himself outnumbered two-to-one. But, believing that the quality of troops mattered more than quantity, Cornwallis was confident nonetheless.[35] His force at Camden was composed of well-trained British regulars while the approaching American force was mostly militia. Cornwallis expected his troops to slice through the Americans like the proverbial hot knife through butter.

In fact, neither commander had a sound grasp on the relative sizes of the opposing forces. Cornwallis's intelligence overestimated the American force. And, amazingly, Gates himself did not know the size of his own command. Colonel Otho Williams, Gates's deputy adjutant, was stunned when Gates remarked that they were leading a force of 7,000 men. Williams immediately asked all units to report actual counts of their manpower, and then relayed the total to Gates. The true size of their force was 3,052. Gates was unfazed. "There are enough for our purpose," he replied.[36]

When, just a few days earlier, Gates had arrived beside Deep River, his army totaled 1,400.[37] These were not militia but Continental troops. They were tired, hungry, and probably dehydrated. "But," writes historian John Buchanan, "the Continental Army was no longer the ill-trained, ill-disciplined force that had taken the field in 1775."[38] These men had acquired battle experience and years of training, including, most famously, by Baron Friedrich von Steuben at Valley Forge. They were now professional soldiers. Moreover, the bulk of the army at Deep River was infantry from Maryland and Delaware, which were among the Continental Army's best.[39] During the march to Camden, however, there were both additions and subtractions to the original force. Gates's army had been joined by 2,100 North Carolina militia commanded by General Richard Caswell and 700 Virginia militia led by Brigadier General Edward Stevens. Meanwhile, because he did not believe he would need cavalry and some other troops on this mission, Gates had sent off several hundred Maryland Continentals and North Carolina militia to Brigadier General Thomas Sumter of the South Carolina militia, who was in command of a militia force further west.[40] As he was nearing Camden, Gates was leading 900 Continentals and 2,500 militia who were ready and fit for duty.[41] The American force, therefore, was about a third larger than its opposition; but the British force was composed exclusively of regulars while more than two-thirds of the American force was militia. If, therefore, there were to be a straight-on battle, it would be decided on how effectively Horatio Gates could deploy his militia.

The actual engagement was precipitated by happenstance. During the moonless night of August 15, Gates ordered a night march to bring his force within about five miles of Camden without being observed by the enemy. Continental Army officers thought this was foolhardy. They thought it inconceivable "that an army consisting of more than two-thirds militia, and which had never been once exercised in arms together, could form columns and perform other maneuvers at night, and in the face of the enemy," Colonel Ortho Williams later wrote.[42] The march was to begin at 10:00 PM. Cavalry that remained with Gates were deployed as screens ahead of the marching columns of soldiers. Meanwhile, Cornwallis ordered a night march to begin at exactly the same hour. His objective was to move his troops into position to attack the Americans in early morning.[43] Acting as screens for his force were cavalry commanded by Major Banastre Tarleton, who had proved himself so effective—and ruthless—a commander that he was known to the Americans as "Bloody Ban."[44] (We met Tarleton in the previous chapter when, as a more junior officer, he captured General Charles Lee.) Tarleton had now become infamous for, literally, taking no prisoners. Tarleton not only instilled fear in his enemies, his viciousness caused embarrassment within his own ranks; at one point Cornwallis cautioned Tarleton against "committing irregularities."[45] (Ultimately, British gratitude won out over embarrassment. Tarleton would ultimately become a general, a baron, and a knight.[46]) In the darkness, cavalry screens from both sides literally bumped into each other. Initial confusion turned into a pitched battle, first among the mounted screens and then among infantry rushing forward from both sides. But eighteenth-century armies generally did not fight at night, and the forces separated to await the dawn.

Horatio Gates was not a creative commander. He performed by rote. He had spent most of his military career in the British army, and it was standard British practice to place the best troops on the right side of the battle line. That was not dictated by tactics but by military etiquette; the right was considered the "post of honor." So, when he formed the American battle line at dawn, that is what Gates did.[47] On the American right stood four Continental Army regiments, three from Maryland and one from Delaware, while most of the center and the left side of the line were composed of militia. Gates positioned himself, about two hundred yards behind the battle line, with a Continental Army brigade from Maryland commanded by Brigadier General William Smallwood.

Following the same tradition, Cornwallis placed the best British troops on the right side of his line. Since Gates's left was opposite Cornwallis's right, and vice versa, this meant that the best British troops would engage North Carolina and Virginia militia.

The Americans had two advantages. In addition to having the larger force, the American battle line was on slightly higher ground and the British had to advance slightly uphill to attack. Gates, mounted on Fearnought, a famous racehorse, positioned himself too far to the rear to observe the action himself and had to rely on reports to know what was happening.[48] Apparently, Gates had given little thought to how to conduct the battle, instead waiting to react to recommendations from aides.[49] When he was advised that the British troops were "displaying"— that is, moving from marching columns into battle lines—on their right (the American left), Colonel Otto Williams recommended that American troops, already deployed, immediately attack on that wing. "Sir, that's right—let it be done," replied Gates.[50] Colonel Williams galloped off to tell General Edward Stevens, whose seven hundred Virginia militia were on the American left wing, to attack.

By the time word had made a roundtrip from the front line to Gates and then, via Williams, back again to the front lines, the British had fully deployed. Williams relayed the order to attack but also had another idea. He asked for volunteers to go forward of the American line, take up positions behind scattered pine trees, and fire at the advancing British while they were still beyond effective musket range. He hoped to provoke the British into returning fire prematurely. Williams personally led a group of nearly fifty volunteers from the Virginia militia on this mission. It did not work. The problem was that British soldiers had been disciplined to fire only on command, and British officers were too well trained and seasoned to order their troops to fire volleys beyond an effective range. But that was far from the most naïve and disastrous element of Williams's recommendations. Ordering the militia to attack the advancing British lines assumed they could perform capably in the face of battle. They could not. It takes rigorous training to prepare men for battle—to prepare them psychologically, to teach them what they must do and to drill them until they are able to do those things not only skillfully but semi-automatically, and to instill the confidence necessary to face an enemy in a deadly encounter. The Continental troops, which had been placed on the right side of the American line and in the rear, had so trained; the militia had not. For example, the Virginia militia had bayonets on their muskets, yet they had never been trained to use them.[51]

The predicable happened, and it happened quickly. As soon as the battle lines closed to within firing range, the British fired a volley, yelled, and began to charge. Immediately, the Virginia militia turned and fled. According to Colonel Williams, at least two-thirds bolted before firing a single shot.[52] They threw away their muskets so they could run as fast as their legs could carry them.[53] Panic spread to the 1,800 North Carolina militiamen positioned immediately to the left of the Virginians. They, too, threw down their weapons and bolted. Because they were hemmed in by wetlands on both sides of the battlefield, fleeing militia tore through the ranks of Continental troops behind them. The Continentals tried valiantly to stand their ground. According to Colonel Williams, "The regular troops, who had the keen edge of sensibility rubbed off by strict discipline and hard service, saw the confusion with but little emotion."[54] But even seasoned professionals could only do so much. Nine hundred jostled and disordered Continentals, standing by themselves in two physically separated groups, were attempting to withstand a tidal wave of two thousand British regulars, energized by their routing of the militia and supported by Bloody Ban's sword-wielding cavalry. The Continentals were forced to retreat.

American casualties totaled 1,900, including approximately 1,000 captured and missing. British casualties totaled 324.[55] Four days later, General Edward Stevens of the Virginia militia described what had occurred in a letter to his state's governor, Thomas Jefferson. "[A]las," wrote Stevens, when the enemy charged "the militia gave way, and it was out of the power of man to rally them."[56] This allowed the entire enemy force to push "their whole force against the Maryland line, who was not able to stand them long." Confusion and panic reigned. If Jefferson were to picture the scene as bad as he possibly could, "it will not be as bad as it really is," said Stevens. He related how fleeing militiamen, rather than reforming into groups after having left the battlefield, continued to race individually through the countryside for more than one hundred miles, relying on the kindness of strangers to take them in. "I am now where scarce a friend is to be found," Stevens wrote. "We are still in such a dispersed situation, that I can't pretend to say, what may be the loss of our men but with respect to the militia, themselves, it matters not, for from their rascally behavior they deserve no pity." And what of the future? "I am doubtful it will be a very difficult matter to collect any number of the militia of this state together again, though if anything else could be done it had better, for militia I plainly see won't do."

In his reply, Jefferson said the misfortune weighed heavier on his mind because it had been brought about by his own countrymen. But how did Jefferson respond to General Stevens's warning that the militia plainly would not do? The past is past, said Jefferson. We must look to the future, and we'll send you two thousand fresh militia.[57] This would hardly be the last time militia would disappoint Jefferson, however. One of his biographers writes that Jefferson's "faith that the militia could be counted on at least to defend home and family was shattered as time and again the raw troops broke ranks and ran from seasoned British regulars."[58]

Among those who fled the field of battle and seemed to never stop was Horatio Gates. It is said that Gates was mounted on the fastest horse in the American military.[59] Gates claimed he rode farther and farther from the battlefield because he was trying to rally fleeing militia. Few believed him. It was more likely he wanted to be sure to outrun the Bloody Ban's cavalry, which was infamous for hot pursuit. Gates did not stop until he reached Hillsborough, 180 miles from Camden. He was a hero of the revolution no longer.

The Southern Department needed a new commander. Having chosen three failed commanders in a row, the Continental Congress decided this time around to take George Washington's recommendation and appointed Nathanael Greene, now thirty-eight. Washington considered Greene his most talented general, and he made it known that, should he fall in battle, Greene ought to succeed him.[60] It was an appointment that may have saved the revolution.

First, Greene had to find the southern army. His most recent information about the army's whereabouts was two months old. Gates, and what remained of his army, had then been in Hillsborough, but they were no longer there when Greene arrived. On December 2, 1780, Greene found Gates and the army in Charlotte, North Carolina, which was then a village of no more than twenty houses. Gates could not be pleased about handing his command over to Greene, and Gates had just learned that his only son, Bob, had died. Nevertheless, he was gracious in introducing Greene to the troops and making the transition. For that Greene was grateful; but everything else he found horrified him. In a letter to his wife, Greene described the soldiers as "half starved" and "remarkable for nothing but poverty and distress."[61] There was no food; there were no tents; clothing was inadequate. The soldiers subsisted on what they could forage on a daily basis.[62] He was informed that 2,307 men were on the rolls, but when Greene ordered an actual count he found only 1,482 present and fit for duty. This included 949 Continentals from Maryland and Delaware, the crème of the American army. Most of the rest were Virginia militia, which Greene described as "literally naked and undisciplined."[63] And only about 800 men were properly clothed. This was the force with which Green would somehow have to outmaneuver General Charles Cornwallis, who commanded 9,000 well-fed, well-equipped, well-trained troops—4,000 of whom were garrisoned at Winnsboro, South Carolina, about sixty miles to the south. The rest were garrisoned at Savannah, Charleston, and other posts.

Greene's first decision was stunningly unorthodox: dividing his tiny force in two. Conventional military doctrine was to never divide one's force when facing a larger enemy. It would be your opponent who wanted to divide and conquer. Greene later explained that his decision flowed "partly from choice and partly from necessity."[64] First, Greene realized that he needed to divide his force to feed them. They were starving and needed to separate geographically to forage more effectively. Second, Greene needed time to train and discipline his militia. Militiamen were coming and going as they pleased; being absent without leave had become commonplace. Greene wasted no time. A month after his arrival, he signed an order to have a man who had deserted three times publicly shot. After writing the date, January 4, 1781, on his order, Greene added, "in the Fifth Year of the Independence of the United States."[65] Greene himself explained his third reason for dividing his force as follows: "It makes the most of my inferior force for it compels my adversary to divide his, and holds him in doubt as to his own line of conduct. He cannot leave Morgan behind him to come at me. . . . And he cannot chase Morgan far, or prosecute his views on Virginia, while I am here with the whole country before me."[66] Years later, Napoleon would articulate a military maxim that captures the spirit of Greene's decision: "divide to live, unite to conquer."[67]

Greene had in his command Brigadier General Daniel Morgan. This may be one of the most fortuitous pairings in American military history. While Greene is considered the Continental Army's most brilliant strategist, Morgan is considered its most talented tactician and battle-field commander—and both men rank among the greatest generals in all of American military history.[68] Greene knew Morgan well. They had served together in Boston and at Valley Forge. Greene gave Morgan 600 of his best troops—300 Continental Army infantrymen, 120 light dragoons led by Colonel William Washington (George Washington's cousin), and 180 Virginia militiamen who had previously served in the Continental Army.[69]

Greene sent his chief engineer, Colonel Thaddeus Kosciuszko, southeast to scout for a new location for his own detachment. He gave Kosciuszko explicit written instructions: follow the Little River twenty or thirty miles to the Pee Dee River, examining water quality, nature of the soil, availability of produce, suitability of the rivers for transportation, and where the rivers could be forded. Based on Kosciuszko's report, Greene selected a site on the Pee Dee River, across from Cheraw, South Carolina, for his army. It was a strategic location in central South Carolina, just south of the North Carolina border. By placing his army there, Greene sought to cut the British off from Tory militia in North Carolina and be in a position to deny the British resources from areas they had not yet plundered. On December 16, Greene set out with 1,100 men, including 650 Continentals. It would take his bedraggled army six days to traverse difficult terrain and reach its new camp. When he arrived, Greene set to work training his army.

Meanwhile, Morgan was to march west, cross the Catawba River, link up with North Carolina militia commanded by Brigadier General William Lee Davidson, and then march southwest across the border into South Carolina. "For the present, I give you the entire command in that quarter, and do hereby require all officers and soldiers engaged in the American cause to be subject to your command," Greene wrote in his orders. That was to make it clear that Brigadier General Thomas Sumter of the South Carolina militia was to take orders from Morgan rather than the other way round. Sumter, known as the "Gamecock," had a sizable force of militia, but he was vain, difficult, and headstrong. Greene hoped, but did not necessarily expect, that Sumter would provide whatever aid Morgan requested.

On Christmas Day, 1780, Morgan set up camp beside the Pacelot River at Grendal's Shoals, South Carolina. That evening sixty South Carolina militiamen rode into Morgan's camp and volunteered their services. Their elected commander, Andrew Pickens, had famously defeated a much larger force at Kettle Creek, Georgia, demonstrating both courage and tactical acumen in the process. Morgan valued not only Pickens's military skills but also his credibility among South Carolina militia. Because of Sumter's irascibility, assistance from the South Carolina militia was a matter of concern. With militia brought by Davidson and Pickens, Morgan's force totaled about 1,200 men.[70] The two American detachments—those under Greene and Morgan— were now about 140 miles apart.[71]

A couple of days after his arrival at Grendal's Shoals, Morgan learned that Tory militia from Georgia were raiding patriot settlements about twenty miles to his south. Morgan found this an opportunity to "spirit up the people," as he put it—that is, to show the people that the Continental Army would come to their aid—and he sent Colonel William Washington with a force of 280 dragoons and mounted militia after the Tories.[72] Washington caught up with the Tories, rode them down, and slashed them to death with large cavalry sabers. It was, writes John Buchanan, "one of the war's more brutal actions."[73] The rebels killed 150 Tory militiamen, severely wounded others, and took 40 prisoners, without suffering a single casualty. It was one more demonstration of the difference in capabilities between regulars and militia, regardless of which side they were on.

Flushed with success, Washington then sent a detachment of 50 mounted men to attack Fort William, a stockade with 150 Tory militiamen that was not far away. This small fort was part of a string of garrisons between Cornwallis's headquarters at Winnsboro and Ninety-Six, a fortified British outpost in the South Carolina Back Country. Fort William was a link in the chain of communications between Cornwallis, Ninety-Six, and points in between.[74] When the commander of Fort William learned that a rebel force was galloping in his direction, he evacuated and fled with his men. This seemed to confirm the previously expressed view of the commander at Ninety-Six—John Harris Cruger, a lieutenant colonel in the British Army who had been born in New York—that their "pusillanimous behavior" made it impossible to rely on militia to defend the region.[75] Around the same time, Greene was suggesting in a letter to Thomas Sumter that it would not be possible to rally people to the American cause as long as they believed they were protected only by the militia. "The enemy will never relinquish their plan, nor the people be firm in our favor until they behold a better barrier in the field than a Volunteer Militia who are one day out and the next day home," Greene wrote.[76] It was not an assessment that Sumter, the commander of the South Carolina militia, received happily.

Meanwhile, word reached Cornwallis not only of William Washington's attacks but also that Daniel Morgan intended to attack Ninety-Six. The latter report, received from a Tory spy, was incorrect; but, either way, Cornwallis needed to deal with Daniel Morgan. On New Year's Day, 1781, Cornwallis ordered Banastre Tarleton to go after Morgan. The next morning, Tarleton led a force of 1,076 British regulars, including 200 cavalry from the British Legion he routinely commanded, in pursuit of Morgan. His force was designed to move quickly. Tarleton told Cornwallis: "When I advance, I must either destroy Morgan's corps, or push it before me over the Broad River, towards King's Mountain."[77] Tarleton rode west from Winnsboro and then turned north. Cornwallis marched a larger force due north from Winnsboro. The two British forces—Tarleton to the west, Cornwallis to the east—were moving north in parallel. They hoped to catch Morgan between them, either at Kings Mountain, just over the border in North Carolina or earlier.

Morgan was now entirely on his own. He had counted on more militia joining the cause, but that was not going to happen. Thomas Sumter had ordered the South Carolina militia to provide Morgan with no military support and no provisions.[78] Moreover, the militia that had joined Morgan was proving troublesome. "[I]t is beyond the art of man to keep the militia from straggling," he wrote Greene.[79] As Morgan had not succeeded in drawing other militia to his force, he believed he should, if possible, avoid a major engagement. He told Greene that he could not count on even two-thirds of the militia to "to assist me, should I be attacked, for it is impossible to keep them collected."

In the early morning of January 12, Tarleton's scouts reported they located Morgan at Grindal's Shoals, and by 5:00 AM Tarleton was leading his force in that direction. The next day Greene sent Morgan a message that read in part: "Col. Tarleton is said to be on his way to pay you a visit. I doubt not that he will have a decent reception and a proper dismission."[80]

Rivers were a key feature of the terrain. They could be used for transportation on boats or barrages. They could also be barriers; there were almost no bridges in the area. Without boats, rivers had to be crossed where they were shallow; hence, Nathanael Greene's instructions to his engineer to identify fording places. Heavy rains in January 1781 had turned the roads to muck and swelled the rivers. Greene reported that during one particular day the Pee Dee River rose twenty-five feet.[81] Tarleton's ability to catch Morgan, or conversely Morgan's ability to evade Tarleton, would depend on how skillfully each used the rivers to maneuver. By the night of January 15, Tarleton had drawn near his quarry. Although it was dark, Tarleton's force marched northwest, along the southern bank of the Pacelot River. Scouts from Colonel Andrew Pickens detachment, on the other side of the river, spotted Tarleton. The scouts moved stealthily, in tandem with the British, watching to see whether the British kept marching northwest or forded the river. If the British crossed the river, they might discover Morgan's camp, which was just six miles away. For three hours, the men kept moving in parallel on opposite sides of the river. At some point, Tarleton became aware he was being shadowed. He ordered his men to halt and pretended to camp. Then he furtively retraced his route back several miles and forded the river.

Morgan and his men were cooking breakfast the next morning when riders galloped in to announce that Bloody Ban had crossed the Pacelot River. Morgan immediately broke camp, formed his men into columns, and moved out behind a screen provided by William Washington's dragoons. Within short order, British scouts located the just-abandoned camp. Tarleton marched his troops there, where they paused to enjoy the Americans' still-warm breakfasts.

Daniel Morgan knew he had to fight, and he had little time to choose his spot. He rode ahead of his troops to reconnoiter. By late afternoon, he selected a pasture called Cowpens. There his force camped for the night, ate a hot dinner, and readied themselves for battle the next morning. Andrew Pickens arrived that night with some additional militia, but there were no reinforcements from Thomas Sumter.[82]

At 2:00 AM on January 17, Tarleton ordered his buglers to blow reveille, and within an hour his force was marching toward Cowpens. One hour before sunrise, a scout informed Morgan that the British were five miles away.[83] When Tarleton grew closer, Morgan roused his men. "Boys!" he yelled. "Get up! Benny's coming!"

Tarleton had 1,076 men, all regulars. Morgan's force totaled somewhere between 800 and 1,000 men, including 300 North Carolina, South Carolina, and Georgia militia. Once again, how well the American commander used his militia could prove decisive. But unlike Horatio Gates, Daniel Morgan had a plan. And he had prepared his militia the preceding night to execute his plan. Morgan decided to position his weakest troops—Georgia and Carolina militia—not on the right, or on the left, or in the rear, but in the center forward position, 300 yards in front of his main line, which was composed of Continentals. But he would ask of his militia just one thing: fire one shot at the enemy when they were 50 yards away. Then, they would fall back, not by fleeing but in an orderly withdrawal, to a second line 150 yards back, composed of Andrew Pickens's more seasoned militiamen. That line would fire one or two rounds at the enemy at 50 yards. Both of the temporary, forward lines of militia were riflemen, and some from the backwoods militia were quite good shots, so Morgan asked them to aim for officers or sergeants, if possible. All of the militia would then withdraw another 150 yards to take up a position to the left of the main line of Continentals, where they would be held in reserve.[84] "Just hold up your heads, boys, three fires and you are free, and when you return home, how the old folks will bless you, and the girls kiss you for your valiant conduct," Morgan told his militiamen on the night before battle.[85]

Morgan, therefore, attempted to use his militia for something he thought they could do—get off one, two, or three targeted shots to enervate the advancing British line—without asking them to do the impossible, namely, stand and fight. Knowing they would withdraw made their temporary stand possible. While Morgan skillfully used his powers of suasion with the militia, he was not going to tolerate what had happened at Camden.

Fifteen minutes before sunrise, the Americans saw columns of British redcoats march out of the woods at the far end of the field, together with Tarleton's British Legion, dressed in their distinctive green jackets. Tarleton, viewing the American lines across the field, was confident of victory. He had easily defeated—indeed, massacred—patriot forces before. He believed his men were superior to the rebels in every dimension. His scouts had reconnoitered the area, and, in his own words, he found the terrain ideally "suitable to the nature of his troops under his command."[86] Tarleton was so eager to engage Morgan that he ordered his main line to march forward even before his officers had all taken their positions. Most of the Americans had never previously witnessed the colorful, fearful sight of British troops advancing toward them. Then, the British let out a yell and began trotting forward. Daniel Morgan rode across his front lines encouraging his men and telling them not to fire until they saw the whites of their enemies' eyes. American officers yelled: "Don't fire! Don't fire!"

In his memoirs, Thomas Young—a young South Carolinian who had volunteered for the American cause after witnessing his brother murdered by Tories—described the scene: "The militia fired first. It was for a time, pop—pop—pop, and then a whole volley, but when the regulars fired, it seemed like one sheet of flame from right to left. Oh! It was beautiful."[87] When the first line of militia started to withdraw, Tarleton thought a rout was in the making and he ordered the captain of the 17th Light Dragoons, a unit of fifty cavalrymen, to attack them. Morgan had promised the militia that his own cavalry would protect their withdrawal, if necessary, and he ordered William Washington to counterattack the Dragoons. According to Thomas Young, "Col. Washington's cavalry was among them, like a whirlwind. . . . The shock was so sudden and violent they could not stand it and immediately betook themselves to flight."[88]

Most militia fired only a single shot before withdrawing, although the South Carolinians stoically fired two.[89] Meanwhile, Daniel Morgan was galloping behind Andrew Pickens's second line—which was in the process of becoming the forward line—to urge on the militia and ensure they did not bolt. "Form, form, my brave fellows!" he yelled.[90]

A few militiamen on horseback did slink off, rode six miles to the Broad River, and swam their horses across, but most militia withdrew to the right wing of the Continental line, as they had been instructed. Morgan was alarmed at one point, when he saw a company of Virginia regulars moving to the rear. Their commander had ordered them to turn, but they misunderstood and thought he had ordered them to retreat. As this officer related it: "Morgan, who had been mostly with the militia, quickly rode up to me and expressed apprehensions . . . but I soon removed his fears by pointing to the line, and observing that men were not beaten who retreated in that order."[91] The British, also seeing what looked like a retreat—and thinking *Camden again!*—charged. "Face about, boys! Give them one good fire, and victory is ours!" shouted Morgan. Officers repeated the order to about-face. "In a minute we had a perfect line," recalled Lieutenant Colonel John Eager Howard, who was commanding the main line of Continentals.[92]

The charging British were now only thirty yards away. Howard gave the order to fire. A devastating volley stopped the British advance cold. "Charge bayonets!" Howard ordered, and within an instant Continental soldiers from Maryland and Delaware were giving the stunned British a taste of their own medicine. Meanwhile, Andrew Pickens rallied his militia, who had fallen back to their designated position beside Howard's main line of Continentals, and ordered them to charge, too. Morgan's army achieved something often dreamed about by military tacticians but actually quite rare: a double envelopment. Washington's cavalry had attacked the British right, Howard's Continentals were attacking their center and left, and Pickens's militia was now also swinging round and joining the attack on the British left flank.

The British infantry broke and started to flee, immune to Bloody Ban's exhortations that they stand their ground. Tarleton sent a message back to a detachment of two hundred cavalry from his own elite British Legion that he had been holding in reserve at rear, ordering them to ride forward to support the redcoats. According to Tarleton, "The cavalry did not comply with the order."[93] Tarleton then galloped to the rear to give the order himself. An American rifleman fired at the galloping British officer, killing Tarleton's horse. A British surgeon rode up, dismounted, and gave Tarleton his horse. When Tarleton gallantly refused, the surgeon insisted. "Your safety is the highest importance to the army," he said.[94] But the battle was over. Tarleton and his remaining forces fled. Morgan's army had killed one hundred of Britain's best soldiers and taken another eight hundred prisoners, plus seventy Blacks the British had been using as slaves. The Americans had also taken from the British eight hundred muskets, one hundred cavalry horses, thirty-five wagons, and—as Morgan reported it to Greene—"all of their music."[95]

When he later suggested that Greene follow his example at future battles, Morgan advised: "Put the militia in the center, with some picked troops in the rear, with orders to shoot down the first man that runs."[96] Greene did not follow that advice. He thought it too draconian. But he did deploy militia in the manner that Morgan devised at Cowpens.[97]

One man did follow Morgan's draconian advice. At the Battle of Guilford Courthouse, which took place near what is now Greensboro, North Carolina, on March 15, 1781, Brigadier General Edward Stevens of the Virginia militia—the man who had written to Governor Thomas Jefferson about the humiliating performance of their state's militia at Camden—did, in fact, post rifleman twenty paces behind the militia line and order them to shoot any men who ran.[98]

Greene had chosen to fight Cornwallis at Guilford Courthouse because, at that moment, he had a pronounced numerical advantage. Greene's forces totaled 4,440 and included 1,762 Continentals, 1,200 Virginia militia commanded by Stevens, two North Carolina militia regiments totaling 1,000, and small units of riflemen, cavalry, and artillery. Cornwallis commanded 1,950 regulars.[99] Greene deployed his troops in three lines. The North Carolina militiamen were placed in the first line, where they were supported by some elite units, including 200 riflemen and about 150 of Light Horse Harry Lee's cavalry. The second line was composed of 1,200 Virginia militia (with 40 of Stevens's riflemen behind with the order to shoot them if they bolted). The third line consisted of 1,400 Continentals.

Greene told the North Carolina militiamen in the first line pretty much what Morgan had told his militia at Cowpens: fire two volleys and then you may withdraw to the rear. Light Horse Harry reinforced Greene's instructions. How well the North Carolina militia performed their first task—firing two volleys at the oncoming British line—is a matter of some dispute. One Continental Army artillery captain said they "behaved well for militia."[100] Greene was more critical; he said some fired twice, some fired once, and some did not fire at all. But there is no dispute about whether the North Carolina militia performed their second task of making an orderly withdrawal: they didn't. Gripped by panic, North Carolina militia threw down their muskets, ammunition boxes, and knapsacks and ran pell-mell to the rear. Light Horse Harry galloped about trying to stop the stampede, but to no avail. Stevens had previously told his Virginia militiamen that the North Carolina militiamen would be "retiring" after their volleys, and when that happened the Virginia line should open and let them through. By following those instructions, the Virginia militia was able to remain in place without being either knocked over or infected by the terror of the North Carolinians. Stevens desperately wanted his Virginia militia to make up for their dastardly performance at Cowpens. His regiment held its ground, but a second Virginia militia regiment commanded by Brigadier General Robert Lawson did not. According to St. George Tucker, then a major in Lawson's regiment, Lawson's militiamen "broke off without firing a single gun and dispersed like a flock of sheep frightened by dogs."[101]

When the dust settled, American casualties totaled 79 killed and 184 wounded, while the British suffered 93 killed and 413 wounded. However, 1,046 Americans were missing—and 885 of them were militiamen who, says military historian John Buchanan, had "gone home."[102]

Virginians were now afraid Cornwallis would invade their state. Virginia was the largest and wealthiest state, and most of its militia was still at home. By this time, however, Virginians had lost faith in militia as a military force. In May 1781, six prominent Virginias submitted an urgent petition to the Virginia Assembly. After making the necessary politic remarks about "the conduct and bravery of our troops, both regular and militia," the petitioners got to the point: militia could not be expected to defend the state from a British army.[103] "Experience now evinces that our regulars have not been enlisted in sufficient numbers . . . to afford a rational prospect of final victory," they said. The petitioners acknowledged that "the militia has been considered as the natural strength of a nation, the cheapest and surest defense, on whose protection we are ultimately to depend." But experience had now shown that "it is impossible that an army chiefly composed of troops without experience should meet an army of veterans upon equal terms." The state, simply, could not depend mainly on militia. Rather, militia "should only be considered as a useful supplement to our armies in cases of emergency."

* * *

We now know three things. First, the South was perpetually terrified of slave revolts. Second, it relied on its militia for slave control—a role so critical that it took precedence over anything else, including the War for Independence. Third, by the end of the Revolutionary War, the rosy image of the citizen-soldier had been destroyed. As military historian Richard H. Kohn says, "Almost universally the framers believed in the superiority of regulars over militia in warfare."[104] This was a conclusion many reached through their own firsthand military experience during the war.[105] Few things are as powerful as such personal experiences; it is not surprising that what many Founders themselves witnessed in war eclipsed prewar—and continuing postwar—oratory about the virtues of the citizen-soldier. This does not mean militia always disgraced themselves. There were times when militia units performed capably, even heroically; but those were exceptions, not the rule. The militia, however, were far from worthless. Quite the contrary. Although militia proved inadequate as a military force, they remained effective and essential to deter and suppress slave insurrections. The evidence for these three propositions—the South was frightened of slave revolts, the South relied on the militia for slave control, and the American Founders had lost faith in the militia as a military force—is overwhelming.

We are now ready to return to James Madison and the story about how he changed his position about a bill of rights, promised to write one, and included what became the Second Amendment to the United States Constitution. Before we resume that story, a brief note about Madison's own militia service is in order. In 1775, at the age of twenty-four, James Madison was commissioned as a colonel in the Orange County militia.[106] The commission resulted not from Madison's military training or interest, for he had neither. It came from his family's status. Madison's father was a wealthy planter, and like other men of his station served as an officer in the county militia. But while Madison's father was personally active to some degree in the county militia—he was involved in procuring arms and supplies—Madison's own participation was, at most, limited to participating in some parades, drills, and target practice.[107] He never mustered for combat. In that sense, Madison's militia stayed home.

When last we left James Madison, he and the federalists had prevailed at the Richmond Convention. The Constitution was ratified and a new government was about to be established. The federalists wanted to celebrate their victory. But they were worried.[108] Although the antifederalists had not succeeded in preventing the Constitution from being ratified, they proved themselves a potent political force nonetheless. And, in fact, George Washington believed that most Americans opposed the new government.[109] In the closing days of the debate, George Mason warned of possible "popular resistance" to the Constitution with "dreadful effects" ensuing.[110] Was he suggesting that he and other antifederalist leaders would attempt to incite violence? This so concerned delegates that in the closing moments of the Convention Patrick Henry felt compelled to state that he would be a "peaceable citizen" and would only seek to "remove the defects" of the new government "in a constitutional way."[111] Yet Henry made clear his adamant, unwavering hostility to the new government. "I despise and abhor it," he declared.[112] Patrick Henry was a powerful and dangerous man. Would he try to strangle the infant nation in its crib? If so, how?

7

Mr. Madison Goes to Congress

ON THE EVENING the Richmond Convention ended, George Mason asked the most stalwart antifederalists to meet him in the Virginia Senate chambers to discuss their next move. When the group was assembled, Mason delivered a speech. What exactly he said is lost to history, probably because Mason himself destroyed his speech, but according to one newspaper account he presented a "fiery, irritating manifesto."[1] Mason's remarks were apparently so over-the-top that some members of the group left the chamber while he was still in the process of delivering them. When Mason finished, he received not applause but stunned silence. Three antifederalists—Benjamin Harrison, John Tyler, and John Lawson—demanded that Mason take back his words. A humiliated George Mason agreed. Patrick Henry had the good sense to avoid the gathering altogether, but the group then sent word entreating him to come. When he arrived, Henry honored his pledge to be a "peaceable citizen." He urged the delegates to seek amendments through the constitutionally mandated process and not to use other means to obstruct the new government.[2] While George Mason was a crank who allowed himself to be swept away by emotion, Henry was a skilled lawyer and savvy politician whose use of emotion to sway an audience was the product of cold calculation. George Mason would never again be influential within the councils of government, but Washington and Madison believed that Henry remained a dangerous enemy of the new government. They worried about what he was up to. In fact, Henry was plotting how to end James Madison's political career.

Immediately after the Richmond Convention ended, Madison left with two other men for Mount Vernon to celebrate ratification of the Constitution and to confer with George Washington. They proceeded there directly, although slowly, due to a relapse of the digestive condition that caused Madison to miss several days of the Convention. When they arrived, Washington told them New Hampshire had also ratified. There must have been joy, toasts, and huzzahs. Still, it was a celebration under a cloud. They had prevailed, but just barely; the antifederalists had proved themselves to be both politically formidable and potentially intransigent; and Patrick Henry was plotting something. Madison and Washington conferred for four days, during which time they were joined by several other federalists, including David Humphreys, who was a loyal aide and occasional ghostwriter for Washington.[3] They focused on next steps for establishing the new government.

While the group at Mount Vernon was conferring, New York surprised everyone by ratifying, becoming the eleventh state to do so. Only two states, North Carolina and much-distained Rhode Island, remained outside the Union. It was heartening news, but storm clouds remained. The antifederalists had been vanquished—for now—but had proved themselves a formidable political force nonetheless. In New Hampshire, 45 percent of the delegates voted against ratification.[4] In New York, 48 percent opposed ratification. Although the New York vote had been breathtakingly close, 30 to 27, the vote did not tell the whole story because the majority of delegates had actually been antifederalists.[5]

In the end, New York had ratified for two reasons. First, the antifederalists agreed on little beyond their opposition to ratification. When it came to listing the ways delegates wanted to amend the Constitution, there seemed to be no end. As historian Pauline Maier described it, "day by day the pile of amendments increased."[6] For Melancton Smith, one of the vocal antifederalists—and someone whose voice was decisive in the end—the most important issue was the size of the House of Representatives. Smith wanted provisions that would guarantee a large House because he believed that a small body would wind up being composed exclusively of "natural aristocrats," which he defined as those on whom nature bestowed "some greater capacities" such as "birth, education, talents, and wealth."[7] Smith argued that a larger body was necessary to "admit those of the middling class" who had walked "the plain and frugal paths of life." Federalist Robert Livingston, himself a dyed-in-the-wool natural aristocrat, mocked Smith's argument. Smith, Livingston argued, would rather "go out in the highways, and pick up the rogue and the robber" than send the learned, wise, virtuous, and wealthy to Congress.[8] Smith argued that including the "respectable yeomanry" in government was "the best possible security to liberty."[9]

That would have been banal if Melancton Smith had stopped there, but he had an interesting—and from today's perspective, insightful— explanation of why that was so. If the common people found themselves excluded from government, argued Smith, they would resort to following "some popular demagogue, who will probably be devoid of principle."[10] Alexander Hamilton entered the debate, too. He said that while there were times it would be "necessary and proper" for representatives to disregard the will of their constituents, they would generally follow popular opinion so as to not be turned out of office.[11] It was a fascinating discussion of political science, but other antifederalists did not long tarry over it. They had other ideas. One proposed no fewer than eight amendments involving jurisdiction of the federal courts. As a group, the antifederalists seemed incapable of deciding what was truly important or cohering in any way. This gave Smith serious second thoughts about voting to approve the Constitution on the condition that it be amended. He told a friend that he would rather vote to ratify the Constitution and recommend a few "substantial amendments" to Congress than vote to approve the Constitution conditioned on Congress agreeing to "unimportant ones."[12]

What finally clinched matters for Melancton Smith and some other antifederalists were the potential consequences of refusing to join the Union. Now that ten states, including Virginia, had decided to join the Union, staying out seemed untenable. They also worried that New York City might secede from New York and join the United States on its own.[13] And so, ultimately, a coalition of nineteen federalists and twelve antifederalists voted to ratify.[14] It was enough to squeak by.

As had Virginia, both New Hampshire and New York sent proposed amendments to Congress along with their formal ratifications. And as had been the case in Virginia, the federalists let the antifederalists compose these proposals without interference as a way to permit the antifederalists to assuage their feelings.

After his four-day stay at Mount Vernon, Madison proceeded on to New York City, the new home of the Confederation Congress, where on July 14 Madison formally presented Virginia's ratification to the Confederation Congress.[15] The future of the nation looked bright, and Madison surely thought his own future looked bright, too. But Patrick Henry had other ideas. When the Virginia Assembly reconvened in October, Henry declared he would do everything he could to obstruct implementing the Constitution and organizing a new government under it—unless such measures provided for a second constitutional convention to consider amendments. Henry did not mince words. He said the Constitution either cancelled "the most precious rights of the people" or rendered those rights insecure, and he accused supporters of the Constitution of betraying the people.[16] Henry wanted a second constitutional convention to take up amendments. But it was not rights of the people with which he was most concerned. He wanted to strangle the new government in its crib by removing its power of direct taxation, unless states failed to meet their financial obligations to the federal government. That would have prevented, or at least greatly impeded, the federal government's ability to raise revenue for its own operations.[17] The United States had been down that road before. Under the Articles of Confederation, the national government had to request states to levy taxes on its behalf—requests that states frequently ignored. That was one of the most important reasons the Founders wrote a new Constitution in Philadelphia. Henry also proposed rewriting the Constitution to require two-thirds majorities (instead of simple majorities) in both houses of Congress to enact any law or raise a standing army. In short, Henry wanted to unwind everything the Founders had accomplished.

Francis Corbin, who we saw in Chapter 2 take on Henry during the Richmond Convention, did so again. "[T]he gentleman tells us he bows to the majesty of the people," Corbin said, looking at Henry and bowing absurdly low.[18] But actually Henry "set himself in opposition to the people," because the people ratified the Constitution, Corbin pointed out. It was a sound argument. But attempting to mock the master debater was treacherous, and attempting it before that audience was foolhardy. The Virginia Assembly was still in Henry's thrall.[19]

When Corbin sat down, Henry took the floor. "[W]hile that gentleman was availing himself of the opportunity which a splendid fortune had afforded him, of acquiring a foreign education," said Henry, reminding everyone that Corbin, the son of wealthy Loyalist parents, had attended Cambridge University during the Revolutionary War while Henry "was engaged in the arduous toils of the revolution."[20] Then, for good measure, Henry drew verbal pictures of King George smiling upon the young Francis Corbin and placing a price on Patrick Henry's head. Henry then faced Corbin and bowed even more absurdly low. "Yet such bow as I can make shall ever be at the service of the people," declared Henry. The chamber exploded in raucous laughter at Corbin's expense. Two-thirds of the Assembly voted to support Henry's proposed constitutional amendments.[21] And Henry had only just begun.

Everyone understood that Madison wanted to represent Virginia in the new Congress. Madison himself originally wanted to stand for election to the House of Representatives.[22] He probably thought of the House as the American analog to the British House of Commons, and therefore a more fitting political home for a politician like himself who— though a blue-blood member of what Melancton Smith called the natural aristocracy—wanted to portray himself as an unpretentious republican.[23] The Senate, however, was designed as the more prestigious chamber. There would be only two Senators from each state, each elected for six-year terms, and the Senate would enjoy advice-and-consent powers over presidential appointments and treaties. Therefore, Madison's friends and advisers urged him to seek election to the Senate rather than the House. George Washington told Madison he did not want Virginia sending two antifederalists to the United States Senate.[24]

The Virginia House of Delegates would nominate candidates for the Senate, and then Virginia's two Senators would be elected by the House and Senate together, with each member casting two votes. On November 6, 1788, the House nominated three men for Virginia's two Senate seats: Richard Henry Lee and William Grayson, both of whom were staunch antifederalists, and James Madison.[25] Although there were only 50 federalists among the 194 members of the Virginia Assembly, Governor Edmund Randolph told Madison he was optimistic about Madison's chances because enough members would place partisanship aside and vote for the most able candidates. But the most influential person among Virginia's legislators was not the sitting governor but the former governor, Patrick Henry. Henry told everyone that Madison was dead set against amending the Constitution. He pointed to a remark that a federalist had made on the floor of the House of Delegates to the effect that Madison would oppose amending the Constitution to eliminate the national government's taxing power even if the Virginia legislature favored such an amendment. "There gentlemen, the secret is out: it is doubted Mr. Madison will obey instructions," Henry declared.[26] On that, Henry was surely right. Madison would go down swinging before he would emasculate the federal government by snuffing out its ability to raise revenue.

Henry had an additional, even more potent argument: Madison would oppose adding a bill of rights to the Constitution. Henry had good reason to believe that was true.[27] Madison had told the Richmond Convention that he thought a bill of rights was both unnecessary and potentially dangerous—unnecessary because the federal government had only expressly authorized powers and could not endanger individual rights, and potentially dangerous because a list of enumerated rights would inevitably be incomplete, thereby implying that rights left off of the list did not exist.[28] Madison, in fact, believed that the only way to effectively protect freedom was through the proper design of government. Structural protections, he believed, were far better than a list of rights, which he dismissed as mere "parchment barriers."[29] The purpose of a bill of rights in a democratic republic is to preserve rights that a political majority wishes to take away. They simply do not work, believed Madison, because the will of the majority is too strong.[30] "In Virginia," he later explained in a letter to Thomas Jefferson, "I have seen the bill of rights violated in every instance where it has been opposed to a popular current."[31] Moreover, "overbearing majorities in every state" had repeatedly done the same thing.[32] Things were different in a monarchy because a bill of rights could serve as a "signal for rousing and uniting the superior force of the community."[33]

Yet Madison had also told the Richmond Convention that he was not against amendments per se. Politics is not a game of subtleties, however, and Patrick Henry repeatedly told everyone who would listen that Madison was opposed to constitutional amendments, pure and simple.[34] Henry warned legislators that the citizenry was so opposed to sending Madison to the United States Senate that, if they did, there would be "rivulets of blood throughout the land."[35]

Legislators cast their votes for Virginia's two Senators on Saturday, November 8. Sixty-two members voted strategically by casting only a single vote for Madison. Even that was not enough. The vote tallies were as follows: Richard Henry Lee, 98; William Grayson, 86; and James Madison, 77.

Madison was reduced to running for election to the House of Representatives. Patrick Henry was not finished, however. He had the General Assembly gerrymander the congressional district in which Madison lived by packing in as many antifederalist precincts as possible. He also had a bill introduced requiring that congressional candidates reside in a congressional district for two years to be eligible to run in that district. Grasping the import of this proposal, Madison's allies resisted it immediately, but they were soundly defeated, 80 to 32.[36] When Madison later learned of this, he must have found it particularly annoying. He, himself, had cogently spoken at the Constitutional Convention in Philadelphia against giving Congress the power to add qualifications for holding congressional office beyond those provided by the Constitution itself, and the arguments he advanced then applied just as well to state legislatures adding qualifications.[37] The Constitution requires that members of the House of Representatives be at least twenty-five years of age, have been a United States citizen for at least seven years, and be an inhabitant of *the state* in which they are chosen. There is no requirement that members live in the *district* that elects them. In the future, courts would, in fact, hold that this kind of provision is unconstitutional.[38] But federal courts did not yet exist, and the doctrine of judicial review had not yet been adopted. No one was going to invalidate that law.

Patrick Henry had two other cards to play. He had the Virginia General Assembly reappoint Madison to represent the state in the now lame-duck Confederation Congress, which then sat in New York City. At first Madison did not himself grasp the full nefariousness of Henry's plot. A friend interpreted Henry's plot for Madison: Henry wanted to keep conscientious James Madison in New York City while the antifederalists recruited a candidate to run against Madison and give that candidate a head start in the election campaign.[39]

They needed a particularly attractive candidate to defeat Madison. After some time, they selected their man. He had just about everything. Standing six feet tall, he would tower over the diminutive James Madison in joint appearances, and he was charming and gregarious while Madison was reserved and, some thought, cold.[40] He was a graduate of William and Mary College, where the best men of Virginia were educated. He was a war hero who fought in the Battles of Harlem Heights, Brandywine, Monmouth Courthouse, and Trenton, and been wounded in combat. He had endured the infamous winter at Valley Forge and risen to the rank of major. After the war, he studied law, was admitted to the bar, and practiced law. He was also an experienced and successful politician: he had, in turns, been elected to the state legislature, the Confederation Congress, and the Richmond Convention, where he had proved himself a reliable antifederalist. He had also won appointment to the state's powerful Executive Committee. Notwithstanding all of these accomplishments, he was only thirty years of age. The antifederalists sent William Cabell to persuade this man to become a candidate.[41] Cabell was a powerful and popular politician from Amherst County, one of the antifederalist enclaves that Patrick Henry had added to the congressional district.[42] Cabell knew the man he was sent to recruit; both had been delegates at the Richmond Convention, and both had voted against ratification. Cabell was delighted to report back that he had succeeded. James Monroe had agreed to run for Congress.

When James Monroe learned what counties had been placed in the Fifth Congressional District, he immediately concluded Madison would lose.[43] The district had been reconfigured to include eight counties. Perhaps the best barometer of public sentiment is how delegates, two from each county, voted at the Richmond Convention. Both delegates from Orange County, where Madison's home, Montpelier was located, and from neighboring Albemarle County, voted to ratify. Delegates from Louisa County split. All of the delegates from the other five counties—including Culpeper, which was, by far, the most populous county in the district—had voted against ratification.[44]

Word of all of these events reached James Madison in New York City. What he needed to do was obvious: return home without delay and begin campaigning. Yet Madison was reluctant to do so. He offered many explanations for his reluctance. He told George Washington his hemorrhoids were inflamed, which made travel painful. Besides, he hated campaigning and was not sure whether active campaigning would help or hurt.[45] He told Jefferson the cards were stacked against him and campaigning would be unlikely to make a difference.[46] He told Randolph he wanted to stay in New York for the winter because he was working on some unidentified project for which he needed access to congressional records.[47] He told friends he was confident that if he lost, Washington would give him an important position in his new administration, even while admitting that both Washington and he considered it preferable that Madison assume a leadership role in Congress.[48] None of this made sense to Madison's friends. Even if he could land a position in the Washington administration, taking a shellacking in an election is bad for a politician's career. And what research project could possibly take precedence over an impending election? Entreaties to return home grew more insistent.[49]

Perhaps there was another explanation for Madison's foot dragging. The preceding year, Thomas Jefferson had written Madison from Paris to urge him to make the acquaintance of the new French minister, Count de Moustier. Jefferson had taught Madison to encode sensitive portions of their letters to prevent them from being read by anyone who intercepted them (which was then not a rare occurrence), and in a coded portion of his letter Jefferson told Madison that getting to know the count could be politically useful because the count was "remarkably communicative" and "[w]ith adroitness he may be pumped of anything."[50] But there was a rather curious feature of Jefferson's letter: it focused more on the count's sister-in-law, Madame de Brèhan, a beautiful and effervescent artist, than on the French minster. Madison must make the acquaintance of this woman, insisted Jefferson, and he proceeded to give his friend tips about how to strike up a relationship with her. Madame Brèhan spoke little English and wanted to learn more. Jefferson suggested that Madison might teach her English and learn French from her. Madame Brèhan's husband, Jefferson noted, would not be in America as he was in the army and stationed elsewhere.

Am I reading too much into Jefferson's letter? Perhaps. But Jefferson had a record of urging on Madison in romantic pursuits. If there was an area in which James Madison lacked self-confidence, it was in relationships with the opposite sex. He was short, pale, frail, and shy.[51] As far as we know, Madison, now thirty-seven, had only had one serious romantic interest in his life so far. Five years earlier, he had become besotted with a fifteen-year-old girl nicknamed Kitty, whom he hoped to marry.[52] Even though courting girls that young was not rare, the age discrepancy suggests a man who was more secure with inexperienced girls than with women. Jefferson had written Madison letters then, encouraging Madison's courtship of the girl. Kitty privately agreed to marry Madison—or at least so Madison thought—but either he was mistaken or she changed her mind, for Kitty terminated the relationship.

In New York, Madison had taken Jefferson's suggestion and struck up a relationship with Madame Brèhan. The relationship was sufficiently successful that a colleague told Madison that Madame Brèhan was making "a thousand inquiries" about him.[53] This had occurred prior to the Richmond Convention. When Madison returned to New York, he brought Madame Brèhan an expensive gift: a Black boy, to be her slave.

If Madison had a romantic interest in Madam Brèhan, it did not last long. To his horror, he realized that the madam was, in fact, the minister's mistress, and worse, they were flouting their relationship. That may have been the way things were done in France, but not in America. On December 8, 1788, Madison reported to Jefferson, in a coded portion of a letter, that Count Moustier had turned out to be an "unlucky appointment" as minister because he was unsocial, proud, and engaged in an "illicit connection with Madame de Brèhan which is universally known and offensive to American manners."[54] The two lovers had been traveling a lot, to Boston, New Hampshire, and Mount Vernon, and on those journeys "it is said they often neglect the most obvious precautions for veiling their intimacy," continued Madison, in code. Word of their scandalous behavior traveled quickly back to New York City, where women in high society now shunned Madam Brèhan, and she unhappily understood why. In the same letter in which Madison reported the distasteful information about the French minister and Madame de Brèhan, Madison told Jefferson he had decided to return home.

On his way back, Madison stopped again at Mount Vernon, where on this occasion he spent a full week.[55] We do not know what Washington and Madison discussed, but we can guess. The election was scheduled for February 2, 1789, just five weeks away. Madison knew that Monroe intended to make a bill of rights his principal campaign issue. A bill of rights was enormously popular with antifederalists, and Madison's congressional district was packed with antifederalists. Monroe favored a bill of rights. Madison was on record as opposing one, and his argument about structural protections versus parchment barriers would be intriguing in a college debate but was far too subtle for a political campaign.

What should Madison do? As a politician, the choice must have seemed obvious; but as a man of principle, Madison wrung his hands. He needed to persuade himself that he was not reversing his carefully considered position solely out of self-interest. A letter he wrote to Jefferson is particularly revealing. "My own opinion has always been in favor of a bill of rights; provided it be so framed as not to imply powers not meant to be included in the enumeration," he began.[56] That was an exaggeration; it would have been more accurate to say he had always been *against* a bill of rights because he feared it would imply the federal government had unenumerated powers, among other reasons. He then went on to say that he never thought the omission of a bill of rights was a "material defect" or wanted to add one "for any other reason than that it is anxiously desired by others." There it was: Madison was reluctantly willing to support a bill of rights because others wanted one. After getting that far, however, Madison felt compelled to state at some length the many reasons why he believed a bill of rights would be ineffectual. For example, should there be a rebellion or insurrection that alarms the public, no written prohibition would prevent the suspension of habeas corpus. Should Britain or Spain station an army in America, no declaration on paper would stop America from raising a standing army for public safety. It is better, argued Madison, to remove the need for such actions in the first place—that is, take care to ensure there is no insurrection, or that a foreign power not secure a foothold in North America. Nevertheless, Madison concluded, he was not against a bill of rights if it could be drafted so as not to be "of disservice." Madison was trying to persuade himself to reverse his position and support a bill of rights. It was a wrenching process.

In reply, Jefferson pointed out that Madison was overlooking something important: a bill of rights could be effective because it would be a legal check in the hands of an independent judiciary.[57] History would prove that to be a remarkably prescient observation. Jefferson was then in Paris, however, and exchanges of letters across the Atlantic took a very long time. By the time Madison received Jefferson's reply, he had already brought himself fully around and stated unequivocal support for a bill of rights on the campaign stump.

As was normal in campaigns at the time, Madison spelled out his position in letters to influential constituents. He sent one such letter to Reverend George Eve, a Baptist minister in Orange County. Madison explained that he had opposed proposing amendments prior to ratification of the Constitution because "the secret enemies of the Union" would exploit the proposals to "throw the States into dangerous contentions."[58] Circumstances had now changed, Madison explained. Eleven states had ratified, and amendments "if pursued with a proper moderation and in a proper mode, will be not only safe, but may serve the double purpose of satisfying the minds of well-meaning opponents, and of providing additional guards in favor of liberty."[59] It was now his "sincere opinion," said Madison, that the new Congress should write a bill of rights at its first session.

What should it include? Madison said it should include all "essential rights," and he listed four. First and foremost was the right of conscience, that is, freedom of religion. This long held a special place for Madison, who, in fact, had worked with George Mason to draft the religious freedom provision of Virginia's 1776 Declaration of Rights.[60] Madison knew this would resonate with Baptists, who were being criminally prosecuted by Virginia for worshiping outside the Anglican Church, the official, established church of the state. Madison told Reverend Eve that he also wanted to guarantee freedom of the press, trial by jury, and security against general warrants. In addition to protecting those freedoms, Madison also said he favored amendments to periodically increase the size of the House of Representatives and to prohibit "vexatious appeals" to federal courts. Although Madison noted that "sundry other alterations" were "eligible" for consideration, he specified nothing else. He made no mention of a right to bear arms, the militia, or standing armies.

Madison's new position, therefore, was essentially as follows: I now favor a bill of rights, and if you send me to Congress, I'll write one.

You can expect it to include four essential rights: freedom of religion, freedom of the press, jury trials, and a protection against warrantless searches and seizures. Armed with Madison's letter, Reverend Eve spoke in support of Madison's election two weeks later at a meeting of antifederalists in Culpeper County. And he surely disseminated Madison's views among his congregants, others in Orange County, and Baptists elsewhere in the district.

It is not entirely clear whether Patrick Henry, William Cabell, and the other antifederalists knew it when they selected their candidate, but James Monroe and James Madison were good friends. They had been introduced to each other three years earlier by their mutual mentor Thomas Jefferson, when they had both been elected to serve in the Confederation Congress. "A better man cannot be," Jefferson had written to Madison about James Monroe in his letter of introduction.[61] Madison and Monroe had even briefly become partners in a real estate venture, although the partnership was short lived because Monroe found himself short of cash and Madison bought out his interest.[62] Their friendship did not diminish their strong desires to win the election—these were, after all, two strong-willed and ambitious politicians—but it did lead to a civil and even cooperative campaign.

The two friends arranged to debate each other in a number of different towns. Not only did they sometimes travel together to the debates, but they even shared a room in inns along the way. Citizens who attended the debates could not have known they were watching two young men who eventually would become the fourth and fifth presidents of the United States! Years later, someone asked Madison how upset he was that Monroe did not vigorously defend him from personal attacks by Henry and other antifederalists during the campaign. Madison said that despite pointed disagreements between him and Monroe on issues and "the considerable excitement" of the campaign, "there never was *an atom of ill will* between us."[63] And, in fact, the two men remained friends for the rest of their lives.

The total non-slave population of the district was 50,857, but things were not very democratic in eighteenth-century America. The only people eligible to vote were males who were at least twenty-one years of age and owned fifty acres of undeveloped land or twenty-five acres with a house. The voting population in the district was only 5,189.[64]

On Friday, January 30, three days before the election, it started to snow. When it stopped on Saturday, ten inches of snow covered the ground, making travel difficult. On Monday, Election Day, it was two degrees Fahrenheit at Montpelier.[65] Only 44 percent of eligible voters went to the polls. When the votes were counted, Madison had won by the comfortable margin of 1,308 to 972. He did particularly well in areas where the two candidates had made joint appearances. Madison nearly shut out Monroe in Orange County; the vote was 216 to 9. Madison also blew Monroe away, 256 to 103, in Culpeper County, where the candidates debated several times. In light of Monroe's advantages in physique and personality, not to mention the advantages from gerrymandering, the election results must be interpreted as a testament to both Madison's credibility and his persuasiveness in argument.

And so Madison was off to Congress, where—he had promised his constituents—he would propose a bill of rights. If he thought this was going to be a walk in the park, however, he was in for a surprise. Madison would discover that, notwithstanding the hullabaloo about the need for a bill of rights during the ratification battles, there would be little interest in a bill of rights in Congress, even among members who had been antifederalists during the ratification battles.[66]

* * *

In the next chapter, we will take up Madison's drafting of the Bill of Rights, and specifically the prevision that ultimately became the Second Amendment, but first we need to step back and take a look at then-existing state constitutions. Twelve states had adopted constitutions, and four of those constitutions contained right-to-bear-arms provisions. Here are those four states and the dates on which they originally adopted those provisions:[67]

Pennsylvania	July 25, 1776
North Carolina	December 17, 1776
Vermont	July 2, 1777
Massachusetts	June 7, 1780

My thesis is that, in the main, Madison drafted the Second Amendment to ensure that Congress could not disarm the militia and thereby undermine the slave system in the South. If that is correct, why did four states—three of them Northern states—adopt right-to-bear-arms provisions in their state constitutions?

The short answer to that question is this: All of those constitutions were adopted during the Revolutionary War. Glorifying the militia during the war was commonplace—arguably, even necessary. The nation had not yet fully grasped how incapable the militia was at fighting professional soldiers.

Look at the dates on which those state bills of rights were adopted. The most important of the four provisions was that of Pennsylvania because the other three states largely copied its provision. Pennsylvania adopted its provision after Lexington, Concord, and Bunker Hill, but before any of the other battles we have discussed took place, including even the Battle of Long Island. Massachusetts, the last of the four states, adopted its provision before the Battles of Camden, Cowpens, and Guilford Courthouse. All four of these provisions were therefore adopted while Americans still held romanticized visions of citizen soldiers. Of course, the South then knew its militia were essential for slave control—and considered that the most important duty of its militia—but while the war was still in progress few beyond the senior officer corps of the Continental Army had fully grasped that the militia were useful only for suppressing insurrections.

It is instructive, however, to take a brief look at special circumstances in these four states.

Pennsylvania. The first of these states, Pennsylvania, was not writing on a blank slate when it included a right-to-bear-arms provision in its constitution. It was undoubtedly inspired by a provision in the English Declaration of Rights of 1689 that we will take up in Chapter 9. That is where a so-called right to have arms originated. Surely, it was the war they were then fighting that motivated these four states to draw upon that history and include a right-to-bear-arms provision in their constitutions. But why did these four states adopt right-to-bear-arms provisions while most states did not? There is no single, self-evident explanation. There is nothing these four states had in common that sets them apart from the other eight states that did not do so.[68] It is possible, however, that each of the four had something unique to itself that led it to adopt a right-to-bear-arms provision. While examining the history and culture of each of these four states in sufficient depth to find their distinguishing characteristics would entail a deeper dive than we can accomplish here, we can take a brief glimpse that might, at least, be suggestive.

Pennsylvania had a unique tradition against a government-regulated militia. Quakers controlled the state government and resisted supporting military organizations.[69] Where others were quick to resolve territorial disputes with American Indians by force, Quakers preferred developing relationships with the Indians and negotiating with them. That left settlers in Pennsylvania's western frontier feeling undefended in conflicts with the native inhabitants. And during King George's War, which began in 1744, Pennsylvanians along the Delaware River also felt undefended from raids by French and Spanish privateers.[70] In 1747, Benjamin Franklin created a plan for forming voluntary militia companies, as well as a Militia Association to purchase artillery and equipment. More than a hundred militia companies organized. The militia companies and the Association were entirely private, with the Association being funded through a lottery rather than by taxes.

Despite its nearly instant success, Franklin's militia did not last long. The Militia Association disbanded within about a year, with the end of King George's War. But the perceived need for defense arose again with the French and Indian War in 1754. This time Franklin persuaded the Pennsylvania Assembly to appropriate funds for defense and to sanction the organization of militia companies.[71] But even though this time the state authorized forming militia, the militia remained more or less independent. The Pennsylvania law provided that it "may be lawful for the freemen of this province *to form themselves*."[72] It also prohibited the governor or any militia officer from making any rule that "shall in the least affect those of the inhabitants of the province who are conscientiously scrupulous of bearing arms." A newspaper of the time described what was happening as follows: "[T]he people of the west side of the Susquehanna . . . are gathering to defend *themselves*."[73] I have added the emphasis to those phrases, and I will explain why shortly.

In early 1764, Pennsylvania experienced an insurrection. It was not a slave insurrection, although more people owned slaves in Pennsylvania than you might think; 10 percent of the people living in Philadelphia were slaves.[74] This insurrection, however, came from disgruntled White frontiersmen. Although the French and Indian War had recently ended, clashes between White settlers and American Indians had left bitter feelings in the backwoods.[75] In December 1763, mobs from the small town of Paxton (near what is today Harrisburg) murdered twenty un-armed American Indians. Then, three hundred armed backwoodsmen, calling themselves the Paxton Boys, marched on the state capital in Philadelphia. They were furious that the Quaker-dominated leg-islature were not protecting them from American Indians, and they threatened to kill another group of 140 Indians who were living peace-ably in the Philadelphia area, together with any Whites who harbored them. Working-class German Lutherans, who lived in Germantown, through which the mob would march, sided with the Paxton Boys. So did Scots-Irish Presbyterians. Quakers rallied to defend the Indians. Some Quakers astonished everyone—even other Friends—by taking up arms. "Look, look!" some boys are said to have shouted. "Quaker carrying a musket on his shoulder!"[76] Anglicans tended to side with the Quakers. As the Paxton Boy mob drew near, Philadelphia erupted into chaos.

Benjamin Franklin, who was then the most prominent member of the Pennsylvania Assembly, demanded that the Paxton Boys, whom he called "barbarous men," be brought to justice for murdering unarmed American Indians. John Penn, grandson of William Penn and the last royal governor of the state, also wanted the Paxton Boys arrested. He called out British troops, but there probably weren't many. Franklin began desperately trying to reorganize militia companies, and Penn asked residents to join them.[77] But Penn decided to try to avoid blood-shed. He sent a delegation of city leaders, including Franklin, to meet with the Paxton Boys. The two sides reached an agreement: Leaders of the Paxton Boys would be allowed to present their grievances to the Assembly, and the rest of the Paxton Boys would return home.

This had been a close call. It demonstrated why Pennsylvania might need a militia to protect itself from riots, insurrections, and other disturbances. There were, after all, no police forces in eighteenth-century America.[78] It was not only Southern states that had to worry about security.

It is against this background that Pennsylvania adopted its first constitution. Here in full is its right-to-bear-arms section:

> XIII. That the people have a right to bear arms for the defence of themselves and the state; and as standing armies in the time of peace are dangerous to liberty, they ought not to be kept up; And that the military should be kept under strict subordination to, and governed by, the civil power.[79]

To the modern ear, declaring that the people have a right to bear arms for the defense "of themselves" as well as the state sounds as if it includes a right of individuals to have arms for their own self-defense. That, in fact, is how it used to sound to me.[80] But one historian has argued that in view of the language highlighted in a statute authorizing people to form militia *themselves* for community defense, and the rest of the history just recited, the section may have been understood at the time as guaranteeing a collective right.[81] That is a reasonable interpretation, especially as the right is to "bear arms," a term of art that was then used almost exclusively in a military context.[82]

One final observation about the Pennsylvania provision is worth making. As we learned in Chapter 3, Virginia adopted a Declaration of Rights on June 12, 1776, about six weeks before Pennsylvania adopted its Declaration of Rights. It is said that in writing Pennsylvania's Declaration of Rights, Benjamin Franklin largely copied Virginia's document.[83] The Virginia Declaration mentions nothing about a right to bear arms, yet it included a provision that clearly served as the template for the Pennsylvania provision. We previously looked at the Virginia language in Chapter 3, but now let's compare it to Pennsylvania's. Here is Virginia's provision, which you will remember was largely written by George Mason:

> XIII That a well-regulated militia, composed of the body of the people, trained to arms, is the proper, natural, and safe defense of a free state; that standing armies, in time of peace, should be avoided as dangerous to liberty; and that in all cases the military should be under strict subordination to, and governed by, the civil power.[84]

The Virginia and Pennsylvania provisions are essentially identical except for the first clause in each. Virginia's reads, "That a well-regulated militia, composed of the body of the people trained to arms, is the proper, natural, and safe defense of a free state." Pennsylvania's says: "That the people have a right to bear arms for the defence of themselves and the state." Why the difference? Even during the Revolutionary War, Quaker Pennsylvania had qualms about endorsing a state-sanctioned military organization. Yet Pennsylvania needed to defend itself. This presented a conflict between protecting freedom of conscience and equitably distributing the burden of defending the community. Some years earlier, Franklin himself wrote a pamphlet in which he explored the dilemma through a dialogue between two fictitious characters. One character said, "Hang me if I'll fight to save the Quakers." The other replied, "That is to say you won't jump ship, because it will save the rats as well as yourself."[85] The tension between freedom of conscience and civic duty was heightened when the Continental Congress asked all able-bodied men to join militia companies.[86] Pennsylvania's solution was to make enrolling in militia associations entirely voluntary, but asking (and not requiring) those who did not join a militia to make an equivalent contribution of some kind. Pennsylvania also ordered anyone who did not join a militia association to turn any weapons they possessed over to those who were willing to bear arms.

Now we can see that the clause "the people have a right to bear arms for the defence of themselves and the state" was Pennsylvania's counterpart to Virginia's clause statement that "a well-regulated militia, composed of the body of the people, trained to arms, is the proper, natural, and safe defense of a free state." These clauses were designed to serve the same purpose. Each—adopted during the early days of the Revolutionary War—expressed how the state would defend itself during the war. While Virginia would rely on its government-regulated militia, Pennsylvania would rely on voluntary militia associations, which all citizens had a right (but not a duty) to join.

North Carolina. The next state constitution to include a right-to-bear-arms provision was that of North Carolina. Here is that provision:

> XVII. That the people have a right to bear arms, for the defence of the State; and, as standing armies, in time of peace, are dangerous to

liberty, they ought not to be kept up; and that the military should be kept under strict subordination to, and governed by, the civil power.[87]

If this provision looks familiar, it is because North Carolina copied the Pennsylvania provision verbatim—except for removing two words, the very words we were just discussing, namely, "of themselves." The North Carolina Congress kept no record of deliberations about this, or about any other provision, of the state constitution.[88] We can only surmise that it dropped those two words because it wanted to make it clear that the right to bear arms for the defense of the state only. With this one modification, it was sensible that North Carolina adopted the Pennsylvania provision. For one thing, the two states had each faced similar insurrectionist threats. In Pennsylvania, it was the Paxton Boys. In North Carolina during the period 1766 to 1768, an even larger mob of backwoodsmen, calling themselves Regulators, had taken up arms to prevent officials from collecting taxes and debts.[89] The Paxton Boys and the Regulators were both manifestations of the same dynamic: back-country animosity toward the elites who controlled the governments.[90] (Some years later, the Whiskey Rebellion in western Pennsylvania would be yet another demonstration of hostility to government by backcountry groups steeped in a violent Greater Appalachian culture.) On one occasion, there was a confrontation between 1,400 militiamen and 3,700 Regulators. As had been the case in Pennsylvania, blood-shed was avoided, but the episode had made a lasting impression. Moreover, when North Carolina considered its constitution shortly be-fore Christmas in 1776, it was in a hurry. The North Carolina Congress devoted only six meetings to a constitution, and only four meetings to a bill of rights. While there are no records of substantive discussions, we know that those few meetings were also filled with pressing issues pertaining to the war.[91]

Vermont. The Green Mountain State had a unique militia his-tory. In fact, early Vermont militia history is almost the history of the state itself. At the risk of oversimplification, here in a nutshell is what happened. In 1741, the English government appointed Benning Wentworth the royal governor of the Province of New Hampshire.[92] His commission empowered him to grant unoccupied land and to create towns. This was supposed to be a means of developing the province. Wentworth, however, was not content to grant lands within New Hampshire. He also granted land in what is today Vermont but was then part of the Province of New York.[93] He chartered 140 townships within that area, created large plots of land within those townships, and granted them—in effect, selling them—to speculators, who in turn sold them to immigrants from England, Scotland, and Connecticut who wanted to establish farms.[94] Within fifteen years, Wentworth had granted nearly three million acres, constituting about a third of present-day Vermont. Wentworth had ideas of using his considerable political influence in England to have the boundary between New York and New Hampshire redrawn and transfer his grants to New Hampshire, but at the time he granted them, those lands were indisputably part of New York. Wentworth had no authority to grant them to anyone. And he knew it. The New Hampshire Grants, as they came to be called, were a scam.[95] They made Wentworth fabulously rich.[96]

Eventually, people from New York who held legal title began eviction proceedings against farmers in the New Hampshire Grants. Those farmers included Ethan Allen and his family, who had previously lived in Connecticut. Ethan Allen was a gifted organizer. Together with other holders of New Hampshire Grants, he hired a top-notch Connecticut lawyer to litigate their right to the lands in the New York courts. They lost. New York's counsel cleverly divided the claims into nine separate lawsuits, each one below the threshold necessary to appeal from New York's courts to London. Allen went to see Wentworth, who promised to lobby the English government to protect holders of the New Hampshire Grants. But Wentworth was simply stringing Allen along. He forwarded to London a petition from Allen and other holders of the New Hampshire Grants without personally endorsing it. With growing awareness of his corruption, the British government forced Benning Wentworth to resign as governor in 1766, replacing him with his nephew John Wentworth. John Wentworth also strung Allen along, telling him he was going to bat for New Hampshire Grant holders while, in fact, he merely sat on his hands.[97] New York continued to aggressively, and successfully, press its claims.

Ethan Allen would not give up. He and his family had been fleeced. His response was righteous indignation, and he focused his resentment not on Wentworth but on New York. That was not entirely without cause. New York governors were also corrupt, and the New York judges who decided the cases had conflicts of interest that, today, would leave us aghast.[98] With legal and political solutions failing him, Allen resorted to force. In 1771, he organized a paramilitary organization which called itself the Green Mountain Boys.[99] It called itself a militia; that sounded so much better than admitting to being a vigilante group. Only the royal governor of a province could lawfully authorize the formation of a militia.[100] Moreover, the Green Mountain Boys were organized not to fight the British, but to fight surveyors, sheriffs, and deputies from New York.[101] Allen characterized the dispute as virtuous farmers versus "designing men," but virtue had little to do with it.[102] It was self-interest all around. The Allen family claimed rights to more than 13,000 acres within the New Hampshire Grants.[103] It was enough to cause an Ethan Allen biographer to wonder: "[W]as America founded, at least in part, on terrorism?"[104]

For Ethan Allen and the Green Mountain Boys, the Revolutionary War was a godsend. It gave them an opportunity to launder their image—an opportunity Allen did not waste. On May 10, 1775, less than a month after Lexington and Concord, Allen and his Green Mountain Boys, in collaboration with Benedict Arnold, seized Fort Ticonderoga, a British fort at the southernmost tip of Lake Champlain, at the New York–Vermont border. It was hailed as an early victory of the Revolution, even though the fort had fewer than fifty British soldiers and surrendered without a fight. Historians have described the attacking force as "eighty-five whooping New England roughnecks" or "tatterdemalions in linsey-woolsey who called themselves the Green Mountain Boys."[105] Four months later, Allen, always the glory seeker, launched a foolishly precipitous attack on Montreal. In less than two hours, 95 of the 130 men he led were killed; all of the rest were wounded, save only seven.[106] Allen surrendered. In 1776, the Green Mountain Boys disbanded. Seth Warner, who had been Allen's second-in-command, was commissioned a colonel in the Continental Army, and many former members of the Green Mountain Boys joined his regiment.[107]

The British released Allen in a prisoner exchange in 1778. He personally saw no further action in the war. Allen's reputation as an American patriot comes largely from a bestselling memoir he wrote about the barbarous conditions he endured as a British prisoner of war. He continued to work on Vermont statehood. His American patriotism might fairly be open to question since, when the American Congress balked at recognizing Vermont as an independent state and incorporating it into the Union, Allen explored whether Vermont could join Canada.

Seventy-two delegates held a convention in Windsor, Vermont, from June 4 to July 2, 1777, for the purpose of adopting a constitution.[108] There is no record of their deliberations.[109] We know, however, that Dr. Thomas Young, who helped draft the Pennsylvania constitution, sent that document to friends in Vermont for use as a model.[110] Foremost in the minds of the delegates was adopting a document and a process that would win the respect of the thirteen existing states and the Continental Congress. Indeed, while the convention was meeting in Windsor, Vermont's petition for recognition as a state and representation in Congress was pending. Vermont had no reason to alter the language Pennsylvania had adopted for its right-to-bear-arms provision, especially since Vermont wanted to legitimize its residents bearing arms, not so much against Britain, as New York. Those struggles were continuing. In fact, Vermont militia would defeat New York forces in a "Border War" in December 1781.[111] Thus, for quite different reasons, Pennsylvania's right-to-bear-arms provision suited Vermont fine, and it adopted it without change.[112]

One postscript worth adding is that while the Vermont convention was underway, the Continental Congress refused Vermont's petition for recognition as an independent state.[113] That would not change for quite a while. Vermont was not admitted to the United States until March 4, 1791—ten months *after* James Madison proposed his bill of rights to the First Congress. North Carolina had not yet joined the Union, either, but at least it was recognized as an independent state.

Massachusetts. The last of the four states to adopt a right-to-bear-arms provision during this time frame was Massachusetts. Probably more than any other state's constitution, the Massachusetts document was almost entirely the work of a single person: John Adams. For ten years—from February 1778 to June 1788—Adams was in Europe on four consecutive assignments: as one of three commissioners sent to negotiate an alliance with France, as minister to the Court of Louis

XIV, as a minister to negotiate a treaty with Great Britain, and as minister to the Court of St. James.[114] He returned home only once, from August to November in 1779, during those ten years. And during those three months, he more or less singlehandedly wrote the Constitution of the Commonwealth of Massachusetts, which, incidentally, is the oldest written constitution in effect today in the world.[115]

How did Adams come to write it nearly alone? Within a week after his arrival back in Massachusetts during his three-month return, the town of Braintree selected Adams as a representative to the state constitutional convention. The selection made eminent sense: two years earlier, Adams had published a pamphlet titled *Thoughts on Government*, recommending how a state should structure its government. When the Massachusetts convention assembled in Cambridge in September 1779, it appointed a thirty-member committee to write an initial draft.[116] That committee, in turn, delegated the work to a three-member subcommittee, consisting of John Adams, John's cousin Samuel Adams, and James Bowdoin, who was president of the convention and would later become the state's second governor. That small subcommittee then delegated the work to John Adams alone, making him, as he himself described it, a "sub-sub" committee of one.[117] Why let John do it all by himself? There were two reasons. First, as the author of *Thoughts on Government*, John was the resident expert on constitution writing. Second, and probably just as important, John Adams was too irascible and self-possessed to work agreeably on a team.

As was characteristic of him, Adams undertook the assignment with great diligence. He read the other existing state constitutions, reread his own pamphlet, and set to work. Adams drafted a constitution that provided for three branches of government; separation of powers; a bicameral legislature; a governor chosen by both houses of the legislature; an independent judiciary; and a governmental duty to "cherish" literature, the sciences, public schools, grammar schools, and higher education—"especially the university at Cambridge," of which Adams was a very proud graduate.[118]

Here is the right-to-bear-arms provision as it was finally approved in the constitution:

Art. XVII. The people have a right to keep and to bear arms for the common defence. And as, in time of peace, armies are dangerous to liberty, they ought not to be maintained without the consent of the legislature; and the military power shall always be held in an exact subordination to the civil authority and be governed by it.[119]

The most important thing to note is that the right to bear arms is granted "for the common defense" only, not for individual reasons. That was no oversight. Two towns wanted to expand the right to embrace bearing arms for one's own defense, too, but they did not prevail.[120]

While no records were kept of the convention's deliberations, we know that it made a single word change from Adams's original draft. Adams had written that "standing armies are dangerous to liberty." The convention deleted the word "standing."[121] Thus, Adams appears to have wanted to condemn maintaining armies in peacetime only, while the convention seems to have condemned armies at any time. Militias are not mentioned, but they were the alternative to armies. As we have learned from Chapters 5 and 6, had America followed that advice and relied exclusively on militia, the Revolutionary War would have turned out differently.

If Adams's—and the convention's—view about armies was naïve, they may be forgiven. Massachusetts militia had fought at Lexington, at Concord, and at Bunker Hill. The war was still in progress, and not everyone was then aware how dismally the militia were performing. It was, in fact, something John Adams would never realize. Perhaps that is understandable, too. Two weeks after the proposed Massachusetts constitution was printed for review, Adams was aboard the vessel *Sensible* sailing back to France. He missed nearly the entire war. Following the war as a diplomat in Paris was hardly the same thing as living through it where it was being fought. Moreover, Adams took great stock in the fact that his father, grandfather, great grandfather, and great, great grandfather had all been "officers in the militia and deacons in the church," which he believed marked them as "independent country gentlemen" though they worked the land as hardscrabble farmers.[122] Adams, in fact, would be an enemy of standing armies throughout his career, including as president.[123]

If others were impressed by something John Adams proposed, James Madison was not among them. In a coded letter to Thomas Jefferson, Madison described Adams as a man of "extravagant self-importance," "unprofitable dignity," and "impatient ambition."[124] Nor was Madison positively impressed by Adams's *Thoughts on Government*. "Adams has made himself obnoxious to many particularly in the Southern states by the political principles avowed in his book," wrote Madison.[125] It is hardly surprising, therefore, that when he sat down to write what would ultimately become the Second Amendment, Madison did not follow Adams's model.

How influential, then, were these four state provisions in the drafting of the Second Amendment? The answer must be: not much. While many years did not separate the writing of these provisions and the Second Amendment, much had changed in that relatively short period of time. One change was what the Founders thought about the militia. While many believed the militia was an effective military force before the Revolution, few knowledgeable Founders believed that when the war concluded. How wise, therefore, would it be to engrave a condemnation of standing armies—the only real alternative to militia before international tensions erupted into active warfare—into a constitution? And, of course, the Second Amendment would not do so.

But, more broadly, do these four state constitutions demonstrate that Americans considered a right to bear arms—not in the defense of the community, state, or country—was one of the great, sacrosanct rights? They do not. First, once we read these provisions more carefully in light of the circumstances in which they were adopted, it is far from clear that they were intended to grant an individual right to keep and bear arms for personal reasons. The reverse seems more likely. Second, and even more importantly, we must bear in mind that right-to-bear-arms provisions were included in just four of twelve state constitutions. Thus, two-thirds of the state constitutions did not protect a right to bear arms of any kind.

* * *

We also need to bear in mind that the number and diversity of rights being enshrined in one place or another was then quite staggering. There were, of course, rights in state constitutions, as we have just been discussing. And, as we know, as a sop to the defeated, federalists in five state ratifying conventions gave antifederalists nearly free reign to write proposed amendments that would be transmitted to the states along with the state's formal ratification of the Constitution. There was no harm in salving antifederalist wounds in this way, the federalists thought, as these lists of proposed amendments had no force. Scholars who tally up the number of rights in these proposals count two hundred rights, and seventy-five different provisions, if one eliminates duplicates.[126] And so, these lists tell us little about what James Madison or his colleagues in the First Congress considered the most important rights, or how those rights should be defined. What matters is what they adopted in what became our Bill of Rights. And that is where we turn in the next chapter.

8

The Ghost of Patrick Henry

JAMES MADISON ARRIVED in New York City, then home to the First Congress, on March 14, 1789.[1] It may seem a strange thing to say about a congressman who would someday become president of the United States, but Madison was then at the height of his personal powers and political influence.[2] Here is one measure of the high regard in which he was held: George Washington decided that his first official act would be to give an inaugural address to Congress, and he asked Madison to ghostwrite his historically important speech.[3] The House of Representatives decided to compose a formal response to the presidential address and, unaware that Madison had written Washington's address, assigned Madison to write the House's reply.[4] Then Washington, probably unaware that Madison wrote the House reply, asked Madison to draft his response to the House, as well as his reply to a separate response from the Senate.

Madison used these opportunities to promote a bill of rights. But he was speaking for others and had to tread carefully. George Washington did not think a bill of rights was necessary, or at least he did not think adopting one was a matter of urgency.[5] Thus, Washington's inaugural address neither asked Congress to draft a bill of rights nor recommended what it should contain should Congress decide to draft one. In fact, Washington's address never even contained the phrase "bill of rights." It is up to you, Washington told Congress, "how far an exercise of the occasional power delegated by the Fifth article of the Constitution is rendered expedient at the present juncture."[6] Article V gave Congress—by a two-thirds vote in each chamber—the ability to propose amendments to the states. Note how Washington described this as an *occasional* power. He wanted to make it clear that amending the Constitution should not be routine business. Washington then succinctly laid out the arguments for, and against, considering amendments. "I assure myself," Washington said, "that whilst you carefully avoid every alteration which might endanger the benefits of an United and effective Government, or which ought to await the future lessons of experience," you will also weigh "a reverence for the characteristic rights of freemen, and a regard for the public harmony."

That was as far as Madison was able to get Washington to go. But it significantly advanced Madison's goal. Although Washington did not recommend that Congress put a bill of rights on its agenda, he suggested that Congress needed to consider whether to place it on its agenda. That was no small matter. Congress, as a whole, had no reason to put a bill of rights on its agenda. After all, the federalists and antifederalists had fought over whether there should be a bill of rights, and the federalists not only won, but won twice: by getting the Constitution ratified, and by winning overwhelming majorities in both houses of Congress. Only one state—Virginia, thanks to Patrick Henry—sent any antifederalists to the United States Senate. Federalists also comprised forty-nine of the fifty-nine members of the House of Representatives. That meant that federalists comprised 91 percent of the Senate and 83 percent of the House. Why even consider taking up a bill of rights? There was no clear reason to do so. The president, however, said they ought to consider it. Madison also persuaded Washington to subtly rebut a key argument against considering amendments now. The prevailing view was that it was wise to gain experience with the new Constitution before amending it. Theory was one thing, but it was no substitute for seeing how the new government actually functioned. But the president suggested that some amendments—those pertaining to "the characteristic rights of freemen"—did not need to "await the future lessons of experience." So Madison had packed a persuasive argument into what superficially seemed like a few uncontroversial sentences.

The formal reply of the House of Representatives, drafted by Madison, included the following: "The question arising out of the fifth article of the Constitution, will receive all the attention demanded by its importance; and will, we trust be decided, under the influence of all the considerations to which you allude."[7] That came pretty close to committing the House to actually considering whether to propose amendments. It was, for Madison, a significant step forward. There was nothing more to be said, so Washington's reply to the House, also drafted by Madison, was merely two sentences expressing thanks.[8]

Notwithstanding this skillful beginning, Madison knew that he faced a steep climb. Few of his colleagues wanted to take up a bill of rights. Establishing a new government was a Herculean task. The First Congress had to immediately take on many difficult and complex matters, for which there was no instruction manual and no precedent. It had to create a revenue system and establish executive departments and a federal judiciary. The Senate had to confirm the President's appointments—Secretary of the Treasury Alexander Hamilton, Secretary of State Thomas Jefferson, Secretary of War Henry Knox, and Attorney General Edmund Randolph, as well as Supreme Court Chief Justice John Jay and the associate justices of the Court. Congress also had to wrestle with fundamental but unprecedented questions such as whether, after a presidential appointment was confirmed, the president could terminate that officer on his own authority or whether he needed Senate consent. This was no small matter. As anyone who has held any job realizes, employees work to please the person who can fire them. (Congress decided the power of removal was the president's alone, a highly consequential decision that established presidential control over executive departments). The federalists believed their constituents would judge them on how well they stood up to the new government. With so many things that had to be done, they did not feel they had time for something that could—and even prudently should—be deferred, especially something as complex as drafting a bill of rights.

Ironically, antifederalists were not interested in taking up a bill of rights either. Their previous laments about the Constitution being defective because it lacked a bill of rights were now revealed to have been primarily a rationale against ratifying the Constitution rather than a genuine concern. They did not admit that, of course. They argued that a bill of rights should be written—but by a second constitutional convention, not Congress. Their principal objective was not a bill of rights; they wanted to make structural changes that would paralyze the national government. Number one on their wish list was removing Congress's power to levy taxes. They also wanted to hamstring Congress's ability to ratify treaties and regulate commerce by requiring unrealistically large supermajorities for those matters.[9] There was no chance Congress, controlled by federalists, would propose such amendments—something Patrick Henry was painfully aware of.[10] A second convention was extremely unlikely, however. The antifederalists were now extremely weak, as reflected by the composition of Congress. Even Virginia voters sent seven federalists and only one antifederalist to the House of Representatives.[11]

On May 4, 1789, only four days after Washington's inaugural address, Madison rose on the House floor and announced that he would introduce a bill of rights three weeks hence.[12] Meanwhile, Patrick Henry was renewing his effort to unravel the Constitution. On the day after Madison promised to introduce a bill of rights, Theodorick Bland, another congressman from Virginia and an antifederalist, presented to the United States House of Representatives a resolution from the Virginia House of Delegates calling for a second constitutional convention.[13] And on the day after that, Congressman John Laurance presented a similar resolution from New York. The petitions did not rattle the federalists unduly. At the time, there were eleven states. (North Carolina and Rhode Island still remained outside the Union, and Vermont was not even yet recognized as a state. Thus, eight states had to call for a new convention, and even if North Carolina were to ratify—which was expected in the not-too-distant future—the number of states needed to ratify would remain eight.) Although Virginia and New York were important states, they were political outliers. Patrick Henry effectively controlled the Virginia legislature, and the antifederalist governor of New York, William Clinton, exercised enormous power in that state. Few expected many more petitions for a second convention. Still, who could be sure?

And so, the two petitions presented Madison with both a small problem and an unintended gift. The problem was one of etiquette. As a Virginia representative, he had to express respect for anything coming from the Virginia House of Delegates. The unintended gift was that the applications strengthened Madison's argument that Congress needed to propose a bill of rights to promote national harmony and avoid a second constitutional convention. In brief remarks, therefore, Madison began by saying the applications merited great respect. He quickly followed that by observing that Congress had no constitutional authority to call a constitutional convention except upon application by two-thirds of the states. Congress had no choice, therefore, but to simply lay the two applications on the desk until such time as the requisite number of applications arrived. He then reminded everyone he would soon propose amendments. He hoped that the applications from Virginia and New York, lying figuratively on the House's desk, would provide incentive to take up a bill of rights.

Madison's desire to put a bill of rights on the agenda experienced further resistance and delay, but on June 8, 1789, he rose on the floor of the House to propose a bill of rights and deliver a speech supporting them. Madison told his colleagues that he considered himself "bound in honor and duty" to propose a bill of rights—he was referring, of course, to the promise he made to his constituents during his election campaign against James Monroe—and moved that the House "resolve itself into a committee of the whole" to consider them.[14] That proposal ran into an immediate buzz saw of opposition. Some members argued that going into a committee of the whole would impede more urgent House business. They were willing to consider a bill of rights, but not then and there. Others, including the highly influential Roger Sherman of Connecticut, argued that it was premature to consider amending the Constitution, no matter what the process. "The Constitution may be compared to a ship that has never yet put to sea," said James Jackson of Georgia.[15] Nothing had been tested: not the sails, not the keel, not the helm. "Upon experiment she may prove faultless, or her defects may be very obvious—but the present is not the time for alterations," Jackson argued. Others echoed those sentiments.

Madison quickly put aside the question of process and delivered a speech on the substance of his proposal—laying out in full his proposed amendments and arguing why Congress should endorse them. Madison would give more than 150 speeches to the first session of Congress; this was one of his most consequential.[16] He had persuaded reluctant colleagues that adopting a bill of rights was both necessary and wise.

Madison began by apologizing to the House for diverting it from the many tasks necessary to establish a new government, and by acknowledging that he had made a political commitment to propose a bill of rights. This was an opportunity for those who supported the Constitution to prove "that they were as sincerely devoted to liberty and a republican government, as those who charged them with wishing the adoption of this Constitution in order to lay the foundation for aristocracy or despotism," said Madison.[17] He noted that although the Constitution had been ratified by eleven of the thirteen states—"in some cases unanimously, in others by large majorities"—there were still "a great number of our constituents who are dissatisfied with it." Congress should "on principles of amity and moderation, conform to their wishes, and expressly declare the great rights of mankind secured under this Constitution," he said. Madison added that adopting a bill of rights might persuade North Carolina and Rhode Island to ratify the Constitution and join the Union. He suggested that "if all power is subject to abuse," it was possible, by proceeding with caution and moderation, to guard further against abuses and have something to gain and nothing to lose.[18] "I will not propose a single alteration which I do not wish to see take place, as intrinsically proper itself, or proper because it is wished for by a respectable number of people," Madison promised.

The first group of amendments Madison would propose "may be called a bill of rights," said Madison, adding: "I will own that I never considered this provision so essential to the federal Constitution" that it should have prevented ratification; but now that the Constitution had been ratified "such a provision was neither improper nor altogether useless."[19] One can't help but smile at that statement. Madison had not been able to fully accommodate himself to his political flip—first opposing a bill of rights, then changing his position during an election—and here his discomfort produces a strikingly lukewarm endorsement for his own proposal. But his colleagues probably saw this as a reflection of Madison's straightforwardness. Even if I had not been an early and fervent advocate of a bill of rights, Madison went on to say, he realized that "a great number of the most respectable friends to the government and champions for republican liberty" did favor it. Madison drew a distinction between the kind of bill of rights he was about to propose and the English Declaration of Rights of 1689—a document the Founders knew well and revered. (The next chapter will take up the English Declaration of Rights and explain the distinction Madison took care to point out.)

Madison got to the meat of his proposal. He began with what he termed "the great rights," which he defined as trial by jury, freedom of the press, and liberty of conscience.[20] What about "the perfect equality of mankind"?[21] (Here Madison may have been taking a bit of a swipe at the Constitution of Massachusetts, drafted by John Adams, which began: "All men are born free and equal, and have certain natural, essential, and unalienable rights.") A representative of a slave state might be expected to tread carefully here; and Madison did tread carefully. "[T]his to be sure is an absolute truth, yet it is not absolutely necessary to be inserted at the head of a constitution," Madison remarked. The United States Constitution would not mention equality or guarantee equal protection of the laws for nearly a century. Trial by jury was not a natural right, observed Madison; it arose from the social contract "but is as essential to secure the liberty of the people as any one of the preexistent rights of nature."

For a while, Madison waxed philosophical. In guarding against abuses of power, it was important to recognize where the greatest power resided. The legislature was the most powerful branch of government, but in a government such as the United States the greatest danger flowed not from the legislature but "in the body of the people, operating by the majority against the minority." Would a paper barrier be sufficient to restrain abuses by the majority? A bill of rights, argued Madison, might help protect rights by forming public opinion in their favor.

Are rights adequately protected by state constitutions? No, suggested Madison, because "some states have no bills of rights" and others have "very defective ones."[22] Madison said he wanted an amendment prohibiting states from passing bills of attainder or ex post facto laws (which the Constitution already prohibited Congress from enacting). And Madison argued that it was important that the federal Constitution provide "that no state shall violate equal right of conscience, freedom of the press, or trial by jury in criminal cases."[23] Even though some state constitutions protected these particular rights, "I cannot see any reason against obtaining even a double security on these points," he said.

Madison also included in his speech two structural amendments he was proposing.[24] He wanted to provide both a floor and a ceiling for the total number of representatives, so that as the nation's population increased, the House of Representatives would not grow to an unwieldly size, and he wanted to prohibit any salary increase for members of Congress from taking effect before the next congressional election. He also wanted to establish that no appeal could be taken from a federal court to the United States Supreme Court unless a certain sum were in dispute, so that litigants were not unfairly required to travel great distances.[25] And he wanted to provide that powers not granted by the Constitution were reserved to the states.

Madison made no mention of a right to bear arms in his speech. We should not make too much of that omission. After all, Madison did not mention many other rights he included in his proposal, including freedom of speech and assembly, and the right of not being deprived of life, liberty, and property without due process of all, to mention just a few. Madison also distributed his proposals in writing at the same time, so members could see everything he proposed. Still, one assumes Madison included in his speech the provisions he thought would draw the greatest attention and support from his colleagues—the headliners, so to speak. There is little doubt that freedom of conscience, freedom of the press, and the right to jury trials in criminal cases were headliners. They were also the rights Madison personally considered important. Madison must have also thought that the two structural amendments he proposed—setting a ceiling and floor on the number of representatives, and prohibiting Congress from giving itself a raise during the current term—would be popular with his colleagues. Representatives might have liked the first because it would provide some stability in their congressional districts. The provision about salary increases would be politically useful to members of Congress. Even the dullest politicians know that political opponents will bludgeon them for voting to raise their own salaries. This amendment would provide some political cover: they would not be voting to raise their own salaries; they would be voting to raise the salaries of a future Congress.

Why was not the right to bear arms a headliner? If my thesis is correct, the answer is obvious: Representatives would have understood Madison's right-to-bear-arms provision as a supplement to the slavery compromise in the Constitution—the tacit compact that included the provisions that counted a slave as three-fifths of a person for purposes of congressional apportionment and taxation, the fugitive slave provision, and the provision prohibiting Congress from ending the slave trade until 1808. About such a provision, the less said the better.

Here is the right-to-bear-arms proposal as it appeared in Madison's original proposal on June 8, 1789:

> The right of the people to keep and bear arms shall not be infringed; a well armed, and well regulated militia being the best security of a free country: but no person religiously scrupulous of bearing arms, shall be compelled to render military service in person.[26]

There is, at this point, probably nothing that seems earth-shaking about Madison's original proposal. If anything, one may be struck by how closely it resembles Congress's final product. Still, a few observations are in order. Madison did not copy verbatim the right-to-bear-arms provision from any prior document—not from the English Declaration of Rights of 1689 (which is the subject of the next chapter), not from any of the four state constitutions that had right-to-bear-arms provisions (which were discussed in the last chapter), and not from proposed amendments submitted by any of the state ratifying conventions, including Virginia's (which was discussed in Chapter 3). Madison's provision more closely resembles the proposal submitted by the Richmond Ratifying Convention than any other right-to-bear-arms provision, as one might expect.

It makes sense, therefore, to focus on how Madison's proposal differs from Virginia's because we can assume that Madison had reasons for making changes. First, Madison eliminated the section stating "[t]hat standing armies in time of peace are dangerous to liberty, and therefore ought to be avoided, as far as circumstances and the protection of the Community will admit."[27] As you will recall from Chapter 2, the question of whether the Constitution should prohibit standing armies, or limit Congress's discretion to create them, was debated at the Philadelphia Convention. The issue was settled when a delegate proposed limiting standing armies to three thousand men, and George Washington whispered that the Constitution ought to limit invading armies to three thousand, too. The Philadelphia Convention decided that Congress should decide, as a policy matter, to what extent to rely on a standing army or militia for national defense. Madison, obviously, was not in favor of reversing that decision. Second, Madison changed "defence of a free State" to "security of a free country." Probably Madison, the careful technician, preferred "country" because this provision would apply to the national government only, not the states. What is most significant for our purposes is Madison's choice of the word *security* rather than *defence*. That makes sense when one considers that Madison is focusing not on defending the nation from external threats but providing security from internal disturbances, especially slave revolts.

Madison also did not include the separate provision in the Virginia recommendations that stated: "That each State respectively shall have the power to provide for organizing, arming, and disciplining it's [sic] own Militia, whensoever Congress shall omit or neglect to provide for the same."[28] Madison did not want to solve his problem that way because he had vowed not to propose an amendment that would change anything in the original Constitution.[29] Virginia's provision would have effectively changed the Constitution. Besides, if adopted, it could have led to future disputes over whether Congress was neglecting the militia. Madison proposed solving the problem raised at Richmond—that is, ensuring that states could have armed militia to provide for their own security—not by giving the states a concurrent power to arm the militia, but by giving it to the people.

Legal historian Noah Feldman makes the point slightly differently. He says Madison's "language left little doubt that the right to bear arms meant neither more nor less than the right to serve in a well-regulated militia. The protection afforded to conscientious objectors at the end of the sentence further underscored the purpose of the amendment."[30] While our formulations are slightly different, as a practical matter they would have led to the same result in eighteenth-century America: Congress could not have prohibited militiamen from supplying their own muskets. Yet I believe my interpretation fits Madison's intention more closely. Here's why: Feldman interprets the language as guaranteeing a right to serve in the militia. But if, for example, Congress enacted a statute enrolling men between the ages of *eighteen* and forty-five in the militia, and Virginia had previously enrolled men starting at age *sixteen*, I doubt Madison would have thought the amendment gave a seventeen-year-old a basis for complaining about being excluded from the militia. By contrast, Madison surely intended his amendment to allow a state to complain if Congress decided militia were not to be armed.

Can one argue that Madison intended the clause "[t]he right of the people to keep and bear arms shall not be infringed" to give the people a right to keep and bear arms outside of and unrelated to service in the militia? Yes, but one can only make that argument by contending that the amendment has three separate and unrelated parts—effectively restyling it as follows:

The right of the people to keep and bear arms shall not be infringed.
A well-armed and well-regulated militia is the best security of a free country.
No person religiously scrupulous of bearing arms shall be compelled to render military service in person.

That restyled provision, however, is not what Madison wrote. He placed all three clauses in one sentence. Why did do that? The most obvious answer is that he was writing a single provision with three interrelated parts, not three separate provisions. As we shall shortly see, Congress reworked Madison's language to make that even more obvious.

The House continued to argue over whether and how to consider Madison's proposal. When his motion to consider a bill of rights in a committee of the whole ran into trouble, Madison withdrew it and moved instead to refer the matter to a select committee.[31] But that, too, turned out to be controversial. By day's end, Madison had withdrawn that motion as well, and simply moved that the House approve his proposed amendments.[32] The procedure to be followed was left up in the air. Only July 21, the House returned to this matter and spent the entire day debating procedure. A frustrated James Madison began the day by once again asking the House to consider his amendments in a committee of the whole. At the end of the day, however, the House decided by a vote of thirty-four to fifteen to refer Madison's proposal to a select committee composed of one member from each state.[33]

The select committee was, therefore, composed of eleven members. Madison was appointed to represent Virginia. The most prominent other member was Roger Sherman of Connecticut. Sherman was a man of contrasts. He was universally considered strikingly ugly, and he moved awkwardly. He came from a modest family, dressed plainly, and lacked both a formal education and eloquence. He was, nevertheless, a figure of stature, both physically, standing six feet tall, and in terms of intellect, judgment, and industriousness. He started out as a shoemaker, yet studied law and gained admission to the bar at thirty-three.[34] He served in the First and Second Continental Congresses, was a member of the Committee of Five charged with drafting the Declaration of Independence (along with Thomas Jefferson, John Adams, Benjamin Franklin, and Robert Livingston), was later appointed to the drafting committee for the Articles of Confederation, and became a member of the Confederation Congress. He was also one of the most influential delegates to the Constitutional Convention. He addressed the Philadelphia Convention more than any other member, save only James Madison and Gouverneur Morris of Pennsylvania, but Sherman's remarks were generally succinct and to the point.

Sherman had a reputation for common sense, and he was first and foremost a pragmatist. In Philadelphia, he originally favored a unicameral legislature, but he became a prime mover behind the compromise between large and small states that produced a Senate with equal representation among the states and a House with proportional representation. He was offended by classifying slaves as property and taxing them as such; but he publicly supported the slave compact in the Constitution because the South had made it a sine qua non to joining the Union, and also because he believed that "the abolition of slavery seemed to be going on in the U.S. and that the good sense of the several states would probably by degrees complete it."[35] (Although the Constitution never used the words *slave* or *slavery*, it nonetheless included a carefully negotiated compact consisting of provisions requiring that slaves who escape across state lines be returned to their owners, prohibiting Congress from abolishing the African slave trade until 1808 or imposing an import tax of more than ten dollars per slave, and counting slaves as three-fifths of free persons for the purposes of apportioning congressional representation or direct taxation.)

Moreover—and this is particularly relevant for our purposes—in Philadelphia Sherman wanted to supplement the slave compact by providing "that no State shall without its consent be affected in its internal police."[36] Sherman said that twice during debate, and he expressly related his proposal to the slavery system.[37] In other words, Sherman wanted the Constitution to guarantee that states had the authority to police their slaves as they deemed necessary, without interference from the national government. And he even wanted to shield that guarantee from any future decision by three-fourths of the states to eliminate it by amending the Constitution. Sherman's interest was not in preserving the slave system. He believed that over time the slave system would end on its own. His interest was in forming—and later preserving—the Union, which he believed required not allowing the potentially explosive issue to divide North and South.

We do not know anything about the discussions within the select committee of the House because it kept no record of its deliberations.[38] On July 28, only one week after it was formed, the select committee reported its recommendations. Here is how it reworked Madison's right-to-bear-arms provision:

> A well regulated militia, composed of the body of the people, being the best security of a free State, the right of the people to keep and bear arms shall not be infringed, but no person religiously scrupulous shall be compelled to bear arms.[39]

The select committee changed Madison's draft in several ways. The sentence now begins by announcing that it is about the militia. Madison's semicolon and colon have been replaced by commas, more clearly signaling pauses rather than separations. And "country" has been replaced by "State," more accurately reflecting that the provision is concerned with state rather than national security. That was a better fit because the concern was not that Congress would neglect the security of the country; it was that Congress might deprive states of armed militia. In view of Roger Sherman's statements at the Constitutional Convention, we know he was sympathetic to a constitutional guarantee that the national government would not interfere with a state's slave control machinery. Indeed, in Philadelphia Sherman had suggested something even stronger: a constitutional guarantee that would have been immune from future amendments agreed to by three-fourths of the states.

We can, therefore, be confident that had Madison told Sherman about the Richmond debate and said he needed an amendment to assure his constituents that Congress could not undermine the slave system by disarming the militia, Sherman would have been supportive. And other members of the House would have been supportive, too, had Madison privately confided in them. As historian William W. Freehling says, "Almost all of the Founding Fathers believed that nothing done about slavery should jeopardize the Union."[40] We shall never know whether such conversations took place. But in all likelihood, neither Roger Sherman nor other members of Congress would have needed James Madison to personally explain his political difficulty or objectives. They were, after all, politicians. Like politicians of any age, they paid a great deal of attention to grapevine news of political drama and intrigue. They were well-versed in the political arts and skilled at inferring the motives of other political actors. And in their sphere, all eyes were constantly on Virginia—the largest state, and home to so many prominent politicians. Four of the first five presidents of the United States were Virginians, which reflects how central that state's politics was to national politics. Did members of Congress know about key events at the Richmond Ratifying Convention and Patrick Henry's efforts to end Madison's political career? Of course they did. In fact, we know they did. One member of the First Congress, Senator Robert Morris of Pennsylvania, said at the time, "Poor Madison got so cursedly frightened in Virginia that I believe he has dreamed of amendments ever since."[41] Another, Congressman Theodore Sedgwick of Massachusetts, said Madison was "constantly haunted by the ghost of Patrick Henry."[42]

On August 13, 1789, the House began eleven days of debate over the amendments proposed by the select committee.[43] One might think that at this stage the House had decided to consider constitutional amendments, but that was, in fact, still a matter of energetic controversy. The debates began with the question of whether the House ought to discuss amendments at all, and the question continued to arise again and again, throughout most of the eleven days of debate.

Another topic that consumed a great deal of time was the issue of whether the amendments should be placed into the main body of the Constitution next to the existing provisions to which they were germane, or whether they should all be added as a supplement at the end. James Madison and Roger Sherman were on opposite sides of this issue. Madison favored incorporating amendments into the original text. "[I]t appears to me that there is a neatness and propriety in incorporating the amendments into the Constitution itself," he argued.[44] "[I]t will certainly be more simple when the amendments are interwoven into those parts to which they naturally belong [and] we shall then be able to determine its meaning without references or comparison." Sherman argued that the amendments should be added to the Constitution "by way of supplement."[45] "We ought not to interweave our propositions into the work itself because it will be destructive of the whole fabric," he argued.[46] "Besides this, sir," Sherman continued, "it is questionable whether we have the right to propose amendments in this way. The Constitution is the act of the people, and ought to remain entire." Representative James Jackson of Georgia also argued that "the original Constitution ought to remain inviolate, and not be patched up from time to time, with various stuffs resembling Joseph's coat of many colors."[47] Several times it appeared that Madison had won this debate; but obviously he did not, as the issue repeatedly came back up. Finally, Roger Sherman made a motion to add the amendments at the end, which passed with a two-thirds majority.[48] By that time, the matter must have been resolved through private discussions as the vote was taken without discussion or debate. Ironically, James Madison is known to history as the father of the Bill of the Rights—and appropriately so, since he was its prime architect and advocate—yet that would have not have come to pass if Madison had prevailed because the amendments would not have comprised a unified bill of rights.

One of the substantive provisions debated at greatest length ultimately became the first amendment proposed by Congress—a provision never ratified by the states. It related to the size of the House of Representatives. Some members argued that a representative could not effectively represent too many people; others believed that to be an effective deliberative body, the House had to fall within certain parameters of size. The House finally adopted an amendment that would have required that the House of Representatives never have "less than one representative for every fifty thousand persons."[49] Under that formulation, the House of Representatives today would have about 6,600 members.

The House also spent considerable time debating whether the people should be given a right "to instruct their representatives."[50] That provision was not proposed by the select committee, but offered by Representative St. George Tucker of Virginia. There was considerable discussion about how the people might instruct their representatives and whether representatives would be bound to vote in accordance with those instructions. "It appears to me that the words are calculated to mislead the people by conveying the idea that they have a right to control the debates of the legislature," argued Roger Sherman.[51] This "would destroy the object of their meeting. I think, when the people have chosen a representative, it is his duty to meet others from different parts of the union, and consult, and agree with them to such acts as are for the general benefit of the whole community; if they were guided by instructions, there would be no use in deliberations." On this, Sherman and Madison were on the same side. "I do not believe the inhabitants of any district can speak the voice of the people, so far from it, their ideas may contradict the sense of the whole people."[52]

The debates had otherwise been civil, but during debate on the right to instruct issue, tempers boiled over. The proposal had a small number of vociferous advocates, who were mostly antifederalists.[53] One was Elbridge Gerry of Massachusetts—one of the three delegates to the Constitutional Convention in Philadelphia who had refused to sign the Constitution (and who also has the dubious distinction of having the word *gerrymander* named after him). After the fifth time Gerry had risen to speak on this subject—twice at considerable length on a single day—John Vining, a federalist from Delaware, could not contain himself any longer. "Is it not inconsistent in that honorable member to complain of hurry when he comes day after day reiterating the same train of arguments, and demanding the attention of this body by rising six or seven times on a question?" demanded Vining.[54] That emptied the benches. Gerry rose again, sarcastically stating that he intended to follow the "example of moderation and laconic and consistent debate" set by Vining.[55] Thomas Sumter of South Carolina (known as "the Gamecock" when he commanded the South Carolina militia) said members who opposed the motion on the floor were not treating it fairly.[56] Then Aedanus Burke went after the antifederalists' principal nemesis, James Madison. And he did so in a way that, in relation to the manners and etiquette of the time, amounted to hitting below the belt. As Madison was surely aware, many of his colleagues—both federalists and antifederalists—had been whispering that Madison was pushing a bill of rights as a "tub to the whale."[57] The phrase, made famous by *Tale of the Tub* by Jonathan Swift, referred to the supposed practice of diverting a whale that was threatening to ram a sailing ship by flinging onto the ocean "an empty tub by way of amusement." This was a snide way of saying that Madison was proposing a bill of rights consisting of uncontroversial, even banal, provisions to distract antifederalists from their goal of weakening the national government through structural amendments. Such comments "out of doors" was one thing; stating it on the floor of the House was quite another. It brought an irate James Madison to his feet, complaining that Burke had insinuated that he, as well as the select committee, was "not acting with candor."[58]

For people of this class in eighteenth-century America, accusing someone of lacking candor was a serious matter. It could even provoke a duel. While there was no such danger in this case—James Madison was a far different person than, say, Aaron Burr—the chamber must have fallen deathly still. Burke quickly deescalated by saying he had not intended to accuse Madison of a lack of candor. Still, he stood his ground. He said the select committee omitted "all the important amendments" required by a number of states, and he proceeded to list states that had right-to-instruct provisions.[59] When Burke sat down, William Loughton Smith of South Carolina, a federalist, rose to say that Burke was wrong in stating that South Carolina had a right-to-instruct provision in its constitution; it did not. With that, the House voted down the motion to include such a provision in its proposed amendments by a vote of 41 to 10.[60]

The House also spent some time debating whether to amend the preamble to the Constitution by inserting at the beginning of the Constitution, before the phrase "We the people," this language: "Government being intended for the benefit of the people, and the rightful establishment thereof being derived from their authority

alone." Although the House approved adding that language to the preamble by a vote of 27 to 33, the proposed addition did not survive
the Senate.[61] Antifederalists pressed—to no avail—for an amendment
to remove Congress's power of direct taxation.[62] And Elbridge Gerry
kept trying the House's patience with hopelessly unpopular proposals
and bizarre conspiracy theories. He wanted a civil magistrate to decide whether troops could be quartered in a home—a modification he
argued was "essential"—and lost 35 to 13.[63] In support of a motion by a
fellow antifederalist to prohibit Congress from interfering in the time,
place, and manner of elections, Gerry raised the specter of Congress
abolishing secret ballots and requiring voters to announce their votes
publicly.[64] Gerry so insistently pressed a motion that the House consider all amendments proposed by state ratifying conventions—a proposal that everyone knew was dead on arrival in the federalist-controlled
Congress, and that was even arguably out-of-order while the House was
still considering the special committee's recommendations—that *The
Daily Advertiser*, which generally attempted to objectively record the
proceedings, wrote: "Mr. Gerry still persisting in his motion."[65] When
Gerry prevailed on the procedural dispute, thus forcing the House to
debate his doomed motion, he exasperated colleagues by beginning
debate with "a lengthy speech" and ending it with a demand for a
rollcall vote, even though a voice vote would have been indisputably
sufficient.[66]

It was, perhaps predictably, Elbridge Gerry who objected to the
right-to-bear-arms provision recommended by the select committee.
He said, in full:

> This declaration of rights, I take it, is intended to secure the people
> against the maladministration of the government; if we could sup-
> pose that in all cases the rights of the people would be attended to,
> the occasion for guards of this kind would be removed. Now I am
> apprehensive, sir, that this clause would give an opportunity to the
> people in power to destroy the Constitution itself. They can declare
> who are those religiously scrupulous, and prevent them from bearing
> arms. What, sir, is the use of the militia? It is to prevent the establish-
> ment of a standing army, the bane of liberty.

Now it must be evident that under this provision, together with their other powers, Congress could take such measures with respect to the militia as to make a standing army necessary. Whenever government meant to invade the rights and liberties of the people, they always attempt to destroy the militia in order to raise an army upon their ruins. This was actually done by Great Britain at the commencement of the late revolution. They used every means in their power to prevent the establishment of an effective militia to the eastward. [When he says "to the eastward," Gerry refers to what we today call the Northern states.] The assembly of Massachusetts, seeing the rapid progress that administration were making to divest them of their inherent privileges, endeavored to counteract them by the organization of the militia, but they were always defeated by the influence of the Crown.[67]

When Gerry sat down, Joshua Seney of Maryland asked what the question on the floor was, "in order to ascertain the point upon which the gentleman was speaking?"[68] Gerry said that "he meant to make a motion" to alter the language "so as to be confined to persons belonging to a religious set, scrupulous of bearing arms."[69] But Gerry had neither actually made a motion nor stated how he wanted the provision rewritten, and thus had failed to put anything on the floor.

James Jackson said that he "[d]id not expect that all the people of the United States would turn Quakers or Moravians," and it would be unjust that "one part would have to defend the other in case of invasion." He moved to amend the clause by adding the italicized language "no one religiously scrupulous of bearing arms shall be compelled to render military service in person, *upon paying the equivalent to be established by law.*"[70] No one seconded Jackson's motion.

William Smith said he would consider seconding Jackson's motion if Jackson could confirm what language was used by Virginia and Carolina. Jackson said he thought it was "No one, religiously scrupulous of bearing arms, shall be compelled to render military service in person, upon paying an equivalent."[71]

Roger Sherman said he thought "it difficult to modify the clause and make it better."[72] He said people who were scrupulous of bearing arms were equally scrupulous of getting substitutes, and he thought a clause of this kind was unnecessary. He said it would be unwise to exclude a whole sect because some Quakers will turn out notwithstanding the religious principles of the Society of Friends. "We do not live under an arbitrary government . . . and the states respectively will have the government of the militia, unless when called into actual service," Sherman added.

John Vining said the clause should stand as written because compelling a man to find a substitute "was the same as if the person himself turned out to fight."[73]

Michael Jenifer Stone of Maryland asked whether "religiously scrupulous" referred to "bearing arms," and said that, if so, that "ought to be expressed."[74]

Egbert Benson, a federalist from New York, moved to have the words "but no person religiously scrupulous shall be compelled to bear arms" struck out from the proposed amendment.[75] He said that being excused from bearing arms was not a natural right "and therefore ought to be left to the discretion of the government." He said that if the clause remained, the judiciary would wind up getting involved "on every regulation you make with respect to the militia." He added that he had no reason to believe the legislature would not be sufficiently humane. His motion was seconded, but it was defeated on a vote of 24 to 22.

Elbridge Gerry rose again and moved that the words "trained in arms" be inserted in the provision as follows: "A well-regulated militia, *trained in arms*, being the best security of a free state. . . ."[76] No one seconded Gerry's motion.

Aedanus Burke then moved to add the following language to the amendment: "A standing army of regular troops in time of peace, is dangerous to public liberty, and such shall not be raised or kept up in time of peace but from necessity, and for the security of the people, nor then without the consent of two-thirds of the members present of both houses, and in all cases the military shall be subordinate to the civil authority."[77] Vining asked whether this should be added to the clause just discussed or stand as a separate amendment. Burke said he feared attempting to add a separate amendment would be "trammeled in rules." Bowing to the inevitable—and unlike Gerry, not consuming undue time in a hopeless endeavor—Burke confessed he made the motion "because he could not help himself."[78] Thomas Hartley, a federalist from Pennsylvania, said that while he thought Burke's motion was in order, he "would always be satisfied with having a majority to govern" and thought that requiring supermajorities of two-thirds (which is what Burke's proposal would have required to raise a standing army) or three-fourths "might put it in the power of a small minority to govern the whole union."[79] Burke's motion was then defeated by a vote of approximately 30 to 17.[80]

With that, the select committee's original proposal was approved by the House.

What are we to make of this discussion? First and foremost, the discussion reflects that the House—or at a minimum, everyone who spoke—considered the amendment to be about military matters. The entire discussion was about whether people we today would call conscientious objectors should be exempt from a draft, and about whether congressional supermajorities should be required to raise a standing army. It is difficult to believe these men thought the amendment was about giving individuals a right to own weapons for their own purposes, unrelated to militia service. Second, the House devoted very little time to this provision. I have described every statement made by every member. While I abbreviated some of them a bit, I preserved the substance of every comment. The unabbreviated record of the discussions takes up just a little over three pages. Third, the House was not only opposed to requiring congressional supermajorities for Congress to raise a standing army but overwhelmingly so. Finally, Madison said nothing during the discussion. He was likely present because he spoke on another topic very shortly after this discussion.[81] His silence on Benson's motion to strike the exemption for conscientious objectors is curious. Madison included the exemption in his original proposal and considered the right of conscience to be of transcendent importance. If he had a good sense of the room, Madison would have realized the outcome of the issue was not preordained. As it turned out, the vote on Benson's motion was very close.

The best guess is that Madison feared that his speaking on the issue might be counterproductive. It appears that sometime during the day Madison read an article in *The New York Daily Advertiser* styled as an open letter to James Madison.[82] The author, identified in print as "Pacificus," was Noah Webster. The piece blisteringly accused

Madison of hypocrisy in "espousing the cause of amendments with so much earnestness?"[83] Webster noted that Madison said he proposed amendments because he pledged to his constituents that he would do so. "But, Sir, who are your *constituents?* Are they electors of a small district in Virginia?" Webster asked. And yet, Webster said, Madison had also declared himself "an enemy to local attachments" and said he considered himself "not merely the representative of *Virginia*, but of the *United States*."[84] The people of your district gave you a place in the federal legislature, but when you took your seat you became a representative of millions of Americans, Webster argued. "We see, in the debates, it is frequently asserted that some amendments will satisfy the opposition and give stability to the government. The people, Sir, in the northern and middle states do not believe a word of this," Webster wrote.[85] Rather, they believe that you have thrown out "an empty tub to catch people, either fractious or uninformed," causing Congress to waste time on amendments that would little affect the Constitution but "may sow the seeds of discord from New Hampshire to Georgia."[86] With this piece circulating throughout the halls of Congress that very day, Madison may have thought it imprudent to rise in defense of a provision he wrote to reassure his constituents that Congress would not interfere with slave control.

The House passed its resolution proposing constitutional amendments on August 24. Although the House had rejected all changes to the select committee's right-to-bear-arms provision, the version passed by the House differed from the select committee's version in a few minor, almost imperceptible ways. Whether that was because someone thought it proper to make tiny, nonsubstantive changes for housekeeping purposes before the final vote in the House, or whether a scribe made the changes inadvertently, we cannot know. They matter little. Nevertheless, for accuracy's sake, here is the provision passed by the House.

> A well regulated militia, composed of the body of the People, being the best security of a free State, the right of the People to keep and bear arms, shall not be infringed, but no one religiously scrupulous of bearing arms, shall be compelled to render military service in person.[87]

We know next to nothing about the Senate debates because that chamber did not open its sessions to the public and did not record its deliberations.[88] Senator William Maclay of Pennsylvania kept a personal journal, which historians often use to glean some knowledge about Senate discussions. Maclay's diary entry for August 25, 1789, tells us that the amendments proposed by the House resolution reached the Senate, where they "were treated contemptuously" by Senators Ralph Izard of South Carolina, John Langdon of New Hampshire, and Robert Morris of Pennsylvania, all federalists, who moved that the Senate postpone taking them until its next session.[89] That motion lost, and the Senate agreed to take them up on the following Monday. However, Maclay fell ill before that date and did not attend Senate proceedings during its debate on the Bill of Rights.[90] Here is all we know:

On September 4, on a vote of nine to six, the Senate defeated a motion, similar to one offered by Aedanus Burke in the House, requiring a two-thirds supermajority in both houses of Congress to raise a standing army or regular troops in peacetime, or enlisting soldiers for longer than the continuance of a war.[91]

On September 9, the Senate tentatively adopted a revised provision, which read as follows: "A well regulated militia, being the best security of a free state, the right of the people to keep and bear arms, shall not be infringed."[92]

Later on September 9, the Senate replaced "the best" with "necessary."

On the same day, the Senate also rejected a motion to insert "for the common defence" after "bear arms."

Two observations are in order. The Senate's decision to retain "security" rather than "defence" reflects that Senators considered the militia to be necessary for internal security rather than for defense from invasion. And by replacing "best" with "necessary to the," the Senate was careful not to imply that the militia were better than a professional force.

The House made no further changes. Except for the words "Militia" and "Arms" becoming capitalized when a conference committee resolved differences between the two chambers in the twelve amendments under consideration, the Senate's language became the right-to-bear-arms provision that Congress officially adopted and proposed to the states on September 25, 1789.

During the time that states were considering the proposed amendments, North Carolina, Rhode Island, and Vermont joined the Union. With fourteen states, ten were required to ratify. Maryland, North Carolina, South Carolina, Rhode Island, New York, and Vermont approved all twelve proposed amendments. Delaware approved all except the first proposed amendment (relating to congressional compensation) while New Hampshire, New Jersey, and Pennsylvania approved all except the second (relating to the size of the House of Representatives). Both houses of the Massachusetts legislature approved amendments three through eleven, but the state failed to so formally notify the president, and Secretary of State Thomas Jefferson therefore did not count Massachusetts as having ratified any of the amendments.[93] Georgia refused to ratify because it considered a bill of rights unnecessary. Connecticut failed to ratify because its House and Senate split over whether to ratify the first two amendments, creating a logjam that blocked ratification of even the amendments on which they did agree.

And so, once again, it eventually would all seem to come down to Virginia. Patrick Henry was still a member of the Virginia House of Delegates when, on October 19, 1789, debate on the amendments began. Henry was determined to have the legislature reject ratification. His first move was to submit a resolution commending Virginia's two United States Senators for trying to have Congress approve all of the constitutional amendments recommended by Virginia. His tactic was to begin with easy vote. Virginia had proposed amendments, its Senators had worked to have Congress approve them, and what Virginia politician would be bold enough to vote against praising them for their efforts? But voting for the resolution would be a first step toward opposing ratification. Senators Richard Henry Lee and William Grayson had sent letters to the governor and the Speaker of the House stating that the amendments adopted by Congress fell "far short" of Virginia's recommendations and would not stop a "tendency to consolidated empire."[94] So voting to praise them might make it more difficult to later disagree with them.

It was a clever ploy; yet it failed. Henry and antifederalists were still firmly in control of the state Senate, but spring elections had considerably improved federalist representation in the House. When Henry tried to count votes, he discovered his resolution was in deep trouble in that chamber. He reversed course and moved to delay debate on his own resolution pending the next election. Henry now argued that members had been elected before Congress proposed amendments, and the voters should have the chance to select members based on how they stood on the amendments. But Henry's sudden reversal smelled like desperation, and his motion to postpone lost by an overwhelming margin.[95] Henry's next move stunned everyone: he packed up, left Richmond, and went home.[96] Three weeks later, the House deadlocked 62 to 62 on a motion to demand that Congress consider all of the amendments the state had proposed. The Speaker of the House broke the tie by voting no. The House then voted 64 to 58 to approve all twelve amendments, but the Senate objected to four of the amendments, and progress stalled.

That is how things stood at the end of 1789. But Patrick Henry's power was broken. In the spring, he declined to stand for reelection. His political career was over.

It was two full years before Virginia again took up the amendments. Meanwhile, antifederalist sentiment continued to subside. George Washington was president; the national government seemed sound and sober. Antifederalists sounded as if they were hyperventilating if they bellowed about federal tyranny. When, on December 15, 1791, majorities in both houses of its legislature voted to approve all twelve of the proposed amendments, Virginia became the tenth state to officially ratify the ten amendments that comprise our Bill of Rights.[97] (There is no time limit on ratification. When, in 1992, a total of thirty-eight of fifty states had ratified it, the First Congress's proposal regarding congressional salaries became the Twenty-Seventh Amendment to the United States Constitution.)

* * *

To understand what was in the minds of James Madison and colleagues in the First Congress when they drafted the Second Amendment, we traveled back in time to understand something of slavery and the mi-. litia as they understood them. We must undertake one final journey. The right to bear arms was not an American invention. All of the American right-to-bear-arms provisions—those in state constitutions, those proposed by ratifying conventions, and, most importantly, the Second Amendment to the Constitution—were inspired by a right-to-possess-arms provision of the English Declaration of Rights of 1689 (also known as the English Bill of Rights).

The American Founders were raised and educated as British subjects. They had been brought up to revere the British constitution as a bulwark of liberty and a shield against tyranny. Unlike the American Constitution, the English constitution was not a single document. It was, in fact, often referred to as an unwritten constitution, but that was not precisely correct. While it included unwritten aspects, including deeply embedded traditions and norms, the English constitution was, in the main, composed of three documents of overarching importance—the Magna Carta of 1215, the Petition of Right of 1628, and the Declaration of Rights of 1689—plus fundamental precepts of English common law, set forth in court opinions. That is how people in the eighteenth century, including the American Founders, understood the British constitution. (And that is how Britons still understand it today, although they may now add other documents such as the Parliament Acts of 1911 and 1949 and the Human Rights Act of 1998.[98])

Our Founders were as familiar with the English Declaration of Rights of 1689 as we are with the Declaration of Independence. They referred to it often. Madison expressly mentioned the Declaration of Rights of 1689 in his speech proposing his bill of the rights in the House of Representatives. To understand the English Declaration of Rights of 1689—and, specifically, its right-to-possess-arms provision—one must understand the context in which it was written. The Declaration arose out of the Glorious Revolution of 1688. The next chapter will, therefore, begin with the story of that revolution. It will take us a bit before we get to the Declaration of Rights, but the context is essential. Happily, it is an exciting story.

9

The English Declaration of Rights of 1689

ON JUNE 10, 1688, the queen gave birth to a baby boy. Normally, that would be a time of rejoicing, especially when a king previously had no heir apparent, as was the situation here. Church bells would have rung throughout the land. Everyone would have toasted the health of the king, queen, and newborn prince. Not this time. There were fireworks and bonfires.[1] But they were required. In truth, England was far from joyous; it was panicked. The birth of the baby meant that when King James II died, the crown would no longer pass to his elder daughter, Mary, the Princess of Orange,[2] as the kingdom had expected—and had hoped. Now, the crown would pass to a son raised by James and his queen, Mary of Modena. And England was frightened.

Few in England had wanted James, himself, to become king. In fact, while James's brother, King Charles II, was on the throne, Whigs in Parliament had twice introduced legislation to exclude James from the line of succession.[3] Hostility to James first arose in 1673, when Charles was still on the throne and James was the Duke of York and Lord High Admiral.[4] Because of fears of Catholic conspiracies to seize control of the government, Parliament enacted the Test Act, which required high government officials, both civil and military, to take an oath denouncing beliefs in "transubstantiation in the sacrament of the Lord's Supper, or in the elements of the bread and wine." The oath was designed to smoke out hidden Catholics. In James's case, it worked: he refused to take the oath and resigned as Lord High Admiral. It was thereby revealed that James had converted to Catholicism years earlier, as a result of his becoming enamored with Catholicism while spending some years in France while a young man. James had kept his conversion secret, even publicly attending Anglican services to keep up appearances. James's wife, Anne, had also secretly converted, and when she was on her death bed in 1671, James kept Anglican clergy out of her bedchamber so that she could receive last rites. The public did know that James's second wife, Mary of Modena, the daughter of an Italian duke, was a devout Catholic. King Charles permitted James and Mary to marry—and do so in a Catholic ceremony—but he stipulated that James's and Anne's two daughters, Mary and Anne, be raised in the Church of England.

In 1678, five years after James's Catholicism became public, hysteria over a Popish Plot swept London. Supposedly, the Pope had sent Jesuit agents to assassinate King Charles II, upon which a Catholic army would appear and seize the kingdom. According to different versions of the theory, Charles was supposed to be stabbed, shot, or poisoned by the queen's physician.[5] Today, most historians agree this was all poppycock.[6] But at the time it was taken seriously enough that three alleged conspirators were hanged, the king banished all Catholics within twenty miles of London, and legislation was introduced to bar Catholics from serving in Parliament. When the rumors of the plot first reached his ears, the king was skeptical, but James urged his brother to take the matter before the Privy Council for investigation.

The king followed James's advice. In an ironic twist of fate, a purported witness implicated James's secretary, Edward Coleman. History had decided that this witness knew nothing about Coleman or a plot—or much else. He was simply making up stories, possibly to divert attention from a homosexual relationship he had with another witness who mysteriously turned up dead.[7] But even a blindfolded darts player sometimes hits the bullseye. His story led to a search of Coleman's correspondence, and that search unearthed a letter that Coleman had written to a cleric within the court of Louis XIV, the Catholic king of France (and James's first cousin) whom many in England considered an adversary. Coleman had written: "We have here a mighty work upon our hands . . . no less than the conversion of three Kingdoms" (referring to England, Scotland, and Ireland). Coleman went on to say that James had been "converted to such a degree of zeal and piety as not to regard anything in the world in comparison to God Almighty's glory, the salvation of his own soul and the conversion of our poor Kingdom."[8]

That cast a dark shadow over James's loyalty to king and country. Members of the House of Commons introduced legislation to exclude Catholics—including James—from the king's court or from Parliament unless they swore allegiance to the Church of England. As a result of pressure from the king and the House of Lords, the bill was amended to exempt James from the requirements. In that emasculated version, it passed the House of Commons with only a two-vote margin. Other legislation was then introduced to drastically curtail the powers and prerogatives of any Catholic king. That also passed, but James vetoed it. Meanwhile, on Charles's instructions, James exiled himself to Brussels and then Scotland. Exclusion bills to remove James from the line of succession were introduced in Parliament.

There was a sharp ideological division over whether Parliament had such authority. While both Whigs and Tories believed in a constitutional monarchy—that is, that the sovereign ruled under and pursuant to law, and Parliament made the law—they differed over whether the line of succession could be determined by law. Whigs believed that Parliament and the king, acting together, could alter the line of succession.[9] Tories believed that monarchs ruled by divine right—a right conferred by heredity, not popular will. On this, Charles sided unequivocally with the Tories. He sent a message to the House of Commons stating that he would not permit legislation altering the line of succession.[10] And when the Commons tested his resolve, Charles repeatedly prevented such bills from becoming law by suspending Parliament.[11]

Meanwhile, belief in the Popish Plot was fading. Many were coming round to the view that there probably had never been such a plot, and if there had been a plot, the conspirators had been executed.[12] In the spring of 1682, Charles recalled his brother from Scotland and made a public display of warmly welcoming him home.[13] When, in November, there was still another attempt to pass an Exclusion Act, Charles vigorously lobbied the peers to vote no and also took the usual step of being personally present in the House of Lords during its debate and vote.[14] The bill failed in that chamber by a more than two-to-one margin. Still, not everyone had become comfortable with the idea of James inheriting the throne. James was considered not only a Catholic but an absolutist—that is, a believer in absolute rule by a monarch rather than rule under law established by Parliament—which was widely considered at least as dangerous to England as James's Catholicism.[15]

In 1683, a radical group of Whigs decided that with Charles effectively blocking passage of an exclusion act to keep James from the throne, they ought to assassinate both Charles and James. They hatched a plan to ambush the royal party, which would include the two brothers, as it passed a medieval castle known as the Rye House on the way back to London after attending horse races in Newcastle. The plot failed. The horse races had been cancelled due to a fire, and the royal party had passed Rye House before the ambush party had assembled. Some weeks later, an informer revealed the plot. Three alleged plotters were arrested. One committed suicide in prison; two were beheaded. Other conspirators fled the country—most prominently, the Duke of Monmouth, the eldest illegitimate son of King Charles.[16] The discovery of the plot stimulated a surge of sympathy for both Charles and James.

On February 6, 1685, after having sat on the throne for twenty-five years, Charles died.[17] He had no legitimate heir, and the crown passed to his brother. James immediately gave what one historian describes as a "passionate and politically brilliant" speech to the Privy Council.[18] "I have been reported to be a man of arbitrary power, but I shall make it my endeavor to preserve this government both in church and state as it is now by law established," James declared. The phrase *as it is now by law established* was critical; the new king was pledging to respect Parliament's laws. He underlined the point by adding: "I know too that the laws of England are sufficient to make the king as great a monarch as I can wish, and I shall never depart from the just rights and prerogatives of the crown, so I shall never invade any man's property." The word *property* covered a lot of bases. To Tories, property was land. To Whigs, it was primarily the fruits of one's labor and thus related to one's right to make a living. To both, property was regulated by Parliament, not the Crown—a principle that James seemed to accept. On the matter of religion, James said: "I know the principles of the Church of England are for monarchy, and the members of it have showed themselves good and loyal subjects, therefore I shall always take care to defend and support it." Not to worry, James seemed to be saying, while I may, myself, choose to worship as a Catholic, I shall do nothing to interfere with the established Anglican Church.

James's speech was printed in newspapers and read aloud in each village and town throughout England.[19] People breathed a sigh of relief. That is just what the country needed to hear. People found other things to like about James. Charles, a notorious libertine who had been derisively called "the Merry Monarch," had lacked the regal bearing. James, by contrast, was stiff, formal, and dignified. In time, those traits would come to be viewed less favorably. In the words of one historian, "James II was rigid, proud, single-minded and self-centered."[20] But if that was not immediately evident, James was fortunate—for just how accepting England was of its new monarch was immediately put to the test.

On June 11, the Duke of Monmouth, who had been in exile in the Netherlands since the unsuccessful Rye House assassination attempt, landed with a small group of rebels at Lyme Regis in the West Country, and asked people to rally to his banner.[21] He was not an especially attractive personality. He had a troubled upbringing that produced an adult who was only semi-literate, violent, and insecure. He was also widely considered a notorious womanizer and a man of low integrity.[22] Upon landing, Monmouth claimed only to be fighting for a free Parliament, but within a week he declared himself the rightful heir to the throne. Monmouth coordinated his landing with the Earl of Argyll of Scotland, who had also been exiled in the Netherlands after having been placed under a death sentence at home. Argyll was to attempt a simultaneous insurrection in the north.[23] Argyll's effort collapsed almost immediately. His small band of rebels dispersed as soon as they were confronted by the Royal Navy. Argyll adopted a disguise and went into hiding, but he was soon captured and executed.

Monmouth had more success in the West Country. As many as four thousand men joined his rebellion.[24] He began marching for Bristol, the largest town in West Country and second largest in all England, where, he hoped, even more dissidents would join his cause.

The first forces sent to engage Monmouth were the county militias, but militias were no more effective in seventeenth-century England than they would be in eighteenth-century America.[25] In fact, their failure to effectively take on Monmouth's ragtag force later helped persuade James that increasing the size of England's professional army was necessary.[26] Things changed when regular forces arrived. After his first skirmish with the Royal Army, Monmouth began to retreat. The king's forces pursued. The first battle, which took place in a pouring rain, was a stalemate. A second battle at Bridgewater was decisive. Monmouth escaped and evaded capture for several days. He was finally apprehended, sent to the Tower of London, and hanged.

The rebellion—such as it was—had lasted one month. There had been no uprising in London, as Monmouth had hoped, and with the exception of perhaps four thousand people who rallied to Monmouth in the West Country, no uprising of significance anywhere. Regardless of whether he was fully trusted or beloved, James appeared to have been accepted by the nation. He was their sovereign, and he had made the right promises to the nation. James, therefore, had good reason to feel confident in the throne. But that feeling of confidence would lead to his undoing. It would all happen with stunning speed. In just three years, James would be gone. The catalyst would be the birth of his son.

* * *

With Monmouth defeated, James proceeded on an ambitious program to fundamentally change England. His true goals flew in the face of the speech he had made to the Privy Council. Moreover, he did not seek to make changes in tandem with efforts to persuade either the people or the elites that the changes he desired were in their in their interests or in the best interest of England. Rather, he sought to force the changes by creating a modern police state.

Since the time, more than a century earlier, when Henry VIII removed England from the Catholic Church and established the Church of England, there had been tension—and worse—between Catholics and Protestants in England. Henry's daughter, Queen Mary I, earned the moniker "Bloody Mary" for brutally attempting to reverse the Reformation and restore Catholicism in England. Her efforts included burning nearly three hundred Protestant leaders at the stake. Mary's half-sister, Queen Elizabeth I, reversed course, returning the Church of England to Protestantism. Elizabeth ruled for forty-four years and was one of England's most skilled and beloved monarchs. Historians credit her with moving a small, weak, and vulnerable nation into a position of commercial and military strength, and for bringing a medieval society into modernity. Although she unequivocally restored Protestantism, she nevertheless attempted to follow a moderate course by allowing the Church of England to lean toward Catholic-style worship. This earned her no credit with Catholics, however. Elizabeth had to fend off Catholic attempts to overthrow her through rebellion, invasion, or—as encouraged by a papal bull—assassination.[27] During Elizabeth's reign, Parliament and the nation as a whole became more deeply committed to Protestantism and more fearful of the Catholic plots, both foreign and domestic, real and imagined. There were constant rumors of Catholic plots and outrages.

Following Elizabeth, Protestantism was cherished by the English people for reasons extending beyond religion. England prided itself on having a limited monarchy. English monarchs did not have absolute power, as did some monarchs on the Continent. England had a balanced government, consisting of the sovereign, the nobility represented in the House of Lords, and the people represented in the House of Commons.[28] The supreme authority in England was law, both statutory law enacted by Parliament and common law handed down in court decisions. The fabric of the ancient constitution dated back until at least 1215 and the Magna Carta. The English constitution was still being woven, and the Glorious Revolution would itself add material, but a limited monarchy, balanced government, and the transcendence of law were already fundamental to the English nation.

The English constitution was composed not merely by documents such as the Magna Carta but, even more so, by traditions, customs, and cherished stories. The people of England knew, for example, how in 1607 James I summoned before him the eminent jurist Sir Edward Coke for the purpose of having the Archbishop of Canterbury publicly inform Coke that the king was the supreme magistrate of the land and, as such, had the right to personally decide a case then pending in the common law court over which Coke presided as chief justice. Coke replied that he "greatly marveled that the Archbishop" would advise the king that such authority "belonged to the king by the word of God." The king was endowed with many excellent things, said Coke, but knowledge of the law was not among them. When the king remarked that he would "ever protect the common law," Coke replied that things were properly the other way around: "The common law protecteth the king." That sent the king into a rage. Coke dropped to his knees and begged to be forgiven for his overzealousness. Yet Coke did not recant. On the bench the very next morning, Coke issued an order prohibiting the king's High Commission from issuing charges against a layman, stating, "Cogitationis poenam nemo emeret" (no man may be punished for his thoughts).[29]

England prided itself on being a country where heroes such as Edward Coke held kings in check. The old maxim "the king can do no wrong" no longer meant the king was infallible; it meant he was required to abide by law.[30] The word *liberty* had different meanings, but as one historian has noted, "[i]n the seventeenth century, many thought 'liberty' as 'the privileges, immunities, or rights enjoyed by prescription or grant,'" that is, not natural rights but rights conferred and defined by Parliament.[31] Freedom is what people enjoyed by living in such a system.

Religious liberty had not yet been accepted, however. A century earlier, Queen Elizabeth declared, "There cannot be two religions in one State."[32] The state and its religion were considered inseparable; each legitimized the other, and dissenting religions were deemed not only wrong but also inherently subversive. England was a country with an established church and prohibitions against dissenting religious worship. Those prohibitions were motivated by fear of weakening the legitimacy of the state, fear of disorder and chaos, and with respect to Catholics, fear of disloyalty and subversion. Many believed, for example, that a fire that destroyed most of London in 1666 had been deliberately set by Catholics. A Catholic king, Louis XIV, sat on the throne in France. Louis XIV was an absolute monarch with imperial ambitions and the most powerful military in Europe. England, therefore, feared Catholics concealed in its government and military positions in much the same way that Americans feared communists during the Cold War. Historians studying seventeenth-century England "put anti-Catholicism in the centre, not the periphery, of events" because it had become intertwined with England's vision of itself.[33]

James portrayed himself as a promoter of religious tolerance. Even though that was, at best, a highly controversial view, it was, in James's case, understandable. James's brother Charles II had had also favored religious toleration. His mother had been Catholic, and he understood what it meant for a Catholic to live in a nation hostile to Catholics. Charles surprised his advisers when—against their advice—he granted a royal charter to the colony of Rhode Island to "hold forth a lively experiment, that a civil state may stand and best be maintained . . . with full liberty in religious concernments," and create a place where "no person . . . shall be any wise molested, punished, disquieted, or called into question, for any differences in opinion in matters of religion."[34] Charles, however, had not pushed his personal belief in religious tolerations beyond all bounds. Allowing religious tolerance in colonies across the ocean was one thing. Allowing it on home soil was another matter. And that is what James wanted to do.

James began lobbying Parliament to repeal the Test Acts and Penal Laws. The Test Acts prohibited anyone who did not declare fidelity to the Church of England from holding government positions, including civil positions, military commissions, even faculty appointments at Oxford and Cambridge universities. The Penal Laws subjected those who failed to attend Anglican services to fines and other punishments.[35] When Parliament failed to do his bidding by repealing these laws, James dissolved it, vowing to seek the election of a new Parliament with more compliant members.[36] Meanwhile, James began issuing warrants to free individuals who were imprisoned for violating the Test Acts and Penal Laws, as well as issuing declarations of indulgence to exempt individuals from having to obey those laws.[37] James hoped to win political support from dissenting Protestant groups, including Baptists, Presbyterians, and Quakers.[38] For a while, his efforts were modestly successful. William Penn, for example, was grateful enough for dispensations granted to him and fellow Quakers to assist James in his efforts to pack Parliament with members who would do James's bidding.[39] But support from dissenters turned out to be neither broad nor durable. They recognized that the king was simply trying to buy them off, and most turned against him.[40]

It also became increasingly obvious that James's support of broad religious tolerance was a smokescreen for Catholicizing England.[41] James surrounded himself with Catholic advisers.[42] He opened a Catholic chapel in Whitehall where members of his court could celebrate mass with a Catholic prelate every morning.[43] With James's encouragement, an elaborate Catholic chapel also opened on Lyme Street in London, and James personally celebrated conversions of prominent English subjects there.[44] While everybody understood that Catholic worship had always occurred in England, it was unlawful and previously had been private and discrete. Now Catholicism came out of the shadows across England. Other Catholic chapels sprung up, Catholic schools opened, Catholic books were published and distributed, and Catholic priests and monks began wearing their robes in public.[45]

James appointed Catholics to the professions. He appointed Catholics to the Inns of Court, the inner sanctum of barristers.[46] He had Catholics appointed to faculty and administrative positions at Oxford and Cambridge. That was especially offensive because those universities educated future theologians and clerics for the Church of England—serving, as a fellow in one of the colleges put it at the time, as "a nursery to the Church of England."[47] When faculty at Oxford's Magdalen College balked at James's Catholic appointments, the king told them: "You have dealt with His Sacred Majesty as if he reigned only by courtesy and you were resolved to have a king under you, but none over you."[48] Unable to resist but unwilling to participate with James's program of Catholicizing the college, twenty-five of its fellows resigned.

James appointed Catholics as officers in the army. By the end of James's reign, about 11 percent of the officer corps and between 12 and 15 percent of rank-and-file soldiers were Catholic.[49] Many of these had come from Ireland. Consider what this meant in England at the time. First, less than 2 percent of England's population was Catholic.[50] Second, it was unlawful for Catholics to serve as officers in the Royal Army or Navy. Third, James was increasing the number of Catholics in the army at the same time he was dramatically expanding the size of the army itself. Indeed, when James ascended to the throne, England's army numbered 9,000 men.[51] Within three years he more than quadrupled to the size of the army to 40,000, with appropriations for the army more than tripling over the same span of time.

Many in England believed they knew why James wanted a larger, more Catholic military. War was looming once again between France and the United Provinces of the Netherlands. France was ruled by Louis XIV, head of the Gallican Catholic Church, an absolute monarch, and a man with territorial ambitions and a powerful military.[52]

The geopolitical counterbalance to him was the Netherlands, which had a mixed government, religious tolerance, and a formidable military of its own.[53] Its leader, William of Orange, Stadtholder of Holland, was considered the defender of Protestantism on the Continent. During open warfare in 1672, the Dutch stopped advancing French troops by breaching their dykes and creating a flood.[54] War, everyone believed, would inevitably resume. When it did, where would England stand? Whigs wanted England to stand with the Netherlands. They believed that if Louis XIV prevailed, Protestant England would face an existential threat.[55] Therefore, an English army should join the fight against France on the Continent. Tories, by contrast, advocated a blue-water policy: stay out of a land war on the Continent and maintain a formidable navy to shield England from invasion.[56]

The Whigs and the Tories were, however, debating how to best defend Protestant England from a militarily powerful, imperialistic Catholic nation. Neither Whigs nor Tories advocated allying with France and sending an English army to help Louis XIV crush the Netherlands, but both parties came to fear that was exactly what James had in mind. Rumors circulated about a secret "holy alliance" between James II and the French monarch.[57] James himself stoked those fears by frequently stating that the Dutch were "enemies in general to all royalty, and in particular that of England."[58] When in late 1687 James recalled troops that were stationed in United Provinces, many interpreted it as a signal that James was ready to go to war with Netherlands.[59]

James was prudent enough not to say he wanted a larger, more Catholic army to create a military alliance with France and go to war with the Netherlands. And Parliament did not openly accuse him of having such a plan. As is often the case in politics, an unspoken dispute was fought out rhetorically by using a surrogate issue—in this case whether James could maintain a "standing army."[60] There had long been debates about whether the king of England was entitled to maintain a sizable, land-based military force during peacetime. The prevailing view was that the king had a right to maintain a standing army if he, rather than Parliament, paid for it.[61] Armies are, of course, expensive, and England—being an island nation—felt reasonably secure as long as it had a powerful navy. As one wag put it: "soldiers in peace are like chimneys in summer."[62] This did not mean that England should not maintain a professional army of some strength.[63] Both kings and parliaments recognized that the only truly capable force was a professional army, and an army of modest size was needed, if only to provide the expertise and training for an expanded army, when that became necessary.[64]

There was, however, always much huffing and puffing about standing armies being dangerous to liberty. "No standing army!" was a cry often repeated on the floor of Parliament and in political speeches and pamphlets. But as one leading historian observed, "there was more propaganda than principle in the regular attacks on the army in the eighteenth century."[65] Beneath the rhetoric were hardnosed concerns about whether an army of a certain size was necessary, how much it would cost, how it was going to be paid for, and to whom the army would be loyal. The principle that a king was entitled to a standing army if he paid for it himself meant, at a practical level, that the king could maintain a force of moderate size to provide for his own security. As a general matter, English kings could not themselves afford to pay for large military. A large army was acceptable provided Parliament appropriated the monies to fund it, which, of course, would mean that Parliament thought it was needed. There was one more principle: armies ought to be under civilian control in peacetime. Thus, the often repeated phrase "No standing army!" meant, at bottom, no standing armies except as approved by Parliament. Many considered these principles part and parcel of the unwritten English constitution. In fact, when he invaded England, the Duke of Monmouth distributed a Declaration designed to persuade the English people to support his rebellion against James II, and one of Monmouth's promises in that document was to support legislation that would "prevent all military standing forces, except what shall be raised and kept up by Authority and consent of Parliament."[66]

On November 9, 1685—four months after defeating Monmouth—James delivered a speech to Parliament that portended what was to come. Standing legislation required disbanding the army that had been assembled to defeat Monmouth.[67] James flatly told Parliament he was going to disregard that law. Moreover, he had unilaterally decided to double the size of the army—and he demanded Parliament appropriate funds to pay for that. Monmouth's rebellion had proved an expanded army was essential, said James, because "the Militia, which hath hitherto been so much depended on, is not sufficient for such occasions; and that there is nothing but a good Force of well-disciplined Troops in constant pay, that can defend us."[68] If this was not arrogant enough, James also told Parliament that he was appointing army officers in violation of the Test Acts—that is, Catholics. "I will deal plainly with you," said James, and he told Parliament that he knew these men, thought them "fit to be employed under me," and would "neither expose them to disgrace, nor myself to the want of them." That was that. The law meant nothing. The king expected Parliament to do his bidding. For good measure, James said Members had better not be "so wicked" as to take exception to his demands.

Following several days of impassioned debate, Parliament settled on a two-pronged reply to the king. First, it decided to give James 700,000 pounds for the army. This was a split-the-difference-right-down-the-middle compromise between the king's demand for 1.2 million pounds and Members who wanted to give the king 200,000 pounds, which presumably would have required shrinking the army. Second, it drafted an Address—taking great care to make the language as diplomatic as possible—begging "leave to acquaint your Majesty" with the law that made it unlawful for Catholics to serve as in the army, and stating that because those men had brought their incapacities to serve upon themselves by refusing to take the oaths prescribed in Test Acts, Parliament found it impossible to change the law.[69] Parliament would enact legislation indemnifying the Catholic officers for any penalties for their unlawful service to date, but the king would have to give the appropriate "Directions," that is, to dismiss the officers.

James was enraged. He prorogued Parliament; that is, he immediately terminated its session and sent members home—losing the 700,000 pound appropriation in the process. James vowed to keep the army, paying for it himself through his annual allowance and by diverting monies that had been appropriated for the militia.[70] He never again summoned Parliament.[71]

The army continued to grow in size. Troops were garrisoned in many towns, including York, Hull, Ailesbury, Leeds, and Hounslow Heath on the western outskirts of London.[72] There were, moreover, insufficient barracks; some soldiers were quartered in inns, public houses, and homes. This was not a new practice; earlier monarchs, including

Charles II, had done much the same.[73] But it was a despised practice nonetheless, one that extracted a heavy form of tax on citizens whose private property was requisitioned without compensation.[74] Soldiers could be unruly, drunk, arrogant, sexually aggressive, and otherwise abusive to civilians. Relations between soldiers and civilians became so troubled that street battles broke out in Oxford, Yarmouth, and even London itself.[75] James response was to decree that private individuals could not carry arms on the public streets, and then to direct Lord Lieutenants (militia who functioned something like local sheriffs) to search for and seize "muskets or guns" in private hands.[76]

James's program of militarization went hand in hand with his program of developing a police state. James employed spies to monitor dissent. The people of England had gotten used to reading newspapers and freely discussing the events of the day in coffeehouses and taverns; now they worried about who was listening.[77] They knew—and hotly resented—that James was also using the mail for political surveillance. Even prominent people privately complained that "all letters are opened," and some people started burning any correspondence that expressed political views.[78]

James may have thought he was successfully bending England to his will. He had no one to tell him differently. When he became king, James vowed that rather than having "divided councils" that he thought had plagued his brother Charles, he would only retain advisers "who were entirely attached to his interests."[79] That was foolish. James was apparently oblivious as to how far he was pushing England, and how much England resented it. It is as if the king stacked a mountain of dry kindling under this throne, and all that was needed was a single spark to set it ablaze.

There would soon be not merely one spark, but two.

* * *

On April 27, 1688, James issued a second Declaration of Indulgence, by which he purported to eliminate the requirements of the Test Acts, thereby allowing Catholics and other dissenters to hold office, and to grant liberty of conscience and free exercise of religion worship throughout the realm.[80] He had issued a Declaration of Indulgence a year earlier, but this time—to ensure that the benefits of his indulgence were not frustrated by the "malice of crafty, wicked men"—James ordered the clergy of the Church of England to read the Declaration aloud in every parish of the kingdom. The Archbishop of Canterbury convened a meeting of bishops at his home to decide how to respond to the king's direction, and seven of the eight bishops who attended that meeting decided to submit a petition, "in the most submissive and respectful manner," to the king, to be excused from reading the Declaration of Indulgence. Most significantly, the bishops did not ground their petition on religion but on law. They were not petitioning, they said, out of "any want of due tenderness to the dissenters," yet were compelled to ask to be excused because the king's claimed power to dispense with the law "hath been often declared illegal in Parliaments."[81]

Simply put, the issue—as framed by the bishops—was: Who makes the law, the king or Parliament? The bishops said Parliament makes the law, and the king has no "dispensing power" to overrule the law of the land.

James promptly had the bishops arrested and imprisoned in the Tower of London. But the bishops did not stand alone. A majority of clergy refused to read the Declaration of Indulgence, in some cases in defiance of bishops who insisted that it be read. James prosecuted the seven bishops for seditious libel, and they were promptly placed on trial. The Seven Bishops Trial—which lasted the better part of May and June—riveted the nation.

The first spark dropped into the dry kindling on June 10, when the queen gave birth to a son. As stated at the outset of this chapter, the kingdom did not celebrate that news. Quite the opposite. Previously, England hoped it was possible to wait James out. He was fifty-five years of age. Life expectancy—including that of English royals—was not nearly what it is today, and James was not considered to be in good health.[82] England had hoped James would be succeeded by his older daughter, Mary, wife of William of Orange, the defender of Protestantism.

The second spark dropped less than three weeks later when the seven bishops were acquitted of all charges. Wild cheering erupted throughout the land. If there had been any doubt about the sentiment of the English people, their reaction to the Seven Bishops verdict settled it.

And so, on that same day, seven prominent members of the House of Lords dispatched an invitation to William of Orange, requesting that he invade England. They pledged to support him if he did, and predicted that nineteen out of every twenty English subjects would support him, too.

William did not send regrets. For him, this was not about saving England; it was about ensuring that England would be an ally, rather than an enemy, of the Netherlands in an imminent war with France. William set at work assembling two forces—an invasion force, plus a second force to defend the United Provinces should Louis XIV attack while Dutch troops were engaged in England. He tried to keep his preparations secret as long as possible. But assembling a large military force draws attention. French intelligence learned something was up, and by August it had warned James about a possible invasion. On August 31, James sent his son-in-law a chatty letter that innocently inquired, "What news from your side of the water?"[83] Prevaricating correspondence crossed the Channel between James and either his daughter Mary or son-in-law for weeks. By the end of September, pretenses were dropped. On September 28, James issued a proclamation ordering all subjects to arm themselves in preparation for invasion. Arm themselves many did—but often to support the expected invaders.[84] James also ordered English troops in Ireland and Scotland to return home. Attempts to assemble militia proved a dismal failure.[85]

On November 2, 1688—flying under the banner of English colors emblazoned with the motto "the Protestant Religion and the Liberties of England"—William set sail for England with more than fifteen thousand troops and sixty-four warships. James hoped the Royal Navy would intercept the invasion force in the English Channel, and Louis promised to send French warships to assist; but winds prevented the English fleet from leaving port and the French force never materialized.[86] On November 15, William landed at Torbay (not far from where Monmouth landed with his much smaller invasion force three years earlier) and began marching toward London. James set forth with his army to meet him. James had significant military experience. Forced into exile during the English Civil War, James had joined the French army, fought gallantly in battle, and rose to the rank of lieutenant general. He also later served as a captain-general with the Spanish army, commanding six regiments of English volunteers in battle. In addition to experience and courage, James also had forty thousand men under arms in England— at least a two-to-one advantage over William. As he rode forth to meet William in battle, James was, at first, confident.

But, as we already know, James had no feel whatever for the sentiment of his own people. William of Orange—who, many months earlier, had secretly sent aides to England to gauge public opinion—had a far better grasp on England's political situation than did England's own king. As James marched westward to engage the invader, he quickly learned that he was in deep trouble. Spies sent ahead to learn about the strength and whereabouts of the enemy failed to return. They had not been captured; they had defected.[87] As a battle commander, James found himself blind. County militia either sat on their hands or joined in spontaneous uprisings.[88] Worst of all, some of the commanders in his main force on whom James counted most began deserting, taking entire regiments with them.[89] It was not the raw numbers of desertions that did him in. Rather, James realized he did not know whom he could trust. Even his own nephew deserted. All of this came as a shock to James. He was, he himself said, stunned "to see so general defection in the officers from a Prince that paid them well and cherished them so much."[90] His situation was untenable, and he knew it. On November 22, James assembled a war council, and following its advice, he retreated back to London. Once there, he learned that even Anne, his youngest daughter, had deserted him.[91]

London was in chaos. It was not the invading army that most Londoners feared; it was the Catholics in their midst. The Mayor of London ordered that all Catholics be searched and disarmed. Mobs began destroying Catholic chapels and pillaging Catholic homes.[92] James called for a new Parliament to convene on January 15, and sent three peers to negotiate with William of Orange. Those were delaying tactics. James had no cards left to play, and he knew it. He sent his wife and son to travel secretly to France. When he learned they had safely made their escape, James burned his writs convening a new Parliament, donned a disguise, and with another companion—Sir Edward Hales, a Catholic politician—climbed into a small skiff by which they made their way down the Thames River to a larger boat, which was to take them to France.[93] En route, James threw into the swirling waters of the Thames the Great Seal of England, without which Parliament could not be lawfully called into session. When the second vessel made what was intended to be a quick stop to take on ballast, sailors recognized Hales, seized both men, and dragged them to the local pub, where they were stripped naked and searched. There, someone noticed that the other captive happened to be the king of England.

When he was informed that the king had been captured, William of Orange was frustrated. He had wanted James to flee the county. James continued presence in England was, of course, intolerable, but regicide has downsides—perhaps especially when the king is your father-in-law. To remedy the situation, William moved James from London to Rochester, which is closer to seaports, and he gave his Dutch guards instructions to look the other way should James try again to escape. Letters to James from his wife were intercepted and read. When William learned Mary's letters begged James to join her in France, he had the guards deliver them to their intended recipient. As further encouragement, James was given a letter from the Earl of Halifax which said that William thought James might no longer be safe if he remained in London.[94] James's second attempt to escape to France was successful.

* * *

William arrived in London on December 28. Since Parliament could not lawfully be convened without the Great Seal, the House of Lords met informally and advised William to summon a Convention. In effect, the Convention was Parliament meeting under a different name. The Convention and William engaged in negotiations as to the terms under which the Convention would offer, and William would accept, the Crown.

The first—and most debated issue—was who would rule as sovereign.[95] There was tension between those (mostly Tories) who believed in an inviolate hereditary monarchy, those (mostly Whigs) who believed that Parliament could select the monarch, and those who held both viewpoints to some degree. William had some English royal blood flowing through his own veins. He was a grandson of King Charles I of England, though from his mother's side of the family; but that did not make him a rightful heir to the throne. As the eldest daughter of James

II, Mary was the rightful heir—provided the throne was vacant, and the fact that James now had a son was ignored. For the most part, Whigs were willing to take the position that, by leaving the kingdom, James had abdicated. That led the way to declaring—or acknowledging—Mary to be queen. Patrimony was strong in seventeenth-century England, however, and everyone more or less understood that William would rule. But should William rule as regent, or should William and Mary be king and queen? Some Tories argued that as long as James lived, there could only be a regency, but they had pretty such the same problem: Should Mary be regent and William consort, or should William and Mary be co-regents? Some argued that even debating these questions was problematic because that, in effect, meant they were substituting a monarch elected by Parliament for a hereditary monarchy.

After several days of unsuccessful debates and votes, William summoned a group of influential peers and brought matters to a head. Louis XIV had declared war on the United Provinces, William's attention was needed elsewhere, and therefore the matter had to be settled immediately. Moreover, said William, he did not intend to hold "anything by apron springs."[96] The Convention would have to declare him king and undisputed sovereign. If that was unacceptable, William would simply take his Dutch army back to the Netherlands. That would have leave Parliament to deal with national chaos on its own—not to mention the potential problem of James returning with French help, reclaiming the throne, and hanging everyone who had supported William for treason. To paraphrase Mario Puzo, William made the Convention an offer it couldn't refuse.[97] Thus, it agreed to Williams's terms. But it got three things in return—things that were important to the Convention but not disagreeable to William. First, William and Mary were to formally share the throne; that is, they were to be king and queen, with the stipulation that William would enjoy the sole and full exercise of the regal power as long as he lived.[98] Second, to ensure that the line of succession would return to England, after William and Mary had both died, the line of succession would run to Mary's children, and if Mary had no children, then to Mary's sister Anne and Anne's children.

The third condition—which we can now properly understand in context—is the one that concerns us, namely Williams and Mary's agreement to the Declaration of Rights of February 1689.

The Convention that negotiated with William of Orange, one must remember, was Parliament, or as close a surrogate for Parliament as could be convened under the circumstances. As such, the Convention was concerned with parliamentary prerogatives. (During the course of these events, the Convention transformed itself back into Parliament by enacting a statute to that effect, and will be referred to as Parliament from this point on.[99]) The primary reason for the revolution was that James II had not recognized Parliament's authority to make law. As we have seen, James repeatedly claimed the authority to nullify Parliament's laws. Moreover, the courts (packed with judges appointed by James) had supported him. In a case challenging James's authority to dispense with the Test Acts, the Court of King's Bench had ruled: "The Laws of England are the King's Laws," and thus the king could dispense with laws enacted by Parliament at his pleasure.[100] As one historian put it, this meant that "[i]nstead of the law being sovereign, it was a sovereign king who was in control of the law." Moreover, "the fact that it was made legal made it that much more menacing."[101] It is almost impossible to overstate the importance of this issue for Parliament and for England.

Parliament wanted to reaffirm its authority by having William and Mary acknowledge that Parliament makes law and English sovereigns must respect Parliament's laws. William and Mary were willing to do that. This was accomplished through a Declaration of Rights. The document was drafted by Whigs, who then made concessions to Tories in the House of Lords to win approval from both houses of Parliament. The document was formally adopted by Parliament at Westminster on February 12, 1689, and accepted by William and Mary at a public ceremony the next day, just before they were declared king and queen.[102] William was, however, permitted to state that he and Mary accepted the Crown before they promised to preserve the laws, religion, and liberties of the England, thereby asserting that they accepted the Declaration voluntarily rather than as a condition of being named sovereigns.[103] When the document was subsequently enacted by statute, it became the English Bill of Rights of 1689.

The document first lists thirteen grievances, each an instance in which James and his "Evil Counsellors, Judges, and Ministers" had endeavored "to Subvert and extirpate" laws and liberties of England.[104]

It then affirms Parliament's authority to make the law, and sets forth, in parallel to the grievances, thirteen rights. Two points must be made to understand the document. First, as has often been stated, nothing in the Declaration of Rights purported to create new rights.[105] The document itself states it is merely "vindicating and asserting . . . antient rights and Liberties."[106] Nor did the document create "rights" in the modern, American sense of that term. We Americans today think of rights as prerogatives possessed by the people, irrespective of what Congress or state legislatures might decide to the contrary, with courts defending those rights from legislative abuses or encroachments. But in England, rights were privileges granted and demarked by Parliament.[107]

The focus on Parliament's right to make the law is evident when one reads the Declaration of Rights in its entirety. The first of thirteen Articles describing these rights reads: "That the pretended power of suspending of Lawes or the execution of Lawes by Regall Authority without Consent of Parliament is illegal."[108] The second Article states: "That levying money for or to the use of the crown by pretense of prerogative without grant of Parliament for longer time or in other manner than the same is or shall be granted is illegal." There was an Article devoted to freedom of speech, but it was only about "freedom of speech and debates or proceedings in Parliament." In fact, only four of the thirteen Articles are not expressly about parliamentary prerogatives—those protecting the right to petition the king; prohibiting excessive bail, fines, and cruel and unusual punishments; protecting jury trials; and prohibiting fines and forfeitures prior to conviction.[109] Even with these, Parliament's concern was probably not as much about denying subjects ancient rights but about who could make those judgments, king or Parliament. As one scholar said, "the Bill of Rights (1689) is frankly nothing but a limitation upon the power of the Crown."[110]

Here are the Articles which are directly relevant to our investigation:

6. "That the raiseing or keeping a Standing Army within the Kingdom in time of Peace unlesse it be with consent of Parliament is against Law."

7. "That the Subjects which are Protestants may have Armes for their defence Suitable to their Condition and as allowed by Law."[111]

These two provisions are, of course, expressly about Parliament. Article 6 does not say that standing armies are prohibited; it says they are prohibited *unless it be with the consent of Parliament.* In other words, Parliament—and only Parliament—has the authority to determine whether an army shall be maintained during peacetime. The parallel grievance in the Declaration made very much the same point. It accused James of abusing the law "[b]y raiseing and keeping a standing army within this Kingdom in time of Peace *without consent of Parliament* and quartering Soldiers *contrary to Law*" (my emphasis).[112]

Article 7 does not say that subjects may have arms for their defense. Nor does it even say that Protestants have such a right. Rather, it provides that Protestants may have weapons *as allowed by law.* The point, quite simply, was that Parliament makes the laws which prescribe what weapons Protestants may possess, and the king must acknowledge and respect Parliament's authority to do so. Once again, the parallel grievance makes the same point. It accused James of subverting the law "[b]y causing several good Subjects being Protestants to be disarmed at the same time when Papists were both armed and Employed *contrary to Law*" (my emphasis).[113]

The term *arms* meant the kinds of weapons that were suitable for war, and it included guns and crossbows.[114] What prompted the provision was that James had been disarming Protestants without Parliament's consent. This provision, therefore, was intended to resolve a dispute between Parliament and the king—not about whether subjects had a right to own weapons—but about who regulated gun ownership. Parliament was, in essence, saying: "We don't care about Catholics. If you want to disarm them, be our guest." And, in fact, while William and Parliament were negotiating the Bill of Rights, the mayor of London was disarming Catholics. By restricting Article VII to Protestants, Parliament made it clear it had no problem with that; but when it came to Protestants, the king was obliged to respect Parliament's gun laws.[115]

Did Parliament have a long and hallowed tradition of allowing Protestants to own firearms for their own defense? It did not. Roughly from the time firearms came to be purchased and sold in England, Parliament regulated them—and regulated them heavily. This is where the term *suitable to their conditions* becomes relevant. Under Parliament's regulatory system, the weapons one could possess, if any, depended on his condition, that is, his socioeconomic status. The laws could and did change depending on currency values and other factors, but for more than a century no one without an annual income of £100 was allowed to possess or use a firearm.[116] Ninety-eight percent of the English population fell below that level. Gun ownership in England, therefore, was not a universal right. Quite the reverse, only a privileged few were permitted to own firearms.

Why was gun ownership so restricted in England? There were two related views: the people, as a whole, were not to be trusted with guns and other dangerous weapons such as crossbows; and only gentry who owned large tracts of land should be permitted to engage in the sport of hunting. As King James I explained it to the House of Commons when he requested they enact such laws in 1610, "it is not fit that clowns should have these sports."[117] (By "clowns," he meant plebeians.) Legislation enacted by Parliament in 1671 increased the amount of land one had to own to hunt, titled "A Bill to preserve the Game." As historian Edmund S. Morgan famously described them, English gun and hunting laws "protected pheasants from peasants."[118] But Parliament was not exclusively focused on the game laws. It was also concerned with public safety. As early as 1541, Parliament enacted legislation restricting handguns, which, because of their small size and concealability were, said Parliament, used in murders, robberies, and riots "to the great peril and continual fear and danger of the King's most loving subjects."[119] Parliament required that guns be at least three-quarters of a yard in length, or in some cases a full yard, to make concealability impossible.[120] Pistols with barrels of six inches or less—often called dags—were considered a particular threat to public safety and Parliament repeatedly enacted legislation banning them, although it failed to entirely eliminate them.[121]

Did the Declaration of Rights in any way restrict Parliament's ability to regulate gun laws? It did not. As Lois G. Schwoerer of George Washington University wrote: "The constitutional right of the individual to hold arms at the end of the eighteenth century had not changed one iota. It remained a right restricted by religion, socioeconomic standing, and law."[122] After the English Bill of Rights, Parliament's statutes, which premised lawful gun ownership with socioeconomic status, continued to allow gun possession by only about 2 percent of the population.[123]

* * *

It is no accident that two of the ten amendments in the American Bill of Rights—namely, the Second and Third Amendments to the United States Constitution—resemble Articles VI and VII in the English Declaration of Rights. The American Founders were, after all, educated as British subjects. The Glorious Revolution and the English Bill of Rights were as familiar to them as the American Revolution and our Bill of Rights are to us. They understood that the English Declaration of Rights was about allocating authority between Parliament and the king.

In the *Federalist Papers*, Alexander Hamilton twice referred to both the Glorious Revolution and the English Declaration of Rights.[124] On one of those occasions, Hamilton made the precise point on which we have been focusing, namely, that, in the main, the Declaration of Rights allocated power between two branches of government and should not be understood to have granted rights directly to the people. It was understandable, said Hamilton, that some people might be confused about that distinction. It was possible to fail to perceive the boundary between "*power* and *priviledge*" or mistakenly collapse questions involving "the energy of government with the security of private rights" (Hamilton's emphasis).[125]

At this point in the *Federalist Papers*, Hamilton was replying to antifederalist arguments that the United States Constitution should have prohibited standing armies. Hamilton found the antifederalist argument foolish. "The idea of restraining the legislative authority in the means of providing for the national defense is one of those refinements which owe their origin to a zeal for liberty more ardent than enlightened," he said. Moreover, the Constitution did not need the same kind of restriction on standing armies contained in the English Bill of Rights. The two situations were not the same. For a long time after the Norman Conquest, English monarchs enjoyed almost unlimited power, explained Hamilton. Gradually some limitations were placed on royal power. "But," he continued, "it was not till the revolution in 1688, which elevated the Prince of Orange to the throne of Great Britain, that English liberty was completely triumphant." Hamilton then stressed that English liberty meant living under laws enacted by Parliament. The English Bill of Rights provided that "'the raising or keeping a standing army within the kingdom in time of peace, *unless with the consent of Parliament*, was against the law,'" Hamilton explained

(Hamilton's emphasis). But under the United States Constitution only the legislature was empowered to raise an army. Including a declaration "that standing armies ought not to be kept up in time of peace *without the consent of the Legislature*" was therefore entirely unnecessary (Hamilton's emphasis).

The Founders had also recognized the same point in the Declaration of Independence. In the list of grievances that, they argued, justified dissolving the political bands which had connected the American colonies with the mother country, the Founders complained that the king "has kept among us, in Times of Peace, Standing Armies, *without the consent of our Legislatures*" (my emphasis).

We know, specifically, that James Madison understood this. In his speech to the United States House of Representatives in which he introduced his proposed bill of rights, Madison brought up the English Declaration of Rights of 1688. It would have been impossible for members of Congress not to make the comparison. English subjects were brought up to venerate the Declaration of Rights, and that included all of the American Founders. Moreover, Madison was proposing an American bill of rights almost exactly one hundred years after Parliament adopted the English Bill of Rights. Comparisons were inevitable. And for that reason, Madison thought it essential to contrast the two. "[T]he truth is," observed Madison, the English Declaration goes "no farther than to raise a barrier against the power of the crown; the power of the legislature is left altogether indefinite."[126] By contrast, his bill of rights would bind Congress, and in some instances state legislatures, too. Madison suggested this was in keeping with American tradition. "The people of many states have thought it necessary to raise barriers against power in all forms and departments of government," he said.

Nevertheless, there was one parallel between Madison's proposed right-to-bear-arms provision and the arms provision in the English Declaration of Rights: Each was designed to resolve distribution-of-power issues. In 1689, Parliament wanted the king to acknowledge that Parliament made the law—specifically, law regulating the possession of arms by Protestants. A century later, Madison wanted to rectify a possible distribution of power as well. In this case, however, the issue was not a tug-of-war issue between two branches of government but between two levels of government, that is, between the national and state governments.

It was an elegant way to use a seventeenth-century template to resolve an eighteenth-century issue. Neither Madison nor his contemporaries could have possibly foreseen twenty-first-century ramifications of their work.

* * *

So far, we have scrupulously avoided moving beyond the time that Madison and his colleagues in the First Congress crafted the Second Amendment. The reason for that is simple: To understand what Madison and his colleagues intended when they wrote the Second Amendment, we should stick exclusively to what they knew then. Nevertheless, it can be helpful to know something about what Madison and the Founders did next. Was there, for example, an effort to reform the militia—to make it into a credible military force or at least ensure it was well armed? So in the final chapter and in the Conclusion, we will venture across the time barrier just a bit.

10

Chimeras of Liberty

ONE YEAR INTO his administration, George Washington told Congress it was time to act on its constitutional responsibility to organize the militia. In his first State of the Union address, Washington told Congress that it should now focus its attention on "providing for the common defense."[1] He then addressed, in turn, both the militia and the army. About the militia, Washington said: "A free people ought not only to be armed but disciplined; to which end a uniform and well digested plan is requisite: And their safety and interest require that they should promote such manufactories, as tend to render them independent on others, for essential, particularly for military supplies." The gist of Washington's remark was that having an armed populace, with all White adult males enrolled in the militia, was not sufficient for national defense. An effective militia had to be disciplined, that is, trained. The latter part of Washington's remark was focused on manufacturing weapons domestically so that the United States was not dependent on other nations—principally, Britain, France, or Spain, each of which was both a potential adversary—for military supplies.

About a professional force, Washington said: "The proper establishment of the Troops which may be deemed indispensable, will be entitled to mature consideration." But as to how large a professional army should be during peacetime, Washington was diplomatically vague. He said: "In the arrangements which may be made respecting it, it will be of importance to conciliate the comfortable support of the officers and soldiers with a due regard to economy." In his speech, therefore, Washington stopped at making the banal observation that the need for professional forces had to be weighed against their cost, taking into consideration the economic ramifications of raising the revenue through import duties or taxes. Washington, however, was suggesting that a professional force was necessary to protect Americans from hostile Indian tribes in the southern and western frontiers.

Things were, in fact, dicey in the western and southern frontiers, especially in the Ohio River Valley (the area comprised by the present states of Ohio and Indiana). Under the Treaty of Paris of 1783, which formally ended the Revolutionary War, Britain recognized the United States and ceded to it all land south of the Great Lakes and east of the Mississippi River. Previously, Britain had forbidden American colonists to settle on land west of the Appalachian Mountains. Now settlers were pressing westward onto land American Indian tribes considered their own. Most of the tribes had been allies of the British during the war, but they had no say in the treaty. On the same year the treaty was signed, thirty-five Indian nations formed a confederation to prevent settlers from seizing lands west of the Ohio River.[2] Washington had hoped to ameliorate the situation with negotiations and treaties, but that had not worked out. By the time of Washington's first State of the Union address, tensions between settlers and Indians in the Ohio River Valley had reached the boiling point. This conflict had geopolitical ramifications. Although Britain had lost the war as a result of French assistance at the Battle of Yorktown, it believed the United States was too weak to survive on its own and retained hopes of regaining its lost colonies. In violation of the treaty, Britain retained forts on the U.S. side of the Canadian border, and it was covertly arming the Indians and encouraging them toward open warfare.[3] Meanwhile, hostilities were also increasing between Creek Indians and Whites in western North Carolina and Georgia.[4] This also had geopolitical ramifications as aggressive Indian tribes provided a buffer between Spanish possessions in western Florida and Louisiana and voracious American settlers. Spain, too, was supplying Indians with arms and ammunition.[5]

The new republic had been born into a treacherous world. Washington strongly believed a credible military force was essential to deter aggression, whether from Indians or European powers. "To be prepared for war is one of the most effectual means of preserving peace," he told

Congress. Yet the United States army then consisted of only 672 men, most of whom were deployed in forts in the Ohio Valley.[6] Despite the hard realities, Washington understood that convincing Congress to appropriate funds for a reliable military would be difficult. Some headwinds came from anti–standing army rhetoric. Politicians still got mileage with speechifying about standing armies and tyranny, although most knowledgeable people knew better. "Our leaders flatter the people by declaiming against standing armies, and pretending to believe that the militia is the best security of a nation, but they are not in earnest, and their own experience may convince them of the futility of this notion," Charles Nisbet, president of Dickenson College, told a friend.[7] But there were broader cultural and economic obstacles, too. Americans were simply unaccustomed to a sizable federal government in any realm. There were then no more than five civilian employees in the War Department and six in the State Department.[8] In fact, even a decade later, civilian employees of the federal government would total just 153, including President Thomas Jefferson.[9] The greatest obstacle, however, was economic. For nearly two decades, the United States economy had been spiraling downward. National income had declined 30 percent since 1774.[10] Five years earlier, to raise desperately needed cash, the Confederation Congress had sold the nation's last warship.[11] Congress was unlikely to spend considerable money on a military unless it believed there was an exigent need.

Washington told Congress there was, in fact, an immediate need for a larger military. Both Britain and Spain had entered into alliances with Native Americans, he told Congress. And both nations were arming the Indians with guns and encouraging them into aggressions against settlers. Washington said a military presence on the western frontier was necessary to prevent and punish what he called "depredations" by Indians.[12]

Soon after Washington's State of the Union address, Secretary of War Henry Knox submitted to Congress the administration's plan for organizing the militia.[13] Knox, like Washington, put little stock in militia. Early in the Revolutionary War, Knox had supported Washington's pleas to Congress to raise a professional army, calling militia "a receptacle for ragamuffins."[14] As we have previously seen, militia shortcomings stemmed, in significant part, from their lack of training. Knox tried to rectify that somewhat by proposing three different classes of militia, with one class—consisting of 32,500 men between the ages of eighteen and twenty—receiving thirty days of training per year in state camps. This Advanced Corps, as it was labeled, would also be armed, clothed, and fed by the federal government. While soldiers who train for thirty days a year cannot be as proficient as professional troops training for three hundred days a year, thirty days was an enormous leap over the little or no training militia were then receiving.[15] The other classes were a Main Corps, consisting of 211,250 men between the ages twenty-one to forty-five, who would be mustered and trained four days a year, and a Reserve Corps of 81,250 men, ages forty-six to sixty, who would muster just twice a year. Obviously, the Advanced Corps was the heart of the Knox Plan. That was the only class to receive significant training, and the only class to be furnished with weapons and uniforms by the government. The other two classes would—by virtue of the amount of training they would receive—be little more than an active roster of additional men who might be called up should the need arise.

Even with a better trained militia, Washington and Knox continued to believe a regular army of some size was essential. Knox told Congress that only regulars "disciplined according to the nature of the service" would possess the qualities necessary to stand up to "the greatest probable combination of Indian enemy."[16] Knox, therefore, asked Congress to add to the existing army five new regiments—four regiments of infantry, one regiment of riflemen, plus a battalion of artillery and a battalion of cavalry—a total of about five thousand men. From our standpoint today, Knox's proposal seems modest. The percentage of Americans who serve in the active military today is three times what it would have been under the Knox Plan. Still, Knox's proposal was radical for its time. The projected price of $1 million per year would have more than tripled what the United States was then spending on its military.

The government had been attempting to negotiate with the Miami and Wabash tribes in the Ohio River Valley. But negotiations were failing, and Washington and Knox came increasingly to the view that force would be necessary.[17] The House approved the Five Regiment Plan. But the Senate refused, with some Senators accusing the administration of exaggerating the threat.[18] Denied five new regiments, the government assembled an expeditionary force consisting of 300 regulars and 1,500 militia drawn from Pennsylvania and Kentucky. In October 1790, Lieutenant Colonel Josiah Harmar led that force on a series of attacks on Indian villages in the Ohio River Valley. During an engagement with about 100 Indians on October 18, Kentucky militiamen bolted and ran at the first sign of the Indians, without firing a single shot. They fled until they had left the Ohio River Valley entirely.[19] Recklessly, Harmar continued his search-and-destroy mission. Three nights later, he sent a 400-man contingent of his larger force to return to a village that they had raided earlier, in the hope of surprising warriors who were returning after they thought the coast was clear. During that operation, some units split off to pursue what appeared to be fleeing warriors. But this was a ploy. With their enemy divided, the Indians attacked.[20] Once again, militia bolted, and most of the regulars, including their commanding officer, Major John P. Wyllys, were killed. Indians then attacked Harmar repeatedly. Over the course of the next two weeks, Harmar retreated from the Ohio River Valley. So hasty and panicked was his retreat that he abandoned soldiers who had become separated from his main force, and violating military tradition, he left behind his dead.

Harmar sent word to Henry Knox that he had been victorious, but Lieutenant Ebenezer Denny, who carried the official dispatches to Knox, told a different story. An analysis by Knox and the War Department confirmed Denny's version: The battles had been lost—and each battle was lost because militia fled, leaving the relatively small number of regulars exposed and overwhelmed. Moreover, when in camp or on marches, militia had been grossly disobedient, even mutinous, and after the crucial battle during the night of October 21 to 22, militia refused to fight again.[21]

While Knox was conducting his analysis, Congress was turning to its constitutional duty to organize the militia. On December 16, the House began several days of debate about the administration's militia proposal.[22] There was little enthusiasm for the Knox Plan, but there was no agreement about what to do instead. Nicholas Gilman of New Hampshire and John Laurance of New York did not want to require anyone to serve in the militia past age forty-five. Gilman and Elias Boudinot of New Jersey believed the active militia should be a smaller, more select force. James Jackson of Georgia disagreed. "In Georgia," he said, "the militia has been as strict as is contemplated by the bill, but they have never complained. In a Republic every man ought to be a soldier, and prepared to resist tyranny and usurpation, as well as invasion, and to prevent the greatest of evils—a standing army."[23] Jackson said that "the people of America would never consent to be deprived of the privilege of carrying arms," by which he meant being excluded from the militia, not being personally disarmed, which no one was suggesting.

Josiah Parker of Virginia argued that requiring militiamen to provide their own arms and military equipment would be impracticable because many could not afford to do so. Jeremiah Wadsworth of Connecticut countered that providing arms to those who could not afford them would "empower the officers to create an enormous charge against the United States."[24] Thomas Fitzsimons of Pennsylvania moved to add language providing "[t]hat every citizen so enrolled, and providing himself with the arms and accoutrements as aforesaid, shall hold the same exempt from all executions, or suits for debt, or for the payment of taxes."[25] Six congressmen, including James Madison, immediately rose in opposition. We do not know what each of them said; the transcript tells us only that they collectively argued that the language might be interpreted to mean that it was optional, to either the states or individuals, whether militiamen were armed. It is easy to understand Madison's concern, however. He wrote the Second Amendment to ensure that states could have armed militia. The practical effect of the Amendment was that if government did not furnish militia arms, the people could do so themselves. Madison would not want legislation that might be interpreted to mean that *only* militiamen themselves could furnish militia arms. The transcript tells us: "This motion was lost by a great majority."[26]

Much debate swirled over the question of who, if anyone, should be exempted from militia service. The question of whether Quakers should be exempted came up briefly, but what most animated members was whether they—that is, members of Congress—should be exempt. Even on this, opinions split.

When the militia debate ended, the House was not ready to vote on a final proposal. Everyone took it for granted that Congress should provide for national uniformity in the militia, but opinions had not gelled around such basic questions as who should serve in the militia; whether the federal government should mandate a certain level of training, and if so, how much; and who should bear the responsibility and cost of supplying arms and equipment: the federal government, state governments, or militiamen.

While Congress could afford to take its time, Washington and Knox did not believe they had that luxury. They were convinced Indians in the Ohio River Valley would be emboldened by their victory over Harmar's expedition, and that tribes might band together to increase raids on settlers. The administration believed, therefore, that it needed to take quick and decisive action to prevent outright war on the western frontier. Washington and Knox had wanted a professional army to deal with the Indians, but Congress had not given them one. So they devised an alternative that they hoped would be an easier sell: "levies," a sort of halfway house between militia and regulars.[27] Volunteers would enlist for the duration of the campaign (expected to be about four months) and serve under the command of regular army officers. In the wake of Harmar's defeat, Congress authorized raising two thousand men through levies and adding one additional regiment of infantry to the regular army.

In March 1791, Knox gave command of the new force to Major General Arthur St. Clair. The plan was for St. Clair to lead a force of three thousand from Fort Washington, where Cincinnati is now located, north into the Ohio River Valley. St. Clair was to build a series of forts as he progressed and then ultimately engage the Miami and Wabash tribes—assuming, that is, that the tribes did not agree to peace on St. Clair's terms. Knox sent a message to the tribes offering peace and warning that war would mean "the absolute destruction to you, your women, and children." If you do not embrace this last opportunity, Knox said, "your doom must be sealed forever."[28] It was precisely the wrong kind of message to encourage the tribes to seek peace through negotiations.

Notwithstanding his arrogant bombast, Knox was far from confident. He was encountering considerable difficulty raising troops through levies. But backing down was not an option, which left no choice but to make up the shortfall with militia. Moreover, the men who volunteered to join the levies were not of the quality that Knox expected, and because recruitment had been slow, they did not receive as much training as had originally been planned. These problems were, in turn, exacerbated by logistical difficulties: As late as June, there were not enough weapons at Ft. Washington to train troops, and when St. Clair's army began their march northward, it lacked adequate rations and quality powder. Instead of the planned force of 3,000, St. Clair's actual force totaled 1,400, which he, himself, described as "the worst and most dissatisfied troops I ever served with."[29] St. Clair was, himself, in less than optimum shape: he was suffering so painful an episode of gout that for periods of time troops were carrying him on a stretcher.[30]

St. Clair's orders were as follows: "Seek the enemy and endeavor by all possible means to strike them with great severity."[31] He realized that he was leading a force of about the same size and composition as had Harmar, so he could not have helped being on edge. On the night of November 3—camped just south of the Wabash River, not far from where Harmar had been attacked—St. Clair kept his entire force on alert for half the night. After becoming satisfied the enemy would not attack, he sent his exhausted soldiers to bed. Then, just before sunrise, one thousand Indians attacked. Once again, the militia immediately bolted. The attacking Indians penetrated quickly into the center of the camp. The regulars coalesced and fought stoutly for three hours, but they ultimately succumbed to a devastating crossfire. When the smoke cleared, six hundred soldiers and militia—more than 40 percent of St. Clair's total force—lay dead. Only about a third of St. Clair's soldiers were unscathed. History would record this as the greatest defeat ever sustained by the United States Army at the hands of American Indians.

According to one account, on the evening of December 9, a courier carrying news of the catastrophe arrived in Philadelphia, then the nation's temporary capital, and insisted upon delivering his dispatch personally, and immediately, to the president of the United States. Washington was in a reception with guests. Upon being told there was a courier who had to see him, Washington excused himself, read the dispatch, returned to his guests, and carried on without giving any hint of the devastating news he had just received. Only after the guests had departed did he allow himself to vent anger and frustration at the news.

As Washington and Knox now saw it, they were in a full-scale war with Indian tribes in the Northwest Territory—a war that could be won only with regular troops.[32] On January 11, 1792, the administration sent a full report to Congress together with a renewed request for the Five Regiment Plan that had failed in the Senate two years earlier.[33] Once again, Knox asked to raise five thousand regular troops, consisting of four infantry regiments, one riflemen regiment, a battalion of artillery, and a battalion of cavalry. The cost was still $1,000,000 per year (the equivalent of about $28,500,000 today—a paltry sum by current standards but then staggeringly large in eyes of members of Congress). To avoid objections about the evils of a standing army, this time the legislation provided for the troops to be disbanded after the Indian threat ended.[34] Congress debated the proposal with a sense of urgency.[35] Some members accused the administration of unnecessarily provoking an Indian war on the frontier. White settlers were just as much the aggressors, they argued. The proper policy was not a full-out war against Indians but employing a small force as a buffer to keep the two sides apart. Others laid all the blame at the feet of the Indians. But most congressmen probably thought questions about the origins of the conflict were now beside the point: A war was underway, and that war had to be won.

There was, again, the usual give and take about the relative merits of militia versus regulars. An unidentified congressman said "that frontier militia are not only unequal, but infinitely superior to any regular troops whatever, in defense of the borders, and that they are, in fact, the only force that can be effectively employed in expeditions against hostile Indians, whose mode of fighting is familiar to them, and does not strike them with the degree of terror with which it inspires those men who enlist on the regular establishment."[36] Another member of Congress, also unidentified, said: "Every man who has ever seen militia in the field cannot but know that a very trifling disaster, or a slight cause of discontent, is sufficient to make them disband and forget all subordination, so far as even to neglect the means of self-defense; whereas regular troops, under proper discipline, and acting with greater steadiness and concert, are much to be depended on."[37] The pro-militia view had to seem hollow in light of the disastrous experiences of Harmar and St. Clair, both of whom had led troops composed largely of militia or of levies resembling militia.

How members voted depended more on how much their constituents wanted protection from Indians than on even their own

rhetoric about standing armies. Two congressmen representing frontier areas in western Pennsylvania voted to raise the professional force,
even though they often pontificated about the evils of standing armies
and the virtues of militia.[38] New England Federalists were generally
opposed. Knox attempted to persuade Elbridge Gerry to introduce
the plan in the House. He thought that would help, both because
Gerry was from Massachusetts and because he was a principal trum-
peter of the virtues of militia and the evils of standing armies. Gerry
declined to sponsor the bill, but he was absent on the day the vote
was taken, thereby avoiding criticism for either voting against the
proposal or being a hypocrite and for voting for it.[39] James Madison
voted for the bill—even though he was beginning to politically drift
away from George Washington and would soon ally himself with the
administration's Republican opponents—while James Monroe, newly
elected by the Virginia legislature to fill a Senate seat vacated upon the
death of William Grayson, voted against it.[40] The Five Regiment bill
passed the House by a comfortable margin, and this time around it
also squeaked through the Senate.[41] The United States started recruiting
and training a five-thousand-man professional force it would call the
Legion of the United States.

Four months later, Congress resolved the other side of the military
equation by passing the Uniform Militia Act of 1792.[42] This legislation
did not resemble the Knox Plan. The Act provided that that "each and
every free able-bodied white male citizen" between the ages of eighteen
and forty-four was to be enrolled in the militia, and that every militiaman was to provide himself with either a "good musket or firelock"
and a bayonet, or "a good rifle," about two dozen rounds of ammunition suited to his particular weapon, and a knapsack. Cavalrymen were
required to provide their own horses, saddles, boots, spurs, sabers, and
pistols. All federal officials, from the president down to people delivering
mail for the post office—and including members of Congress—were
exempt from militia service. While the Act did not provide a blanket
exemption for Quakers or other conscientious objectors, it exempted
anyone who was exempted from militia service by the law of his state.
A couple of states exempted those religiously opposed to bearing arms;
a number of states exempted teachers, students, clergy, and local and
state officials.[43] In an invasion, the president could call out the militia

on his own authority. If the laws of the United States were obstructed "by combinations too powerful to be suppressed by the ordinary course of judicial proceeds," the president could call out the militia after being notified of the need to do so by a federal judge. In the case of an insurrection in any state, the president could—upon a request from either the legislature or the governor of that state—call out militia from other states to suppress the insurrection. Implicit in the Act was the authority of a state to call out its own militia in the event of an insurrection or other internal need.

A weaker militia act could not have been enacted. There was no select militia who would undergo meaningful training. Indeed, no training was required whatsoever.[44] Brigade inspectors were to attend militia musters, inspect their arms and ammunition, and report the results of their inspection "at least once every year." As a practical matter, therefore, Congress required nothing more than maintaining an annual roster of militiamen and their weapon. And since militiamen supplied their own weapons, there was no uniformity of arms, which meant there would be no uniformity of ammunition—a supply nightmare in a military conflict. Moreover, the federal government was to provide no assistance in procuring arms, even though many men did not have muskets, rifles, or the money to buy them. Two years later, when President Washington called up 15,000 militiamen to suppress the Whiskey Rebellion, only a little more than one-third of them had weapons.[45] And according to a War Department estimate at the time, less than one-quarter of all militiamen in the United States possessed arms required by the Act.[46]

Some believe that George Washington expressed his displeasure at so feeble an Act by not signing it until the very last day permitted under the Constitution.[47] Washington had little regard for militia. But as we know from his "Sentiments on a Peace Establishment" prepared in 1783, and from the Knox Plan, he believed that a relatively small, select militia could be chosen, armed, and given at least some degree of meaningful training. While such a force would never be the equal of more highly trained regulars, Washington believed it could nonetheless contribute to national defense. However, a universal militia comprised of everyone, without meaningful training, was worse than worthless because it lulled the nation into a false sense of security. Washington had originally come to his views about the militia while himself serving as a Virginia militia officer during the French and Indian War. His views had been painfully confirmed during the Revolutionary War. Now they reconfirmed yet again on the western frontier.

Washington was not the only person who found the Uniform Militia Act of 1792 wanting. One commentator said its provisions "were unworkable when they were adopted; they were soon obsolete; [and] as measures of national defense, they were worthless."[48] And according to a leading military historian, "By the 1790s, the old colonial militia had become an obsolete," and yet Congress simply continued that institution, without reform, even though "many Americans sensed the inability of state institutions, poorly coordinated, badly disciplined, and casually armed to meet the needs of the republic."[49]

What was Congress thinking when it passed the Militia Act of 1792? Congress, of course, was not a single mind. Its members did not all think alike. But to the extent there was a collective view, it had to be this: "The militia, as we know it, is not and cannot become an effective military force. To the extent that we need a military force, we must raise, equip, and train a professional force. And because of the geographic advantages we enjoy, should war loom on the horizon, we are likely to have time to raise and train a professional force." Nor would Congress's thinking quickly change. The Uniform Militia Act of 1792 remained in effect until 1903.[50]

Raising a professional army to meet a current threat is what Congress did in 1792. To defeat the hostile Indian tribes in the Ohio River Valley, Congress authorized a five-thousand-man professional army, to be named the Legion of the United States. The commander of that force, General Anthony Wayne, was given two full years to recruit and train his Legionnaires. When he was ready to march, Wayne assured Henry Knox that the Legion had been well trained and rigorously disciplined, and was therefore capable of victory. The decisive engagement, known as the Battle of Fallen Timbers, occurred on August 20, 1794. Wayne's force in that battle—nine hundred Legionnaires, who were well trained and highly disciplined but not combat veterans—defeated an opposing force of two thousand Indians assisted by a company of Canadian militia.[51] The Battle of Fallen Timbers (followed by a vicious scorched-earth campaign against Indian villages) marked the end of Indian military challenges in the Northwest Territory, as well as British efforts to provoke those challenges.[52]

Military historian Richard H. Kohn titled a book chapter devoted to the Uniform Militia Act "The Murder of the Militia System [1792]."[53] Congress, however, did not murder the militia system. It continued it. The militia remained exactly what they had previously been: a highly effective instrument of slave control. If anything, the South was relieved that Congress had not interfered with its militia.

When, in 1807, it appeared that the United States and Britain were moving toward war, the U.S. Army had 3,287 men.[54] President Thomas Jefferson wanted a credible force to threaten an invasion of Canada. That possibility, Jefferson believed, would incentivize Britain to make concessions and avoid war with the United States. But Jefferson was reluctant to ask Congress to expand the army, so he directed the nation's governors to prepare for his calling 100,000 militiamen to federal service. Could Jefferson have been surprised when his secretary of the treasury told him they could not expect to draw militia from states south of Pennsylvania because "none can be spared from the Negro country"?[55] Or, considering how the Virginia militia performed during the Revolutionary War, could Jefferson have been surprised when the mayor of Norfolk privately told him that the local militia were almost totally useless as a defense force, adding: "If feasts, popular toasts, fine speeches, patriotic professions, and self-important airs were weapons . . . we should drive all our enemies into the red sea!"[56]

The Norfolk mayor's remark is telling. Institutions often develop the culture they need. Pomposity, inflated self-importance, toasts, and feasts are not compatible with a hard and disciplined military organization. But a slave-control militia did not need rigorous discipline and training. It needed ways to attract and retain men who were willing to spend a great deal of time patrolling in the night, often with little or no financial compensation.[57] There are men for whom feasts, toasts, camaraderie, and patriotic posturing will go a long way. Maybe this partly explains why men who were assigned a year of slave patrol duty in Norfolk County, Virginia, often continued on for a number of years.[58]

Meanwhile, James Madison had experienced a political transformation.[59] At the Constitutional Convention in Philadelphia in 1787, and at the Virginia Ratifying Convention in 1788, Madison was a committed nationalist. He recognized that a mere confederation of states had been an abject failure and believed that a strong national government— deriving its authority directly from the people—was essential. Madison had even wanted a national government powerful enough to veto state laws. Madison had not only been a federalist, but a federalist leader— one of the strongest advocates for the Constitution, one of George Washington's most intimate political friends and advisers, and the man antifederalists such as Patrick Henry and George Mason considered their principal nemesis. Then, during the Washington administration, Madison changed. He became one of the founders of the Republican Party, the opposition party to George Washington and the Federalists (with a capital *F* because it designates not the informal group who wanted to ratify the Constitution but members of a political party).

The divisions between Republicans and Federalists were personal, sectional, ideological, and international. They were personal because they arose, in part, from competing personal ambitions between Thomas Jefferson, Washington's secretary of state, and Alexander Hamilton, Washington's secretary of the treasury. Both men were ambitious; both men wanted to be Washington's primary protégé and eventual successor; and both men developed personal antipathies for the other. The divisions were sectional because, in the main, the Republicans represented the interests of the agricultural South and the Federalists those of the manufacturing and commercial North. (This does not mean, however, that all Northerners were Federalists and all Southerners were Republicans.) The sectional affiliations bled into the ideological divisions. The Republicans believed that an agriculturally based society would produce a more virtuous and humble people. The Federalists believed a mercantile-based nation would be stronger, more vibrant, and more cosmopolitan.

This, in turn, affected political philosophies. The North was growing more quickly in population than the South, which meant that as time marched on, the North was more likely to control both the House of Representatives and the presidency. The Republicans, therefore, became champions of state rights. They argued that the national government had no powers beyond those specifically enumerated in the Constitution. Federalists, by contrast, remained proponents of a strong national government. They stressed that the Constitution gave Congress the power to enact whatever legislation was "necessary and proper" to execute the broad powers that the Constitution granted it, including the power to provide for the "general welfare." This division came to the fore when Alexander Hamilton proposed creating a national bank to put capital to use financing projects in support of government and commerce. The Federalists agreed with Hamilton. The Republicans thought that debt and borrowing led to decadence and corruption. They also feared that a national bank would increase national power at the expense of the states.

Views about domestic policy intertwined with views about foreign relations. Britain and France were superpowers and almost constant enemies. Toward which would America lean? The Federalists wanted good relations with Britain because it was America's principal commercial trading partner. As Republicans saw it, America fought a war against British oppression, and France had been America's ally in that war. They also saw the French Revolution as following in the anti-monarchial spirit of the American Revolution. Jefferson had become such a Francophile that he even argued that the rise of Napoleon Bonaparte would be good for republics like the United States.[60] Republicans promoted conspiracy-minded theories that Federalists wanted to either reunite America with Britain or create a British-styled monarchy in America. A peril of dabbling in paranoid propaganda is coming to believe it yourself. This occurred surprisingly quickly. On May 5, 1792, Madison privately told George Washington that Secretary of the Treasury Alexander Hamilton, Vice President John Adams, and Chief Justice John Jay were all closet monarchists. In his personal notes, Madison observed that Washington seemed "not to be in any wise satisfied with what I had urged."[61]

On the question of where to strike the balance between national and state power in the federal system, Madison's transformation took him across the spectrum from the position he advocated at the Constitutional Convention of wanting to give the national government a veto over state laws to the position he advocated in 1789 that the states had the right to "interpose" themselves between federal laws they considered to be unconstitutional and their citizens.[62] To be fair, Madison advocated for interposition as a way of tempering Jefferson's contention that states could nullify federal laws that they considered to be unconstitutional. Madison did not want to support Jefferson's radical theory, but he did not want to undercut his friend and ally, either. Still, the Madison of 1787 would not have argued such a thing under any circumstances.

* * *

Standing armies were too expensive for both Republicans and Federalists, but Republicans, especially, made speeches praising militia and condemning standing armies.[63] That turned out to be a double-edged sword. In June 1812, President James Madison asked Congress to declare war against Great Britain. Congress obliged, although not by overwhelming margins.[64] We shall not delve into the complex events leading up to this, other than to say that through a series of diplomatic missteps and miscalculations, Madison painted himself into a corner and felt compelled to declare war against Britain.[65] The United States then had an army of 6,744 men in active service.[66] The U.S. Navy had six frigates. Britain had more than three hundred frigates plus dozens of even more formidable ships of the line. Congress authorized expanding the army to 35,603, but it would take time to recruit, equip, and train that force, and there was no surge of men seeking to enlist. Congress also authorized Madison to call up 100,000 militia for six months of service. As one military historian observed, the militia figure was "impressive but deceiving, for most of the militia was poorly trained and equipped."[67] The secretary of war found that in the Pennsylvania militia only one man in five had a musket.[68]

Madison's strategy was to use large militia forces to invade Canada and seize Montreal before Britain could send an army to defend them, and then negotiate peace from a position of strength. It did not work. The United States launched two separate attacks—one near Detroit in August, the other near Niagara Falls in October. In the Battle of Detroit, 300 U.S. regulars and 1,200 Ohio militiamen were immediately outmaneuvered by a combined British-Shawnee force. The entire American force surrendered without firing a shot.[69] The plan for the Battle of Niagara was for 3,500 New York militiamen and a single detachment of regulars to cross the Niagara River and attack Queenston, Canada. The British commander was killed at the very outset of the battle, throwing his force into temporary disarray. Notwithstanding that advantage, two-thirds of the militia balked and refused to cross the river, leaving the advance force unsupported. More than a thousand Americans were killed or captured by the British and Chippewa defenders.[70] Although there would be later engagements in which the United States took pride—including Oliver Hazard Perry's naval victory on Lake Erie ("We have met the enemy, and he is ours")—they did not have sufficient strategic value to revive Madison's hopes of conquering Canada.

In attempting to rally the nation, Madison, more than once, found himself hung on his own Republican petards. Massachusetts and Connecticut refused to send militia for the Canadian campaign.[71] They argued that the Constitution only empowered the national government to call forth the militia to "suppress Insurrections and repel Invasions." There was no power to use the militia to invade another country. Madison must have found it galling to have Federalist states thumb their noses at him with Republican arguments about limited, enumerated powers. Madison called their strict construction of the constitutional language "novel and unfortunate."[72] He argued that if the federal government could not use the militia for national defense, its only alternative would be "those large and permanent military establishments which are forbidden by the principles of our free government, and against the necessity of which, the militia were meant to be a constitutional bulwark." This was not the James Madison of the Constitutional Convention or the Virginia Ratifying Convention. That James Madison understood that the Constitution gave Congress the authority to raise armies and maintain a navy, and the discretion to decide on which kinds of forces to rely. Madison was surely also frustrated by Congressman John Randolph of Virginia, a cousin of Thomas Jefferson, who was gaining a great deal of attention by claiming to be a better republican than the president. Randolph used his considerable oratorical skills on the House floor to argue that invading Canada was inconsistent with republican principles because Canada could not be conquered without a standing army, and that raising a standing army violated republican principles.[73] It must have been especially vexing that on the first point, Randolph was proved right.

During the early stages of the war, Britain was distracted by its war against Napoleonic France. A main feature of its war with the United

States was harassing Chesapeake coastal areas with raiding parties from British warships. This fit hand in glove with keeping the United States guessing about whether, and where, it might land a sizable ground force. It also brought slavery to the forefront of the war. When the federal government ordered new recruits to the northern front, Virginia's governor complained this exposed his state to "great dangers to be apprehended from our Black population," whether "from their violence" or "by their desertion."[74] The militia were needed for slave control, but no one felt they would provide an effective defense if they had to tangle with British regulars. A Virginia congressman described the militia as badly equipped, badly disciplined, and not at all as portrayed "by the patriotic puffs of the newspapers and orators."[75] The commander of the York County militia reported that only one man in five or six had a musket. Many of those men had been given muskets during a potential crisis five years earlier, but they had sold them, lost them, and allowed them to corrode.[76]

In April 1813, British warships sailed into the Chesapeake Bay, effectively closing it to American maritime traffic. The ships bombarded Havre de Grace with cannon fire, and raiding parties burned and looted several towns on both sides of the Bay.[77] Virginia wanted the national government to do something to protect it from the British warships menacing its coastline, but to leave its militia alone to attend to its slave control duties. Some slaves were running away, trying to make their way to British raiding parties or ships and pleading to be taken in. And, of course, Virginians became increasingly fearful slaves might revolt. Slave patrolling went into hyper-drive. Prior to the war in Lancaster County, Virginia, four men had spent thirty hours per month patrolling. In July 1813, thirty-seven men spent 1,544 hours on slave patrol duty.[78] In April 1814, the commander of the British fleet in the Chesapeake publicly offered freedom to slaves, and their families, if they ran away, reached British forces, and agreed to either enter the British army or navy or accept relocation to British possessions in Canada or the West Indies.[79] He expected only a small number of slaves to take him up on the offer. After all, how many slaves would even learn of the offer? And how many would risk getting past slave patrols and somehow make their way to British warships offshore? But during the course of the war, 3,400 slaves did just that.[80]

* * *

We are ready for a few concluding thoughts. But we shall begin that with one short, final story.

Conclusion

ON AUGUST 17, 1814, the enemy landed about four thousand soldiers where the Patuxent River flows into the Chesapeake Bay and began slowly marching north.[1] Not knowing where the British were headed, the Americans decided to place their forces on commanding heights at Bladensburg, Maryland, nine miles northeast of Washington. They were positioned there to defend either the nation's capital or Baltimore. The Americans destroyed bridges crossing the Potomac south of Washington so that, if the federal capital were their goal, the British would have to cross the Anacostia River at Bladensburg, where both the river was fordable and the Eastern Branch Bridge remained.

When fully assembled, the American forces consisted of about four hundred regular Army soldiers, five hundred U.S. Navy sailors, and between six thousand and seven thousand militia from Virginia, Maryland, and Pennsylvania. In light of his numerical advantage, General William H. Winder, the American commander, thought that the British would retreat back to their ships. But at midnight on August 24, a rider arrived with a note from James Monroe, the secretary of state (and future president) who was personally serving as an Army scout. Monroe reported that the British were heading for Washington, DC. Around 10:00 AM, President James Madison met with his cabinet secretaries at General Winder's camp in southeast Washington. The president asked Secretary of War John Armstrong whether he had any final advice in the face of the current emergency. As Madison himself recorded it, Armstrong answered "no." Then Armstrong added that "as the battle would be between militia and regular forces, the former would be beaten."[2]

Madison was upset by the remark, but for many good reasons he had long since lost faith in his secretary of war. He ordered Armstrong to proceed to Bladensburg and assist General Winder in any way possible. Shortly afterward, the president himself bravely rode on horseback to Bladensburg. He wanted to be on hand to resolve disputes of authority among American commanders, who had been feuding. Among other things, state militia had been refusing to take orders from General Winder of the federal army.[3] When he arrived, Madison misunderstood where the opposing forces were and rode straight through the American lines and toward British vanguards. An alert sentry called out to him, and the president—dangerously close to being captured—wheeled around and rode quickly back to American lines. Madison then rode to a hilltop where he and American commanders could view the impending battle. From that vantage point, the president watched what to this day is still considered one of the most humiliating defeats in American military history. As Ralph Ketcham put it, "The British regulars pushed ahead, driving first one detachment of militia and then another before them."[4]

Even though they outnumbered their enemy, the relatively untrained, undisciplined, and inexperienced militia were simply no match for professional soldiers who had been battle-tested in the Napoleonic wars. Entire companies of militia threw down their weapons and fled in panic.[5] According to one witness, "the militia ran like sheep chased by dogs."[6] By contrast, the small contingent of U.S. Navy commanded by Captain Joshua Barney held its ground. They fought on determinately as militia disappeared, leaving them to face the British nearly alone. The sailors quit the field only after running out of ammunition; for some reason, their ammunition train had departed without notice.[7] British casualties totaled one hundred dead and three hundred to four hundred wounded; American casualties were twenty-six dead and fifty-one wounded.[8] The striking discrepancy was due, in significant part, to Navy fighters inflicting large casualties on the enemy while militiamen saved their skins by running away.

After setting fire to the Capitol building, British Rear Admiral Cockburn literally ate the president's dinner. Upon entering the White

House, he found a well-set table and meat roasting on spits, awaiting Madison.[9] "To Jemmy's health!" toasted Cockburn as he raised a glass of the president's favorite Madeira wine, which was sitting on a side table. After dinner, Cockburn and his officers piled up tables and chairs and set the president's mansion ablaze. They then moved on to other government buildings and set them on fire, too.

Who was responsible for this disaster? There was plenty of blame to go around. Armstrong had been an incompetent and disloyal secretary of war; Winder had been a dithering military commander whose preparations to meet the invaders had been slow and chaotic; and although President Madison had understood that Armstrong and Winder had been deficient, he sat on his hands while things moved inexorably to calamity. But one wonders whether—as he watched the flames and columns of smoke from a distant hilltop—Madison thought back to political choices he had made during the course of his career and how some of them helped lead to this shameful day. For, in terms of political philosophy and alliances, the James Madison of 1814 was not the same man who earned the reputation as Father of the Constitution for his brilliant work during the Constitutional Convention in Philadelphia in 1788. He was not the same man who collaborated with Alexander Hamilton and John Jay to produce *The Federalist*. He was not the same man who had eloquently defended the Constitution at his state's ratifying convention against the attacks of the antifederalists who did not want Virginia to ratify that document and join the Union. Madison knew that he was, in at least small part, responsible for the United States having strong slave control but weak national defense.

James Madison did not need Secretary of War John Armstrong to tell him militiamen would be unable to go toe to toe with professional soldiers. Madison knew that. All of the Founders knew it. Even Thomas Jefferson, who had every inclination to glorify the citizen soldier as a more virtuous and superior warrior, and who originally believed it, watched with horror at how incompetently the militia performed during the Revolutionary War.[10] After the war, the Federalists—Washington and Hamilton especially—wanted America to retain a professional military. Jefferson, however, believed that America, protected by a vast ocean, did not need a strong military.[11] Moreover, Jefferson and his party, the Republicans, had political reasons for opposing a robust military. For one thing, a military is expensive. Maintaining one would require the federal government to raise significant revenue through taxes. Once such a revenue stream was established, it might easily be incrementally enlarged to fund broader ambitions of the national government. For Republicans, that was anathema. And if that was inconvenient to admit directly, there was another argument—fatuous yet rhetorically appealing—to deploy: the worn, two-sided coin of standing armies leading to tyranny, and the militia providing a bulwark against standing armies.

The militia were, in fact, a bulwark—but not a bulwark of national defense. They were a bulwark against slave insurrections.

When James Madison sat down with his quill pen in 1789 to protect the right of states to maintain armed militia to provide for their own security, he was still almost entirely the James Madison of the Constitutional Convention and *The Federalist*. He was still a friend and political ally of George Washington and Alexander Hamilton, and he still believed in a strong national government. (He was a friend of Jefferson, too, but Madison's bitter, irrevocable break with Washington and Hamilton would not come until 1796.[12]) The task Madison set for himself then was a limited one. He wrote what became the Second Amendment to solve a political problem, not a governmental problem. At the Virginia Ratifying Convention, Patrick Henry and George Mason had accused Madison of handing Northern abolitionists a way to undermine the slave system: Congress could disarm the militia. Madison thought that to be nothing but a dark fantasy—a bugbear conjured by Patrick Henry. But Henry had touched a nerve. "Haunted" by Henry's ghost, Madison wrote the Amendment to assure his constituents, and the South generally, that Congress could not deprive states of armed militia.

In all likelihood, Madison paid relatively little attention to his right-to-bear-arms provision. It was a small part of the larger project of writing twelve proposed amendments to the Constitution. The Amendment can be seen as a supplement to the slavery compact and the militia clauses in the Constitution, but when Madison wrote it and his colleagues modified and adopted it, they all probably considered it uncontroversial. Even a Connecticut Yankee such as Roger Sherman was willing to assure the South that Congress would not interfere with slave control. Madison surely thought more about other provisions in the Bill of Rights that he considered more important, particularly those protecting what he considered "the great rights." In fact, dear reader, it is a good bet that by now you have spent more time thinking about what James Madison thought about the Second Amendment than Madison, himself, spent thinking about the provision. That does not mean he was cavalier. Madison was not only brilliant; he was invariably diligent. He was mindful about what he was doing. He wanted to accomplish something; and he did not want to accomplish more than that. He gave thought to every word and phrase. So, too, did some of his colleagues. The House and the Senate changed Madison's draft slightly to create what ultimately became the Second Amendment.

Did Madison reconsider the Second Amendment later in life? Probably not. He did not expect it to have significant practical effects when he wrote it, and it would be difficult to argue that it did have significant effects during Madison's lifetime. When he watched Washington burn, Madison may well have had regrets about his contributing to an overreliance on the militia, by succumbing to rhetoric demonizing standing armies and glorifying militia. Consider the subtle difference in the language that James Madison used when, in the message he sent Congress announcing that the War of 1812 had ended, he praised "the public spirit of the militia" but the "valor of the military and naval forces of the country."[13] Experience had been a hard teacher, Madison conceded. Now he recommended that Congress maintain an "adequate regular force" in peacetime, gradually expand the navy, and discipline the militia. Cries of "No standing armies!" would disappear. Henceforth, America would maintain an army and navy at all times. But there were still reasons (which had always been primary) for not maintaining sizable military forces in peacetime. Bordered by two great oceans, America still believed it had time to expand its military when that became necessary. Its strategy, now, was to maintain a well-trained military that could be quickly expanded should the need arise.

That did not change until the Cold War when nuclear weapons, long-range bombers, aircraft carriers, and missiles changed the calculus. In his farewell address to the nation, delivered in January 1961, President Dwight David Eisenhower expressed a modern concern about the political power of large, permanent armed forces and the corporations that supply them when he warned the nation about "unwarranted influence, whether sought or unsought, by the military-industrial complex."[14] As President Eisenhower observed, the size of the United States armed forces and the money spent on defense in peacetime were unprecedented. The United States was then spending about 9 percent of its gross domestic product on defense and 2,472,166 Americans were serving on active duty in the four branches of the nation's armed forces.[15]

On one occasion, Congress did disarm the Southern militia. In 1867, in the wake of the Civil War, Confederate Army regiments began reorganizing as militia to intimidate and control emancipated slaves. Congress responded by adding a provision to an appropriations bill to prohibit the nine states that had rebelled (and which were then unrepresented in Congress) from "further organization, arming, or calling into service" the militia.[16] During debate over this provision in the Senate, some members argued this violated the Second Amendment, but most members felt the restriction was reasonable because it was necessary and essential. President Andrew Johnson could not block the provision without vetoing the entire appropriations bill, so he signed the legislation under protest, complaining that it denied the Southern states "their constitutional right to protect themselves, in any emergency, by means of their own militia."[17]

After serving two terms as president, James Madison retired to Montpelier, where one hundred slaves worked his plantation. He was sufficiently embarrassed about being a slaveholder to build showcase slave cabins in a prominent spot fifty yards from the main house. These were to impress visitors.[18] Most of his slaves continued to live in worse cabins near the fields. The South remained in perpetual fear of slave revolts throughout his life. In 1822, for example, an elaborately planned insurrection led by a free Black named Denmark Vesey in Charleston, South Carolina, was discovered and foiled before it was launched. The plotters, who it was rumored may have numbered in the hundreds, or even thousands, had collected 250 pikes and bayonets and 300 daggers for the revolt.[19] At least 139 Blacks were arrested; following trials, 35 were hanged. Slave patrols in Charleston were permanently increased to 150 men, and the state legislature appropriated funds for a fortified patrol headquarters, named The Citadel.

It is impossible to know what Madison would have made of the Civil War, Abraham Lincoln, and the Emancipation Proclamation. And what would James Madison and his colleagues in the First Congress—who, in their discussions about the Second Amendment, focused exclusively on military concerns related to the militia—have made of the United States Supreme Court declaring, for the first time in the year 2008, that the Second Amendment grants individuals a right to have guns for their own purposes, entirely divorced from the militia?

Surely, they would have been astounded.

AUTHOR'S NOTE

To make this book as readable as possible, I have modernized spelling, punctuation, capitalization, and other elements of style (such as replacing ampersand signs with the word "and") in transcribed oral statements, letters, and diaries from the seventeenth century, eighteenth century, and early nineteenth century. I have indicated where I have made such changes by including the notation "spelling and style modernized" in an endnote. I have made no such changes in constitutions, statutes, resolutions, or other documents formally adopted or promulgated by an official body, or in proposed drafts of such documents.

My thanks to Hannah Pfeiffer, Zoe Sperber, and Edward Gencarelli, all of whom are now alumni of the Roger Williams University School of Law, for their diligent research assistance, valuable feedback, and perpetual good cheer on this project.

NOTES

———⟡———

Introduction

1. Peter H. Wood, *Black Majority: Negroes in Colonial South Carolina from 1670 through the Stono Rebellion* (W.W. Norton, 1974), 222 (spelling and style modernized).
2. Peter Charles Hoffer, *Cry Liberty: The Great Stono River Slave Rebellion of 1739* (Oxford University Press, 2012), 41.
3. Jack Shuler, *Calling Out Liberty: The Stono Slave Rebellion and the Universal Struggle for Human Rights* (University Press of Mississippi, 2009), 70.
4. Hoffer, *Cry Liberty*, 21–23.
5. Peter Hoffer speculates that one of the men may have been the night watchman. The other was a prominent landowner. Hoffer, *Cry Liberty*, 78–79.
6. Hoffer, *Cry Liberty*, 87–98; Shuler, *Calling Out Liberty*, 70–71.
7. Shuler, *Calling Out Liberty*, 70.
8. Hoffer, *Cry Liberty*, 103–4.
9. Wood, *Black Majority*, 312 (quoting Bull's letter to the Duke of Newcastle; spelling and style modernized).
10. According to Peter Hoffer, Bull did not personally ride to Wiltown but sent one of the men with him. Hoffer, *Cry Liberty*, 110.
11. Hoffer, *Cry Liberty*, 111–19; Shuler, *Call Out Liberty*, 71–73.
12. Hoffer, *Cry Liberty*, 121.
13. Hoffer, *Cry Liberty*, 124.
14. Wood, *Black Majority*, 220–21 (quoting from the diary of Captain Philip Friedrick von Reck; spelling and style modernized).
15. Hoffer, *Cry Liberty*, 122.

16. Wood, *Black Majority*, 276.
17. Wood, *Black Majority*, 277.
18. Wood, *Black Majority*, 274 (quoting doctoral dissertation of David William Cole).
19. Wood, *Black Majority*, 221.
20. Letter from Samuel Eveleigh to Mr. Martyn (September 10, 1735), available at https://classroom.monticello.org/view/74235 (spelling and style modernized).
21. Wood, *Black Majority*, 221.
22. Martin S. Flaherty, "History 'Lite' in Modern American Constitutionalism," 95 *Columbia Law Review* 523, 553–54 (1995).
23. Don Higginbotham, "The Second Amendment in Historical Context," 16 *Constitutional Commentary* 263, 263–64 (1999). Professor Higginbotham was referring to my article "The Hidden History of the Second Amendment," 31 *U.C. Davis Law Review* 309 (1998).
24. Nathan Kozuskanich, "Originalism, History, and the Second Amendment: What Did Bearing Arms Really Mean to the Founders," 10 *University of Pennsylvania Journal of Constitutional Law* 413, 446 (2008).
25. Quentin Skinner, "Meaning and Understanding in the History of Ideas," 8 *History and Theory* 3, 39 (1969).
26. Skinner, "Meaning and Understanding," 39 (Skinner quoting J. Hingham; italics eliminated).
27. David Hackett Fisher, *Historians' Fallacies: Toward a Logic of Historical Thought* (Harper Torchbooks, 1970), 214.
28. Fisher, *Historians' Fallacies*, 215.
29. Richard Beeman, *Plain, Honest Men: The Making of the American Constitution* (Random House, 2009), 369.
30. Beeman, *Plain, Honest Men*, 412.
31. Beeman, *Plain, Honest Men*, 374.
32. See generally Saul Cornell, *The Other Founders: Anti-Federalism and the Dissenting Tradition in America, 1788–1828* (University of North Carolina Press, 1999); and Ralph Ketcham, ed., *The Antifederalist Papers and the Constitutional Convention Debates* (Mentor, 1989).
33. Colin Woodard, *American Nations: A History of the Eleven Rival Regional Cultures of North America* (Penguin Books, 2011), 119.

Chapter 1

1. George Morgan, *The Life of James Monroe* (Boston, Small, Maynard and Co., 1921) (reporting weather of opening day), 131.
2. Pauline Maier, *Ratification: The People Debate the Constitution 1787–1788* (Simon & Schuster, 2010), 223–25, 458–59.
3. Maier, *Ratification*, 217–23.
4. Maier, *Ratification*, 222.
5. Maier, *Ratification*, 218, 314.

6.   Maier, *Ratification*, 320. Regarding Clinton generally, see Maier, *Ratification*, 320–28, and Ron Chernow, *Alexander Hamilton* (Penguin Books, 2004), 108–9, 217–22, and 236–38.

7.   Harlow Giles Unger, *Lion of Liberty: Patrick Henry and the Call for a New Nation* (Da Capo, 2010), 208.

8.   Chernow, *Alexander Hamilton*, 220.

9.   Chernow, *Alexander Hamilton*, 236 (quoting Clinton).

10. Chernow, *Alexander Hamilton*, 237 (quoting an unsigned article attributed to Hamilton).

11. Chernow, *Alexander Hamilton*, 237 (quoting an unsigned article attributed to a "Clinton henchman").

12. Chernow, *Alexander Hamilton*, 262 (quoting Hamilton).

13. https://gunstonhall.org/learn/george-mason/mason-slavery. Cf. Jeff Broadwater, *George Mason: Forgotten Founder* (University of North Carolina Press, 2006), 6 (placing the number at around ninety slaves), and Richard Beeman, *Plain, Honest Men: The Making of the American Constitution* (Random House, 2009), 320 (placing the number at three hundred slaves).

14. Ralph Ketcham, *James Madison: A Biography* (University Press of Virginia, 1990), 12.

15. Chernow, *Alexander Hamilton*, 628.

16. Paul Finkelman, *Supreme Injustice: Slavery in the Nation's Highest Court* (Harvard University Press, 2018).

17. Ron Chernow, *Washington: A Life* (Penguin Books, 2010), 800.

18. Unger, *Lion of Liberty*, 257.

19. Ketcham, *James Madison*, 89 (regarding Madison's natural shyness).

20. Ketcham, *James Madison*, 407 (quoting Coles), 471, 474–75.

21. See, e.g., Unger, *Lion of Liberty*, 203 and 234.

22. Chernow, *Washington*, 546; Unger, *Lion of Liberty*, 203.

23. Maier, *Ratification*, 232–333.

24. Maier, *Ratification*, 275–76.

25. Maier, *Ratification*, 276 (quoting Pendleton reciting Jefferson's letter).

26. Ketcham, *James Madison*, 232–37, 253.

27. Ketcham, *James Madison*, 235.

28. Ketcham, *James Madison*, 236 (quoting Madison).

29. Ketcham, *James Madison*, 236 (quoting Madison).

30. Maier, *Ratification*, 266.

31. Chernow, *Washington*, 546–47.

32. Broadwater, *George Mason: Forgotten Founder*, 57–58.

33. Broadwater, *George Mason: Forgotten Founder*, 109, 125–31.

34. Broadwater, *George Mason: Forgotten Founder*, 213 (quoting Washington).

35. Broadwater, *George Mason: Forgotten Founder*, 228.

36. Broadwater, *George Mason: Forgotten Founder*, 242.

37. See, e.g., Broadwater, *George Mason: Forgotten Founder*, 137 and 245.

38. Broadwater, *George Mason: Forgotten Founder*, 251.
39. Broadwater, *George Mason: Forgotten Founder*, 69 (regarding being drafted), and 78 (regarding being elected "with great difficulty").
40. Broadwater, *George Mason: Forgotten Founder*, 80.
41. Broadwater, *George Mason: Forgotten Founder*, 85.
42. See, e.g., https://www.archives.gov/founding-docs/virginia-declaration-of-rights (referring to Mason as the author of the Virginia Declaration of Rights), and Broadwater, *George Mason: Forgotten Founder*, 81 (describing how Mason exaggerated his role to a correspondent two years later, leading to confusion among historians).
43. https://www.archives.gov/founding-docs/virginia-declaration-of-rights.
44. Ketcham, *James Madison*, 181; Broadwater, *George Mason: Forgotten Founder*, 97.
45. Broadwater, *George Mason: Forgotten Founder*, 103.
46. Broadwater, *George Mason: Forgotten Founder*, 153–55.
47. The three others were George Wythe, James Blair, and James McClurg. Governor Randolph appointed James McClurg to the delegation after Patrick Henry, whom the legislature had appointed to be a delegate, declined to serve. Broadwater, *George Mason: Forgotten Founder*, 157–58.
48. "Opposition to the Constitution (September 7, 10, 15)," in Ralph Ketcham, ed., *The Anti-Federalist Papers and the Constitutional Convention Debates* (Mentor, 1986), 171–75. See also Beeman, *Plain, Honest Men*, 320–23; Broadwater, *George Mason: Forgotten Founder*, 183–84.
49. Ketcham, *Anti-Federalist Papers*, 175.
50. Some of Mason's remarks were made at the Constitutional Convention, others in a 1773 essay. See Beeman, *Plain, Honest Men*, 322–23 (quoting Mason).
51. Beeman, *Plain, Honest Men*, 323; Broadwater, *George Mason: Forgotten Founder*, 194.
52. Ketcham, *James Madison*, 224.
53. Ketcham, *Anti-Federalist Papers*, 175.
54. Ketcham, *James Madison*, 212 (quoting Madison). See also Maier, *Ratification*, 24.
55. Ketcham, *James Madison*, 226.
56. Maier, *Ratification*, 24–25 (quoting Madison). See also Ketcham, *James Madison*, 216.
57. Beeman, *Plain, Honest Men*, 228.
58. Catherine Drinker Bowen, *Miracle at Philadelphia: The Story of the Constitutional Convention May to September 1787* (Atlantic—Little, Brown, 1966), 279.
59. Broadwater, *George Mason: Forgotten Founder*, 198 (quoting Mason).
60. Broadwater, *George Mason: Forgotten Founder*, 210.

61. Letter of George Washington to Patrick Henry, September 24, 1787, https://teachingamericanhistory.org/library/document/letter-to-patrick-henry/.

62. Letter from George Washington to James Madison, November 17, 1788, https://founders.archives.gov/documents/Washington/05-01-02-0090 (spelling and style modernized).

63. Letter from George Washington to James Madison, November 17, 1788.

64. Unger, *Lion of Liberty*, 116, 142.

65. Unger, *Lion of Liberty*, 5.

66. Unger, *Lion of Liberty*, 11; Maier, *Ratification*, 229.

67. Unger, *Lion of Liberty*, 229.

68. Unger, *Lion of Liberty*, 23.

69. Unger, *Lion of Liberty*, 24.

70. Unger, *Lion of Liberty*, 38.

71. Unger, *Lion of Liberty*, 40 (quoting Jefferson).

72. Unger, *Lion of Liberty*, 63–64, 95.

73. Unger, *Lion of Liberty*, 97 (spelling and style modernized).

74. Unger, *Lion of Liberty*, 282.

75. Unger, *Lion of Liberty*, 100.

76. Unger, *Lion of Liberty*, 62. Thomas Jefferson came to despise Patrick Henry. On one occasion he described Henry as "avaricious & rotten hearted." Maier, *Ratification*, 231.

77. Unger, *Lion of Liberty*, 11 (regarding Henry's education).

78. Unger, *Lion of Liberty*, 55.

79. Unger, *Lion of Liberty*, 55.

80. Chernow, *Alexander Hamilton*, 229.

81. Clinton Rossiter, ed., *The Federalist Papers* (Mentor, 1961), vii and xi.

82. Regarding Henry's refusal to attend the Convention, see Ketcham, *James Madison*, 180; Unger, *Lion of Liberty*, 186.

83. Jonathan Elliot, ed., *The Debates in Several State Conventions on the Adoption of the Federal Constitution*, vol. 3, 2nd ed. (J.B. Lippincott Co., 1891), 2 [hereinafter Elliot's Debates], https://memory.loc.gov/ammem/amlaw/lwed.html.

84. Elliot's Debates, 3:128.

85. Letter from George Washington to Henry Knox, February 25, 1787, https://www.mountvernon.org/library/digitalhistory/digital-encyclopedia/article/shays-rebellion/?gclid=CjwKCAjwi_b3BRAGEiwAemPNU6mzmi4I7fzdDpYJK7U76WqICmdtU4IVoGAHBgvakNVw7QovnV8nwBoCPioQAvD_BwE#note3.

86. Ketcham, *James Madison*, 186. Hamilton had a slightly different view. He believed Shays' Rebellion demonstrated the need for a national government that could distribute tax burdens more equitably than states so that someone like Daniel Shays did not become "a *desperate debtor*"

in the first place. Chernow, *Alexander Hamilton*, 225 (quoting Hamilton; Hamilton's emphasis).

87. Virginia Ratifying Convention, Proceedings on Wednesday, June 4, 1788.

Chapter 2

1. Harlow Giles Unger, *Lion of Liberty: Patrick Henry and the Call to a New Nation* (Da Capo, 2010), 210.
2. Harlow Giles Unger, *The Last Founding Father: James Monroe and a Nation's Call to Greatness* (Da Capo, 2009), 79.
3. Jonathan Elliot, ed., *The Debates in Several State Conventions on the Adoption of the Federal Constitution*, 2nd ed., vol. 3 (J. B. Lippincott Co. 1891), 45 [hereinafter Elliot's Debates], available at https://memory.loc.gov/ammem/amlaw/lwed.html.
4. Petition of Robert Poage and Others to the General Assembly of Virginia, May 1781, https://founders.archives.gov/documents/Jefferson/01-06-02-0058 (spelling and style modernized). See also Don Higginbotham, *The War of American Independence: Military Attitudes, Policies, and Practices 1763–1789* (1971), 377.
5. Elliot's Debates, 3:50.
6. Charles Watson-Wentworth, the Marquis of Rockingham. See Russell Kirk, *Edmund Burke: A Genius Reconsidered* (Intercollegiate Studies Institute, 1967), 32–36.
7. *Notes of Debates in the Federal Convention of 1787 Reported by James Madison* 478 (Ohio University Press, 1966) [hereinafter Madison's Notes of the Federal Convention].
8. Madison's Notes of the Federal Convention, 482.
9. Chernow, *Washington: A Life* (Penguin Books, 2011), 537–38. See also Carl Riehl, "Uncle Sam Has to Want You: The Right of Gay Men and Lesbians (and All Other Americans) to Bear Arms in the Military," 26 *Rutgers Law Journal* 343, 354 n.41 (1995), citing James H. Hutson, ed., "Supplement to Max Farrand's *The Records of the Federal Convention of 1787*" (Yale University Press, 1987), 229.
10. Madison's Notes of the Federal Convention, 482.
11. Madison's Notes of the Federal Convention, 484 (spelling and style modernized).
12. Madison's Notes of the Federal Convention, 516 (spelling and style modernized).
13. Madison's Notes of the Federal Convention, 514 (spelling and style modernized).
14. Madison's Notes of the Federal Convention, 515.
15. Madison's Notes of the Federal Convention, 639.
16. Madison's Notes of the Federal Convention, 639–40. See also Richard Beeman, *Plain, Honest Men: The Making of the American Constitution* (Random House, 2009), 353–54. New York did not vote. By this point, two

of New York's three delegates had left the Convention. The sole remaining New York delegate, Alexander Hamilton, could not vote because the rules required a state have at least two delegates present to vote. See Ron Chernow, *Alexander Hamilton* (Penguin Books, 2004), 235–36.

17. Elliot's Debates, 3:48 (spelling and style modernized).
18. Elliot's Debates, 3:51 (omitting a question mark after the word "state," which appears to be a typographical error).
19. Elliot's Debates, 3:52.
20. Elliot's Debates, 3:72.
21. Elliot's Debates, 3:73.
22. Elliot's Debates, 3:76.
23. See Chapter 5, in this volume.
24. Elliot's Debates, 3:77. Randolph also argued that a navy is necessary.
25. Elliot's Debates, 3:77 (emphasis added).
26. Elliot's Debates, 3:80.
27. Pauline Maier, *Ratification: The People Debate the Constitution, 1787–1788* (Simon & Schuster, 2010), 227; Catherine Drinker Bowen, *Miracle at Philadelphia: The Story of the Constitutional Convention May to September 1787* (Atlantic—Little, Brown, 1966), 297; Unger, *Lion of Liberty*, 223; https://www.lva.virginia.gov/public/dvb/bio.php?b=Corbin_Francis.
28. https://www.encyclopediavirginia.org/Braxton_Carter_1736-1797#start_entry.
29. Elliot's Debates, 3:112–13 (spelling and style modernized).
30. Elliot's Debates, 3:104.
31. Unger, *Lion of Liberty*, 223–24.
32. E.g., "On so important an occasion, and before so respectable a body, I expected a new display of [Henry's] powers of oratory; but, instead of proceeding to investigate the merits of the new plan of government, the worthy character informed us of horrors which he felt, and apprehensions of his mind, which made him tremblingly fearful of the fate of the commonwealth. Mr. Chairman, was it proper to appeal to the fears of this house?" Remarks of Henry "Light Horse Harry" Lee, Elliot's Debates, 3:42.
33. Elliot's Debates, 3:31 (Mason) and 3:56–57 (Henry).
34. Elliot's Debates, 3:115–16.
35. Elliot's Debates, 3:117.
36. Maier, *Ratification*, 3:271.
37. Elliot's Debates, 3:138.
38. Elliot's Debates, 3:168 (spelling and style modernized).
39. Elliot's Debates, 3:169.
40. Elliot's Debates, 3:169–70.
41. U.S. Constitution, Article I, Section 5, Clause 3.
42. Regarding Henry (Light Horse Harry) Lee Jr., see John Buchanan, *The Road to Guilford Courthouse: The American Revolution in the Carolinas* (John Wiley & Sons, 1997), 352–54.

43. Elliot's Debates, 3:178.
44. Elliot's Debates, 3:178.
45. Elliot's Debates, 3:187 (original emphasis).
46. Unger, *Lion of Liberty*, 226.
47. Elliot's Debates, 3:188.
48. Elliot's Debates, 3:188.
49. Elliot's Debates, 3:188.
50. Elliot's Debates, 3:188 (spelling and style modernized).
51. Elliot's Debates, 3:189.

Chapter 3

1. https://founders.archives.gov/documents/Washington/04-06-02-0295.
2. Letter from James Madison to George Washington, June 4, 1788, https://founders.archives.gov/?q=Author%3A%22Madison%2C%20Ja mes%22%20Recipient%3A%22Washington%2C%20George%22%20Per iod%3A%22Confederation%20Period%22%20Dates-From%3A1788-06-01%20Dates-To%3A1788-06-30&s=1111311111&r=2.
3. Pauline Maier, *Ratification: The People Debate the Constitution, 1787–1788* (Simon & Schuster, 2010), 279.
4. Jonathan Elliot, ed., *The Debates in Several State Conventions on the Adoption of the Federal Constitution*, vol. 3, 2nd ed. (J.B. Lippincott Co., 1891), 628 [hereinafter Elliot's Debates], available at https://constitution.org/rc/rat_va.htm.
5. Elliot's Debates, 3:482.
6. Elliot's Debates, 3:485.
7. Elliot's Debates, 3:486.
8. Elliot's Debates, 3:486.
9. Elliot's Debates, 3:521.
10. Tuesday, June 17, 1788.
11. Elliot's Debates, 3:248.
12. Elliot's Debates, 3:249.
13. Elliot's Debates, 3:251 (spelling and style modernized).
14. Elliot's Debates, 3:249–50.
15. Elliot's Debates, 3:225.
16. For example, as late as November 1810, despite British ships seizing American vessels just as predicted by Madison twenty-two years earlier, the Republican-controlled Congress refused to continue the Bank of the United States and cut funding for both the army and the navy. Ralph Ketcham, *James Madison: A Biography* (University of Virginia, 1990), 506. Funding for the military had been so woeful beforehand that Madison knew that "the navy was unfit for sea" and "the army was virtually nonexistent." Ketcham, *James Madison*, 498. None of this was because of a preference for a strong militia, which was also, according to Thomas Jefferson's secretary of war in 1807, in a "really deplorable" condition

throughout the Union. Ketcham, *James Madison*, 455 (quoting Henry Dearborn).

17. Elliot's Debates, 3:378.
18. See David P. Szatmary, *Shays' Rebellion: The Making of an Agrarian Insurrection* (University of Massachusetts, 1980), 78–79.
19. Elliot's Debates, 3:379 (spelling and style modernized).
20. Elliot's Debates, 3:380.
21. Elliot's Debates, 3:380.
22. Elliot's Debates, 3:381 (spelling and style modernized).
23. Madison's Notes of the Federal Convention, 514 (spelling and style modernized).
24. Clement Eaton, "The Freedom of the Press in the Upper South," 18 *The Mississippi Valley Historical Review* 479, 484 (1932).
25. Elliot's Debates, 3:383.
26. Elliot's Debates, 3:382.
27. Elliot's Debates, 3:386.
28. Elliot's Debates, 3:385.
29. Elliot's Debates, 3:388.
30. Elliot's Debates, 3:386.
31. Elliot's Debates, 3:421.
32. Elliot's Debates, 3:590 (spelling and style modernized).
33. Elliot's Debates, 3:590 (spelling and style modernized; original emphasis).
34. Ron Chernow, *Washington: A Life* (Penguin, 2010), 333–34; Gerald M. Carbone, *Nathanael Greene* (self-published, 2008), 101–2.
35. Carbone, *Nathanael Greene*, 209–10.
36. Chernow, *Washington*, 399–400.
37. Chernow, *Washington*, 440–42.
38. Elliot's Debates, 3:590 (spelling and style modernized).
39. Elliot's Debates, 3:590.
40. Elliot's Debates, 3:590.
41. Jack N. Rakove, *Original Meanings: Politics and the Ideas in the Making of the Constitution* (Knopf, 1996), 124.
42. Elliot's Debates, 3:621.
43. Elliot's Debates, 3:622.
44. See, e.g., remarks of James Madison at Elliot's Debates, 3:470.
45. Maier, *Ratification*, 292.
46. Elliot's Debates, 3:632 (remarks of Innes); Maier, *Ratification*, 302 (about Innes).
47. Elliot's Debates, 3:645 (remarks of Johnson); Maier, *Ratification*, 303 (about Johnson).
48. Elliot's Debates, 3:646.
49. Elliot's Debates, 3:650–51.
50. Elliot's Debates, 3:650.
51. Elliot's Debates, 3:652.

52. Harlow Giles Unger, *Lion of Liberty: Patrick Henry and the Call to a New Nation* (Da Capo, 2010), 210.
53. Unger, *Lion of Liberty*, 234.
54. Elliot's Debates, 3:652.
55. Elliot's Debates, 3:653.
56. Maier, *Ratification*, 306.
57. Unger, *Lion of Liberty*, 233–34.
58. Maier, *Ratification*, 306; Richard Labunski, *James Madison and the Struggle for the Bill of Rights* (Oxford University Press, 2006), 113.
59. Jeff Broadwater, *George Mason: Forgotten Founder* (University of North Carolina, 2006), 234–36.
60. Elliot's Debates, 3:593.
61. Maier, *Ratification*, 309 (quoting Corbin).
62. Maier, *Ratification*, 309 (quoting Madison).
63. Maier, *Ratification*, 313.
64. https://www.archives.gov/founding-docs/virginia-declaration-of-rights.
65. Elliot's Debates, 3:659.
66. Maier, *Ratification*, 311.
67. The following August, Mason resigned from an important local position in Fairfax County because he refused to take an oath supporting the Constitution of the United States. Broadwater, *George Mason*, 240. He held no positions of importance, state or local, after that.
68. Unger, *Lion of Liberty*, 235 (quoting Madison).
69. Even before leaving Richmond, Henry recruited James Monroe to run for Congress from Madison's district. Unger, *Lion of Liberty*, 242.

Chapter 4

1. Vincent Brown, *Tacky's Revolt: The Story of an Atlantic Slave War* (Belknap, 2020), 127–31.
2. Brown, *Tacky's Revolt*, 2, 89–90, and 130.
3. Brown, *Tacky's Revolt*, 72–73. In 1720, Easter fell on March 31. Tacky's revolt occurred about one week later.
4. Brown, *Tacky's Revolt*, 52.
5. R. B. Sheridan, "The Wealth of Jamaica in the Eighteenth Century," 18 *The Economic History Review* 292, 297 (1965). I have converted hundredweights (cwt.) into pounds at the rate of 112 pounds per one cwt.
6. Sheridan places the number of sugar plantations at ninety-seven; Brown says there were more than sixty. Brown, *Tacky's Revolt*, 164.
7. Brown, *Tacky's Revolt*, 53.
8. Brown, *Tacky's Revolt*, 56.
9. Brown, *Tacky's Revolt*, 53.
10. Brown, *Tacky's Revolt*, 58.
11. Brown, *Tacky's Revolt*, 55.

12. John Hope Franklin, *From Slavery to Freedom: A History of Negro Americans*, 3rd ed. (Vintage, 1969), 60–70, 90; Jill Lepore, *New York Burning: Liberty, Slavery, and Conspiracy in Eighteenth-Century Manhattan* (Vintage, 2005), 147.
13. Brown, *Tacky's Revolt*, 63.
14. Brown, *Tacky's Revolt*, 60 (quoting Governor Robert Hunter).
15. Regarding the militia and British army and navy forces, see Brown, *Tacky's Revolt*, 175–82.
16. Sheridan, "Wealth of Jamaica," 297.
17. Brown, *Tacky's Revolt*, 108–9.
18. Brown, *Tacky's Revolt*, 110.
19. Brown, *Tacky's Revolt*, 111–15.
20. Brown, *Tacky's Revolt*, 115–17.
21. Brown, *Tacky's Revolt*, 130–33.
22. Brown, *Tacky's Revolt*, 133–37.
23. Brown, *Tacky's Revolt*, 140.
24. Brown, *Tacky's Revolt*, 140–41.
25. Brown, *Tacky's Revolt*, 60 (quoting Pierre Eugène du Simitière).
26. Brown, *Tacky's Revolt*, 141.
27. See Brown, *Tacky's Revolt*, 125 (regarding Moore being acting governor) and 142–44 (regarding Moore's actions upon learning of the revolt).
28. Brown, *Tacky's Revolt*, 144–48.
29. Brown, *Tacky's Revolt*, 153.
30. Brown, *Tacky's Revolt*, 151–54.
31. Brown, *Tacky's Revolt*, 158.
32. Brown, *Tacky's Revolt*, 34–36, 70–78.
33. For location of Masemure, see Brown, *Tacky's Revolt*, 168 (map).
34. See Brown, *Tacky's Revolt*, 58–59 (regarding Thomas Thistlewood, an overseer in Westmoreland Parish) and 164–66 (regarding Westmoreland Parish generally).
35. Brown, *Tacky's Revolt*, 167–72.
36. Brown, *Tacky's Revolt*, 168–74.
37. Brown, *Tacky's Revolt*, 174.
38. Brown, *Tacky's Revolt*, 176.
39. Brown, *Tacky's Revolt*, 177.
40. Brown, *Tacky's Revolt*, 178 (quoting Long).
41. Brown, *Tacky's Revolt*, 179.
42. Brown, *Tacky's Revolt*, 182–83.
43. Brown, *Tacky's Revolt*, 185–87.
44. Brown, *Tacky's Revolt*, 187–89.
45. Brown, *Tacky's Revolt*, 194–95.
46. Brown, *Tacky's Revolt*, 194.
47. Brown, *Tacky's Revolt*, 197–203.

48. Brown, *Tacky's Revolt*, 204.
49. Brown, *Tacky's Revolt*, 220–24.
50. Brown, *Tacky's Revolt*, 1–2.
51. Eugene D. Genovese, *From Rebellion to Revolution: Afro-American Slave Revolts in the Making of the Modern World* (Louisiana State University Press, 1979), 112; Jill Lepore, *These Truths: A History of the United States* (W.W. Norton, 2018), 58. See also Sally E. Haddon, *Slave Patrols: Law and Violence in Virginia and the Carolinas* (Harvard University Press, 2001), 152.
52. Susan Eva O'Donovan, "William Webb's World," *New York Times*, February 18, 2001, https://opinionator.blogs.nytimes.com/2011/02/18/will iam-webbs-world. See also Brown, *Tacky's Revolt*, 244.
53. Lepore, *These Truths*, 58.
54. Franklin, *From Slavery to Freedom*, 67–69.
55. Brown, *Tacky's Revolt*, 210.
56. To some extent, the 1718 date for Jamaica is arbitrary. There was an uprising in St. Elisabeth Parish then, but it was one of a series of revolts. Vincent Brown writes that following the 1718 rebellion more and more slaves joined rebels hiding in the mountains until, in 1733, planters told London they were no longer able to defend themselves. Brown, *Tacky's Revolt*, 108–15. Regarding revolts in St. John's and Antigua, see Brown, *Tacky's Revolt*, 105.
57. Alan Taylor writes that slave insurrections in the British West Indies in both 1772 and 1791 caused Virginians to be become more terrified about slave insurrections at home. See Taylor, *Internal Enemy*, 22 (regarding 1772) and 42 (regarding 1791).
58. Eugene D. Genovese, *From Rebellion to Revolution: Afro-American Slave Revolts in the Making of the Modern World* (Vintage, 1979), 112.
59. Lepore, *New York Burning*, 53; Taylor, *Internal Enemy*, 42.
60. Genovese, *From Rebellion to Revolution*, 42.
61. Stanley M. Elkins is particularly associated with this view. Peter Kolchin, *American Slavery 1619–1877*, rev. ed. (Hill and Wang, 2003) (describing Elkins's belief that the South did not have large insurrections like those in the Caribbean because Southern slaveholders successfully turned slaves "into childlike 'Sambos'"), 135–36.
62. Genovese, *Roll, Jordon, Roll*, 588.
63. Genovese, *Roll, Jordon, Roll*, 595 (quoting southern historian Ulrich Bonnell Phillips).
64. Edmund S. Morgan, *American Slavery American Freedom: The Ordeal of Colonial Virginia* (W.W. Norton, 1975), 309.
65. Franklin, *From Slavery to Freedom*, 75.
66. Kolchin, *American Slavery*, 30.
67. By Eastern Virginia, I refer generally to the Tidewater region, that is, that portion of Virginia that lies east of the Fall Line, the imaginary line where

the coastal region meets the foot of the higher-elevated Piedmont region. According to the official 1790 census, slaves constituted 51 percent of the total population in thirty-one counties that lay partially or entirely east of the Fall Line. (There were thirty-five such counties, but no census data for four of them. For a map depicting the Fall Line and Virginia counties, see Alan Taylor, *The Internal Enemy: Slavery and War in Virginia 1772–1832* [W.W. Norton, 2013], xvi.) Slaves also constituted the majority in about half of the counties that were adjacent to and west of the Tidewater counties, including Cumberland County, where Richmond was located. Of course, slaves did not have to be a majority to comprise a threateningly large portion of the population. For example, slaves comprised 37 percent of the population in Fairfax County, where Mount Vernon (Washington's home) and Gunderson Hall (George Mason's home) were located, and 44 percent of the population in both Orange County, where Montpelier (James Madison's home) was located, and Albemarle County, where Monticello (Jefferson's home) was located. For 1790 Virginia census data by county, see page 9 at https://www2.census.gov/prod2/decennial/docume nts/1790m-02.pdf.

68. The Charleston District was composed of twelve parishes and constituted the second most populous district in the state. For 1790 South Carolina census data by district, see page 9 at https://www2.census.gov/library/publi cations/decennial/1790/heads_of_families/south_carolina/1790k-02.pdf. For population of the largest U.S. cities, see https://www2.census.gov/libr ary/working-papers/1998/demo/pop-twps0027/tab02.txt.

69. Kolchin, *American Slavery*, 31.
70. Kolchin, *American Slavery*, 254 (Appendix, Table 3).
71. Kolchin, *American Slavery*, 64.
72. Genovese, *Roll, Jordon, Roll*, 7.
73. Ralph Ketcham, *James Madison: A Biography* (University Press of Virginia, 1990), 12.
74. Paul Finkelman, *Slavery and the Founders* (M.E. Sharpe, 1996), 105. Peter Kolchin writes that forty-five slaves were at Monticello and the rest at Jefferson's other holdings. Kolchin, *American Slavery*, 33. However, the Monticello website says, "At any given time, around 130 people were enslaved at Monticello" itself, with additional slaves at Jefferson's other properties. https://www.monticello.org/slavery/slavery-faqs/property/#bea ten.
75. Ron Chernow, *Washington: A Life* (Penguin Books, 2010), 800. Mount Vernon was comprised of five farms located some distance apart. Chernow, *Washington*, 141. According to Peter Kolchin, sixty-seven slaves were at the Home House and the rest at the other farms. Kolchin, *American Slavery*, 33.
76. Brown, *Tacky's Revolt*, 86–89.

77. Some had similar views about Africans imported from Guinea. See Peter H. Wood, *Black Majority: Negroes in Colonial South Carolina from 1670 through the Stono Rebellion* (W.W. Norton, 1974), 301.

78. Brown, *Tacky's Revolt*, 1, 34–37 (regarding Wager), 89–90 (regarding Tacky).

79. Kolchin, *American Slavery*, 57.

80. Franklin, *From Slavery to Freedom*, 69.

81. Kolchin, *American Slavery*, 23, 34, 37–39; Genovese, *From Rebellion to Revolution*, 12, 82–83. The word "Creole," especially when capitalized, also has other meanings, including people who were descended from both Black slaves and White Spanish or French colonists along the Gulf of Mexico. Kolchin, *American Slavery*, 82–83.

82. Kolchin, *American Slavery*, 38.

83. Taylor, *Internal Enemy*, 36–37. There were political and economic, as well as public safety, reasons for the ban: Virginia could look somewhat progressive by forbidding the slave trade, and the ban economically benefitted Virginia, which had a slave surplus and was a slave-exporting state.

84. Kolchin, *American Slavery*, 37–38.

85. Brown, *Tacky's Revolt*, 101.

86. Genovese, *Roll, Jordon, Roll*, 595; Kolchin, *American Slavery*, 156.

87. Genovese, *Roll, Jordon, Roll*, 53–54; Colin Woodard, *American Nations: A History of the Eleven Rival Regional Cultures of North America* (Penguin Books, 2011), 87–91.

88. See Kolchin, *American Slavery*, 35 (regarding Southern slaveholders); Brown, *Tacky's Revolt*, 55–56 (regarding Jamaican slaveholders).

89. See Franklin, *From Slavery to Freedom*, 205 (stating that Southerners "almost always sought to convey the impression that their human chattel was docile, tractable, and happy").

90. Taylor, *Internal Enemy*, 259.

91. See, e.g., Herbert Aptheker, *American Negro Slave Revolts* (Columbia University Press, 1943; International Publishers, 6th ed., 1993), 11. Citations refer to the International Publishers edition; and Franklin, *From Slavery to Freedom*, 205; Genovese, *From Rebellion to Revolution*, xxii, 20.

92. John H. Bracey, Foreword in Aptheker, *American Negro Slave Revolts*, 4 (quoting Morrison and Commager).

93. "The panic of the slaveholders at the slightest hint of slave insurrection revealed what lay beneath their endless self-congratulations over the supposed docility, contentment, and loyalty of their slaves. Almost every slaveholder claimed to trust his own slaves but to fear his neighbor's. Genovese, *Roll, Jordon, Roll*, 596.

94. Genovese, *Roll, Jordon, Roll*, 64.

95. Kolchin, *American Slavery*, 58.

96. See Fawn M. Brodie, *Thomas Jefferson: An Intimate Biography* (Bantam Doubleday, 1974), 377 (regarding whip) and 378 (quoting Jefferson's letter to Steven T. Mason).

97. https://www.monticello.org/slavery/slavery-faqs/property/#beaten.
98. Kolchin, *American Slavery*, 57–58.
99. Lepore, *New York Burning*, 52–53. See also Aptheker, *American Negro Slave* Revolts, 172; Franklin, *From Slavery to Freedom*, 92.
100. https://www.nycurbanism.com/blog/2019/6/18/a-short-history-of-slavery-in-nyc. See also Kolchin, *American Slavery*, 252 (Table 1), estimating the Black population in New York State at 15.5 percent in 1720.
101. Lepore, *New York Burning*, 6, 21.
102. Lepore, *New York Burning*, 159.
103. Lepore, *New York Burning*, 43 (quoting shoemaker Isaac Gardner).
104. Lepore, *New York Burning*, 59.
105. Lepore, *New York Burning*, 61.
106. Lepore, *New York Burning*, 62.
107. Lepore, *New York Burning*, 9–10, 188, 201, 220. Regarding possible torture, see 91–92. Regarding a comparison to Salem witch trials made at the time, see 203–10. Regarding transporting accused to the West Indies, see Andy Doolen, "Reading and Writing Terror: The New York Conspiracy Trials of 1741," 16 *American Literary History* 377, 400 (2004).
108. For a summary of differing conclusions by historians, see Lepore, *New York Burning*, at 279–81 n.11.
109. David Eltis and Stanley L. Engerman, "Shipboard Slave Revolts and Abolition," in *Who Abolished Slavery? Slave Revolts and Abolitionism*, ed. Seymour Drescher and Pieter C. Emmer (Berghahn Books, 2010), 149.
110. Eltis and Engerman, "Shipboard Slave Revolts and Abolition," 149, 152.
111. Genovese, *Roll, Jordan, Roll*, 587.
112. In 1969, Bryn Mawr College hired Aptheker. Although Aptheker said, "I have waited thirty-one years for this moment," Bryn Mawr hired him as an instructor, not a tenured or tenure-track professor. Emma Ruth Burns, "The Birth of the Bryn Mawr College Black Studies Program and the Herbert Aptheker Appointment," 1 *Swarthmore Undergraduate History Journal* 1, 10 (2020), available at https://works.swarthmore.edu/cgi/view content.cgi?article=1002&context=suhj.
113. An academic brouhaha erupted in 1975 when Yale would not let Aptheker teach a single course, just once. Although Yale historian C. Van Woodward said that was because Aptheker's scholarship did not meet Yale standards, there were good reasons to believe the decision was politically motivated. Gary Murrell, *"The Most Dangerous Communist in the United States"* (University of Massachusetts Press, 2015), 227–44. See also Dennis McLelan, "Herbert Aptheker, 87; Scholar of Slave History, Quit U.S. Communist Party," *Los Angeles Times*, March 21, 2003, available at https://www.latimes.com/archives/la-xpm-2003-mar-21-me-aptheker21-story.html. Herbert's daughter accused him of sexually abusing her as a child. However, her accusation only became public after Herbert's death and could not have affected his failure to win a university appointment. See Christopher Phelps, "Bettina Aptheker's Recent Memoir Has Incited

Fierce Debate over Her Father s Legacy," *The Nation*, October 18, 2007, available at https://www.thenation.com/article/archive/father-history.

114. E.g., Genovese, *Roll, Jordon, Roll*, 587; João Pedro Marques, "History or Ideology?" in *Who Abolished Slavery?*, ed. Drescher and Emmer, 70 .

115. Genovese, *Roll, Jordon, Roll*, 162.

116. Aptheker, *American Negro Slave Revolts*, 192–93 (citations omitted).

117. Aptheker, *American Negro Slave Revolts*, 183.

118. Aptheker, *American Negro Slave Revolts*, 202–3. All quotations are from a letter by the chairman of the Pitt County Committee of Correspondence. Aptheker, *American Negro Slave Revolts*, n.111. See also Sally E. Hadden, *Slave Patrols: Law and Violence in Virginia and the Carolinas* (Harvard University Press, 2001), 156–57.

119. Aptheker, *American Negro Slave Revolts*, 202.

120. Aptheker, *American Negro Slave Revolts*, 198–99.

121. Franklin, *From Slavery to Freedom*, 76; Genovese, *Roll, Jordon, Roll*, 616; Wood, *Black Majority*, 289–92.

122. Genovese, *Roll, Jordon, Roll*, 361.

123. Lepore, *These Truths*, 93–94; https://encyclopediavirginia.org/entries/madison-ambrose-ca-1696-1732/.

124. The legislation was enacted in 1741. Wood, *Black Majority*, 290.

125. Franklin, *From Slavery to Freedom*, 208.

126. Wood, *Black Majority*, 289.

127. Franklin, *From Slavery to Freedom*, 208.

128. Like Herbert Aptheker, Moses Finley catalogued about 250 slave revolts in the United States. Olivier Pétré-Grenouilleau, "Slave Resistance and Abolitionism: A Multifaceted Issue," in *Who Abolished Slavery?*, 159.

129. One South Carolinian believed that physicians occasionally covered their own shortcomings by attributing a patient's death to poisoning. Wood, *Black Majority*, 290–91.

130. Wood, *Black Majority*, 298–99; Genovese, *Roll Jordon, Roll*, 616.

131. Taylor, *Internal Enemy*, 99, 415–16.

132. Wood, *Black Majority*, 298.

133. Peter Charles Hoffer, *Cry Liberty: The Great Stono River Slave Rebellion of 1739* (Oxford University Press, 2012), xv; Jack Shuler, *Calling Out Liberty: The Stono Slave Rebellion and the Universal Struggle for Human Rights* (University Press of Mississippi, 2009), 71–72.

134. Franklin, *From Slavery to Freedom*, 210.

135. Genovese, *From Rebellion to Revolution*, 4.

136. Hadden, *Slave Patrols*, 6. Hadden also writes: "Even though actual rebellions happened infrequently, their effects loomed large in the sanguinary imaginations of Southern whites." Hadden, *Slave Patrols*, 139.

137. Taylor, *Internal Enemy*, 72 (quoting Austin Steward).

138. Taylor, *Internal Enemy*, 408 (quoting Jefferson).

139. Taylor, *Internal Enemy*, 408.

140. Genovese, *Roll, Jordon, Roll*, 41, 98 (relating a story of a slave who learned to read but kept that secret from his master), 561–63; Kolchin, *American Slavery*, 127–29.

141. Hadden, *Slave Patrols*, 98.

142. Genovese, *Roll, Jordon, Roll*, 618; Hadden, *Slave Patrols*, 123; Wood, *Black Majority*, 275.

143. Hadden, *Slave Patrols*, 43, 219.

144. Hadden, *Slave Patrols*, 121.

145. Hadden, *Slave Patrols*, 111–12, 117; Wood, *Black Majority*, 272.

146. Wood, *Black Majority*, 273.

147. Genovese, *Roll, Jordon, Roll*, 23–24, 619.

148. Genovese, *Roll, Jordon, Roll*, 618; Hadden, *Slave Patrols*, 130.

149. Hadden, *Slave Patrols*, 125.

150. Hadden, *Slave Patrols*, 131; Wood, *Black Majority*, 275.

151. Hadden, *Slave Patrols*, 147.

152. Hadden, *Slave Patrols*, 106.

153. Hadden, *Slave Patrols*, 37.

154. Hadden, *Slave Patrols*, 19, 31, 168, 198.

155. Hadden, *Slave Patrols*, 107–9.

156. Hadden, *Slave Patrols*, 14–24 (South Carolina), 24–32 (Virginia).

157. Hadden, *Slave Patrols*, 19, 31, 168, 198.

158. Hadden, *Slave Patrols*, 32–40.

159. This is Sally Hadden's supposition. Hadden, *Slave Patrols*, 36.

160. North Carolina courts used militia rolls or tax rolls to staff the slave patrols. Hadden, *Slave Patrols*, 42. Nevertheless, every patroller came from the militia because all White men between the ages of sixteen and sixty were enrolled in the militia. The national Militia Act of 1792 fixed militia ages at eighteen to forty-five. Hadden, *Slave Patrols*, 74.

161. Hadden, *Slave Patrols*, 37.

162. Wood, *Black Majority*, 274.

163. Hadden, *Slave Patrols*, 65, 102–4.

164. Hadden, *Slave Patrols*, 73. At times (e.g., during the Yamasee War in South Carolina), elites maneuvered to be assigned slave patrol duty to avoid being sent to war with their militia units. Hadden, *Slave Patrols*, 21.

165. Hadden, *Slave Patrols*, 94.

166. Hadden, *Slave Patrols*, 65, 102–4.

167. Hadden, *Slave Patrols*, 78.

168. Hadden, *Slave Patrols*, 29–30, 137–66.

169. Charles Royster, *A Revolutionary People at War: The Continental Army and American Character, 1775–1783* (University North Carolina Press, 1979), 39. Just seven weeks later, Adams said: "We cannot all be soldiers." Royster, *A Revolutionary People at War*, 39.

170. Virginia Declaration of Rights §17 (1776), available at https://www.archives.gov/founding-docs/virginia-declaration-of-rights.

Chapter 5

1. Rick Atkinson, *The British Are Coming: The War for America, Lexington to Princeton, 1775–1777* (Henry Holt, 2019), 90–112.
2. Atkinson, *The British Are Coming*, 113.
3. Atkinson, *The British Are Coming*, 101.
4. John Ferling, *Independence: The Struggle to Set America Free* (Bloomsbury, 2011), 44.
5. Atkinson, *The British Are Coming*, 77, 113.
6. Atkinson, *The British Are Coming*, 70 ("unmanly barbarity").
7. Ferling, *Independence*, 60.
8. Atkinson, *The British Are Coming*, 104 (noting the British vanguard was to be a bayonet charge). John Buchanan writes: "The sight of a line of disciplined British infantry, advancing at a trot and shouting huzzas, muskets leveled and protruding from them some eighteen inches of cold steel at charge bayonet, was known to turn American militia bowels to jelly and heels to quicksilver, British officers were well aware of this." John Buchanan, *The Road to Guilford Courthouse: The American Revolution in the Carolinas* (John Wiley & Sons, 1997), 160.
9. Don Higginbotham, *The War of American Independence: Military Attitudes, Policies, and Practices* (Northeastern University, 1971), 72–73.
10. Atkinson, *The British Are Coming*, 101; Ferling, *Independence*, 161.
11. Atkinson, *The British Are Coming*, 94–95.
12. Atkinson, *The British Are Coming*, 94; Higginbotham, *War of American Independence*, 70–71.
13. Robert Leckie, *George Washington's War: The Saga of the American Revolution* (HarperPerenial, 1992), 161.
14. Atkinson, *The British Are Coming*, 103.
15. Atkinson, *The British Are Coming*, 103.
16. Priya Satia, *Empire of Guns: The Violent Making of the Industrial Revolution* (Penguin, 2018), 230–31. See also Atkinson, *The British Are Coming*, 61–62 (stating "the musket was marginally accurate at fifty yards, hopeless beyond a hundred") and 79 (the "shot heard round the world likely missed"); John Buchanan, *The Road to Valley Forge: How Washington Built the Army that Won the Revolution* (Barnes & Noble, 2004), 34 (stating the single-shot musket had an effective range of about eighty yards). For a particularly good description of the flintlock musket and the British bayonet, see Buchanan, *Road to Guilford Courthouse*, 158–61.
17. Lois G. Schwoerer, *Gun Culture in Early Modern England* (University of Virginia, 2016), 184. Although Schwoerer may be referring specifically to research on earlier guns, she notes that guns did not change until the nineteenth century. Schwoerer, *Gun Culture in Early Modern England*, 185.
18. Atkinson, *The British Are Coming*, 79.
19. Atkinson, *The British Are Coming*, 132–33; Satia, *Empire of Guns*, 278, 282; Lois G. Schwoerer, *Gun Culture in Early Modern England* (University

of Virginia, 2016), 184–85; John W. Wright, "The Rife in the American Revolution," 29 *American Historical Review* 293 (1924). Because of the rifle's many disadvantages as an eighteenth-century military weapon, one historian observed: "The British could hardly have asked for a better war than facing an army made up solely of riflemen." Charles Royster, *A Revolutionary People at War: The Continental Army and American Character, 1775–83* (University of North Carolina, 1979), 34.

20.   In civilian hands, rifles were used for hunting. Satia, *Empire of Guns*, 278. They were, therefore, more prevalent among backwoodsmen in the mid-Atlantic region, and during the war ten rifleman companies were formed in Maryland, Pennsylvania, and Virginia. Higginbotham, *War of American Independence*, 102–3, 120 n.9.

21.   Buchanan, *Road to Guilford Courthouse*, 126, 286.

22.   Atkinson, *The British Are Coming*, 104.

23.   Atkinson, *The British Are Coming*, 105.

24.   Atkinson, *The British Are Coming*, 105–6 (quoting a diary entry from a soldier in the 47th Foot Regiment).

25.   Atkinson, *The British Are Coming*, 106.

26.   Atkinson, *The British Are Coming*, 106.

27.   Robert Leckie, *George Washington's War*, 161.

28.   Atkinson, *The British Are Coming*, 107; Leckie, *George Washington's War*, 162.

29.   Leckie, *George Washington's War*, 162.

30.   Atkinson, *The British Are Coming*, 106.

31.   Atkinson, *The British Are Coming*, 107.

32.   Atkinson, *The British Are Coming*, 110.

33.   Gerald M. Carbone, *Nathanael Greene: A Biography of the American Revolution* (self-published, 2008), 23.

34.   Atkinson, *The British Are Coming*, 239.

35.   Atkinson, *The British Are Coming*, 133.

36.   Atkinson, *The British Are Coming*, 239.

37.   Atkinson, *The British Are Coming*, 256–62.

38.   Atkinson, *The British Are Coming*, 263–64.

39.   Higginbotham, *War of American Independence*, 36–39, 55 n.25.

40.   See, e.g., Atkinson, *The British Are Coming*, 193 (reporting that nine Virginia regiments were mustered into the Continental Army).

41.   See Ron Chernow, *Washington: A Life* (Penguin Books, 2010), 203 ("Washington's favorite general") and Atkinson, *The British Are Coming*, 448 ("one of the finest commanders in American military history").

42.   Carbone, *Nathanael Greene*, 15–16.

43.   He had, however, been barred from attending Quaker meetings, probably for frequenting alehouses. Atkinson, *The British Are Coming*, 203.

44.   Carbone, *Nathanael Greene*, 17.

45.   Carbone, *Nathanael Greene*, 19–20.

46. Chernow, *Washington*, 196 (quoting a letter from Washington to his brother Sam).
47. Chernow, *Washington*, 197.
48. Carbone, *Nathanael Greene*, 24.
49. Carbone, *Nathanael Greene*, 22.
50. The formal name was then Army of the United Colonies. Carbone, *Nathanael Greene*, 25.
51. Greene's full quote also includes: "The policy of Congress has been the most absurd and ridiculous imaginable pouring in militia men who come and go every month. A military force established upon such principles defeats itself." Carbone, *Nathanael Greene*, 41. See also Buchanan, *Road to Valley Forge*, 96.
52. David Hackett Fisher, *Paul Revere's Ride* (Oxford University Press, 1994), 149–56.
53. Atkinson, *The British Are Coming*, 229.
54. Chernow, *Washington*, 71.
55. Chernow, *Washington*, 196.
56. Fisher, *Paul Revere's Ride*, 151.
57. Atkinson, *The British Are Coming*, 101.
58. Buchanan, *Road to Valley Forge*, 304.
59. David McCullough, *John Adams* (Simon & Schuster, 2001), 219.
60. Higginbotham, *War of American Independence*, 247.
61. Ron Chernow, *Washington: A Life* (Penguin Books, 2010), 187.
62. Atkinson, *The British Are Coming*, 230.
63. Chernow, *Washington*, 234–35.
64. Don Higginbotham, *The War of American Independence: Military Attitudes, Policies, and Practices* (Northeastern University, 1971), 151.
65. Carbone, *Nathanael Greene*, 30.
66. Atkinson, *The British Are Coming*, 180–81, 243–45.
67. Chernow, *Washington*, 235.
68. John Buchanan, *The Road to Valley Forge: How Washington Built the Army that Won the Revolution* (Barnes & Noble, 2004), 78.
69. Buchanan, *Road to Valley Forge*, 2–5; Higginbotham, *War of American Independence*, 68–77; Chernow, *Washington*, 239.
70. Chernow, *Washington*, 16–17.
71. Buchanan, *Road to Valley Forge*, 21 (regarding Lord Richard Howe); Buchanan, *Road to Guilford Courthouse*, 76 (regarding Cornwallis).
72. Buchanan, *Road to Valley Forge*, 22.
73. Buchanan, *Road to Valley Forge*, 23.
74. Buchanan, *Road to Valley Forge*, 28 (quoting letter from Clinton to Washington) (spelling and style modernized).
75. Buchanan, *Road to Valley Forge*, 29–33; Chernow, *Washington*, 239–41.

76. For the Battle of Long Island, I rely on Buchanan, *Road to Valley Forge*, 41–76; Atkinson, *The British Are Coming*, 348–79; Chernow, *Washington*, 244–56; Higginbotham, *War of American Independence*, 152–59.

77. Buchanan, *Road to Valley Forge*, 49 (quoting Washington's written instructions to Putnam); and Chernow, *Washington*, 246 (quoting Washington and commenting on Putnam's semi-coherence).

78. Buchanan, *Road to Valley Forge*, 49 (quoting Washington's written instructions to Putnam).

79. Buchanan, *Road to Valley Forge*, 57.

80. Chernow, *Washington*, 243.

81. Buchanan, *Road to Valley Forge*, 55.

82. Buchanan, *Road to Valley Forge*, 58 (quoting Major Carl Leopold Baurmeister).

83. Chernow, *Washington*, 248.

84. Chernow, *Washington*, 249.

85. Buchanan, *Road to Valley Forge*, 67.

86. Chernow, *Washington*, 250 (quoting Private Joseph Plumb Martin).

87. Letter from George Washington to John Hancock (September 2, 1776), available at https://founders.archives.gov/documents/Washington/03-06-02-0162 (spelling and style modernized).

88. Atkinson, *The British Are Coming*, 387.

89. Buchanan, *Road to Valley Forge*, 77–78.

90. Atkinson, *The British Are Coming*, 389.

91. Buchanan, *Road to Valley Forge*, 81–87.

92. Buchanan, *Road to Valley Forge*, 83 (quoting Captain Frederick Mackenzie). For identifying information about Mackenzie, see https://quod.lib.umich.edu/c/clementsead/umich-wcl-M-1066mac?view=text.

93. Buchanan, *Road to Valley Forge*, 84. See also Atkinson, *The British Are Coming*, 392.

94. Carbone, *Nathanael Greene*, 39.

95. Letter from George Washington to John Hancock (September 16, 1776) (spelling and style modernized), available at https://founders.archives.gov/documents/Washington/03-06-02-0251.

96. Washington's statement was recounted by Major General William Heath. See n.5 at https://founders.archives.gov/documents/Washington/03-06-02-0251.

97. Atkinson, *The British Are Coming*, 394–97.

98. Letter from George Washington to Patrick Henry (October 5, 1776) (spelling and style modernized), available at https://founders.archives.gov/documents/Washington/03-06-02-0367.

99. Buchanan, *Road to Valley Forge*, 84. See also Atkinson, *The British Are Coming*, 439 (putting the figure at 13,000).

100.   Militia units on Chatterton Hill were from Massachusetts, New York, and New Jersey. Atkinson, *The British Are Coming*, 108.

101.   Buchanan, *Road to Valley Forge*, 108; Atkinson, *The British Are Coming*, 445.

102.   Atkinson, *The British Are Coming*, 445.

103.   Atkinson, *The British Are Coming*, 446.

104.   Buchanan, *Road to Valley Forge*, 108–9; Atkinson, *The British Are Coming*, 446–47.

105.   Atkinson, *The British Are Coming*, 448.

106.   Buchanan, *Road to Valley Forge*, 110.

107.   Buchanan, *Road to Valley Forge*, 64, 72, 86–87, 122–23, and 130–31.

108.   Buchanan, *Road to Valley Forge*, 122–23 (quoting Lieutenant General Johann von Ewald).

109.   Atkinson, *The British Are Coming*, 451. See also Buchanan, *Road to Valley Forge*, 112–14.

110.   Atkinson, *The British Are Coming*, 459.

111.   Carbone, *Nathanael Greene*, 44.

112.   Atkinson, *The British Are Coming*, 459 (quoting diary entry of Captain Frederick Mackenzie).

113.   Atkinson, *The British Are Coming*, 510.

114.   Atkinson, *The British Are Coming*, 460–61. Regarding the canon loss, see Carbone, *Nathanael Greene*, 46.

115.   Buchanan, *Road to Valley Forge*, 131.

116.   Atkinson, *The British Are Coming*, 485.

117.   Atkinson, *The British Are Coming*, 488. See also Buchanan, *Road to Valley Forge*, 125 (stating that Washington ordered Lee to come with 3,400 Continentals).

118.   Carbone, *Nathanael* Greene, 50. Lee tried to augment his force by ordering Heath to give him 2,000 of Heath's force at Hudson Heights. That directly contravened Washington's explicit instructions, and Heath courageously refused, even though Lee was his superior officer. Buchanan, *Road to Valley Forge*, 126–30.

119.   See note 1 at https://founders.archives.gov/documents/Washington/03-07-02-0171.

120.   Atkinson, *The British Are Coming*, 485.

121.   Letter from George Washington to John Hancock (November 30, 1776) (spelling and style modernized), available at https://founders.archives.gov/?q=Author%3A%22Washington%2C%20George%22%20Recipient%3A%22Hancock%2C%20John%22%20Dates-To%3A1776-12-15%20Dates-From%3A1776-11-25&s=1111311111&r=2.

122.   Atkinson, *The British Are Coming*, 489; Buchanan, *Road to Valley Forge*, 135.

123.   Letter from George Washington to John Hancock (December 1, 1776) (spelling and style modernized), available at https://founders.archives.

gov/?q=Author%3A%22Washington%2C%20George%22%20Recipi
ent%3A%22Hancock%2C%20John%22%20Dates-From%3A1776-12-
01%20Dates-To%3A1776-12-15&s=1111311111&r=1. See also note 8 by the
National Archives.

124. Buchanan, *Road to Valley Forge*, 135.

125. Buchanan, *Road to Valley Forge*, 125.

126. Atkinson, *The British Are Coming*, 495.

127. Atkinson, *The British Are Coming*, 492–93.

128. Atkinson, *The British Are Coming*, 493–94; Buchanan, *Road to Valley Forge*, 139.

129. Atkinson, *The British Are Coming*, 502. See also Buchanan, *Road to Valley Forge*, 142 (stating that while there is no evidence that Lee spent the night at the tavern for an assignation with an unnamed woman, "it certainly would have been in character").

130. Atkinson, *The British Are Coming*, 502. See also Buchanan, *Road to Valley Forge*, 142–43.

131. Carbone, *Nathanael Greene*, 50.

132. Atkinson, *The British Are Coming*, 546; Buchanan, *Road to Valley Forge*, 177.

133. Atkinson, *The British Are Coming*, 546; Buchanan, *Road to Valley Forge*, 177.

134. Atkinson, *The British Are Coming*, 546.

135. Atkinson, *The British Are Coming*, 546.

136. Letter from George Washington to John Hancock (January 7, 1777) (spelling and style modernized), available at https://founders.archives. gov/documents/Washington/03-08-02-0008.

137. Atkinson, *The British Are Coming*, 84.

138. Additional casualties were inflicted on loyalists and a regiment composed of former slaves who were promised liberty in return for fighting for Britain. It is not clear how well armed or trained these two groups were. Atkinson, *The British Are Coming*, 190–91. Regarding the group of former slaves, called the "Ethiopian Regiment," see Atkinson, *The British Are Coming*, 185; and Alan Taylor, *The Internal Enemy: Slavery and War in Virginia 1772–1832* (W.W. Norton, 2013), 24.

139. Letter from George Washington to Major General Joseph Spencer (March 11, 1777), available at https://founders.archives.gov/?q=%20Aut hor%3A%22Washington%2C%20George%22%20Recipient%3A%22Spen cer%2C%20Joseph%22&s=1111311111&r=9.

Chapter 6

1. See Ralph Ketcham, *James Madison: A Biography* (University Press of Virginia, 1990), 12 (stating the family had at least 118 slaves by 1782) and 34 (stating that Bradford was Madison's closest friend at Princeton). Bradford later became the second attorney general of the United States.

2. Letter from James Madison to William Bradford (November 26, 1774) (spelling and style modernized), available at https://founders.archives.gov/documents/Madison/01-01-02-0037.

3. Letter from James Madison to William Bradford (June 19, 1775), available at https://founders.archives.gov/?q=Author%3A%22Madison%2C%20James%22%20Recipient%3A%22Bradford%2C%20William%22%20Dates-From%3A1775-01-01%20Dates-To%3A1775-12-31&s=1111311111&r=5.

4. Harlow Giles Unger, *Lion of Liberty: Patrick Henry and the Call to a New Nation* (Da Capo, 2010), 74.

5. Unger, *Lion of Liberty*, 75.

6. Unger, *Lion of Liberty*, 75.

7. Gerald Horne, *The Counter-Revolution of 1776: Slave Resistance and the Origins of the United States of America* (New York University Press, 2014), 241.

8. Unger, *Lion of Liberty*, 102–5; Alan Taylor, *The Internal Enemy: Slavery and War in Virginia 1772–1832* (W.W. Norton, 2013), 22–23; Jill Lepore, *These Truths: A History of the United States* (W.W. Norton, 2018), 93–95; Ketcham, *Madison*, 64.

9. See David Hackett Fisher, *Paul Revere's Ride* (Oxford University Press, 1994), 85 (stating the British objective in Massachusetts had been to seize gunpowder in Concord).

10. Unger, *Lion of Liberty*, 103.

11. Ron Chernow, *Washington: A Life* (Penguin, 2010), 177; Ketcham, *Madison*, 64.

12. See Chernow, *Washington*, 177, for Madison's quotation. See Ketcham, *Madison*, 64–65, for a report by one participant that Madison was one of the members of the Orange County militia joining the march. With respect to exactly what "property" Madison was referring to, Ketcham says Madison believed Washington "feared reprisals on their property by British warships or other forces commanded by Dunmore." Ketcham, *Madison*, 65. However, what was most salient at this moment in time was Dunmore interfering with slaves. It was after Dunmore retreated to a British warship that British marines began raiding coastal towns and plantations for supplies and plunder, as well as slaves who would fight for Britain in return for freedom. Unger, *Lion of Liberty*, 110.

13. Unger, *Lion of Liberty*, 103.

14. https://www.gilderlehrman.org/history-resources/spotlight-primary-source/lord-dunmores-proclamation-1775.

15. Taylor, *The Internal Enemy*, 24.

16. Taylor, *The Internal Enemy*, 26.

17. Lepore, *These Truths*, 94.

18. See Colin Woodward, *American Nations: A History of the Eleven Rival Regional Cultures of North America* (Penguin Books, 2011), 134 (quoting the physician).

19. John Buchanan, *Road to Guilford Courthouse: The American Revolution in the Carolinas* (John Wiley & Sons, 1997), 25–26, 307; Don Higginbotham, *The War of American Independence: Military Attitudes, Policies, and Practice 1763–1789* (Northeastern University Press, 1971), 354.

20. https://www.battlefields.org/learn/revolutionary-war/battles/savannah.

21. Buchanan, *Road to Guilford Courthouse*, 70.

22. Jon Meacham, *Thomas Jefferson: The Art of Power* (Random House, 2013), 135.

23. John Buchanan, *The Road to Charleston: Nathanael Greene and the American Revolution* (University of Virginia Press, 2019), 166. On another occasion, Greene said: "[It] is almost impossible to draw the militia out of one district into another." Buchanan, *The Road to Charleston*, 161 (spelling and style modernized in both quotations).

24. https://encyclopediavirginia.org/entries/journals-of-the-continental-congress-march-29-1779/.

25. See Gerald M. Carbone, *Nathanael Greene: A Biography of the American Revolution* (self-published, 2008), 210, and Ron Chernow, *Alexander Hamilton* (Penguin Books, 2004), 121 (regarding Rhode Island's uniqueness as only state to allow slaves to serve in its regiments) and Chernow, *Alexander Hamilton*, 355 (stating that "with a heavy influx of black soldiers from New England, the Continental Army had become a highly integrated force").

26. Carbone, *Nathanael Greene*, 209.

27. Buchanan, *Road to Guilford Courthouse*, 142–49 (regarding Gates's biography).

28. Buchanan, *Road to Guilford Courthouse*, 285.

29. Buchanan, *Road to Guilford Courthouse*, 129.

30. Buchanan, *Road to Guilford Courthouse*, 153 (quoting Gates with original emphasis).

31. Buchanan, *Road to Guilford Courthouse*, 154.

32. Buchanan, *Road to Guilford Courthouse*, 161 (quoting Sergeant Major Seymour of Delaware).

33. Buchanan, *Road to Guilford Courthouse*, 156.

34. Buchanan, *Road to Guilford Courthouse*, 157.

35. Banastre Tarleton would have the same confidence when he attacked a larger American force at Cowpens. See Carbone, *Nathanael Greene*, 165 (explaining that "superior numbers did not guarantee victory over better-trained troops).

36. Buchanan, *Road to Guilford Courthouse*, 161.

37. Higginbotham, *War of American Independence*, 357.

38. Buchanan, *Road to Guilford Courthouse*, 126.

39. Higginbotham, *War of American Independence*, 357.

40. Buchanan, *Road to Guilford Courthouse*, 155.

41. Buchanan, *Road to Guilford Courthouse*, 162. Shortly before the
     engagement, a British prisoner informed the Americans that Cornwallis's
     force totaled about 3,000 men. Buchanan, *Road to Guilford Courthouse*,
     162. The actual number appears to have been somewhat less.
42. Buchanan, *Road to Guilford Courthouse*, 161 (spelling and style
     modernized).
43. Buchanan, *Road to Guilford Courthouse*, 161.
44. See Buchanan, *Road to Guilford Courthouse*, 58–72 (regarding Tarleton's
     background) and 161 (regarding Tarleton's dragoons leading the way). See
     also Carbone, *Nathanael Greene*, 161, and Higginbotham, *War of American
     Independence*, 361 (regarding the sobriquets "Bloody Ban" and "Bloody
     Tarleton").
45. Buchanan, *Road to Guilford Courthouse*, 85 (quoting Cornwallis).
46. Buchanan, *Road to Guilford Courthouse*, 388.
47. Buchanan, *Road to Guilford Courthouse*, 162–70; Higginbotham, *War of
     American Independence*, 359–60. For a diagram, see https://www.battlefie
     lds.org/learn/maps/camden-august-16-1780.
48. Regarding Fearnought, see Carbone, *Nathanael Greene*, 134. Regarding the
     Battle of Camden generally, see Buchanan, *Road to Guilford Courthouse*,
     157–72; Higginbotham, *War of American Independence*, 359–64.
49. Buchanan, *Road to Guilford Courthouse*, 163 (stating, "There is no
     indication that Gates had a plan or put his mind seriously to work").
50. Buchanan, *Road to Guilford Courthouse*, 166.
51. Buchanan, *Road to Guilford Courthouse*, 155.
52. Higginbotham, *War of American Independence*, 360.
53. Buchanan, *Road to Guilford Courthouse*, 167.
54. Buchanan, *Road to Guilford Courthouse*, 167 (quoting Williams).
55. https://www.battlefields.org/learn/revolutionary-war/battles/camden.
56. Letter from Edward Stevens to Thomas Jefferson, August 20, 1780 (spelling
     and style modernized), available at https://founders.archives.gov/?q=
     %20Author%3A%22Stevens%2C%20Edward%22%20Recipient%3A%22Je
     fferson%2C%20Thomas%22&s=1111311111&r=1.
57. Letter from Thomas Jefferson to Edward Stevens, September 3, 1780,
     available at https://founders.archives.gov/?q=%20Author%3A%22Jeffer
     son%2C%20Thomas%22%20Recipient%3A%22Stevens%2C%20Edw
     ard%22&s=1111311111&r=4.
58. Fawn M. Brodie, *Thomas Jefferson: An Intimate History* (Bantam Books,
     1974), 166–67.
59. Buchanan, *Road to Guilford Courthouse*, 171.
60. Buchanan, *Road to Guilford Courthouse*, 260.
61. Carbone, *Nathanael Greene*, 153 (quoting Greene's letter).
62. For these events through and including the Battle of Cowpens, see
     Carbone, *Nathanael Greene*, 150–67, and Buchanan, *Road to Guilford
     Courthouse*, 275–77 and 288–333.

63. Carbone, *Nathanael Greene*, 156 (quoting Greene's letter to Baron von Steuben, December 7, 1780).

64. Buchanan, *Road to Guilford Courthouse*, 292.

65. Carbone, *Nathanael Greene*, 160.

66. Carbone, *Nathanael Greene*, 157 (quoting Greene's letter to an unknown recipient).

67. Carbone, *Nathanael Greene*, 157 (quoting Napoleon Bonaparte).

68. See, e.g., Buchanan, *Road to Guilford Courthouse*, 260 (stating that Greene "was one of the great generals in American history, and could have held his own on any stage. . . . He made his mark as a brilliant strategist"), and 276 (stating that Morgan "was by far the Continental Army's finest battle captain. If one were to judge him by all who have led Americans into battle, he would have no superiors and few peers").

69. Carbone, *Nathanael Greene*, 157–58. See also Buchanan, *Road to Guilford Courthouse*, 296 (stating that this contingent of Virginia militiamen had previously served in the Continental Army).

70. Buchanan, *Road to Guilford Courthouse*, 296.

71. Buchanan, *Road to Guilford Courthouse*, 311.

72. Buchanan, *Road to Guilford Courthouse*, 302.

73. Buchanan, *Road to Guilford Courthouse*, 302.

74. Regarding Ninety-Six, see Buchanan, *Road to Guilford Courthouse*, 92–93.

75. Buchanan, *Road to Guilford Courthouse*, 303 (quoting Cruger; spelling and style modernized).

76. Buchanan, *Road to Guilford Courthouse*, 304 (quoting a letter from Nathanael Greene to Thomas Sumter) (spelling and style modernized).

77. Buchanan, *Road to Guilford Courthouse*, 309 (spelling and style modernized).

78. Carbone, *Nathanael Greene*, 163.

79. Buchanan, *Road to Guilford Courthouse*, 312.

80. Buchanan, *Road to Guilford Courthouse*, 313 (quoting Greene's letter to Morgan of January 13, 1781).

81. Buchanan, *Road to Guilford Courthouse*, 310.

82. Buchanan, *Road to Guilford Courthouse*, 315.

83. Carbone, *Nathanael Greene*, 164.

84. Higginbotham, *War of American Independence*, 367.

85. Buchanan, *Road to Guilford Courthouse*, 318.

86. Buchanan, *Road to Guilford Courthouse*, 320.

87. Buchanan, *Road to Guilford Courthouse*, 322 (spelling and style modernized).

88. Buchanan, *Road to Guilford Courthouse*, 323.

89. Carbone, *Nathanael Greene*, 165–66.

90. Buchanan, *Road to Guilford Courthouse*, 323.

91. Buchanan, *Road to Guilford Courthouse*, 324 (quoting Lieutenant Colonel John Eager Howard).

92. Buchanan, *Road to Guilford Courthouse*, 324.
93. Buchanan, *Road to Guilford Courthouse*, 325.
94. Buchanan, *Road to Guilford Courthouse*, 325 (quoting Doctor Robert Jackson).
95. Carbone, *Nathanael Greene*, 66.
96. Charles Royster, *A Revolutionary People at War: The Continental Army and the American Character, 1775–1783* (University of North Carolina Press, 1979), 322 (spelling and style modernized).
97. Buchanan, *Road to Guilford Courthouse*, 370.
98. Buchanan, *Road to Guilford Courthouse*, 372.
99. Buchanan, *Road to Guilford Courthouse*, 372–74.
100. Buchanan, *Road to Guilford Courthouse*, 375 (quoting Captain Anthony Singleton and Greene).
101. Buchanan, *Road to Guilford Courthouse*, 377. Tucker identifies Holcombe's regiment and his own as fleeing from the battle. Colonel John Holcombe commanded troops in Lawson's regiment. https://www.carolana.com/NC/Revolution/revolution_battle_of_guilford_courthouse.html
102. Buchanan, *Road to Guilford Courthouse*, 380.
103. Petition of Robert Poage and Others (May 1781), available at https://founders.archives.gov/documents/Jefferson/01-06-02-0058 (spelling and style modernized).
104. Richard H. Kohn, *Eagle and Sword: The Beginnings of the Military Establishment in America* (Free Press, 1975), 77.
105. Kohn, *Eagle and Sword*, 13, 42.
106. Ketcham, *Madison*, 64.
107. Madison boasted that although he was far the best shot in his militia company, he could generally hit a target the size of a man's face at one hundred yards. Ketcham, *Madison*, 64. This would have been impossible with a musket, and one wonders how likely it could have been even with a rifle. American marksmanship was as much lore as reality. See Priya Satia, *Empire of Guns: The Violent Making of the Industrial Revolution* (Penguin Books, 2018), 278–89.
108. Ketcham, *Madison*, 269.
109. Jeff Broadwater, *George Mason: Forgotten Founder* (University of North Carolina Press, 2006), 213.
110. Jonathan Elliot, ed., *The Debates in Several State Conventions on the Adoption of the Federal Constitution*, vol. 3, 2nd ed. (J.B. Lippincott Co., 1891), 585 [hereinafter Elliot's Debates], available at https://memory.loc.gov/ammem/amlaw/lwed.html.
111. Elliot's Debates, 3:652.
112. Elliot's Debates, 3:547.

Chapter 7

1. Jeff Broadwater, *George Mason: Forgotten Founder* (University of North Carolina Press, 2006), 230 (quoting an unnamed newspaper).

2. Richard Labunski, *James Madison and the Struggle for the Bill of Rights* (Oxford University Press, 2006), 115–16.

3. Sources differ on whether Madison arrived at Mount Vernon on July 3 or 4 and, therefore, whether he stayed with Washington for three or four days. See Ralph Ketcham, *James Madison: A Biography* (University Press of Virginia, 1990), 268 (stating Madison arrived on July 4) and Ron Chernow, *Washington: A Life* (Penguin Books, 2010), 546 (stating Madison arrived on July 3).

4. The New Hampshire ratification vote was 57 to 47. Pauline Maier, *Ratification: The People Debate the Constitution, 1787–1788* (Simon & Shuster, 2010), 316.

5. The key vote was on a motion of Melancton Smith to ratify the Constitution unconditionally rather than on the condition that a second convention be called for the purpose of considering amendments. Smith finessed things by proposing that New York express "full confidence" that there would be a second convention instead of ratifying "upon the condition" that there be a second convention. The vote on that motion was 31 to 29. From that point on, the matter had been effectively decided. The formal vote on ratification, which carried 30 to 27, took place three days later. Maier, *Ratification*, 392–98.

6. Maier, *Ratification*, 371.

7. Speech of Melancton Smith (June 21, 1788), in *The Antifederalist Papers and the Constitutional Debates*, ed. Ralph Ketcham (Mentor, 1986), 343.

8. Maier, *Ratification*, 357.

9. Maier, *Ratification*, 343, 345.

10. Maier, *Ratification*, 344, 354–57.

11. Maier, *Ratification*, 355.

12. Maier, *Ratification*, 375.

13. Maier, *Ratification*, 381.

14. Maier, *Ratification*, 393.

15. Ketcham, *James Madison*, 270.

16. See letter to George Washington from Charles Lee (October 29, 1788) (reporting Henry's remarks to the Virginia Assembly). Charles Lee, brother of Henry "Light Horse Harry" Lee, was an attorney who did legal work for George Washington. Charles Lee was not a member of the Assembly in 1788, and it is not clear whether he personally heard Henry's remarks or was reporting secondhand. In 1795, Washington appointed Lee the third attorney general of the United States.

17. Harlow Giles Unger, *Patrick Henry and the Call to a New Nation* (Da Capo, 2010), 239.

18. Unger, *Patrick Henry*, 336–39.

19. Most of its members were antifederalists. J. Gordon Hylton, "Virginia and the Ratification of the Bill of Rights, 1789–1791," 25 *University of Richmond Law Review* 433, 442 (1991).

20. Unger, *Patrick Henry*, 238–39.

21. Hylton, "Virginia and the Ratification," 442.

22. Labunski, *James Madison*, 135.

23. See, e.g., Harlow Giles Unger, *James Monroe: The Last Founding Father* (Da Capo, 2009), 47 (describing Madison as "to the manor born").

24. Labunski, *James Madison*, 34–35.

25. Labunski, *James Madison*, 136.

26. Labunski, *James Madison*, 136.

27. Labunski, *James Madison*, 121.

28. Jonathan Elliot, ed., *The Debates in Several State Conventions on the Adoption of the Federal Constitution*, vol. 3, 2nd ed. (J.B. Lippincott Co., 1891), 626–27, available at https://memory.loc.gov/ammem/amlaw/lwed.html.

29. Labunski, *James Madison*, 159; Ketcham, *James Madison*, 274, 290.

30. Ketcham, *James Madison*, 290.

31. Letter from James Madison to Thomas Jefferson (October 17, 1788), available at https://founders.archives.gov/documents/Madison/01-11-02-0218.

32. Letter from Madison to Jefferson (October 17, 1788) (spelling and style modernized).

33. Letter from Madison to Jefferson (October 17, 1788) (spelling and style modernized).

34. Labunski, *James Madison*, 158.

35. Labunski, *James Madison*, 136.

36. Labunski, *James Madison*, 140–41. At the time, one could only run for election in the congressional district in which one resided. Today, one may run in any congressional district in the state in which one resides.

37. See U.S. Term Limits, Inc. v. Thornton, 514 U.S. 779, 790–91 (1995) (describing Madison's argument at the Constitutional Convention and holding that a state may not add any requirements beyond those set forth in the Constitution).

38. E.g., Hellmann v. Collier, 141 A.2d 908 (Md. 1958).

39. Labunski, *James Madison*, 142 (quoting Madison's friend George Lee Turberville).

40. See Labunski, *James Madison*, 152 (comparing the candidates), and Ketchum, *James Madison*, 471 (describing Madison as "[c]old and reserved in the presence of strangers or large crowds, small in stature, and weak voiced").

41. Labunski, *James Madison*, 144.

42. Labunski, *James Madison*, 150 (stating that when he stood for election in Amherst County to be a delegate to the Richmond Convention, William

Cabel received 327 votes, his son Samuel received 313 votes, and the next closest candidate received 23 votes).

43. Labunski, *James Madison*, 150.

44. Labunski, *James Madison*, 149–51.

45. Labunski, *James Madison*, 144.

46. Labunski, *James Madison*, 144–45.

47. Labunski, *James Madison*, 142.

48. Ketcham, *James Madison*, 275–76.

49. See Labunski, *James Madison*, 145 (stating "quoting letters from Alexander White and Andrew Shepherd).

50. Letter from Thomas Jefferson to James Madison (October 8, 1787), available at https://founders.archives.gov/?q=Author%3A%22Jeffer son%2C%20Thomas%22%20Recipient%3A%22Madison%2C%20Ja mes%22%20Dates-From%3A1787-07-01%20Dates-To%3A1788-07-31&s=111 1311111&r=7.

51. A woman described Madison as "a small man quite devoid of dignity in his appearance. . . . His skin looks like parchment." Ketchum, *James Madison*, 476 (quoting Frances Few). This description accords with that of Madison's personal secretary, who described him as follows: "In height he was about five feet six inches, of small and delicate form, of a tawny complexion . . . his form, features, and manner were not commanding)." Ketchum, *James Madison*, 407 (quoting Edward Coles). Other sources place Madison at five feet, four inches tall. Labunski, *James Madison*, 2, 89.

52. Ketcham, *James Madison*, 108–11 (regarding Madison's relationship with Catherine Floyd).

53. Ketcham, *James Madison*, 272.

54. Letter from James Madison to Thomas Jefferson (December 8, 1788), available at https://founders.archives.gov/documents/Jefferson/ 01-14-02-0119.

55. Ketcham, *James Madison*, 147.

56. Letter from James Madison to Thomas Jefferson (October 17, 1788), available at https://founders.archives.gov/documents/Madison/ 01-11-02-0218.

57. Letter from Thomas Jefferson to James Madison (March 15, 1789), available at https://founders.archives.gov/?q=Author%3A%22Jefferson%2C%20Tho mas%22%20Recipient%3A%22Madison%2C%20James%22%20Dates- From%3A1788-10-15&s=1111311111&r=5.

58. Letter from James Madison to George Eve (January 2, 1789), available at https://founders.archives.gov/documents/Madison/01-11-02-0297.

59. Letter from James Madison to George Eve (January 2, 1789) (spelling and style modernized).

60. Labunski, *James Madison*, 163.

61. Unger, *Last Founding Father*, 53 (quoting Jefferson's letter).

62. Ketchum, *James Madison*, 46–47; Labunski, *James Madison*, 154.

63. Labunski, *James Madison*, 155.

64. Labunski, *James Madison*, 152.

65. Labunski, *James Madison*, 172.

66. As early as December 1788, Madison realized federalists were going to dominate the First Congress. He had then written Jefferson: "Of the seven states which have appointed their Senators, Virginia alone will have antifederal members in that branch." Letter of James Madison to Thomas Jefferson (December 8, 1788) (spelling and style modernized), available at https://founders.archives.gov/documents/Jefferson/01-14-02-0119.

67. Regarding Pennsylvania, see Nathan Kozuskanich, "Originalism, History, and the Second Amendment: What Did Bearing Arms Really Mean to the Founders?" 10 *Journal of Constitutional Law* 413, 442–43 (2008). Regarding North Carolina, see Earle H. Ketcham, "The Sources of the North Carolina Constitution of 1776," VI *The North Carolina Historical Review* 215, 218 (1929). Regarding Vermont, see Gary J. Aichele, "Making the Vermont Constitution: 1777–1824," 56 *Vermont History: Proceedings of the Vermont Historical Society* 166, 179 (1988). Regarding Massachusetts, see George C. Homans, "John Adams and the Constitution of Massachusetts," 125 *Proceedings of the American Philosophical Society* 286, 287 (1981).

68. Vermont was the fourteenth state. It did not join the Union until March 4, 1791. Meanwhile, two states—Connecticut and Rhode Island—continued to operate under their royal charters and did not adopt constitutions during this time frame.

69. Saul Cornell, *A Well-Regulated Militia: The Founding Fathers and the Origins of Gun Control in America* (Oxford University Press, 2006), 20–23; Walter Isaacson, *Benjamin Franklin: An American Life* (Simon & Schuster, 2003), 123–26, 169–72; Nathan Kozuskanich, "Defending Themselves: The Original Understanding of the Right to Bear Arms," 38 *Rutgers Law Journal* 1041 (2007).

70. Isaacson, *Benjamin Franklin*, 123.

71. Isaacson, *Benjamin Franklin*, 169–72; E. Digby Baltzell, *Puritan Boston and Quaker Philadelphia* (Beacon, 1979), 158.

72. Pennsylvania Militia Act (November 25, 1755) (spelling and style modernized), available at https://founders.archives.gov/documents/Franklin/01-06-02-0116.

73. Kozuskanich, "Defending Themselves," 1048 (quoting the *New York Mercury* of August 4, 1754).

74. Isaacson, *Benjamin Franklin*, 463.

75. Isaacson, *Benjamin Franklin*, 210–14; Kozuskanich, "Defending Themselves," 1051–53.

76. Kozuskanich, "Defending Themselves," 1051. See also Arthur J. Mekeel, *The Quakers and the American Revolution* (Sessions Book Trust, York, England, 1996), 108 (noting that other Quakers were horrified that some among them had taken up arms).

77. Isaacson, *Benjamin Franklin*, 212.

78. Carl T. Bogus, "Race, Riots and Guns," 66 *Southern California Law Review* 1365, 1378 (1993).

79. Constitution of Pennsylvania (September 28, 1776), available at https://avalon.law.yale.edu/18th_century/pa08.asp.

80. See Carl T. Bogus, "The Hidden History of the Second Amendment," 31 *U.C. Davis Law Review* 309, 364–65 (1998).

81. Kozuskanich, "Defending Themselves," 1047–48; Kozuskanich, "Originalism," 439–40.

82. Searches of three databases of American documents from 1763 to 1791 found that the phrase "bear arms" was used to connote a military meaning 98 percent of the time (general documents), 96 percent of the time (newspapers), and 92 percent of the time (letters and speeches by members of Congress). Kozuskanich, "Originalism," 416.

83. E.g., Jeff Broadwater, *George Mason: Forgotten Founder* (University of North Carolina Press, 2006), 90.

84. Virginia Declaration of Rights (June 12, 1776), available at https://avalon.law.yale.edu/18th_century/virginia.asp.

85. Isaacson, *Benjamin Franklin*, 169–70.

86. Kozuskanich, "Defending Themselves," 1057–59.

87. Constitution of North Carolina (December 18, 1776), available at https://avalon.law.yale.edu/18th_century/nc07.asp.

88. E. H. Ketcham, "Sources of the North Carolina Constitution," 218.

89. Willard Sterne Randall, *Ethan Allen: His Life and Times* (W.W. Norton, 2011), 207.

90. Colin Woodard, *American Nations: A History of the Eleven Rival Regional Cultures of North America* (Penguin Books, 2011), 105–11. See also Thomas P. Slaughter, *The Whiskey Rebellion: Frontier Epilogue to the American Revolution* (Oxford University Press, 1986), 28 (labeling the culture "cis-Appalachian"), and 32 (stating "The Paxton riots in eighteenth-century Pennsylvania and the Regulator movements of Revolutionary North Carolina were only the latest in a series of frontier protests against the perceived inadequacy of East–West relations").

91. E. H. Ketcham, "Sources of the North Carolina Constitution," 218.

92. Randall, *Ethan Allen*, 155.

93. Randall, *Ethan Allen*, 154–55.

94. Randall, *Ethan Allen*, 156.

95. Randall, *Ethan Allen*, 189–90.

96. Randall, *Ethan Allen*, 155.

97. Randall, *Ethan Allen*, 178.

98. Randall, *Ethan Allen*, 174 (regarding the New York governors) and 181–82 (regarding the judges).

99. Randall, *Ethan Allen*, 205.

100. Randall, *Ethan Allen*, 208.

101. Randall, *Ethan Allen*, 193–94.
102. Randall, *Ethan Allen*, 218.
103. Randall, *Ethan Allen*, 224.
104. Randall, *Ethan Allen*, 205.
105. Rick Atkinson, *The British Are Coming: The War for America, Lexington to Priceton, 1775–1777* (Henry Holt, 2019), 84, 588 n.84. "Roughnecks" is Atkinson's term. "Tatterdemalions" is Donald Barr Chidsey's term. See also Don Higginbotham, *The War of American Independence: Military Attitudes, Policies, and Practice 1763–1789* (Northeastern University Press, 1983), 67 (referring to the Green Mountain Boys as vigilantes).
106. Randall, *Ethan Allen*, 291. See also Atkinson, *The British Are Coming*, 147.
107. Aichele, "Making the Vermont Constitution," 173.
108. Aichele, "Making the Vermont Constitution," 173.
109. Aichele, "Making the Vermont Constitution," 173.
110. Young also suggested the name Vermont would be better than New Connecticut for the new state. Aichele, "Making the Vermont Constitution," 179.
111. Aichele, "Making the Vermont Constitution," 184.
112. Constitution of Vermont (July 8, 1777), available at https://avalon.law. yale.edu/18th_century/vt01.asp.
113. Aichele, "Making the Vermont Constitution," 181.
114. See David McCullough, *John Adams* (Simon & Schuster, 2001), 174 (regarding appointment in 1777 as a commissioner to France), 210 (regarding appointment in 1778 as minister to the Court of Louis XVI), 225 (regarding appointment as a minister to negotiate a peace treaty with Great Britain), 328 (regarding appointment in 1779 as minister to the Court of St. James), 218–27 (regarding this three-month stay back in Massachusetts in 1779), and 389 (regarding his having been in Europe for ten years, except only for the three-month return to Massachusetts in 1779).
115. McCullough, *John Adams*, 225.
116. Paul C. Reardon, "The Massachusetts Constitution Marks a Milestone," 12 *Publius: The Journal of Federalism* 45, 51–52 (1982).
117. The description of serving as a "sub-sub" committee of one was John Adams's. McCullough, *James Adams*, 220.
118. See George C. Homans, "John Adams and the Constitution of Massachusetts," 125 *Proceedings of the American Philosophical Society* 286, 289 (1981) (noting that although Adams was merely a farmer's son, "he had graduated from Harvard, and that made him a gentleman").
119. Constitution of Massachusetts (1780), available at http://www.nhinet.org/ ccs/docs/ma-1780.htm.
120. Stephen P. Halbrook, "The Right to Bear Arms in the First State Bills of Rights: Pennsylvania, North Carolina, Vermont, and Massachusetts," 10 *Vermont Law Review* 255, 303 (1985).
121. Halbrook, "The Right to Bear Arms in the First State Bills of Rights," 302.

122. McCullough, *John Adams*, 414 (quoting Adams).
123. McCullough, *John Adams*, 499.
124. Letter from James Madison to Thomas Jefferson (October 17, 1788).
125. Letter from Madison to Jefferson (October 17, 1788).
126. Labunski, *James Madison*, 199.

Chapter 8

1. Richard Labunski, *James Madison and the Struggle for the Bill of Rights* (Oxford University Press, 2006), 184.
2. See also Ralph Ketchum, *James Madison: A Biography* (University Press of Virginia, 1990), 293 (stating that Madison "was at the pinnacle of his career as a nation builder").
3. Ketchum, *James Madison*, 278.
4. Ketchum, *James Madison*, 284; Noah Feldman, *The Three Lives of James Madison: Genius, Partisan, President* (Picador, 2017), 262.
5. Labunski, *James Madison*, 188–89.
6. First Inaugural Address of George Washington (April 30, 1789), available at https://www.archives.gov/exhibits/american_originals/inaugtxt.html.
7. Address of the House of Representatives to the President (May 5, 1789), available at https://founders.archives.gov/?q=%20Author%3A%22Ho use%20of%20Representatives%22%20Recipient%3A%22Washing ton%2C%20George%22%20Dates-From%3A1789-04-30%20Dates-To%3A1789-06-30&s=1111311111&r=1.
8. Reply of the President to the House of Representatives (May 8, 1789), available at https://founders.archives.gov/?q=%20Author%3A%22Washing ton%2C%20George%22%20Recipient%3A%22House%20of%20Represen tatives%22&s=1111311111&r=1.
9. Ketcham, *James Madison*, 289. See also Letter from Edmund Randolph to James Madison (August 18, 1789), and Helen E. Veit, Kenneth R. Bowling, and Charlene Bangs Bickford, eds., *Creating the Bill of Rights: The Documentary Record from the First Federal Congress* (Johns Hopkins University Press, 1991), 281 (stating that although Patrick Henry favored some of the amendments proposed by Congress, he "still asks for the great desideratum, the destruction of direct taxation").
10. See, e.g., letter of Patrick Henry to William Grayson (March 31, 1789), in which Henry states that the differences between federalists and antifederalists "seem now scarcely to exist" because "even our highest toned Feds say we must have amendments," but that agreement ended regarding direct taxation, treaties, and trade. Veit et al., Creating the Bill of Rights, 226.
11. The single antifederalist was Theodorick Bland. The seven federalists were John Brown, Samuel Griffin, Richard Bland Lee, James Madison, Andrew Moore, John Page, and Alexander White. See Biographical Gazetteer in Veit et al., Creating the Bill of Rights, 301–14.
12. Ketcham, *James Madison*, 290.
13. Lebunski, *James Madison*, 189–90.

14. Remarks of James Madison in the House of Representatives (June 8, 1789), in Veit et al., Creating the Bill of Rights, 69.
15. Veit et al., *Creating the Bill of Rights*, 64.
16. See Feldman, *The Three Lives of James Madison*, 259 (stating Madison would speak more than 150 times to the first session of Congress).
17. Veit et al., *Creating the Bill of Rights*, 78 (spelling and style modernized). The substantive portion of Madison's remarks is available at https://www.let.rug.nl/usa/documents/1786-1800/madison-speech-proposing-the-bill-of-rights-june-8-1789.php.
18. Veit et al., *Creating the Bill of Rights*, 79.
19. Veit et al., *Creating the Bill of Rights*, 80.
20. Veit et al., *Creating the Bill of Rights*, 80.
21. Veit et al., *Creating the Bill of Rights*, 81.
22. Veit et al., *Creating the Bill of Rights*, 83.
23. Veit et al., *Creating the Bill of Rights*, 85.
24. Veit et al., *Creating the Bill of Rights*, 84.
25. Veit et al., *Creating the Bill of Rights*, 85.
26. Veit et al., *Creating the Bill of Rights*, 12; also available at https://www.let.rug.nl/usa/documents/1786-1800/madison-speech-proposing-the-bill-of-rights-june-8-1789.php.
27. Veit et al., *Creating the Bill of Rights*, 19.
28. Veit et al., *Creating the Bill of Rights*, 20.
29. Labunski, *James Madison*, 199.
30. Feldman, *Three Lives of James Madison*, 269.
31. Veit et al., *Creating the Bill of Rights*, 77.
32. Veit et al., *Creating the Bill of Rights*, 95.
33. Veit et al., *Creating the Bill of Rights*, 102–3.
34. Regarding Roger Sherman, see Richard Beeman, *Plain, Honest Men: The Making of the Constitution* (Random House, 2009), 114–18; John Ferling, *Independence: The Struggle to Set America Free* (Bloomsbury, 2011), 284–96.
35. See James Madison, *Notes of Debates in the Federal Convention of 1789* (Ohio University Press, 1966), 532 (Sherman offended at categorizing slaves as property) and 503 (Sherman's quotation; spelling and style modernized). See also Beeman, *Plain, Honest Men*, 325; Catherine Drinker Bowen, *Miracle at Philadelphia: The Story of the Constitutional Convention May to September 1787* (Atlantic—Little, Brown, 1966).
36. Madison, *Notes of Debates*, 649–50.
37. Madison, *Notes of Debates*, 648.
38. Labunski, *James Madison*, 216.
39. Labunski, *James Madison*, 270.
40. William W. Freehling, *The Road to Disunion: Secessionists at Bay 1776–1854* (Oxford University Press, 1990), 135.
41. Letter from Robert Morris to Francis Hopkinson (August 15, 1789), in Veit et al., *Creating the Bill of Rights*, 278 (spelling and style modernized). See

also Labunski, *James Madison*, 235; Pauline Maier, *Ratification: The People Debate the Constitution, 1787–1788* (Simon & Shuster, 2010), 455.

42. Letter from Theodore Sedgwick to Benjamin Lincoln (July 19, 1789) (spelling and style modernized), in Veit et al., *Creating the Bill of Rights*, 263–64. See also Labunski, *James Madison*, 208; Maier, *Ratification*, 455.

43. The House of Representatives opened its sessions to the public. Three newspapers covered House debates, and one, the Congressional Register, employed a shorthand writer to record the debates verbatim, as much as possible. Nevertheless, there was only a single shorthand writer (Thomas Lloyd) working with poor acoustics and a quill pen. Thus, the reports of the three papers do not, even collectively, provide a full and complete transcript, and we cannot know what they omit. Veit et al., *Creating the Bill of Rights*, 55–56. Therefore, when I say that a topic was debated only briefly, or not at all, I always mean *so far as we know*.

44. Viet et al., *Creating the Bill of Rights*, 118.

45. Veit et al., *Creating the Bill of Rights*, 197.

46. Veit et al., *Creating the Bill of Rights*, 117.

47. Veit et al., *Creating the Bill of Rights*, 124.

48. Veit et al., *Creating the Bill of Rights*, 197–98.

49. Article the First, Amendments Passed by the House of Representatives (August 24, 1789), in Veit et al., *Creating the Bill of Rights*, 272.

50. Veit et al., *Creating the Bill of Rights*, 161.

51. Veit et al., *Creating the Bill of Rights*, 164.

52. Veit et al., *Creating the Bill of Rights*, 167.

53. Antifederalist supporters included Aedamus Burke (SC), Elbridge Gerry (MA), Thomas Sumter (VA), and St. George Tucker (VA). For identifications of them as antifederalists, see Biographical Gazetteer in Veit et al., *Creating the Bill of Rights*, 301 et seq. See also Saul Cornell, *A Well-Regulated Militia: The Founding Fathers and the Origins of Gun Control in America* (Oxford University Press, 2006)(describing Tucker as a moderate antifederalist), 75.

54. Veit et al., *Creating the Bill of Rights*, 170–71.

55. Veit et al., *Creating the Bill of Rights*, 171.

56. Veit et al., *Creating the Bill of Rights*, 174.

57. Veit et al., *Creating the Bill of Rights*, xv.

58. Veit et al., *Creating the Bill of Rights*, 176.

59. The record here is not verbatim and we do not know what state provisions Burke identified. Veit et al., *Creating the Bill of Rights*, 176–77.

60. Veit et al., *Creating the Bill of Rights*, 177.

61. Veit et al., *Creating the Bill of Rights*, 139.

62. Veit et al., *Creating the Bill of Rights*, 206–13.

63. Veit et al., *Creating the Bill of Rights*, 185–86.

64. Veit et al., *Creating the Bill of Rights*, 201.

65. Veit et al., *Creating the Bill of Rights*, 191.

66. Veit et al., *Creating the Bill of Rights*, 193–94.
67. Veit et al., *Creating the Bill of Rights*, 182 (spelling and style modernized).
68. Veit et al., *Creating the Bill of Rights*, 182.
69. Veit et al., *Creating the Bill of Rights*, 183.
70. Veit et al., *Creating the Bill of Rights*, 183 (spelling and style modernized).
71. Veit et al., *Creating the Bill of Rights*, 183.
72. Veit et al., *Creating the Bill of Rights*, 183.
73. Veit et al., *Creating the Bill of Rights*, 183.
74. Veit et al., *Creating the Bill of Rights*, 184.
75. Veit et al., *Creating the Bill of Rights*, 184.
76. Veit et al., *Creating the Bill of Rights*, 184.
77. Veit et al., *Creating the Bill of Rights*, 184.
78. Veit et al., *Creating the Bill of Rights*, 185.
79. Veit et al., *Creating the Bill of Rights*, 185.
80. The record states the motion was defeated by a majority of 13. Veit et al., *Creating the Bill of Rights*, 185. Other votes taken very shortly beforehand and afterward show that between forty-six and forty-eight members were then present and voting. Veit et al., *Creating the Bill of Rights*, 184, 186. It is therefore reasonable to conclude that the vote on Burke's motion was approximately 30 to 17.
81. Veit et al., *Creating the Bill of Rights*, 189.
82. Labunski, *James Madison*, 228–29.
83. "'Pacificus' [*Noah Webster*] to James Madison" (August 14, 1789), in Veit et al., *Creating the Bill of Rights*, 275–76.
84. Veit et al., *Creating the Bill of Rights*, 275 (original emphasis).
85. Veit et al., *Creating the Bill of Rights*, 276 (spelling and style modernized).
86. Veit et al., *Creating the Bill of Rights*, 277 (spelling and style modernized).
87. Labunski, *James Madison*, 273.
88. Saul Cornell, *A Well-Regulated Militia*, 61; Labunski, *James Madison*, 235.
89. Veit et al., *Creating the Bill of Rights*, 289.
90. H. Richard Uviller and William G. Merkel, "The Second Amendment in Context: The Case for the Vanishing Predicate," 76 *Chicago-Kent Law Review* 403, 506 (2000).
91. Veit et al., *Creating the Bill of Rights*, 38 n.13. See also Stephen P. Halbrook, *The Founders' Second Amendment: Origins of the Right to Bear Arms* (Ivan R. Dee, 2009), 274–75.
92. Veit et al., *Creating the Bill of Rights*, 39 n.13.
93. See Labunski, *James Madison*, 246 and 314 n. 16.
94. Labunski, *James Madison*, 247 (quoting letters by Lee and Grayson).
95. Labunski, *James Madison*, 248.
96. Labunski, *James Madison*, 250.
97. Labunski, *James Madison*, 253. There is no time limit on ratification of amendments by states. In 1992, the First Congress's second proposed amendment, regarding congressional salaries, became the Twenty-Seventh

Amendment to the United States Constitution when thirty-eight of the then-existing fifty states had ratified.

98. Ernest A. Young, "The Constitution Outside the Constitution," 117 *Yale Law Journal* 408, 410 (2007).

Chapter 9

1. Edward Vallance, *The Glorious Revolution: 1688—Britain's Fight for Liberty* (Pegasus Books, 2008), 100.
2. Vallance, *Glorious Revolution*, 73, 85–86.
3. Vallance, *Glorious Revolution*, 17.
4. Vallance, *Glorious Revolution*, 80.
5. Vallance, *Glorious Revolution*, 26.
6. Vallance, *Glorious Revolution*, 30.
7. Vallance, *Glorious Revolution*, 30–34.
8. Vallance, *Glorious Revolution* (quoting letter from Coleman to La Chaise, confessor to Louis XIV), 33. Regarding Louis XIV being James's first cousin, see J. S. Bromley, ed., *The New Cambridge Modern History*, vol. VI (Cambridge University Press, 1970), 195.
9. Vallance, *Glorious Revolution*, 45.
10. Vallance, *Glorious Revolution*, 36.
11. On several occasions, Charles prorogued Parliament. Vallance, *Glorious Revolution*, 37, 38, 40–41. I use the term *suspended* rather than *prorogated* because it is more readily understood by American readers. On one occasion, Charles dissolved Parliament. Vallance, *Glorious Revolution*, 41.
12. Vallance, *Glorious Revolution*, 39.
13. Vallance, *Glorious Revolution*, 39.
14. Vallance, *Glorious Revolution*, 40.
15. See Steve Pincus, *1688: The First Modern Revolution* (Yale University Press, 2009), 92 and 132 (regarding James's reputation as an absolutist), and Howard Nenner, "The Later Stuart Age," in *The Varieties of British Political Thought 1500–1800*, ed. J. G. A. Pocock (Cambridge University Press, 1993), 181–83 (regarding absolutism).
16. Vallance, *Glorious Revolution*, 47.
17. Pincus, *1688*, 91–92.
18. Pincus, *1688*, 96.
19. Pincus, *1688*, 96.
20. Bromley, *New Cambridge Modern History*, 6:194.
21. Vallance, *Glorious Revolution*, 51–64.
22. Vallance, *Glorious Revolution*, 52, 56.
23. Vallance, *Glorious Revolution*, 51.
24. Vallance, *Glorious Revolution*, 54.
25. In 1677, Parliament passed legislation to reorganize the military. It decided to disband the army, and at the same time it paid lip service to making the militia more effective. But, as Lois G. Schwoerer noted: "Members,

however, were not really serious about making the militia more useful."
While Parliament took some steps with respect to the militia, Professor
Schwoerer concluded that the "significance of these steps was polemical
rather than substantive, for nothing concrete was done about the condition
of the militia." Lois G. Schwoerer, *"No Standing Armies!" The Antimilitary
Ideology in Seventeenth-Century England* (Johns Hopkins University Press,
1974), 131–32.

26. Vallance, *Glorious Revolution*, 60, 73. See also Pincus, *1688*, 104.
27. John M. Barry, *Roger Williams and the Creation of the American Soul:
     Church, State, and the Birth of Liberty* (Penguin Books, 2012), 12.
28. Schwoerer, *No Standing Armies*, 180.
29. Barry, *Roger Williams*, 29–31.
30. Nenner, "The Later Stuart Age," 196.
31. Vallance, *Glorious Revolution*, 18–19. Sir Edward Coke made this point
     when he said during debate in the House of Commons: "The freedom
     of this House is the freedom of the whole land." Lois G. Schwoerer,
     "British Lineages and American Choices," in *The Bill of Rights: Government
     Proscribed*, ed. Ronald Hoffman and Peter J. Albert (University of Virginia
     Press, 1998), 9.
32. Barry, *Roger Williams*, 12.
33. William M. Lamont, "The Puritan Revolution: A Historiographical Essay,"
     in *Varieties of British Political Thought 1500–1800*, 129.
34. Charles was so pleased with granting religious toleration to Rhode Island
     that he repeated similar language in charters for New Jersey and Carolina.
     See Carl T. Bogus, "Is This a Christian Nation? An Introduction," 26 *Roger
     Williams University Law Review* 237 at 275, 277 (2021), and sources cited
     therein.
35. Pincus, *1688*, 201.
36. Pincus, *1688*, 157.
37. Pincus, *1688*, 166, 199–201; Vallance, *Glorious Revolution*, 83–84.
38. Vallance, *Glorious Revolution*, 79, 83.
39. Pincus, *1688*, 204; Vallance, *Glorious Revolution*, 83.
40. Sir Isaac Newton said that accepting James's indulgences was "to throw up
     all the laws for liberty and property," that is, to throw over fundamentals
     of the English government—including Parliament's authority to make the
     laws and the monarch's obligation to respect the laws—in return for get-
     out-of-jail cards. Pincus, *1688*, 205.
41. See Carl T. Bogus, "The Hidden History of the Second Amendment," 31
     U.C. Davis Law Review 379–82 (1998), 379–82 and sources cited therein.
42. Pincus, *1688*, 155.
43. Pincus, *1688*, 162; Vallance, *Glorious Revolution*, 83.
44. Pincus, *1688*, 163; Vallance, *Glorious Revolution*, 83.
45. Pincus, *1688*, 163–65.
46. Pincus, *1688*, 173.

47. Pincus, *1688*, 173.
48. Pincus, *1688*, 175.
49. Pincus, *1688*, 174.
50. Pincus, *1688*, 174.
51. Pincus, *1688*, 144.
52. Pincus, *1688*, 323.
53. In particular, the Netherlands had developed a strong navy, which it needed to support its considerable commercial trade in the Indies. Pincus, *1688*, 311.
54. Vallance, *Glorious Revolution*, 111–12.
55. Pincus, *1688*, 354–55.
56. Pincus, *1688*, 353–54.
57. Pincus, *1688*, 336; Vallance, *Glorious Revolution*, 152–53.
58. Pincus, *1688*, 323.
59. Pincus, *1688*, 329.
60. See, e.g., Schwoerer, *No Standing Armies*, 104 (distinguishing armies raised during times of war from those maintained during times of peace, only the latter of which were called "standing armies").
61. Schwoerer, *No Standing Armies*, 102, 110–11.
62. Schwoerer, *No Standing Armies*, 11 (quoting William Cecil, Lord Burghley, an adviser to Queen Elizabeth).
63. Schwoerer, *No Standing Armies*, 192.
64. In parliamentary debate, one member observed that being "a Soldier is a Trade, and must (as all other Trades are) be learned," which was why the militia had repeatedly failed. Remark of the Earl of Ranelagh, Debates from the Reign of James II, Thursday, November 12, 1685, https://www.british-history.ac.uk/greys-debates/vol8/pp343-372#h3-0004. See also Schwoerer, *No Standing Armies*, 143.
65. Schwoerer, *No Standing Armies*, 191–92. See also Schwoerer, *No Standing Armies*, 4 (calling the slogan "a propaganda tool").
66. Schwoerer, *No Standing Armies*, 131.
67. The relevant statute was the Disbanding Act of 1677. Schwoerer, *No Standing Armies*, 131.
68. Debates from the Reign of James II, Monday, November 5, 1685, https://www.british-history.ac.uk/greys-debates/vol8/pp343-372#h3-0004. See also Schwoerer, *No Standing Armies*, 139–46; and Pincus, *1688*, 181.
69. Debates from the Reign of James II, November 16, 1685, https://www.british-history.ac.uk/greys-debates/vol8/pp343-372#h3-0004.
70. Schwoerer, *No Standing Armies*, 4, 144–45.
71. Vallance, *Glorious Revolution*, 74.
72. Pincus, *1688*, 182.
73. Schwoerer, *No Standing Armies*, 99.
74. During debates in Parliament, one member said: "The King declared, 'That no soldiers should quarter in private houses;' but that they did:

'That they should pay for all things they took;' but they paid nothing for almost all they took. And for Officers to be employed not taking the Tests, it is dispensing with all the Laws at once; and if these men be good and kind, we know not whether it proceeds from their generosity, or principles: For we must remember, it is Treason for any man to be reconciled to the Church of Rome; for the Pope, by Law, is declared an enemy to this Kingdom." Debates from the Reign of James II, Thursday, November 12, 1685, https://www.british-history.ac.uk/greys-debates/vol8/pp343-372#h3-0004.

75. Pincus, *1688*, 182.
76. James speciously invoked the Game Act of 1671 as justification for this action. Vallance, *Glorious Revolution*, 103–4.
77. Pincus, *1688*, 77–81, 309.
78. Pincus, *1688*, 150–51.
79. Pincus, *1688*, 155.
80. http://www.jacobite.ca/documents/16880427.htm. See also Pincus, *1688*, 191–95; Vallance, *Glorious Revolution*, 85–86, 88–89, 91–101. See also Bromley, *New Cambridge Modern History*, 199 (describing contents of the Indulgence).
81. Pincus, *1688*, 193.
82. See Sheila Ryan Johansson, "Medics, Monarchs and Mortality, 1600–1800: Origins of the Knowledge-Driven Health Transition in Europe," July 7, 2010, 9, available at http://dx.doi.org/10.2139/ssrn.1661453; and Lois G. Schwoerer, *Gun Culture* (University of Virginia Press, 2016), 158 (regarding James's health).
83. Vallance, *Glorious Revolution*, 109–110.
84. Vallance, *Glorious Revolution*, 117.
85. Vallance, *Glorious Revolution*, 121.
86. *The New Cambridge Modern History*, 6:203–4. When the winds and tides were favorable, however, Royal Navy commanders unanimously decided that the Dutch "fleet was much superior to ours" and that it would be futile to engage it in battle. Pincus, *1688*, 237. Their assessment may have been influenced by defections in the navy, although Steve Pincus believes it was principally due to overestimating the strength of the Dutch fleet.
87. Vallance, *Glorious Revolution*, 131.
88. Pincus, *1688*, 230, 238.
89. Vallance, *Glorious Revolution*, 131.
90. Pincus, *1688*, 235. The total number of desertions probably did not exceed 2,000. Pincus, *1688*, 237.
91. Vallance, *Glorious Revolution*, 137, 140.
92. Vallance, *Glorious Revolution*, 144, 147; Pincus, *1688*, 258.
93. Vallance, *Glorious Revolution*, 145. Other sources say James traveled with three companions.

94. Whether the letter was from the Earl of Halifax is not certain. Vallance, *Glorious Revolution*, 158–59.
95. Vallance, *Glorious Revolution*, 163–75; Pincus, *1688*, 284–86.
96. Vallance, *Glorious Revolution*, 173.
97. Mario Puzo, *The Godfather* (G.P. Putnam's Sons, 1969), 397.
98. See Declaration of Rights, February 12, 1689, set forth at Appendix 1 to Lois G. Schwoerer, *The Declaration of Rights, 1689* (John Hopkins University Press, 1981), 297 (spelling and style modernized). English Bill of Rights 1689: An Act Declaring the Rights and Liberties of the Subjects and Settling the Succession of the Crown, https://avalon.law.yale.edu/17th_century/england.asp. See also Schwoerer, *Declaration of Rights*, 297.
99. Vallance, *Glorious Revolution*, 178.
100. Godden v. Hales, 11 Howell's State Trials 1165, 89 Eng. Rep. 1050 (K.B. 1686). See Pincus, *1688*, 183–84; Vallance, *Glorious Revolution*, 104; and Bogus, "The Hidden History of the Second Amendment," 382.
101. Nenner, "The Later Stuart Age," 182.
102. Schwoerer, *The Declaration of Rights, 1689*, 295. See also Pincus, *1688*, 292–93; Vallance, *Glorious Revolution*, 176.
103. Vallance, *Glorious Revolution*, 176.
104. The Declaration of Rights (February 12, 1689), available in Schwoerer, *Declaration of Rights*, Appendix 1, 295–98 (original spelling and style retained). Also available at https://avalon.law.yale.edu/17th_century/england.asp.
105. For example, Howard Nenner writes, Parliament was "attempting a settlement that would rid them of James while keeping the foundations of their government intact." Nenner, "The Later Stuart Age," 202–3. Thomas Macaulay famously wrote: Not a single new right was given to the people. The whole English law . . . was exactly the same after the Revolution as before it." Schwoerer, *Declaration of Rights*, 5 (quoting Macaulay).
106. See Schwoerer, *Declaration of Rights*, 296 (original spelling and style retained).
107. One commentator explains what William Blackstone meant when he used the term "rights" in eighteenth-century England: "The term 'absolute rights' may suggest to a modern reader that these liberties could not be altered even by legislation enacted for the public good. Blackstone meant no such thing: all of these absolute rights could be regulated and defined by Parliament." Stuart Jay, "Origins of the Privileges and Immunities of State Citizenship under Article IV," 45 *Loyola University Chicago Law Journal* 1, 39 (2013). The difference between American and British rights largely remains. "According to the conventional view, constitutional rights in the United States are protected by the courts 'against' the interests of the majority, whereas in the United Kingdom, constitutional rights are defined by Parliament in the best interests of

the British people." Douglas E. Edlin, "The Constitutional Logic of the Common Law," 53 *Vanderbilt Journal of Transnational Law* 79, 82 (2020).

108. See Schwoerer, *Declaration of Rights*, 296 (original spelling and style retained).

109. Article 3 provides: "That the Commission for erecting the late Courte of Commissioners for Ecclesiasticall Causes and all other Commissions and Courts of like nature, are illegall and pernicious." See Schwoerer, *Declaration of Rights*, 296 (original spelling and style retained). This, too, was about parliamentary prerogatives. Parliament abolished this court, which was designed to punish religious dissenters, in 1641. James II reinstituted it on his own, without parliamentary consent, in 1686.

110. Eugene Wambaugh, "War Emergency Legislation—A General View," 30 *Harvard Law Review* 663, 665 (1917).

111. The Declaration of Rights (February 12, 1689), available in Schwoerer, *Declaration of Rights*, 296–97. Also available at https://avalon.law.yale.edu/17th_century/england.asp.

112. Grievance 5. Schwoerer, *Declaration of Rights*, 295 (original spelling and style retained).

113. Grievance 6. Schwoerer, *Declaration of Rights*, 296–97 (original spelling and style retained).

114. Schwoerer, *Gun Culture*, 48, 175. By contrast, there was a recognized right to own a longbow, and in 1511 Parliament passed legislation requiring householders to furnish longbows and arrows to all boys between seven and seventeen years of age. Schwoerer, *Gun Culture*, 54.

115. About a month later, Parliament enacted legislation "disarming Papists and reputed Papists," although it allowed Catholics to possess weapons to defend themselves and their homes if they obtained an order by a justice of the peace. Schwoerer, *Gun Culture*, 161.

116. Schwoerer, *Gun Culture*, 171.

117. Schwoerer, *Gun Culture*, 50.

118. Schwoerer, *Gun Culture*, 50 (quoting Morgan).

119. 33 Hen. 8, c. 6, § 1, An Act Concerning Crossbows and Handguns (1541), available at https://firearmslaw.duke.edu/years/1541/?print=print-search. See also Schwoerer, *Gun Culture*, 59.

120. Schwoerer, *Gun Culture*, 59.

121. Schwoerer, *Gun Culture*, 182, 187.

122. Schwoerer, *Gun Culture*, 169.

123. Schwoerer, *Gun Culture*, 170.

124. *The Federalist Papers* Nos. 26 and 84 (Hamilton).

125. *The Federalist Papers* No. 26 (Hamilton).

126. James Madison's second speech to Congress on June 8, 1789, available at http://www.let.rug.nl/usa/documents/1786-1800/madison-speech-proposing-the-bill-of-rights-june-8-1789.php (spelling and style modernized).

Chapter 10

1. Washington's First State of the Union Address (January 8, 1790) (spelling and style modernized), available at https://www.mountvernon.org/educat ion/primary-sources/state-of-the-union-address.
2. The confederation was formed in 1783, the same year as the Treaty of Paris. Alan Taylor, *American Republics: A Continental History of the United States, 1783–1859* (W.W. Norton, 2021), 26.
3. Taylor, *American Republics*, 26.
4. Richard H. Kohn, *Eagle and Sword: The Beginnings of the Military Establishment in America* (Free Press, 1975), 96.
5. Taylor, *American Republics*, 30.
6. Colonel William L. Shaw, "The Interrelationship of the United States Army and the National Guard," 31 *Military Law Review* 39, 46 (1966).
7. Nisbet made this statement in 1792. Kohn, *Eagle and Sword*, 122 (spelling and style modernized).
8. These are 1791 figures. Treasury was, by far, the largest department; by 1791, it had 204 employees, more than half of whom were customs collectors and surveyors. Ron Chernow, *Alexander Hamilton* (Penguin Books, 2004), 339. However, the growth of the Treasury fueled suspicions about the ambitions of Treasury Secretary Alexander Hamilton and contributed to the growth of the opposition Republican Party.
9. Taylor, *American Republic*, 2.
10. Taylor, *American Republic*, 33.
11. Taylor, *American Republic*, 33.
12. Washington's First State of the Union Address (January 8, 1790); Taylor, *American Republic*, 665.
13. Shaw, "Interrelationship," 45. In 1783, at the invitation of a committee chaired by Alexander Hamilton in the Confederation Congress, Washington, with assistance of his top officers in the Continental Army, submitted a detailed plan for organizing a peacetime military. Shaw, "Interrelationship," 40–48. "[W]e are too poor to maintain a standing army adequate to our defense," Washington had then said. Fortunately, America's "distance from the European States" gave her the ability to retain a small standing force with plans for quickly expanding it should the need arise. Washington had then recommended a standing army of 2,631, plus classes of militia, roughly consistent with the Knox Plan of 1790. "Washington's Sentiments for a Peace Establishment" (May 1, 1783), available at https://founders.archives.gov/documents/Washington/ 99-01-02-11202.
14. Ron Chernow, *Washington: A Life* (Penguin Books, 2010), 256.
15. I cannot help but compare thirty days of annual training to my experience in the modern militia, that is, the National Guard (and Army Reserve) during the period 1970 to 1976. National Guardsmen then initially received 120 days of basic and advanced individual training in a military

specialty (in my case, artillery) alongside regular Army trainees. Thereafter, we trained two days per month plus two weeks every summer: a total of 38 days per year. From my perspective as a low-ranking enlisted soldier, the 38 days of annual training seemed largely designed to maintain the proficiency acquired during the initial 120 days of training.

16. Kohn, *Eagle and Sword*, 120.
17. Chernow, *Washington*, 665; Kohn, *Eagle and Sword*, 101–2.
18. Kohn, *Eagle and Sword*, 100–107.
19. Thomas P. Slaughter, *The Whiskey Rebellion: Frontier Epilogue to the American Revolution* (Oxford University Press, 1986), 94–95; Shaw, *Eagle and Sword*, 106–7.
20. Sources I consulted disagree about which American Indian tribe defeated Harmar. See Kohn, *Eagle and Sword*, 106 (suggesting it was Shawnee); Chernow, *Washington: A Life*, 666 (suggesting it was Miami). Other sources are even more specific yet also disagree: some identify Chief Little Turtle of the Miami tribe as leading the force that defeated Harmar; others identify Chief Blue Jacket of the Shawnee tribe as leading that force. For this reason, I only identify Harmar's opponents as Indians.
21. Kohn, *Eagle and Sword*, 107–8.
22. 2 Annals of Congress 1851–60 (December 16, 1790). For membership of the First Congress, Third Session, see https://history.house.gov/Congressional-Overview/Profiles/1st/.
23. 2 Annals of Congress 1852–53.
24. 2 Annals of Congress 1851–53.
25. 2 Annals of Congress 1855–56.
26. 2 Annals of Congress 1855–56.
27. Kohn, *Eagle and Sword*, 109–10.
28. Kohn, *Eagle and Sword*, 112 (spelling and style modernized).
29. Kohn, *Eagle and Sword*, 114.
30. Chernow, *Washington*, 665.
31. Chernow, *Washington*, 666.
32. Kohn, *Eagle and Sword*, 120.
33. Kohn, *Eagle and Sword*, 120.
34. Chernow, *Washington*, 668.
35. See 2 Annuals of Congress 337–54 (January 1791).
36. 2 Annals of Congress 341 (January 26, 1791) (spelling and style modernized).
37. 2 Annals of Congress 348 (January 26, 1791).
38. The congressmen were William Findley and Albert Gallatin. Kohn, *Eagle and Sword*, 121.
39. Kohn, *Eagle and Sword*, 121.
40. Kohn, *Eagle and Sword*, 121.
41. It passed 29 to 19 in the House and 15 to 12 in the Senate. Kohn, *Eagle and Sword*, 122. Debate over the bill was extensive, and a previous motion

to instead raise a force of only three regiments, totaling 1,800 men, was defeated. Annuals of Congress 337–55 (1792).

42. What is commonly referred to as the Militia Act of 1792 actually consists of two Acts, one enacted on May 2, 1792, and the other enacted on May 8, 1792. Both are available at https://www.mountvernon.org/education/prim ary-sources-2/article/militia-act-of-1792. While most descriptions of the Act say that it enrolled everyone between the ages of eighteen and forty-five, the Act actually enrolls everyone "who is or shall be of age of eighteen, and *under* the age of forty-five years" (emphasis added).

43. Shaw, "Interrelationship," 47.

44. The Act adopted "the rules of discipline, approved and established by Congress" on March 29, 1779, which in turn adopted the "Regulations for the Order and Discipline of the Troops of the United States," developed by Baron Von Steuben during the Revolutionary War, and commonly referred to as the Blue Book.

45. Kohn, *Eagle and Sword*, 135.

46. Kohn, *Eagle and Sword*, 135.

47. Kohn, *Eagle and Sword*, 135.

48. Frederick Bernays Wiener, "The Militia Clause of the Constitution," 54 *Harvard Law Review*, 181, 187 (1940).

49. Kohn, *Eagle and Sword*, 137.

50. Wiener, "Militia Clause," 187.

51. Slaughter, *Whiskey Rebellion*, 175–76; Kohn, *Eagle and Sword*, 156–57. The force that Wayne led into the Ohio River Valley totaled 3,500 and was comprised of 2,000 regulars and 1,500 Kentucky volunteers. According to Slaughter, only 900 regulars were involved in the Battle of Fallen Timbers.

52. Chernow, *Washington*, 717.

53. Kohn, *Eagle and Sword*, chapter 7.

54. Taylor, *Internal Enemy*, 129.

55. "Memorandum of preparatory measures which may be adopted by the Executive in relation to War," an enclosure of letter from Albert Gallatin to Thomas Jefferson (July 25, 1807), available at https://founders.archi ves.gov/?q=%20Author%3A%22Gallatin%2C%20Albert%22%20Recipi ent%3A%22Jefferson%2C%20Thomas%22%20Dates-From%3A1807- 07-01%20Dates-To%3A1807-07-31&s=1111311111&r=7 (spelling and style modernized).

56. Taylor, *Internal Enemy*, 126 (spelling and style modernized).

57. South Carolina slave patrollers were not paid except during the years 1734 to 1737. Sally E. Hadden, *Slave Patrols: Law and Violence in Virginia and the Carolinas* (Harvard University Press, 2001), 21–22, 66. Virginia slave patrollers were compensated with tax breaks and tobacco. Hadden, *Slave Patrols*, 31–32, 91. North Carolina slave patrollers were allowed to keep weapons they confiscated and to claim rewards for capturing runaway slaves. Hadden, *Slave Patrols*, 37, 39.

58. Haddon, *Slave Patrols*, 94.

59. See, e.g., Alan Gibson, "The Madisonian Madison and the Question of Consistency: The Significance and Challenge of Recent Research," 64 *The Review of Politics* 311, 334 (2002); Jack N. Rakove, "James Madison's Political Thought: The Ideas of an Acting Politician," in *A Companion to James Madison and James Monroe*, ed. Stuart Leibiger (John Wiley & Sons, 2013).

60. Noah Feldman, *The Three Lives of James Madison: Genius, Partisan, President* (Picador, 2017), 412.

61. Feldman, *James Madison*, 361.

62. Feldman, *James Madison*, 414–21; Ralph Ketcham, *James Madison: A Biography* (University Press of Virginia, 1990), 394–97. See also Garry Wills, *James Madison* (Times Books, 2002), 48–49, 162–63.

63. Ketcham, *James Madison*, 351–52, 471, 521–22.

64. The declaration of war passed by votes of 19 to 13 in the Senate and 79 to 48 in the House. Feldman, *James Madison*, 545.

65. For a recounting of the events, see Feldman, *James Madison*, 514–43. See also Ketcham, *James Madison*, 532 (observing that Madison "often spoke loudly while carrying no stick at all").

66. Steven J. Rauch, *The Campaign of 1819* (U.S Army Center for Military History, 2013), 8.

67. Rauch, *Campaign of 1819*, 9.

68. Ketcham, *James Madison*, 455.

69. Feldman, *James Madison*, 549.

70. Feldman, *James Madison*, 550.

71. Feldman, *James Madison*, 551; Rauch, *Campaign of 1819*, 9.

72. James Madison's Fourth Annual Address to Congress (November 4, 1812), available at https://founders.archives.gov/documents/Madison/03-05-02-0334 (spelling and style modernized).

73. See Feldman, *James Madison*, 484–85 (regarding Randolph's background) and 539 (regarding Randolph's speech).

74. Taylor, *Internal Enemy*, 149 (quoting Governor James Barbour) (spelling and style modernized).

75. Taylor, *Internal Enemy*, 150 (quoting Congressman Walter Jones) (spelling and style modernized).

76. Taylor, *Internal Enemy*, 150–51.

77. Feldman, *James Madison*, 562.

78. Taylor, *Internal Enemy*, 269.

79. Taylor, *Internal Enemy*, 211.

80. Taylor, *Internal Enemy*, 359.

Conclusion

1. My principal source for this section is Ralph Ketcham, *James Madison: A Biography* (University Press of Virginia, 1990), 573–89. I also consulted

Garry Wills, *James Madison* (Times Books, 2002), 126–41; Harlow Giles Unger, *The Last Founding Father: James Monroe and a Nation's Call to Greatness* (Da Capo, 2009), 218–36, and other sources cited later.

2. https://www.loc.gov/exhibits/out-of-the-ashes/transcript. See also Ketcham, *James Madison*, 577.

3. Ketcham, *James Madison*, 583.

4. Ketcham, *James Madison*, 578.

5. Bladensberg, American Battlefield Trust, https://www.battlefields.org/learn/war-1812/battles/bladensburg.

6. Alan Taylor, *The Internal Enemy: Slavery and War in Virginia 1772–1832* (W.W. Norton, 2013), 300.

7. https://www.battlefields.org/learn/maps/bladensburg-august-24–1814.

8. Ketcham, *James Madison*, 578.

9. Peter Snow, "The Man Who Burned Washington D.C.," available at https://www.thehistoryreader.com/military-history/man-who-burned-washington-dc.

10. Fawn M. Brodie, *Thomas Jefferson: An Intimate History* (Bantam Books, 1974), 166–67.

11. Brodie, *Thomas Jefferson*, 568.

12. Ron Chernow, *Washington: A Life* (Penguin Books, 2010), 741–43.

13. .James Madison's Message to Congress (November 18, 1815), available at https://founders.archives.gov/documents/Madison/03-08-02–0523.

14. President Dwight D. Eisenhower's Farewell Address (1961), available at https://www.ourdocuments.gov/doc.php?flash=false&doc=90&page=transcript.

15. The United States was spending 8.99 percent of its GDP on military and defense. https://www.macrotrends.net/countries/USA/united-states/military-spending-defense-budget. For numbers in the four military branches, see *World Almanac and Book of Facts 2020* (World Almanac Books, 2020), 120–21.

16. Carl T. Bogus, "What Does the Second Amendment Restrict? A Collective Rights Analysis," 18 *Constitutional Commentary* 485, 493–94 (2002).

17. Bogus, "What Does the Second Amendment Restrict?,"494.

18. Feldman, *James Madison*, 616–17.

19. John Hope Franklin, *From Slavery to Freedom: A History of Negro Americans*, 3rd ed. (Vintage Books, 1967), 212; Alan Taylor, *American Republics: A Continental History of the United States, 1783–1850* (W.W. Norton, 2021), 184. One historian argues that the plot was widely exaggerated or even fabricated out of whole cloth by White investigators. Michael P. Johnson, "Denmark Vesey and His Co-Conspirators," LVIII *William and Mary Quarterly* 915 (2001). Johnson does not represent the consensus view, but even if he is correct, Whites believed the conspiracy was real.

INDEX

―――⧫―――

For the benefit of digital users, indexed terms that span two pages (e.g., 52–53) may, on occasion, appear on only one of those pages.